We Started As Farmers In Prussia

Michael Tieman Family
Vol.1 - Descendants of G.W. Tiemann

Compiled by Michael Tieman

ISBN-13: 978-0-9910977-5-3
Design by Michael L. Tieman, Artists Gallerie, LLC

Printed in the United States
Published by Michael Tieman Publishing
15724 SW Flagstone Dr., Beaverton, OR 97007 United States, www.artistsgallerie.com

Prologue

When I am asked why do I do this, why am I so interested in the past, that only the future is important?

I ask … "Tell me about your family, your grandparents, and great-grandparents." Half-way through their stories they begin to understand. Our stories and memories will die with us if we do not pass it on to the future generations.

This is why I do it.

If I do not write down my stories, my parents and theirs, my children and their children will only remember us as someone they saw when they were very young, or as a photo in an album, and they will miss out on the real us. I am selfish in that I want my descendants to remember me and know that I had the same ups and downs in life as they are going through and maybe my experiences will give them some guidance.

My hope is that this small document will grow over the decades and become volumes containing the stories of who we all were.

How it all started

The quest for Nancy and my history, or roots, began innocently enough, Christmas, 1982.

Nancy's maternal grandmother, Dede gave us a book for Christmas titled *The History of Our Family.* A book of empty pages with headings like: Our Children, Husband's Parents' Family and Where Our Ancestors Have Lived.

As Nancy and I started to fill it out, we found that we knew almost nothing of our family starting with our great-grandparents. My family when I asked them for information would tell me nothing as though our ancestors never existed.

I am an artist, and artists are a curious lot by nature and we love knowledge. So, there it is, I was hooked.

First, my quest was "Who were my great-grandparents and where they came from?" All I knew was that they came from Prussia in the early 1800's and that because they were of German descent living in the U.S. during two great wars; their past was never talked about. I then took it upon myself to try and fill in the blanks. First, I talked to my parents, and great-grand aunts, as no one else would tell me squat. I slowly began to fill in the names of our ancestors, with some questionable dates and stories. As time went on, I spent hundreds of hours in the archives and library of the Mormon Church. I was lucky that we lived in cities that had local libraries of the main church.

Back then, I had to search actual books and newspapers and scroll through hundreds of rolls of microfiche, searching out our ancestor's records of birth, censuses and parish records. It took a long time back then in the 80's, and money as I had to order the loan of papers records and history books from the Mormon Church archives in Salt Lake City, which I could only look at in their local church library. Anything I wanted copies of, I had to get their permission and pay them to copy. Their genealogical library is extensive, the largest in the world, and in the case of Prussia where my ancestors came from, they had the only info available as most of it was destroyed.

My list of ancestors started to become impressive, in the thousands. Then I asked, "Who were these people?" I started to collect stories from our relatives about our family. Oh, the stories I heard when the family finally decided to share. Some info turned out accurate as I researched, others, not so much. Like all families we were descended from kings and leading scholars and vice presidents and famous inventors. Or, so the stories went on that were handed down.

Then with the stories, I became interested in the towns, farms and countries our ancestors came from. What was Millom, England like in the 1600's when Nancy's ancestors lived there? Or "What was my Prussian ancestor's diet in the late 1700's?" So, I looked into the town histories, and when was Prussia a country, country histories, and maps of the periods when our ancestors lived. Plot maps where I actually found our family names.

Curious more, what did my ancestors wear and eat in the 18th century on their farms and what did they grow? What church did they attend and why were there no birth records in a particular period of the 1600's but there were baptism records instead? How did the family name change from Tiemann to Tieman? Was Nancy or my family in London during the Great London Plague in 1665/66 or in the original Black Death in Europe in the years 1346-53?

Because of *The History of Our Family* book and asking who the great-grandfather was I never knew, this project has now over 5400 people in our two families, over 1500 source documents dating back to the 1600's (some originals pre-19th century), and a collection of over 2000 original photos some dating back to the beginning of photography.

I hope you enjoy reading this project of mine, this labor of love. Are you in it?

Contents

Tieman Family Portrait

Sometime in the 1980's my father showed me this photo the only one of the Tieman Clan. There were no names on the back of the photo and he could not remember where or when the photo was taken, and only knew that his grandmother Anna (my great-gramdma) was in the photo. I am the last male of my father's line and how sad is it that in only three generations our family was disappearing.

Imagine if you took a photo today of three generations of your family at a reunion and did not put names on the file. Your great-grandson looks at the photo and could not identify anyone. It's like you never existed.

It has taken me decades to track down the names of the people in this photo. I hope I am right; the problem is that I have very few people I can ask. By the way, my great-grandmother Anna is in the back row far left and her husband Henry is in the back row second from right. This photo I think was taken at the family farm in 1902.

Front: L-R: Florence Gerdom, Matilda Wuellner, Unknown, Unknown, Frank Wuellner, Alvin Wuellner, Unknown
Row 2: Mildred Wuellner, Reuben Wuellner, Paul Wuellner, Unknown, Unknown, Unknown
Row 3: Margret?, Fred Wuellner, Magdalene Wuellner, Unknown, Unknown, Luise Rethmeier Tieman, Wilhelm Tieman
Row 4: All Unknown
Back Row: Anna Tieman, William Tieman, Ann Wedertz?, Norman Wedertz?, Henry Tieman, Marjorie Duermeyer?

Linage Chart

Lineage Chart for Michael LaVerne Tieman

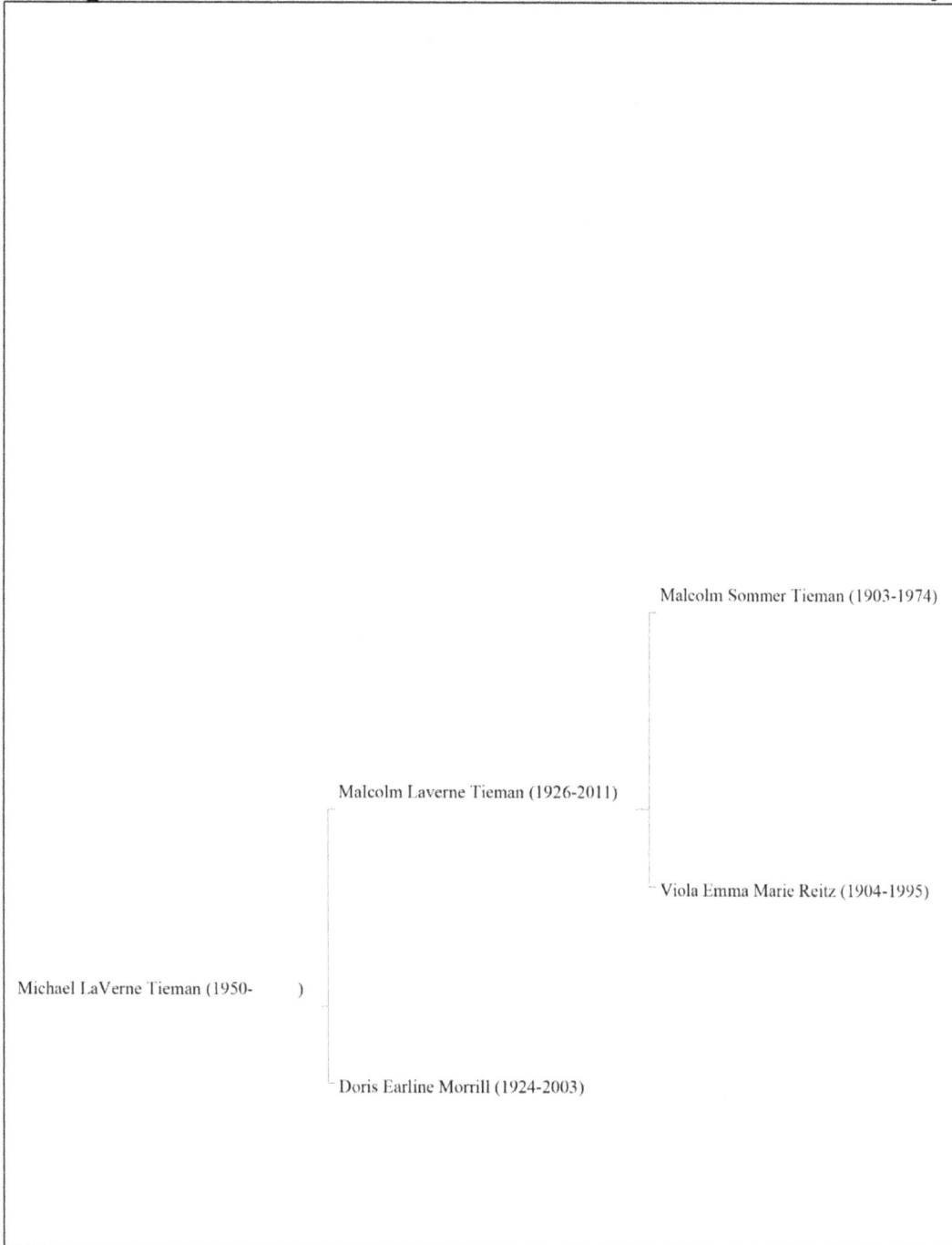

Malcolm Sommer Tieman (1903-1974)

Malcolm Laverne Tieman (1926-2011)

Viola Emma Marie Reitz (1904-1995)

Michael LaVerne Tieman (1950-   )

Doris Earline Morrill (1924-2003)

Lineage Chart for Michael LaVerne Tieman

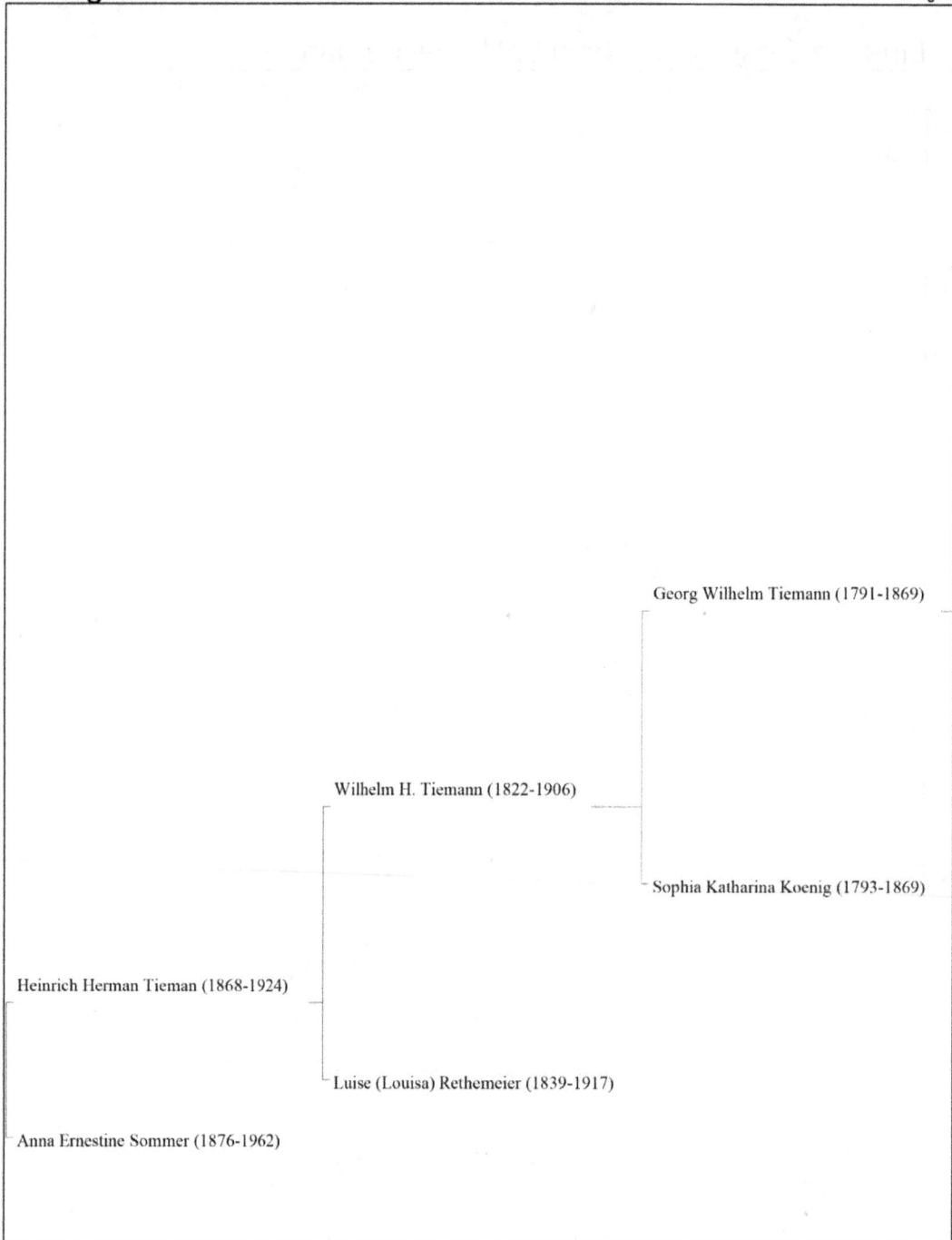

```
                                                                          Georg Wilhelm Tiemann (1791-1869)

                                      Wilhelm H. Tiemann (1822-1906)

                                                                          Sophia Katharina Koenig (1793-1869)

Heinrich Herman Tieman (1868-1924)

                                      Luise (Louisa) Rethemeier (1839-1917)

Anna Ernestine Sommer (1876-1962)
```

Descendants of Georg Wilhelm Tiemann

Descendants of Georg Wilhelm TIEMANN

1-Georg Wilhelm TIEMANN [846]
born: 1791, Lengerich, Steinfurt, Nordrhein-Westfalen, Germany
died: Oct 1869, Benton Township, Des Moines, Iowa, USA

+Sophia Katharina KOENIG [847]
born: 1793, Lienen, Prussia
marr: 8 Aug 1817, Evangelisch, Lengerich, Westfalen, Prussia
died: 1869, Benton Township, Des Moines, Iowa, USA

 2-Wilhelm H. TIEMANN [788]
 born: 2 May 1822, Tecklenburg, Westfalen, Germany
 died: 11 May 1906, Benton Township, Des Moines, Iowa, USA

 +Luise (Louisa) RETHEMEIER [789]
 born: 30 Nov 1839, Minden, Westphalia, Germany
 marr: 13 Feb 1859, Benton Township, Des Moines, Iowa, USA
 died: 5 Jan 1917, Burlington, Des Moines County, Iowa, USA

 3-Johann Heinrich TIEMANN [840]
 born: 15 May 1860, Benton Township, Des Moines, Iowa, USA
 died: 19 Aug 1939

 +Wilhelmina GAISER [841]
 born: 28 Aug 1870
 died: 21 Apr 1952, Burlington, Kane, Illinois, USA

 4-Chester TIEMANN [845]
 born:

 4-Wesley TIEMANN [844]
 born:

 4-Margaret TIEMANN [843]
 born:

 4-Esther TIEMANN [842]
 born:

 3-Maria Karoline TIEMANN [825]
 born: 27 Nov 1861, Benton Township, Des Moines, Iowa, USA
 died: 22 Jun 1947, Burlington, Kane, Illinois, USA

 +Henry J. GERDOM [824]
 born: 23 Jul 1856, Nettlestedt, Germany
 marr: 31 Mar 1887
 died: 1 Aug 1935, Burlington, Kane, Illinois, USA

 4-Florence GERDOM [835]
 born:

 +-- DEIRKUPP [834]
 born:

Produced by Legacy

Descendants of Georg Wilhelm TIEMANN

```
          5-Janet DEIRKUPP [836]
            born:

      4-Alvine GERDOM [833]
        born:

          +Frank G. NEBIKER [832]
          born:

      4-Bertha GERDOM [831]
        born:

          +Otto S. DAUM [830]
          born:

      4-Helen GERDOM [829]
        born:

          +John KLAPPMEIER [828]
          born:

      4-Albert F. GERDOM [827]
        born:

      4-Norman GERDOM [826]
        born:

      4-Selma GERDOM [838]
        born: 26 Oct 1895, Burlington, Kane, Illinois, USA
        died: 17 May 1935, Burlington, Kane, Illinois, USA

          +Arthur RENTZSCH [837]
          born:
          marr: 1917, Chicago, Cook, Illinois, USA
          died: 1920

            5-Arthur RENTZSCH Jr. [839]
              born:

3-Karoline Sarah TIEMANN [823]
    born: 27 Oct 1863, Benton Township, Des Moines, Iowa, USA
    died: 13 Apr 1865

3-Karoline Maria TIEMANN [819]
    born: 21 Dec 1865, Benton Township, Des Moines, Iowa, USA
    died: 26 Oct 1946

      +Fred DUERMEYER [818]
      born: 25 Feb 1857, Mittengen, Germany
      marr: 24 Jan 1889
      died: 7 Oct 1938, Burlington, Kane, Illinois, USA
```

Produced by Legacy

Descendants of Georg Wilhelm TIEMANN

```
    4-Margaret DUERMEYER [822]
      born:

    4-Caroline DUERMEYER [821]
      born:

    +-- KLEIN [820] (see Karoline Maria TIEMANN [819] on page 2)
    born:

3-Heinrich Herman TIEMAN [771]
   born: 16 Mar 1868, Benton Township, Des Moines, Iowa, USA
   died: 19 Aug 1924, Keokuk, Lee, Iowa, USA

   +Anna Ernestine SOMMER [772]
   born: 1 May 1876, Dresden, Saxony, Germany
   marr: 20 Nov 1902, Keokuk, Lee, Iowa, USA
   died: 15 Jun 1962, Keokuk, Lee, Iowa, USA

    4-Malcolm Sommer TIEMAN [716]
      born: 26 Sep 1903, Keokuk, Lee, Iowa, USA
      died: 16 Sep 1974, Keokuk, Lee, Iowa, USA

      +Viola Emma Marie REITZ [1382]
      born: 15 Jan 1904, Van Buran Twp., Lee County, Iowa, USA
      marr: 13 Jun 1925, Keokuk, Lee, Iowa, USA
      died: 22 Mar 1995, Columbia, Boone, Missouri, USA

       5-Malcolm Laverne TIEMAN [26]
         born: 20 Feb 1926, Keokuk, Lee, Iowa, USA
         died: 5 Jan 2011, Stow, Summit, Ohio, USA

         +Doris Earline MORRILL [27]
         born: 12 Nov 1924, Nevada, Story, Iowa, USA
         marr: 30 Dec 1944, Kahoka, Clark, Missouri, USA
         died: 9 Mar 2003, Akron, Summit, Ohio, USA

          6-Beverly Dianne TIEMAN [893]
            born: 15 Mar 1947, Keokuk, Lee, Iowa, USA

            +William James STARR [892]
            born: 16 May 1946, Cowanshannock, Armstrong, Pennsylvania, USA
            marr: 1 Sep 1968, Akron, Summit, Ohio, USA

             7-Amy Christine STARR [916]
               born: 20 Nov 1969, Rochester, Monroe, New York, USA

               +Bryan Keith STEWART [915]
               born: 18 Aug 1969, Boiceville, Ulster, New York, USA
               marr: 3 Nov 1990

                8-Jacob Bryan STEWART [1022]
                  born: 1997, Ft. Lenoardwood, MO
```

Descendants of Georg Wilhelm TIEMANN

```
7-Nicole Renee STARR [914]
   born: 19 Aug 1973, Rochester, Monroe, New York, USA

   +Kyle A. METCALF [3087]
   born: 1966
   marr: 4 May 2002, Akron, Summit, Ohio, USA

      8-Jessica METCALF [3088]
         born: 16 Jun 2003, Texas, USA

      8-Blake METCALF [3217]
         born: 19 Feb 2007, Allen, Collin, Texas, USA

6-Richard Laverne TIEMAN [891]
   born: 28 Jan 1948, Keokuk, Lee, Iowa, USA
   died: 28 Jan 1948, Keokuk, Lee, Iowa, USA

6-Michael LaVerne TIEMAN [1]
   born: 20 Aug 1950, Keokuk, Lee, Iowa, USA

   +Nancy Lee MARSHALL [2]
   born: 5 Mar 1952, Vancouver, British Columbia, Canada
   marr: 16 Jun 1972, Columbus, Franklin, Ohio, USA

   7-Heather Anne TIEMAN [920]
      born: 17 May 1976, North Vancouver, British Columbia, Canada

      +Phillip ERWIN [921]
      born: 30 May 1971, Boise, Ada, Idaho, USA
      marr: 22 Jun 1996, Lake Oswego, Clackamas, Oregon, USA

         8-Riley James ERWIN [1197]
            born: 27 Sep 1999, Portland, Clackamas, Oregon, USA

         8-Jackson Davis ERWIN [3091]
            born: 26 Jul 2005, Portland, Clackamas, Oregon, USA

   7-Katherine Jane TIEMAN [919]
      born: 25 Jun 1979, North Vancouver, British Columbia, Canada

      +Shawn SCHULBERG [3015]
      born:
      marr: 4 Nov 2000, Portland, Clackamas, Oregon, USA

         8-Connor Shamas TIEMAN-WOODWARD [3086]
            born: 28 Oct 2002, Portland, Clackamas, Oregon, USA

      +Samuel Patrick WOODWARD [3089]
      born: 16 Sep 1975, T'ai-Pei, Taiwan
      marr: 25 Jul 2009, Portland, Clackamas, Oregon, USA

         8-Alexis Jean TIEMAN-WOODWARD [3090]
            born: 12 Nov 2006, Portland, Clackamas, Oregon, USA
```

Descendants of Georg Wilhelm TIEMANN

```
                    8-Owen Richard TIEMAN-WOODWARD [3268]
                        born: 18 Feb 2010, Portland, Clackamas, Oregon, USA

              6-Constance Sue TIEMAN [851]
                  born: 5 Aug 1958, Freeport, Stephenson, Illinois, USA
                  died: 29 Jul 2008, Akron, Summit, Ohio, USA

                  +John DROTOS [850]
                  born: 27 Mar 1954
                  marr: 30 Jul 1983, Akron, Summit, Ohio, USA

          4-Thelma Louisa TIEMAN [849]
              born: 12 Sep 1907, Keokuk, Lee, Iowa, USA
              died: 18 Sep 1997, Keokuk, Lee, Iowa, USA

          4-Magdalene TIEMAN [848]
              born: 28 Nov 1912, Keokuk, Lee, Iowa, USA
              died: 2 Jun 2007, Keokuk, Lee, Iowa, USA

    3-Magdalena Christine "Martha" TIEMANN [802]
        born: 29 Apr 1870, Benton Township, Des Moines, Iowa, USA
        died: 17 Feb 1955, Burlington, Kane, Illinois, USA

        +Fred WUELLNER [801]
        born: 2 Mar 1860, Minden, Westphalia, Germany
        died: 17 Sep 1936

          4-Frank WUELLNER [814]
              born:

          4-Matilda WUELLNER [813]
              born:

          4-Alvin WUELLNER [812]
              born:

          4-Mildred WUELLNER [806]
              born:

              +Herbert JACOBSON [805]
              born:

              5-Glenn JACOBSON [808]
                  born:

                  +UNKNOWN [809]
                  born:

                  6--- JACOBSON [811]
                      born:

                  6---- JACOBSON [810]
                      born:
```

Descendants of Georg Wilhelm TIEMANN

5-Neal JACOBSON [807]
born:

4-Reuben WUELLNER [804]
born:

4-Paul WUELLNER [803]
born:

3-Ernst H. Wilhelm TIEMANN [815]
born: 10 Jun 1873, Benton Township, Des Moines, Iowa, USA
died: 10 Mar 1914

+Anna KAMPMEIER [816]
born: 7 Mar 1876
died: 13 Oct 1969

4-Arthur TIEMANN [817]
born: 1905
died: 1934

3-Ernst H. Samuel TIEMANN [799]
born: 5 Jan 1876, Benton Township, Des Moines, Iowa, USA
died: 2 Apr 1930

+Ida ZACHMEYER [800]
born:

4-Walter TIEMANN [3043]
born:

4-Ruth Marie TIEMANN [3044]
born: 1909
died: 2002

4-Helen TIEMANN [3045]
born:

4-Warren TIEMANN [3046]
born:

4-Laura TIEMANN [3047]
born:

4-Richard Frederick TIEMANN [3048]
born: 1916
died: 1999

4-Edith Armeda TIEMANN [3049]
born: 1919
died: 2008

Produced by Legacy

Descendants of Georg Wilhelm TIEMANN

    +WEYRICK [3814] (see Edith Armeda TIEMANN [3049] on page 6)
      born:

   4-Cecil Samuel TIEMANN [3050]
     born: 1921
     died: 2003

3-Emilie Louise TIEMANN [794]
   born: 24 Apr 1881, Benton Township, Des Moines, Iowa, USA
   died: 21 Mar 1939

   +Chris SCHMIDT [793]
   born: 1 Nov 1875, Burlington, Kane, Illinois, USA
   died: 17 Oct 1937

   4-Frieda SCHMIDT [798]
     born:

   4-Raymond SCHMIDT [797]
     born:

   4-Frances SCHMIDT [796]
     born:

   4-Viola SCHMIDT [795]
     born:

    +MARSHALL [3945]
     born:

Produced by Legacy

Name Index

Produced by Legacy

Name Index

Produced by Legacy

TimeLine

Timeline: Descendants of Georg Wilhelm TIEMANN

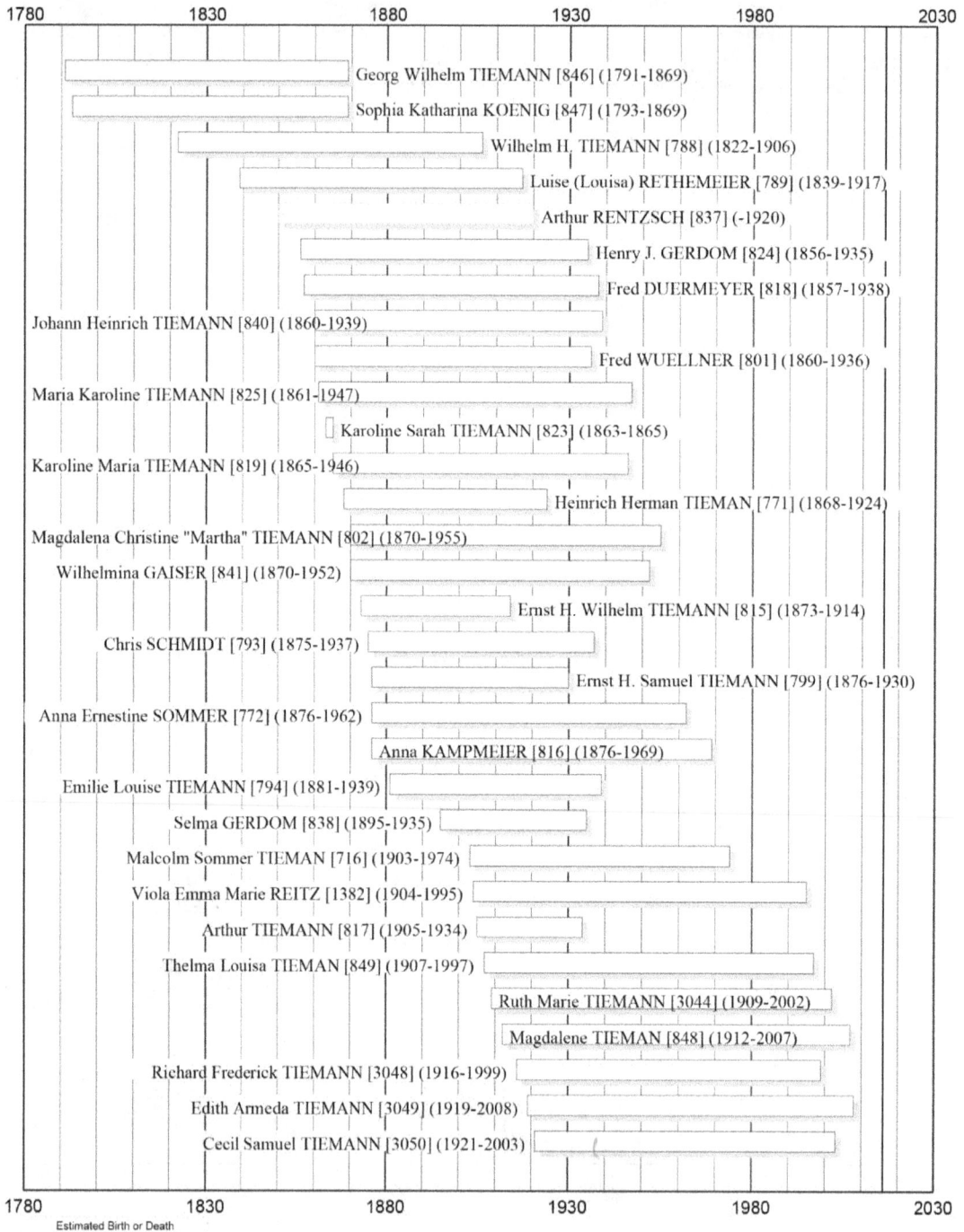

Page 1

1780	1830	1880	1930	1980	2030

Georg Wilhelm TIEMANN [846] (1791-1869)

Sophia Katharina KOENIG [847] (1793-1869)

Wilhelm H. TIEMANN [788] (1822-1906)

Luise (Louisa) RETHEMEIER [789] (1839-1917)

Arthur RENTZSCH [837] (-1920)

Henry J. GERDOM [824] (1856-1935)

Fred DUERMEYER [818] (1857-1938)

Johann Heinrich TIEMANN [840] (1860-1939)

Fred WUELLNER [801] (1860-1936)

Maria Karoline TIEMANN [825] (1861-1947)

Karoline Sarah TIEMANN [823] (1863-1865)

Karoline Maria TIEMANN [819] (1865-1946)

Heinrich Herman TIEMAN [771] (1868-1924)

Magdalena Christine "Martha" TIEMANN [802] (1870-1955)

Wilhelmina GAISER [841] (1870-1952)

Ernst H. Wilhelm TIEMANN [815] (1873-1914)

Chris SCHMIDT [793] (1875-1937)

Ernst H. Samuel TIEMANN [799] (1876-1930)

Anna Ernestine SOMMER [772] (1876-1962)

Anna KAMPMEIER [816] (1876-1969)

Emilie Louise TIEMANN [794] (1881-1939)

Selma GERDOM [838] (1895-1935)

Malcolm Sommer TIEMAN [716] (1903-1974)

Viola Emma Marie REITZ [1382] (1904-1995)

Arthur TIEMANN [817] (1905-1934)

Thelma Louisa TIEMAN [849] (1907-1997)

Ruth Marie TIEMANN [3044] (1909-2002)

Magdalene TIEMAN [848] (1912-2007)

Richard Frederick TIEMANN [3048] (1916-1999)

Edith Armeda TIEMANN [3049] (1919-2008)

Cecil Samuel TIEMANN [3050] (1921-2003)

1780	1830	1880	1930	1980	2030

Estimated Birth or Death

Produced by Legacy

Timeline: Descendants of Georg Wilhelm TIEMANN

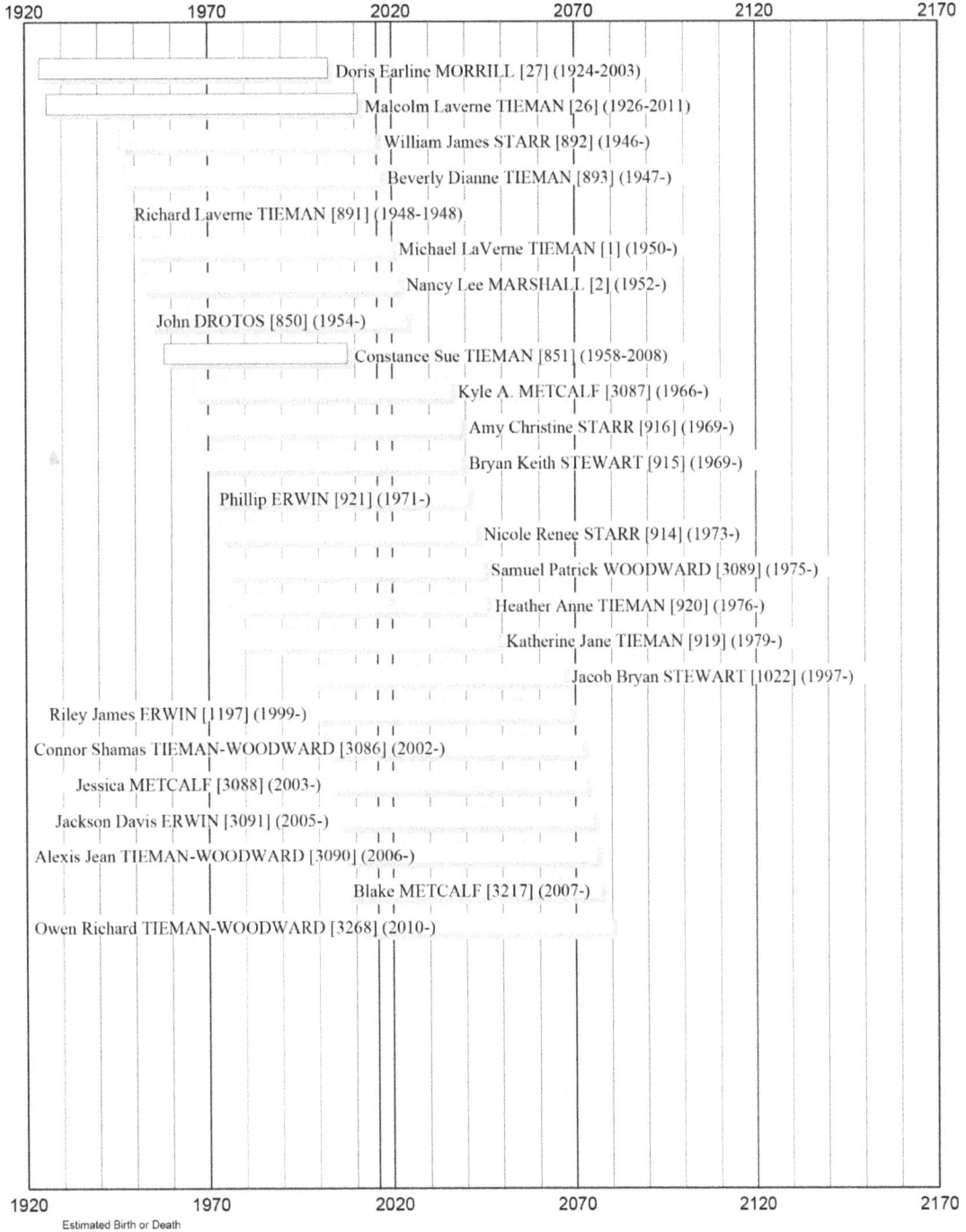

Page 2

| 1920 | 1970 | 2020 | 2070 | 2120 | 2170 |

Doris Earline MORRILL [27] (1924-2003)

Malcolm Laverne TIEMAN [26] (1926-2011)

William James STARR [892] (1946-)

Beverly Dianne TIEMAN [893] (1947-)

Richard Laverne TIEMAN [891] (1948-1948)

Michael LaVerne TIEMAN [1] (1950-)

Nancy Lee MARSHALL [2] (1952-)

John DROTOS [850] (1954-)

Constance Sue TIEMAN [851] (1958-2008)

Kyle A. METCALF [3087] (1966-)

Amy Christine STARR [916] (1969-)

Bryan Keith STEWART [915] (1969-)

Phillip ERWIN [921] (1971-)

Nicole Renee STARR [914] (1973-)

Samuel Patrick WOODWARD [3089] (1975-)

Heather Anne TIEMAN [920] (1976-)

Katherine Jane TIEMAN [919] (1979-)

Jacob Bryan STEWART [1022] (1997-)

Riley James ERWIN [1197] (1999-)

Connor Shamas TIEMAN-WOODWARD [3086] (2002-)

Jessica METCALF [3088] (2003-)

Jackson Davis ERWIN [3091] (2005-)

Alexis Jean TIEMAN-WOODWARD [3090] (2006-)

Blake METCALF [3217] (2007-)

Owen Richard TIEMAN-WOODWARD [3268] (2010-)

| 1920 | 1970 | 2020 | 2070 | 2120 | 2170 |

Estimated Birth or Death

Produced by Legacy

First Generation G.W. Tiemann Timeline 1780-1870

			Tieman Family 1780-1870			
Year		**Rulers**	**World History**	**U.S. History**	**Science/Technology**	**Art**
1780		Catherine II - Rus. 1762	American Revolution	American Revolution	Bifocals 1784	Neoclassicism
		Louis XVI -Fr. 1774	U.S. Independence 1783	U.S. Independence 1783	1st Parachute 1783	*Federalist Pub. 1788*
		Carlos IV - Sp. 1788				
		George III - Eng. 1760			Steamboat 1786	
		Frederick II - Ger. 1740		Constitution Ratified 1788		
		Frederick Wm. II - Ger. 1786				
		Pres. George Washington 1789	French Revolution			
1790		Pres. John Adams 1797	Canada Act 1791	Irish Catholics Migration	Gas Turbine 1791	*Rights of Man 1791*
	Georg William Tiemann Born 1791 - Married. 1817 - Immigrated US 1833 - Died 1869	Paul - Rus. 1796	France/Netherlands	Vermont 1791	Cotton Gin 1793	
				Kentucky 1792		
				Fugitive Slave Act 1793		
				Tennessee 1796		
1800		Pres. Thomas Jefferson 1801	Irish Potato Famine	Ohio 1803	Electric Cell 1800	Romanticism
		Ferdinand VII - Sp. 1808	Battle of Trafalgar	Lib. Of Congress 1800		*Webster Dictionary 1806*
		Napolean - Fr. 1804	Peninsular War in Spain	Lousiana Purchase 1803	1st Submarine 1801	Fifth Symphony 1808
		Alexander I - Rus. 1801		Louis & Clark Exp. 1804	Oil lamp 1804	
		Pres. James Madison1809		African Slaves Act 1808	Braille 1809	
1810		Pres. James Monroe 1817	British American War	Lousiana 1812	1st Photograph 1814	
		Louis XVIII -Fr. 1814	Napolean defeated	Indiana 1816	Steam Locomotive 1814	
				Mississippi 1817	Stethoscope 1819	
				Illinois 1818	Erie Canal 1817	
				Alabama 1819		
1820		Pres. J. Q. Adams 1825	Peru Freedom	Maine 1820	Microphone 1827	Hudson River Sch. 1825
		George IV - Eng. 1820	Greek War of	Missouri 1821	Typewriter 1829	Audubon
		Charles X - Fr. 1824	Independance	Monroe Doctrine 1823		
		Nicholas I - Rus. 1825	Spanish Revolution			
			Russia/Turkey			
		Pres. Andrew Jackson 1829	Uruguay Freedom	Arkansas 1836		
1830		William IV - Eng. 1830		German Migration	Sewing Machine 1830	*Hunchback of ND 1831*
		Queen Victoria 1837		Michigan 1837	Calculator 1835	*Oliver Twist 1837*
		Isabel II- Sp. 1833				
		Pres. M. Van Buren 1837		Mormons 1830	Telegraph 1837	
		Louis-Philippe- Fr. 1830	Britian/China -Opium	Trail of Tears 1838	Bicycle 1839	
1840		Pres. Harrison & Tyler 1841	Britian Factory Act	Florida 1845	Anesthetic 1842	Edgar A. Poe
		Pres. James Polk 1845	U.S./ Mexico	Texas 1845		
		Pres. Taylor & Fillmore 1849	Communist Manifesto	Iowa 1846		*3 Muskateers 1844*
				California Gold Rush 1848		
				Wisconsin 1848		Karl Marx
1850		Louis Napolean III - Fr. 1852	Crimean War 1853-56	California 1850	Jeans 1850	Realism
		Pres. Franklin Pierce 1853	Britain/China 1856	Minnesota 1858	Pasteurisation 1856	*Scarlet Letter 1850*
		Pres. J. Buchanan 1857		Oregon 1859	Smith & Wesson 1854	*Moby Dick 1851*
		Alexander II - Rus. 1855			Darwin 1859	*Walden 1854*
						Leaves of Grass 1855
1860		Pres. Abraham Lincoln 1861	U.S. Civil War 1861-65	Kansas 1861	Dynamite 1867	
				U.S. Civil War 1861-65		*War & Peace 1865*
				West Virginia 1863		
				Emancipation Proc. 1863		Dostoevsky
				Nevada 1864		
				Navajo Long Walk 1864-68		
				Lincoln Assassinated 1865		
				South Reconstruction 1865		
		Pres. Lincoln & Johnson 1865		Nebraska 1867	Tungsten Steel 1868	
		Pres. Ulysses S. Grant 1869			Suez Canal 1869	
1870			Franco-Prussian War	Brooklyn Bridge 1872	Color Photo 1873	Impressionism 1874

First Generation
Georg Wilhelm Tiemann 1791-1869

GEORG WILHELM TIEMANN was born in 1791 in Lengerich, Prussia, died in Oct 1869 in Benton Township, Iowa, at age 78, and was buried in Benton Township, Iowa. Georg married **Sophia Katharina KOENIG,** on 8 Aug 1817 in Lengerich, Prussia. Sophia was born in 1793 in Lienen, Prussia, died in 1869 in Benton Township, Iowa at age 76, and was buried in Benton Township.

The first mention of the Tieman Family that I found when I started in 1983 was in the Prussian passport of **G.W. Tiemann** dated 18th of March 1833:

> Age of 41, his wife and eight-year-old son Emigrated from the government district of Muenster Georg W. Tiemann from Lengerich, emigrated with Family 1833 to Nordamerika.

The wife mentioned in the passport was **Sophia Koenig** aged 39 and the son was **Wilhelm** who I found later was baptized in 1822 so he would have been eleven not eight.

In the letter from the Evangelical Church of Westfalen parish they were able to find the following information on Georg, if I translated the records correctly:

> There was no single boy Tiemann born or baptized in Lengerich from 1785-1795. However, most children were born on the property where they lived; no records kept except maybe a family Bible, and people were baptized if at all when the family could afford it and when they were able to get into a town. The parish assumes that the parents owned or worked on a farm nearby and moved to Lengerich soon after Georg was born. They say this because according to more parish records G.W. and Sophia were married in 1817 in the Evangelic church in Lengerich, Westfalen, Prussia. In the records he was born in Lengerich and was 26 and she was born in Lienen and was 24.

We lose track of this couple until a parish record of their son Wilhelm being baptized in Lengerich on 16 May 1822. This baptism complete with parents' names is also confirmed in the *Germany, Births and Baptisms 1558-1898* records. The interesting thing about this is that according to his tombstone he was born on 2 May 1825, but the 1880 US Census puts him born in 1826. I am going with the parish baptisim records of the day.

Why did the family pack up and leave their home in Lengerich? The wave of emigration from Prussia from 1820-71 was caused by unemployment, religious fracturing, escaping high taxes, the military - wheat crop failures, poor wine harvests and a potato blight. Could it be that the Tiemann farm had too many years of crop failures and G.W. had enough?

According to G.W. passport in 1833 they went to Munster which is a large city, but inland. I have not found anything telling which port town they traveled to from Munster and when they actually left Prussia. The port cities at that time were Hamburg which did not start keeping records until 1852, and Bremen who started making lists in 1832 but most lists were destroyed in 1835 as there were so many records of emigrants leaving previous to 1835 they were burned to make room for newer records. So, I may never find the information I am looking for.

216

Where the family landed in America also is not known. I have checked immigration records such as there is for New York, Boston, Baltimore, Philadelphia and New Orleans but with no success.

When we pick up the family wanderings again, they have left Virginia in a covered wagon and taking the National Road migration route, started their six-month trek west to an unknown future in Burlington, Iowa.

Not much is known about Georg and Sophia after they came to Iowa except from an excerpt from the Latty Church of Christ Centennial Book 1853-1953:

> "The family came to this country in March 1833. They stopped in Virginia before going to Burlington where they resided there for ten years until they moved to a farm on the Irish Ridge Road in Benton Township. They were good neighbors and one of the pioneer families who organized the German Evangelical Zion Church of Benton Township in 1853. The church was built nearby on the Irish Road. Both William and his wife died in 1869, he was 77 and she was 72. They were buried in the church cemetery. The son William survived."

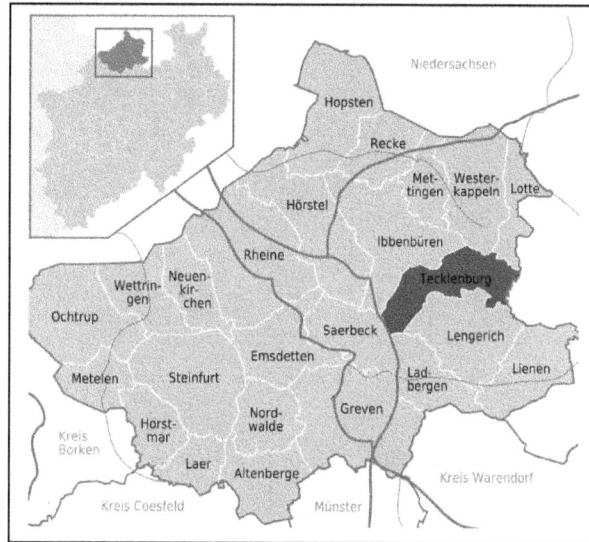

Prussian farmers in 1800's

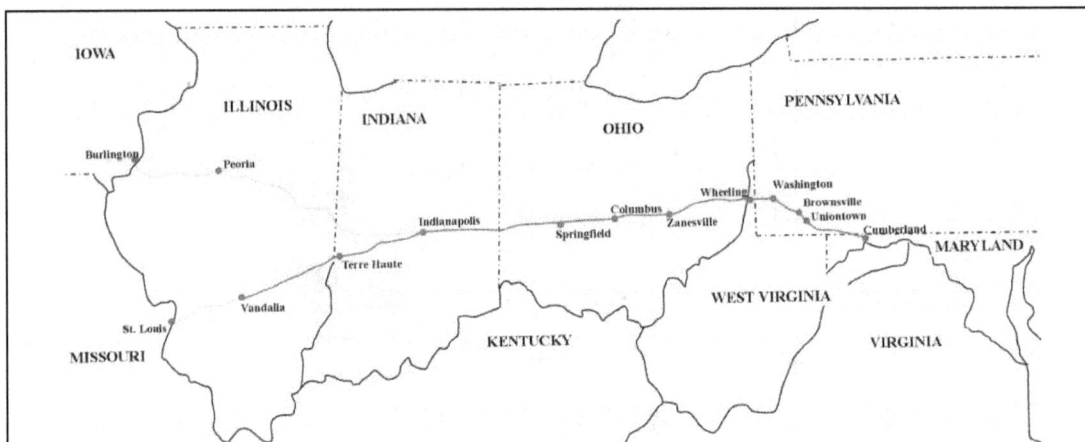

The National Road Extending 600 miles from Cumberland, Maryland, it crossed the states of Pennsylvania, West Virginia, Ohio, Indiana, and Illinois, terminating at Vandalia. The Road served as a major migration route for pioneers heading west in the first half of the 19th century.

The first construction contracts for the National Road were granted in the spring of 1811; the road pushed west in varying degrees over the next forty years, incorporating older trails like the Cumberland Road and Zane's Trace.

Some eastern sections were "macadamized" using crushed rock to create a hard, durable surface, but many western portions were never fully developed. In the 1830s the federal government began turning the Road over to states' control.

Between 1835 and 1865 pioneers headed to Iowa would have had plenty of company as thousands of settlers streamed west over the National Road. Some travelers probably picked up the route at Zanesville, then traveled west at least as far as Indianapolis. They may have left the main road there and cut across Illinois on lesser-known trails, perhaps through Peoria to Burlington, Iowa. Or they could have traveled all the way to Vandalia then on to St. Louis where they would have found transportation north on the Mississippi River to Keokuk or Burlington. Either way, it would have been an arduous journey.

Their New Life in Iowa

I have found a plat map of Benton Township in Des Moines Co, Iowa that shows the Tiemann family farm. It is 93.18 acres in the far western plot #32. The Irish Ridge Road, two rivers and the railroad go through the family land. Looks like a good piece of property that G.W. purchased in 1833. The Irish Ridge Road, the name given to an early highway running north from the city of Burlington to the Round Prairie settlements in Yellow Spring Township in the north. The name has reference to Irish settlers along the road.

The American Fur Company of John Jacob Astor established a post in the area in 1829. Settlement began in 1833, shortly after the Black Hawk Purchase.

In the spring of 1834 John Gray, who purchased the first lot with his wife Eliza Jane, renamed the town. Gray chose to name it Burlington in honor of his hometown in Vermont. The Grays' daughter Abigail was born in Burlington that same year, the first American settler child born on Iowa soil.

Iowa's earliest white settlers soon discovered an environment different from that which they had known back East. Most northeastern and southeastern states were heavily timbered; settlers there had material for building homes, outbuildings, and fences. Moreover, wood also provided ample fuel. Once past the extreme eastern portion of Iowa, settlers quickly discovered that the state was primarily a prairie or tall grass region. Trees grew abundantly in the extreme eastern and southeastern portions, and along rivers and streams, but elsewhere timber was limited. In most portions of eastern and central Iowa, settlers could find sufficient timber for construction of log cabins, but substitute materials had to be found for fuel and fencing. For fuel, they turned to dried prairie hay, corn cobs, and dried animal droppings. In southern Iowa, early settlers found coal outcroppings along rivers and streams. People moving into northwest Iowa, an area also devoid of trees, constructed sod houses. Some of the early sod house residents wrote in glowing terms about their new quarters, insisting that "soddies" were not only cheap to build but were warm in the winter and cool in the summer.

Many people complained that the prairie looked bleak and desolate. These newcomers also discovered that the prairies held another disadvantage - one that could be deadly. Prairie fires were common in the tall grass country, often occurring yearly. Diaries of pioneer families provide dramatic accounts of the reactions of early Iowans to prairie fires, often a mixture of fear and awe. When a prairie fire approached, all family members were called out to help keep the flames away. One nineteenth century Iowan wrote that in the fall, people slept "with one eye open" until the first snow fell, indicating that the threat of fire had passed.

Constructing a farmstead was hard work in itself. Families not only had to build their homes, but often they had to construct the furniture used. Newcomers were often lonely for friends and relatives. Pioneers frequently contracted communicable diseases such as scarlet fever. Moreover, pioneers had few ways to relieve even common colds or toothaches.

But for the pioneers who remained on the land, the rewards were substantial. These early settlers soon discovered that prairie land, although requiring some adjustments, was some of the richest land to be found anywhere in the world. By the late 1860s, most of the state had been settled and the isolation and loneliness associated with pioneer living had quickly vanished.

The earliest settlers shipped their agricultural goods down the Mississippi River to New Orleans, but by the 1850s, Iowans had caught the nation's railroad fever.

What Families Left In Prussia

The population of Prussia grew from about 20 million in 1750 to 33 million in 1816, and up to 52 million by 1865. This created dreadful urban slums. Almost three-quarters of the population though continued to live in communities of fewer than 2,000 people. Infant and child mortality rates remained high, and illegitimate births rose from 15 percent in the early 19th century to 25 percent by mid-century.

Prussia had freed its peasantry in 1807 but had then given much of the land to landowners to compensate them for lost labor, leaving many peasants without the means to sustain themselves. Although serfdom was threatened, it only collapsed following the revolutions of 1848.

What The Family Ate In Prussia

The food of the individual working-man varies according to his wages. The better-paid workers eat meat daily and bacon and cheese for supper. Where wages are less, meat is used only two or three times a week, and the proportion of bread and potatoes increases. Descending in income, animal food is reduced to a small piece of bacon cut up with the potatoes; lower still, even this disappears, and there remain only bread, cheese, porridge, and potatoes, until on the lowest round of the ladder, potatoes form the sole food, As an accompaniment, weak tea, with perhaps a little sugar, milk, or spirits, is universally drunk.

The cultivation of potatoes resulted in change in the daily diet and replaced bread and porridge in many parts of Europe. It took a long time for the potato to integrate into the cuisine of southern Germany, which had been dominated by flour-based dishes. In northern Germany, the potato replaced bread as an accompaniment to the main dish very quickly. In the Central German Uplands, the potato was used as an ingredient in soups and in the form of mash, which was comparable in texture and consistency to the porridge which had long been a part of the local diet. By the mid-19th century, the idea of the potato as the food of the impoverished classes had changed, and middle-class cuisine increasingly added the potato.

The distilling trade also expanded, with the potato and other substances increasingly being used in the distilling process. For example, in Prussia, the amount of liquor distilled doubled between 1820 and 1840.

Changes in farming techniques and land usage (such as the use of artificial fertilizers and the development of agricultural machinery) and the easier circulation of goods, these developments made it possible for the first time since the Middle Ages to ensure that the masses of the population had a dependable food supply. Around 1800 the work of four peasants had been required to provide sufficient food for one non-agrarian consumer, 100 years later one farmer was able to provide for four consumers. The last famine that was not caused by war occurred in Europe in 1846/1847.

Lengerich Prussia - Where G.W. Was Born

The first written source in which Lengerich is mentioned dates back to 1147. In this first written source the place is referred to as "Liggerkerke". It received its "City Rights" (Stadtrechte) in 1727.

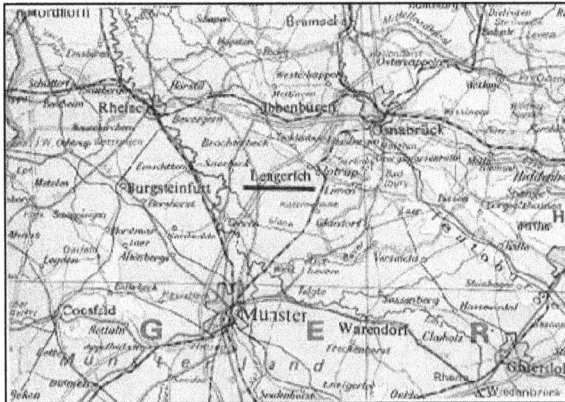

In 1591 Lengerich counted 41 houses; in 1728 it counted 150 houses, with altogether 614 inhabitants and in 1821 the village had 1173 inhabitants in the town, and in the surrounding territory there were 4408 inhabitants.

Between 1832 and 1891, however, more than 1000 inhabitants emigrated, most of them to Canada and the USA.

Children of G. W. and Sophia:

WILHELM H. b. 2 May 1822 Tecklenburg, Prussia; bap. 16 May 1822 Lengerich, Prussia; d. 11 May 1906 Benton Township, Iowa, at age 84; m. Luise RETHEMEIER, 13 Feb 1859 Benton.Township, Iowa.

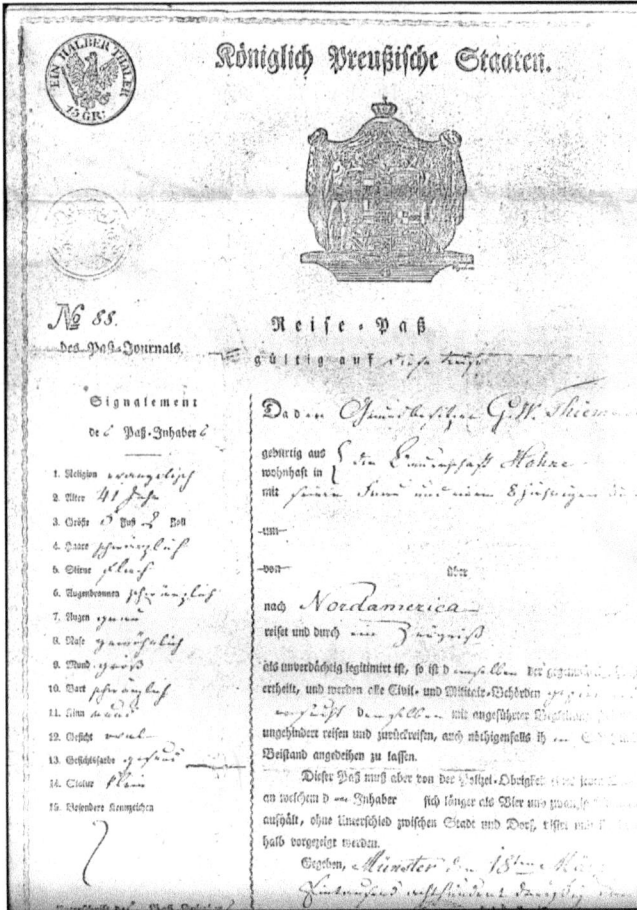

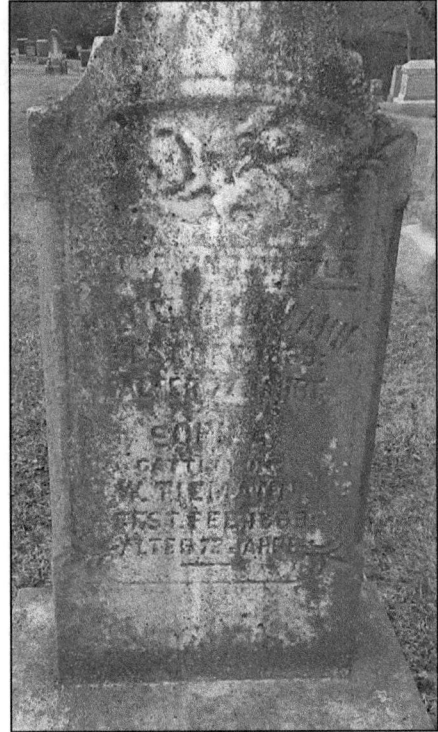

Prussian Passport

**"Germany, Marriages, 1558-1929,"
Georg Wilhelm Tiemann, 1817**

« Back to search results

No image available

- Search collection
- About this collection

Groom's Name:	Georg Wilhelm Tiemann
Groom's Birth Date:	
Groom's Birthplace:	
Groom's Age:	26
Bride's Name:	Sophie Katharina Koenig
Bride's Birth Date:	
Bride's Birthplace:	
Bride's Age:	24
Marriage Date:	08 Aug 1817
Marriage Place:	Evangelisch, Lengerich, Westfalen, Prussia
Groom's Father's Name:	
Groom's Mother's Name:	
Bride's Father's Name:	
Bride's Mother's Name:	
Groom's Race:	
Groom's Marital Status:	
Groom's Previous Wife's Name:	
Bride's Race:	
Bride's Marital Status:	
Bride's Previous Husband's Name:	
Indexing Project (Batch) Number:	M95279-4
System Origin:	Germany-ODM
Source Film Number:	526392
Reference Number:	

Source Citation

"Germany, Marriages, 1558-1929," index, FamilySearch
(https://familysearch.org/pal:/MM9.1.1/JHQ4-JPK : accessed 15 May 2012), Georg
Wilhelm Tiemann, 1817.

U.S. Federal Census Mortality Schedules, 1850-1885 record for William Teeman

Second Generation Wilhelm H. Tiemann Timeline
1820-1910

Tieman Family 1820-1910

(Vertical margin note spanning 1840–1880: William Tiemann Born 1822 - Immigrated US 1833 - Married - 1859 - Died 1906)

Year	Rulers	World History	U.S. History	Science/Technology	Art
1820	Pres. J. Q. Adams 1825	Peru Freedom	Maine 1820	Microphone 1827	Hudson River Sch. 1825
	George IV - Eng. 1820	Greek War of	Missouri 1821	Typewriter 1829	Audubon
	Charles X - Fr. 1824	Independance	Monroe Doctrine 1823		
	Nicholas I - Rus. 1825	Spanish Revolution			
		Russia/Turkey			
	Pres. Andrew Jackson 1829	Uruguay Freedom	Arkansas 1836		
1830	William IV - Eng. 1830		German Migration	Sewing Machine 1830	Hunchback of ND 1831
	Queen Victoria 1837		Michigan 1837	Calculator 1835	Oliver Twist 1837
	Isabel II- Sp. 1833				
	Pres. M. Van Buren 1837		Mormons 1830	Telegraph 1837	
	Louis-Philippe- Fr. 1830	Britian/China -Opium	Trail of Tears 1838	Bicycle 1839	
1840	Pres. Harrison & Tyler 1841	Britian Factory Act	Florida 1845	Anesthetic 1842	Edgar A. Poe
	Pres. James Polk 1845	U.S./ Mexico	Texas 1845		
	Pres. Taylor & Fillmore 1849	Communist Manifesto	Iowa 1846		3 Muskateers 1844
			California Gold Rush 1848		
			Wisconsin 1848		Karl Marx
1850	Louis Napolean III - Fr. 1852	Crimean War 1853-56	California 1850	Jeans 1850	Realism
	Pres. Franklin Pierce 1853	Britain/China 1856	Minnesota 1858	Pasteurisation 1856	Scarlet Letter 1850
	Pres. J. Buchanan 1857		Oregon 1859	Smith & Wesson 1854	Moby Dick 1851
	Alexander II - Rus. 1855			Darwin 1859	Walden 1854
					Leaves of Grass 1855
1860	Pres. Abraham Lincoln 1861	U.S. Civil War 1861-65	Kansas 1861	Dynamite 1867	
			U.S. Civil War 1861-65		War & Peace 1865
			West Virginia 1863		
			Emancipation Proc. 1863		Dostoevsky
			Nevada 1864		
			Navajo Long Walk 1864-68		
			Lincoln Assassinated 1865		
			South Reconstruction 1865		
	Pres. Lincoln & Johnson 1865		Nebraska 1867	Tungsten Steel 1868	
	Pres. Ulysses S. Grant 1869			Suez Canal 1869	
1870		Franco-Prussian War	Brooklyn Bridge 1872	Color Photo 1873	Impressionism 1874
	Pres. R. Hayes 1877	Unification of Germany	Colorado 1876	Telephone 1876	Lewis Carroll
	Amadeo I - Sp. 1870	Russo-Turkish War ends	Little Big Horn 1876		Wagner
	Pres. Diaz -Mex.	War in Pacific 1879	Danish, Icelandic,	Record Player 1877	Gilbert & Sullivan
	Alfonso XII - Sp. 1874	Triple Alliance 1882	Norwegian, Swedish	Light Bulb 1879	
1880			Migration		1st US Film 1889
	Alexander III - Rus. 1881		North Dakota 1889	Freud 1899	
			South Dakota 1889	Rabies Vaccine 1885	
	Pres. Garfield & Arthur 1881		Montana 1889	1st Motion Picture	
	Pres. G. Cleveland 1885		Washington 1889	Camera 1889	
	Alfonso XIII - Sp. 1886				
	Pres. B. Harrison 1889			CP Railway opens 1885	
1890	Pres. G. Cleveland 1893	Chili Civil War 1891	Wyoming 1890	Telegraph 1895	Time Machine 1895
	Nicholas II - Rus. 1894	Modern Olympics 1896	Utah 1896	X-Rays Discovered 1895	
	Pres. W. McKinley 1897	Spanish/American 1898	Wounded Knee 1890	Radium/Polonium	
				Discovered 1898	
1900	Pres. McKinley & Roosevelt 190	Titanic Sinks 1912	Eastern Europe, Italian	1st Airplane 1903	Expressionism
	Pres. T. Roosevelt 1905	Boxer Rebellion 1900	Migration		Cubism 1907
	Edward VII -Eng. 1901	Russo/Japanese War	Tribes become US Cit. 1901		Jack London

Second Generation
Wilhelm H. Tiemann 1822-1906

WILHELM H. TIEMANN was born on 2 May 1822 in Tecklenburg, Prussia, was baptized on 16 May 1822 in Lengerich, Westfalen, Germany, died on 11 May 1906 in Benton Township, Iowa, at age 84, and was buried in Benton Township, Iowa. Wilhelm married **Luise (Louisa) RETHEMEIER** , on 13 Feb 1859 in Benton Township, Iowa. Luise was born on 30 Nov 1839 in Minden, Prussia, died on 5 Jan 1917 in Burlington, Iowa, at age 77, and was buried in Benton Township, Iowa,

TIEMAN - LOUISE AND WILHELM

Now we pick up the story of Wilhelm the son of G.W. and Sophia. I'm afraid I have not found much about **Wilhelm** and his wife **Louise Rethemeier** other than the church booklet and an obituary. Time hopefully will add more info to this section.

If you read the previous section on his father, you will remember that William's date of birth in his father's passport from Prussia stated he was eight in 1833, his tombstone and the *Latty Church Centennial Booklet* say he was born May 2, 1825, but the 1880 U.S. Census puts him at 54 (b.1826) and the *Germany Births and Baptism Records* and the parish records of the time state he was baptized in 1822. Again, until I have other more credible proof, I am going with the parish records of the time.

On February 13, 1859 William was married to Louise Rethemeier, who was born November 30, 1839 in Minden, Germany. They were married in the German Evan. Zion Church, Benton Township. The Pastor was Jakob Schmeiser.

Naturalization Index of Des Moines Co. shows that William became a U.S. citizen on Sept. 4, 1875 at the age of 53. At this period since William became a citizen his wife automatically became one. The downside to this is that if they divorced, she would lose her citizenship.

Burlington Hawkeye Newspaper:
William Tiemann Dead - Worthy Pioneer Had Lived Here Fully Seventy Years - Is Survived by a Large Number of Descendants
Another of the worthy and highly respected pioneers of this county has gone to his well-earned rest. William Tiemann passed away yesterday morning at 6 o'clock at his residence near Latty. Deceased was a native of Germany, but had spent fully seventy of his eighty years in this country, his family having come here from Virginia seventy years ago. They lived in the city for about ten years and then they removed to the farm near Latty, which remained the family home and eventually became the property of the deceased, and he never left it for any considerable time and who never dreamed of parting with it. He was honest, industrious and economical and hence prospered. He was fortunate in more than one sense of the word, for until a week ago he enjoyed that priceless possession almost perfect health. The old gentleman and his good wife had very many friends in the city and country and their home was famed far and wide for a genuine open-handed hospitality. They really found pleasure in entertaining their friends. William Tiemann is survived by the following relatives: The good wife and eight children; John, Henry, William and Samuel Tiemann, Mrs. Henry Gerdom, Mrs. F.J. Duermeyer, Mrs. Fred Wuellner and Mrs. Chris Schmidt all of whom except Henry who is a resident of Keokuk, live

in this city or county. There are twenty grandchildren and one great-grandchild. The funeral will be held from the residence near Latty at 2p.m. Sunday. There will be a service at the Evangelical church at Latty.

Children:

JOHN H. b. May 15, 1860; d. Aug 19, 1939; m. Wilhelmina Gaiser

MARY K. b. Nov. 27, 1861; d. June 22, 1947; m. Henry Gerdom

CAROLINE M. b. Dec. 21, 1865; d. Oct 26, 1946; m. Fred Duermeyer

HENRY H. b. March 16, 1868; d. Aug 19, 1924; m. Anna Sommer b. May 1, 1876; d.June 15, 1962

MAGDELENE C. b. April 29, 1870; d. Feb. 17, 1955; m. Fred Wuellner

E. WILLIAM b. June 10, 1873; d. March 10, 1914; m. Anna Kampmeier

H. SAMUL b. Jan. 5, 1876; d. April 2, 1930; m. Ida Zachmeyer

LOUISE E. b. April 24, 1881; d. March 21, 1939; m. Chris Schmidt

TIEMAN - LOUISE AND WILHELM

Front: L-R: Florence Gerdom, Matilda Wuellner, Unknown, Unknown, Frank Wuellner, Alvin Wuellner, Unknown
Row 2: Mildred Wuellner, Reuben Wuellner, Paul Wuellner, Unknown, Unknown, Unknown
Row 3: Margret?, Fred Wuellner, Magdalene Wuellner, Unknown, Unknown, Luise Rethmeier Tieman, Wilhelm Tieman
Row 4: All Unknown
Back Row: Anna Tieman, William Tieman, Ann Wedertz?, Norman Wedertz?, Henry Tieman, Marjorie Duermeyer?

NAME	PLACE OF [BIRTH]	DATE BIRTH	DATE MARRIED	DATE DIED
Tiemann Wilhelm	Lengerich, Kreis Tecklenburg Regbz. Münster — Deutschland	2. May 1825	13. February 1859	May 11, 1906
Rethemeier Luise	Falldorf, Kreis Herford Regbz. Minden — Deutschland	30. Novbr. 1839	"	Jan. 5. 1917
Tiemann Johann Heinrich	Benton Township, Des Moines Co. Iowa	15. May 1860		Aug 19, 1939
d° Maria Karoline	d°	27. Novbr. 1861	31. March 1887	June 22, 1947
d° Karoline Sarah	d°	27. Oktober 63 10-18-63		13. April 1865
d° Karoline Maria	d°	21. Febr. 1865	24. January 1889	Oct 28, 1946
d° Heinrich Hermann	d°	16. March 1868		17 August 1924
d° Magdalena	d°	29. April 1870		Feb 17, 1955
d° Ernst H. Wilhelm	d°	10. June 1873		10 March 1914
d° Ernst H. Samuel	d°	5 Jany 1876		April 2 1930
d° Emilie Luise	d°	24 April 1881		21 March 1939

Copied from the Tiemann Family bible

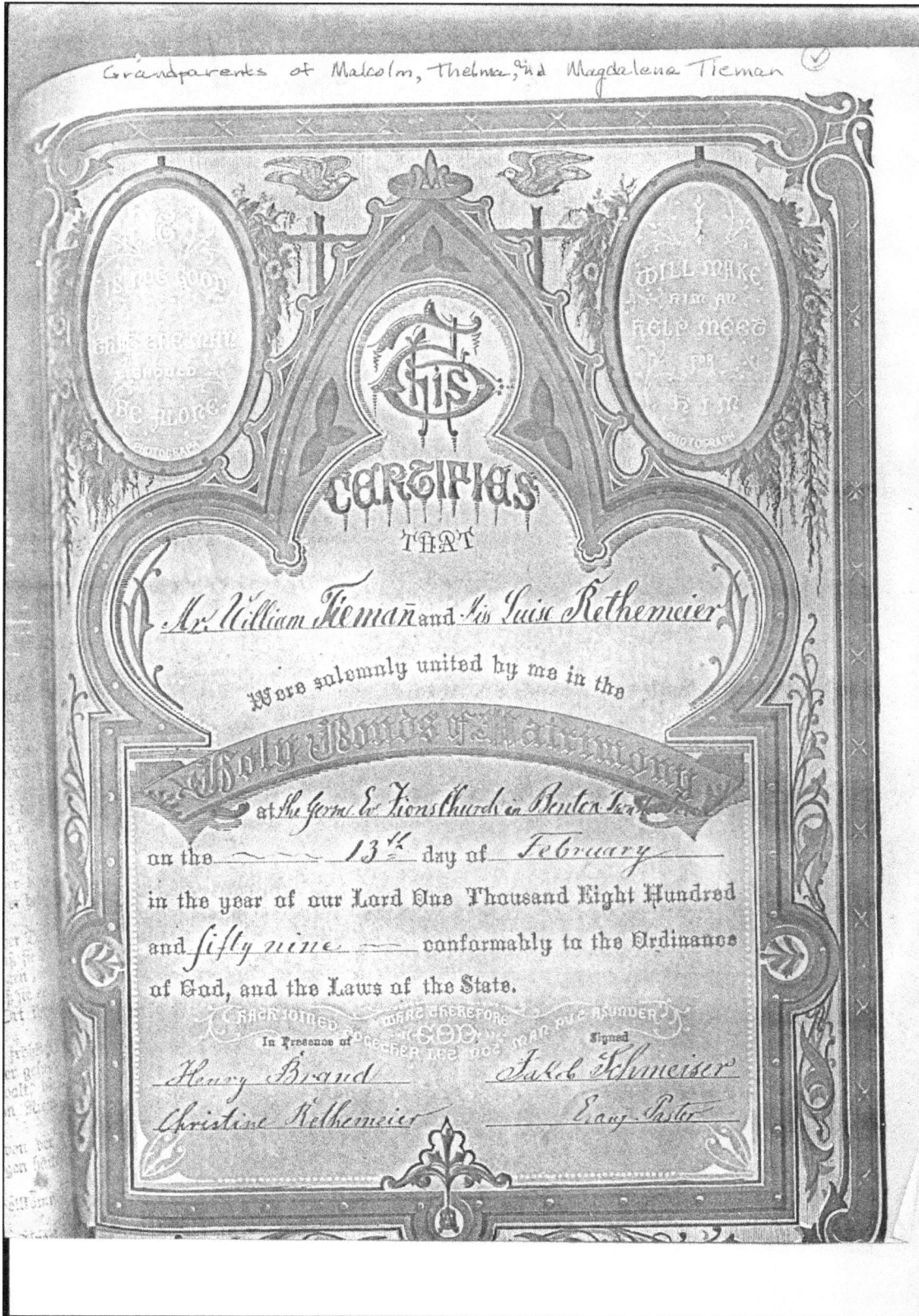

Grandparents of Malcolm, Thelma, and Magdalena Tieman

CERTIFIES

THAT

Mr. William Tieman and Mrs. Luise Rethemeier

Were solemnly united by me in the

Holy Bonds of Matrimony

at the Germ. Ev. Zions Church in Benton Co.

on the 13th day of February

in the year of our Lord One Thousand Eight Hundred

and fifty nine conformably to the Ordinance

of God, and the Laws of the State.

In Presence of

Henry Brand

Christine Rethemeier

Signed

Jakob Schmeiser

Evang. Pastor

"Germany, Births and Baptisms, 1558-1898," Georg Wilhelm Tiemann in entry for Heinrich Wilhelm Tiemann, 1822

« Back to search results

No image available

- Search collection
- About this collection

Name:	Heinrich Wilhelm Tiemann
Gender:	Male
Baptism/Christening Date:	16 May 1822
Baptism/Christening Place:	EVANGELISCH,LENGERICH,WESTFALEN,PRUSSIA
Birth Date:	
Birthplace:	
Death Date:	
Name Note:	
Race:	
Father's Name:	Georg Wilhelm Tiemann
Father's Birthplace:	
Father's Age:	
Mother's Name:	Catharina Sophia Koenig
Mother's Birthplace:	
Mother's Age:	
Indexing Project (Batch) Number:	C95277-9
System Origin:	Germany-ODM
Source Film Number:	526387
Reference Number:	

Source Citation

"Germany, Births and Baptisms, 1558-1898," index, FamilySearch (https://familysearch.org/pal:/MM9.1.1/N69J-J5J : accessed 15 May 2012), Georg Wilhelm Tiemann in entry for Heinrich Wilhelm Tiemann, 1822.

THE BURLINGTON HAWK-EYE: SATURDAY MORNING MAY 12, 1906

MING

fugees
ere.

for La-
es Are

er Bur-
le indi-
uilding,
it pres-
ate and
there
e that
es from
id that
urgent
ds and
conse-
stricken
desired
one in
se who
now up
o has
nen for
ruction
up for
nstruc-
er and
ity of
reatest
n who
of the
aller
to hash
om the
ent as
places
ments
read-
of the
to go
degree
t come
k and
work
come
utdoor
uni-
coun-
com-
resent
r em-

ing n

in St.
itte's
posts,
call

Of Local Interest.

German Baptists Helped—Among the contributions for the sufferers at San Francisco, recently forwarded direct, and not heretofore noted, was one by the German Baptist church, amounting to $45.13.

Married in Connecticut.—Evidently complying with a Connecticut law the authorities at Hartford sent to Dr. J. P. Harrell, the local keeper and compiler of vital statistics, the following notice: "Married at Hartford, Conn., Carl W. Stone, aged twenty-three, and Sarah Louise Buhrmeister, aged twenty-one." Both are formerly of Burlington, Ia., but Mr. Stone's present home is Philadelphia. He is in the navy. Mr. and Mrs. Stone has many friends in the city, who wish the young couple well.

Camp Jackson Day.—Thursday, May 10, was the forty-fifth anniversary of the taking of Camp Jackson at St. Louis by Capt. Nathaniel Lyon with his handful of regulars and a small army of loyal German volunteers. Captain Osterhaus commanded Company II, of the Rifles, on that occasion. He is the same Osterhaus who rose to high rank and was the guest of the city at a German day celebration several years ago. A number of Burlingtonians were members of Captain Osterhaus' company forty-five years ago. The only one who remains here is Joseph Voelker, a former member of the police force and an old resident.

Much Warmer.—After hovering near freezing point for a few days the mercury took a different notion yesterday and tried to climb to the top of the tube. It went above one hundred in the sun, and the sudden change made it almost uncomfortable. As to whether or not there are to be more frosts the local authorities are not agreed. One predicts another frost for Monday night, and still another for the end of the month. Others again are of the opinion that the backbone of winter has been broken, and that yesterday morning marked his final retreat from this city and section of the country.

Heard Kubelik—In the audience that were delighted by Kubelik the great Bohemian violinist at Galesburg Thursday evening were several Burlington musicians. One of these said: "His technique and versatility are admirable, but what pleased the audience more than anything else was a dreamy, tender, pathetic composition labeled a romanza. You could not only hear the proverbial pin drop, but the silence was so intense that you might have heard that pin playing the air. As an encore he gave Schumann's Traeumerei. Everybody had heard that played, and almost everybody has heard it well played. But really, none of us ever heard it played until we heard Ku-

WILLIAM TIEMANN DEAD

Worthy Pioneer Had Lived Here Fully Seventy Years.

Is Survived by a Large Number of Descendants—Mrs. Robert Safely Dead at Cedar Rapids.

Another of the worthy and highly respected pioneers of this county has gone to his well-earned rest. William Tiemann passed away yesterday morning at 8 o'clock at his residence near Latty. Deceased was a native of Germany, but had spent fully seventy of his eighty years in this county, his family having come here from Virginia seventy years ago. They lived in the city for about ten years and then they removed to the farm near Latty, which remained the family home and eventually became the property of the deceased, who never left it for any considerable time and who never dreamed of parting with it. He was honest, industrious and economical and hence he prospered. He was fortunate in more than one sense of the word, for until a week ago he enjoyed that priceless possession almost perfect health. The old gentleman and his good wife had very many friends in city and county and their home was famed far and wide for its genuine, open-handed hospitality. They really found pleasure in entertaining their friends. William Tiemann is survived by the following relatives: The good wife and eight children: John, Henry, William and Samuel Tiemann, Mrs. Henry Gerdau, Mrs. F. J. Duermeyer, Mrs. Fred Wuelfner and Mrs. Chris. Schmidt, all of whom, except Henry, who is a resident of Keokuk, live in this city or county. There are twenty grandchildren and one great-grandchild. The funeral will be held from the residence near Latty at 2 p. m. Sunday. There will be services at the Evangelical church at Latty.

Barnickel.

Mr. and Mrs. Nicholas Barnickel, of No. 1418 Third street, mourn the death of their son Clayton W., who passed away at the tender age of 11 months and 29 days. He was one of twins.

Safely.

Friends in this city received word yesterday of the death of Mrs. Robert Safely, a former well-known resident of the city. Mr. Safely was engaged in the railroad service prior to his removal to Cedar Rapids.

The Cedar Rapids Times had the following concerning the life and death of

PROF. RICKER REGRET

Burlington Has Been Very Kind, But the Proposition Was Too Tempting to Be Rejected.

Professor Maurice Ricker was an interested spectator at the performance last evening, justly of the success of the performance the hearty applause which his proteges were winning. He said: "I am going to Des Moines. I have fine positions in view, and this is the better. Of course, I do not like the idea of leaving Burlington. The old town has been very good to me. I have grown very fond of her. But the proposition was so flattering, salary so much better than I have been receiving here that I feel it my duty to accept. I regret the step I have taken will take us from the many kind friends whom we have won, but we believe it will be for the best. And, of course we shall always look back with pleasure upon our years in Burlington."

Professor Ricker will remain at his old post during the present school year. Whether or not he will again take his vacation in the mountains of Montana, upon that point he is still undecided.

LET THE BEES WORK.

What a Very Busy Man Considers Ideal Existence—for a While

One of Burlington's busiest professional men, a man who has not in the year which he can call his own and who responds as quickly and pleasantly, where perhaps a good word of thanks is a grateful reward, with his only recompense for those days of the hardest kind of work, one of those weary "spells" that come to the most indefatigable workers, he pictured an ideal existence, somewhere in the foot hills; perhaps California, or somewhere in the south or on the southern slope of a range of Georgia or Tennessee, and not too far from town to miss civilization if longing for that came on, plenty of fruit and flowers and books and birds and sunshine and laughter and skies and bird song and perfect so hour that had a claim, no duty would interfere with the mere enjoyment of air and sunshine, of mere trivial existence. Not even light farming of a fruit ranch. Absolutely nothing to do unless it became necessary for sake of the neighbors to have an obligation of some sort. And then the came to him, "Let the bees do the work." Perhaps the bee ranch will afford just that pretense at work without which life would be scarce endurable. And perhaps he will put the idea into practice.

Don't be fooled and made to believe that rheumatism can be cured

Third Generation Heinrich Herman Tieman Timeline
1860-1930

Year		Rulers	World History	U.S. History	Science/Technology	Art
		Tieman Family 1860-1930				
1860		Pres. Abraham Lincoln 1861	U.S. Civil War 1861-65	Kansas 1861	Dynamite 1867	
				U.S. Civil War 1861-65		War & Peace 1865
				West Virginia 1863		
				Emancipation Proc. 1863		Dostoevsky
				Nevada 1864		
				Navajo Long Walk 1864-68		
				Lincoln Assassinated 1865		
				South Reconstruction 1865		
		Pres. Lincoln & Johnson 1865		Nebraska 1867	Tungsten Steel 1868	
		Pres. Ulysses S. Grant 1869			Suez Canal 1869	
1870			Franco-Prussian War	Brooklyn Bridge 1872	Color Photo 1873	Impressionism 1874
		Pres. R. Hayes 1877	Unification of Germany	Colorado 1876	Telephone 1876	Lewis Carroll
		Amadeo I - Sp. 1870	Russo-Turkish War ends	Little Big Horn 1876		Wagner
		Pres. Diaz -Mex.	War in Pacific 1879	Danish, Icelandic,	Record Player 1877	Gilbert & Sullivan
	Henry Tieman Born 1868 - Married 1902 - Died 1924	Alfonso XII - Sp, 1874	Triple Alliance 1882	Norwegian, Swedish	Light Bulb 1879	
1880				Migration		1st US Film 1889
		Alexander III - Rus. 1881		North Dakota 1889	Freud 1899	
				South Dakota 1889	Rabies Vaccine 1885	
		Pres. Garfield & Arthur 1881		Montana 1889	1st Motion Picture	
		Pres. G. Cleveland 1885		Washington 1889	Camera 1889	
		Alfonso XIII - Sp. 1886				
		Pres. B. Harrison 1889			CP Railway opens 1885	
1890		Pres. G. Cleveland 1893	Chili Civil War 1891	Wyoming 1890	Telegraph 1895	Time Machine 1895
		Nicholas II - Rus. 1894	Modern Olympics 1896	Utah 1896	X-Rays Discovered 1895	
		Pres. W. McKinley 1897	Spanish/American 1898	Wounded Knee 1890	Radium/Polonium	
					Discovered 1898	
1900		Pres. McKinley & Roosevelt 1901	Titanic Sinks 1912	Eastern Europe, Italian	1st Airplane 1903	Expressionism
		Pres. T. Roosevelt 1905	Boxer Rebellion 1900	Migration		Cubism 1907
		Edward VII -Eng. 1901	Russo/Japanese War	Tribes become US Cit. 1901		Jack London
		Ferdinand of Bulgaria 1908	Russia Revolution	McKinley Assassinated 1901		
			Young Turk Revolution	Forest Conservation 1902		
				NAACP 1909		
		Pres. William Taft 1909		Oklahoma 1907		
1910		Pres. Woodrow Wilson 1913	World War I 1914	New Mexico 1912	Theory of Relativity 1916	Stravinsky
		George V - Eng. 1910		Arizona 1912		
				Select. Service Draft 1917		
1920		Mussolini - Italy 1922	Hague Court 1920	18th Ammend. No Alcohol		James Joyce
		Pres. C. Coolidge 1925	Spain Dictatorship	19th Ammend. Women Vote		T.S. Eliot
			Stalin Expands Russia			Disney 1st Cartoon 1924
		Pres. Herbert Hoover 1929		Stock Market Crash 1929		Surrealism 1924
1930		Pres. F. D. Roosevelt 1933	World War II 1939	New Deal 1933	Plastics 1937	Hitchcock

Third Generation
Heinrich Herman Tieman 1868-1924

HEINRICH HERMAN TIEMAN was born on 16 Mar 1868 in Benton Township, Iowa, died on 19 Aug 1924 in Keokuk, Iowa at age 56, and was buried on 21 Aug 1924 in Keokuk, IA. Heinrich married **Anna Ernestine SOMMER** on 20 Nov 1902 in Keokuk, Iowa, USA. Anna was born on 1 May 1876 in Dresden, Germany, died on 15 Jun 1962 in Keokuk, at age 86, and was buried in Keokuk, Lee, Iowa.

Wedding photo, Henry Tieman & Anna Sommer Nov. 1902

This was my great-grandfather **Henry**, born in Benton Township probably at the family farm, 16 Mar 1868. My dad never knew Henry (since he died 19 Aug 1924 in Keokuk, Iowa), and he was never spoken of by his wife, **Anna Sommer** (married 20 Nov. 1902 in Keokuk, Iowa) and their daughters.

The reason finally came out in a conversation I had with his daughter Maggie before her sister Thelma died in 1997. It seems that her father, Henry, went mad and they put him in the asylum and was considered dead by the family. This was an illness that carried down to his daughter Maggie. Back in the early and mid-1900's the only diagnosis they had was "mad" and they were stuck away in an asylum. The family of course did not talk about those shut away as there was shame attached. My family it seems was no different. Poor Maggie had to live not only with the stigma of her father's illness, but her own as well.

In the late 1990's the diagnosis was bi-polar 2 and with medication it allowed sufferers to live a more normal life.

Another story my sister Beverly heard, was that Henry had syphilis and was hospitalized, but again never talked about. Either way, it is very sad that my great grandfather "disappeared" and we never knew about him.

Correspondence from his oldest daughter Thelma Tieman in 1989:
Favorite saying of her father, Henry..." Kleine kinder, kleine sorgen; grosse kinder, grosse sorgen" (small children small problems; big children big problems) Henry lost parts of all fingers left hand in a saw mill accident a few days before he was married. A carpenter, he was able to hold a nail between thumb and little finger. He built the little house his family lived in at 1628 Palean in Keokuk in the early 1900's. *That house was still in the family until Maggie died in 2007.

Obit *Daily Gate City Newspaper*:
Henry H. Tieman of 1628 Palean street, died today at 1am at Mt. Pleasant, Iowa. He has been seriously ill since May of this year. Harry Herman Tieman was born in Latty, Iowa near Burlington, on March 16, 1868, and had made his home in Keokuk for the past twenty-five years. On November 20, 1902, he was united in marriage to Miss **Anna Sommer**, who survives her husband with three children, Malcolm, Thelma and Magdalene, all living at home. He is also survived by two brothers and four sisters, John Tieman, Sam Tieman, Mrs.

Fred Duermeyer, Mrs. Henry Gerdom, and Mrs. Fred Wuellner, all of Burlington, and Mrs. Chris Schmidt of Morning Sun, Iowa, and a number of nieces and nephews. Mr. Tieman was a member of St. Paul's Evangelical church, of the Modern Woodmen of America and the Carpenter's Union. The funeral will be held from St. Paul's Evangelical church Thursday afternoon at 3 o"clock.

Iowa 20c.

In 1917, the United States entered World War I and farmers as well as all Iowans experienced a wartime economy. For farmers, the change was significant. Since the beginning of the war in 1914, Iowa farmers had experienced economic prosperity. Along with farmers everywhere, they were urged to be patriotic by increasing their production. Farmers purchased more land and raised more corn, beef, and pork for the war effort. It seemed that no one could lose as farmers expanded their operations, made more money, and at the same time, helped the Allied war effort.

After the war, however, Iowa farmers soon saw wartime farm subsidies eliminated. Beginning in 1920, many farmers had difficulty making the payment for debts they had incurred during the war. The 1920s were a time of hardship for Iowa's farm families and for many families, these hardships carried over into the 1930s.

As economic difficulties worsened, Iowa farmers sought to find local solutions. Faced with extremely low farm prices, including corn at 10 cents a bushel and pork at three cents a pound, some Iowa farmers joined the Farm Holiday Association. This group, which had its greatest strength in the area around Sioux City, tried to withhold farm products from markets. They believed this practice would force up farm prices. The Farm Holiday Association had onlylimited success as many farmers did not cooperate and the withholding itself did little to raise prices. Farmers experienced little relief until 1933 when the federal government, as part of Franklin Roosevelt's New Deal, created a federal farm program.

In 1933, native Iowan Henry A. Wallace went to Washington as secretary of agriculture and served as principle architect for the new farm program. Wallace, former editor of the Midwest's leading farm journal, Wallace's Farmer, believed that prosperity would return to the agricultural sector only if agricultural production was curtailed. Further, he believed that farmers would be monetarily compensated for withholding agricultural land from production. These two principles were incorporated into the Agricultural Adjustment Act passed in 1933. Iowa farmers experienced some recovery as a result of the legislation but like all Iowans, they did not experience total recovery until the 1940s.

Since World War II, Iowans have continued to undergo considerable economic, political, and social change. In the political area, Iowan experienced a major change in the 1960s when liquor by the drink came into effect. During both the nineteenth and early twentieth centuries, Iowans had strongly supported prohibition, but in 1933 with the repeal of national prohibition, Iowans established a state liquor commission. This group was charged with control and regulation of Iowa's liquor sales. From 1933 until the early 1960s, Iowans could purchase packaged liquor only. In the 1970s, Iowans witnessed a reapportionment of the General Assembly, achieved only after a long struggle for an equitably-apportioned state legislature. Another major political change was in regard to voting. By the mid-1950s, Iowa had developed a fairly competitive two-party structure, ending almost 100 years of Republican domination within the state.

In the economic sector, Iowa also has undergone considerable change. Beginning with the first farm-related industries developed in the 1870s, Iowa has experienced a gradual increase in the number of business and manufacturing operations. The period since World War II has witnessed a particular increase in manufacturing operations. While agriculture continues to be the state's dominant industry, Iowans also produce a wide variety of products including refrigerators, washing machines, fountain pens, farm implements, and food products that are shipped around the world.

Children:

MALCOLM S., b.26 Sep 1903 Keokuk, Iowa; m. Viola Emma Marie REITZ; d. 16 Sep 1974 Keokuk, Iowa at age 70; buried in Keokuk, Iowa,
THELMA, b.12 Sep 1907 Keokuk, Iowa; d.18 Sep 1997 Keokuk, Iowa, at age 90, buried on 22 Sep in Keokuk, Iowa.
MAGDALENE, b. 28 Nov 1912 Keokuk, Iowa; d. 2 Jun 2007 Keokuk, Iowa, at age 94.

Wedding photo, Henry Tieman & Anna Sommer Nov. 1902

Front: L-R: Florence Gerdom, Matilda Wuellner, Unknown, Unknown, Frank Wuellner, Alvin Wuellner, Unknown

Row 2: Mildred Wuellner, Reuben Wuellner, Paul Wuellner, Unknown, Unknown, Unknown

Row 3: Margret?, Fred Wuellner, Magdalene Wuellner, Unknown, Unknown, Luise Rethmeier Tieman, Wilhelm Tieman

Row 4: All Unknown

Back Row: Anna Tieman, William Tieman, Ann Wedertz?, Norman Wedertz?, Henry Tieman, Marjorie Duermeyer?

1880 United States Federal Census record for Henry Teiman

Anna Sommer Tieman at her 96th Birthday Party, May 1, 1962

TIEMAN - ANNA SOMMER - MAY 1 YEAR UNKNOWN

TIEMAN - ANNA SOMMER AGE 62 IN 1948

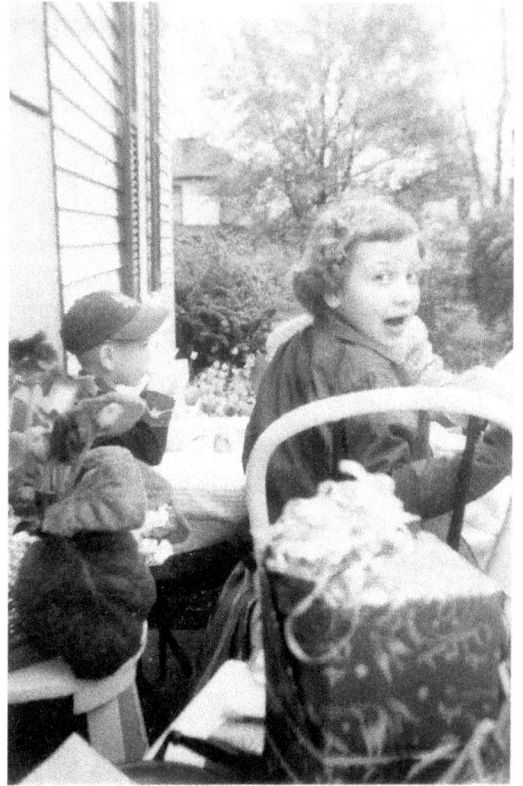

TIEMAN - MICHAEL & BEVERLY AT GR. GRANDMA
ANNA TIEMAN BIRTHDAY MAY 1, 195?

TIEMAN - MICHAEL AND BEVERLY WITH GRANDMA VIOLA TIEMAN AND
GR. GRANDMA ANNA AT HER BIRTHDAY BREAKFAST OUTSIDE HER HOME
MAY 1 195?

Fourth Generation Malcolm Sommer Tieman Timeline
1900-1977

		Tieman Family 1900-1980				
Year		**Rulers**	**World History**	**U.S. History**	**Science/Technology**	**Art**
1900		Pres. McKinley & Roosevelt 1901	Titanic Sinks 1912	Eastern Europe, Italian	1st Airplane 1903	Expressionism
		Pres. T. Roosevelt 1905	Boxer Rebellion 1900	Migration		Cubism 1907
		Edward VII -Eng. 1901	Russo/Japanese War	Tribes become US Cit. 1901		Jack London
		Ferdinand of Bulgaria 1908	Russia Revolution	McKinley Assassinated 1901		
			Young Turk Revolution	Forest Conservation 1902		
				NAACP 1909		
		Pres. William Taft 1909		Oklahoma 1907		
1910		Pres. Woodrow Wilson 1913	World War I 1914	New Mexico 1912	Theory of Relativity 1916	Stravinsky
		George V - Eng. 1910		Arizona 1912		
	Malcolm Tieman Born 1903 - Married 1925 - Died 1974			Select. Service Draft 1917		
1920		Mussolini - Italy 1922	Hague Court 1920	18th Ammend. No Alcohol		James Joyce
		Pres. C. Coolidge 1925	Spain Dictatorship	19th Ammend. Women Vote		T.S. Eliot
			Stalin Expands Russia			Disney 1st Cartoon 1924
		Pres. Herbert Hoover 1929		Stock Market Crash 1929		Surrealism 1924
1930		Pres. F. D. Roosevelt 1933	World War II 1939	New Deal 1933	Plastics 1937	Hitchcock
		Edward VIII - Eng. 1936				
		George VI - Eng. 1936				
		Hitler - Germany 1933	Spain Civil War	Social Security 1935		Faulkner
1940		Pres. Roosevelt & Truman 1945	United Nations 1945	Marshall Plan 1947	Radar 1940	Hemmingway
		Pres. Harry S. Truman 1949	A-Bomb of Japan 1945		Transistor 1948	Sartre
		Gandhi Assass. 1948	NATO 1949			Jazz
			India Freedom 1947			
1950		Charles de Gaulle France 1958	Korean War 1950	Asian Migration	Sputnik - 1957	Abstract Expressionism
		Elizabeth II - Eng. 1952	Argentine Military 1955	Blacks Boycott Buses 1955	H Bomb 1951	
				School Segregation 1955	DNA 1953	
		Pres. D. Eisenhower 1953		Alaska 1959		
		Khrushchev - Russia		Hawaii 1959		
1960		Pres. Kennedy & Johnson 1961/63	Vietnam War 1964	Peace Corps 1961	Laser 1960	Pop Art
		Pres. L. Johnson 1965	Brazil Military 1964	Civil Rights Move. 1960-65		Bob Dylan
		Pres. Richard Nixon 1969		Kennedy Assass. 1963		Beatles
		Brezhnev - Russia 1964		Anti War Dem. 1965-70		1968 Movie 2001
					US -Moon Landing 1969	
				Hippies 1966-69		
1970		Juan Carlos- Sp. 1975		Many Cultures Migration	Personal Computer 1978	Post Modern
		Pres. Nixon & Ford 1973/74		War Powers Act 1973	Viking I & II on Mars	Solzhenitsyn
		Pres. Jimmy Carter 1977		Nixon Resigns 1973-74		Star Wars 1977
				Wounded Knee 1973		Punk Rock
				Feminism 1970's		

Fourth Generation
Malcolm Sommer Tieman 1903-1974

MALCOLM SOMMER TIEMAN was born on 26 Sep 1903 in Keokuk, Iowa, died on 16 Sep 1974 in KeokukIowa at age 70, and was buried in Keokuk, Iowa. Malcolm married **Viola Emma Marie REITZ** on 13 Jun 1925 in Keokuk, Iowa. Viola was born on 15 Jan 1904 in Van Buran Twp., Iowa, died on 22 Mar 1995 in Columbia, Missouri at age 91, and was buried on 27 Mar 1995 in Keokuk, USA. Children: **Malcolm LaVerne.**

VIOLA & MALCOLM TIEMAN - WEDDING PHOTO
JUNE 13, 1925

Like Beverly, I do not have many memories of Papa and Viola (see her memories below). Papa was an electrician and loved to putter at home on small projects. He was about 6', and thin, a very quiet, gentle man who died at the age of 71 of a heart attack after repainting the interior of their home. Viola was a Christian Scientist a large lady also close to 6', (large boned from farmer stock), loved to cook. Several years after Papa died, she went to a nursing home in MO. close to her family where she died in 1995 at the age of 91.

Memories: Grand-Daughter
Beverly Dianne Tieman Starr, 2009

On very hot summer nights in Iowa on the river with nothing but maybe a small fan at home, we would take a ride along the river road with all the car windows down to cool off. Or sleep in the front yard on blankets when the house got too hot. There must have been mosquitoes the size of aircraft carriers! We lived near a Dairy Queen and in the summer had ice cream cones and Caesar always got one too.

PaPa and Grandma Tieman would take either Michael or I on rides on the river road to try to cool off. They never took us both at the same time and that always upset my mother. Our grandparents Viola (Rietz) and Malcolm Tieman also lived in Keokuk in an upstairs apartment on Franklin Street. They were Christian Scientists although my grandmother had to take insulin for her diabetes (the religion doesn't believe any medicine in necessary). She worked at Swift's meat packing plant for a few years before my dad was born and he was an electrician at the Hoopinger's plant.

Grandma made the best yeast donuts from scratch and I used her recipe for years.

They were both very quiet and dad was an only child. I don't remember too much about them. They would never have Michael and I over there at the same time and that was really upsetting to our mother. The women didn't get along very well. Grandma did come twice to see us in NY with Maggie and Thelma when Amy and Nicole were little after PaPa died.

Obit - *Daily Gate City Newspaper:*
Malcolm Sommer Tieman, 70, 1023 Palean, died at 3:05 pm Monday at Graham hospital. Born Sept. 26, 1903 in Keokuk, he was the son of Henry H. and Anna Sommer Tieman, and was a lifelong resident of Keokuk. He was first employed by the Standard Four Tire Co. then

by its succeeding companies. He retired from Sheller-Globe in 1968. He married Viola Reitz, June 13, 1925 in Keokuk. He was a member of the First Church of Christian Scientist and served as an usher. Mr. Tieman is survived by his wife: one son, Malcolm L. of Akron, Ohio; three grandchildren; two great grandchildren; two sisters, Thelma Tieman of Keokuk and Magdalene Tieman of Keokuk and other relatives. The funeral will be held at 2pm Thursday at the DeJong Funeral Home with Reader Mrs. Paul DeVries officiating. Interment will be in Oakland Cemetery. Visitation will begin at 2pm Wednesday.

Keokuk (pronounced /kiːəkuk/) is named for Chief Keokuck, a chief of the Sac and Fox Indians. His bones were brought here in 1883 from Franklin County, Kansas, and reinterred in Rand Park beneath a massive stone pedestal which is surrounded by a life-sized statute of an Indian chieftain. On the east side of this monument is embedded the marble slab taken from the grave in Kansas which is lettered as follows: "Sacred to the memory of Keokuck, a distinguished Sac chief born at Rock Island in 1788. Died in April 1848." Keokuck, "The Watchful Fox", was not a hereditary chief, but raised himself to the dignity by the force of talent and enterprise. He was a man of extraordinary eloquence in council and never at a loss in an emergency. He was a noble looking man about six feet tall, portly and weighing over 200 pounds. He had an eagle eye, dignified bearing, and a manly, intelligent expression of countenance.

On November 23, 1985 a new Keokuk Hamilton (IL) bridge was opened. This bridge which is 3,340 feet long and 64 feet wide eliminates the tie up of traffic from the former swing span bridge, allowing both automobile and barge traffic to move more efficiently.

Children:
MALCOLM L. b. 20 Feb 1926 Keokuk, Iowa; d. 5 Jan 2011 Stow, Ohio at age 84; buried 8 Jan 2011 Hillside Memorial Park Cemetary - Akron, OH.; m. Doris Earline MORRILL 30 Dec 1944 Kahoka, Missouri.

Anna Sommer Tieman and Son Malcolm Sommer Tieman
Photo 1903-1905?

Malcolm Tieman

Viola & Malcolm Tieman - Wedding Photo
June 13. 1925

Tieman- Malcolm, LaVerne, Viola

Malcolm Tieman - far right
Christmas Day 1951 as BW boiler broke
down

Malcolm & Viola Tieman
Date ?

STATE OF IOWA

IOWA STATE DEPARTMENT OF HEALTH
DIVISION OF VITAL STATISTICS
Delayed Certificate of Birth

3 7 0 3 5 2

Full name
at birth Malcolm Sommers Tieman Date of birth September 26, 1903 Sex Male
(Month) (Day) (Year)

Birthplace Keokuk Lee Iowa Color or Race White
(City or Town) (County) (State)

Father: Full Name Henry Herman Tieman Birth place Iowa
(State or Country)

Mother: Maiden Name Anna Sommers Birth-place Germany
(State or Country)

Affidavit: I hereby declare upon oath that the above statements are true.
Signature Malcolm Sommers Tieman Address 717 Franklin St. Keokuk, Iowa
(To be signed by registrant if possible)

Subscribed and sworn to before me on January 21, 19 42
My commission expires on July 4th, 19 42
(SEAL) Notary Public

Applicant—do not write below this line.

	ABSTRACT OF SUPPORTING EVIDENCE	Date original document was made
	Name and kind of document, and by whom issued and signed	
1	Hospital Record. St. Joseph's Hospital, Keokuk, Iowa. Sister M. Elicia	July 28, 1929
2	School Record, Independent School District Keokuk, Iowa J.C.Wright, Supt. of Public Schools	-----
3	Voting Registration Record, City of Keokuk, Iowa, Carl L. Mundy, Comm. of Registration	Sept. 16, 1932
4	Return of Marriage, Record No.13, page 466 Records of Lee Co. Iowa at Keokuk	June 13, 1925

Information Concerning Registrant as Stated in Documents

	Birth date or age	Birthplace	Name of Father	Maiden Name of Mother
1	25 years			
2	Sept. 26,1903	Keokuk,Iowa		
3	1903	Iowa		
4	22 next birthday	Keokuk, Ia.	Henry Tieman	Anna Sommers

Additional information: School record shows registrant attended Carey School in Keokuk, Iowa.

Statement of Reviewing Official

I certify that no prior certificate has been found in the State Bureau of Vital Statistics for this registrant and that documentary evidence has been seen and read which substantiates the facts as set forth in the foregoing abstract.

For Genealogical Purposes Only

Walter L. Bierring M.D.
(State Registrar)

Signature _____ M.D.
(Director Division of Vital Statistics)

Date signed FEB 3 1942 Date filed FEB 3 1942

This is to certify that this is a true and correct reproduction of the original record as recorded in this state, issued under the authority of Chapter 144, Code of Iowa.
This copy is not valid unless prepared on engraved border displaying state seal and signature of the Registrar.
THIS COPY NOT VALID UNLESS UNALTERED AND PREPARED ON CERTIFIED SECURITY PAPER

This form recommended by the U. S. Bureau of the Census.

DATE ISSUED
AUG 18 2016
S2012643

Terry E. Branstad
GOVERNOR, STATE OF IOWA
Kim Reynolds, Lt. Governor

Melissa R. Bird
DEPUTY STATE REGISTRAR

FORM #588-0328S (Rev. 01/2016)

ANY ALTERATION OR ERASURE VOIDS THIS CERTIFICATE

STATE OF IOWA
CERTIFICATION OF VITAL RECORD

*** FOR GENEALOGICAL PURPOSES ONLY ***
IOWA DEPARTMENT OF PUBLIC HEALTH
CERTIFICATE OF DEATH

STATE OF IOWA
DEPARTMENT OF HEALTH
CERTIFICATE OF DEATH

114-
74-020030

DECEASED — NAME (First Middle Last)	MALCOLM SOMMER TIEMAN
SEX	MALE
DATE OF DEATH	SEPTEMBER 16, 1974
RACE	WHITE
AGE	70
DATE OF BIRTH	SEPT 26, 1903
COUNTY OF DEATH	LEE
CITY, TOWN, OR LOCATION OF DEATH	KEOKUK
INSIDE CITY LIMITS	YES
HOSPITAL OR OTHER INSTITUTION	GRAHAM HOSPITAL
STATE OF BIRTH	IOWA
CITIZEN OF WHAT COUNTRY	U.S.A.
MARRIED, NEVER MARRIED, WIDOWED, DIVORCED	MARRIED
SURVIVING SPOUSE	VIOLA REITZ
SOCIAL SECURITY NUMBER	479-10-2240
USUAL OCCUPATION	MILL WORKER SHELLER GLOBE CO
KIND OF BUSINESS OR INDUSTRY	RETIRED
WAS DECEASED EVER IN U S ARMED SERVICES?	NO
RESIDENCE — STATE	IOWA
COUNTY	LEE
CITY, TOWN, OR LOCATION	KEOKUK
INSIDE CITY LIMITS	YES
STREET AND NUMBER	1023 PALEAN St
FATHER — NAME	HENRY H. TIEMAN
MOTHER — MAIDEN NAME	ANNA SOMMER
INFORMANT — NAME	MRS VIOLA TIEMAN
MAILING ADDRESS	1023 PALEAN XT KEOKUK, IOWA 52632

PART I. DEATH WAS CAUSED BY

(a) IMMEDIATE CAUSE: Coronary occlusion — sudden

CERTIFICATION: I ATTENDED THE DECEASED FROM 9 16 74 TO 9 16 74 — did not — DEATH OCCURRED AT 3:05 P.M.

CERTIFICATION BY: MEDICAL EXAMINER — THE DECEDENT WAS PRONOUNCED DEAD Sept. 20, 1974 3:05 P M

CERTIFIER — NAME: F. R. Richmond, M. D. — SIGNATURE: F.R. Richmond M.D. 9/20/74

MAILING ADDRESS — CERTIFIER: 61- 10th, Ft. Madison, Ia. 52627

BURIAL: BURIAL — CEMETERY OR CREMATORY: OAKLAND CEMETERY — LOCATION: KEOKUK, IOWA

DATE: SEPT 19, 1974 — FUNERAL HOME: DeJong's Funeral Home 917 Blondeau St Keokuk, Iowa 52632

DATE RECEIVED BY LOCAL REGISTRAR: Sept. 23 1974

07/20/2016 DATE ISSUED
Terry E. Branstad — GOVERNOR, STATE OF IOWA — Kim Reynolds, Lt. Governor
DEPUTY STATE REGISTRAR

S1949510

FORM #588-0328S (Rev. 01/2016)

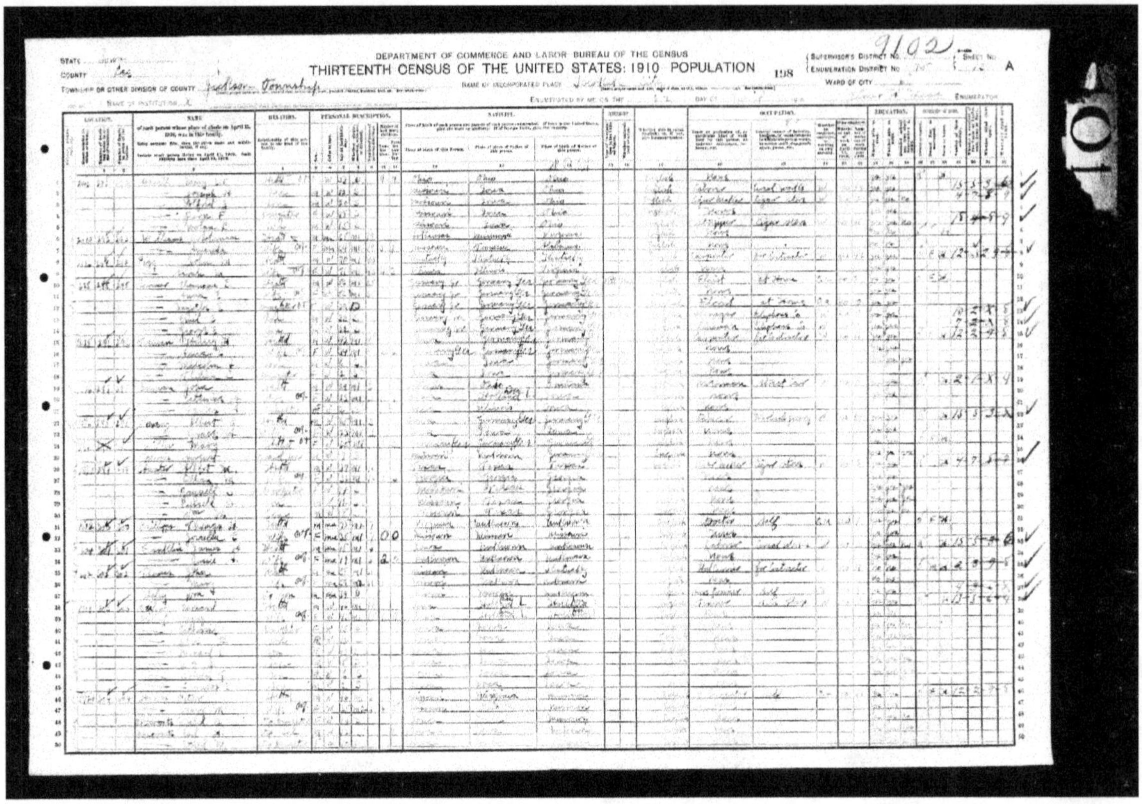

DEPARTMENT OF COMMERCE AND LABOR—BUREAU OF THE CENSUS
THIRTEENTH CENSUS OF THE UNITED STATES: 1910—POPULATION

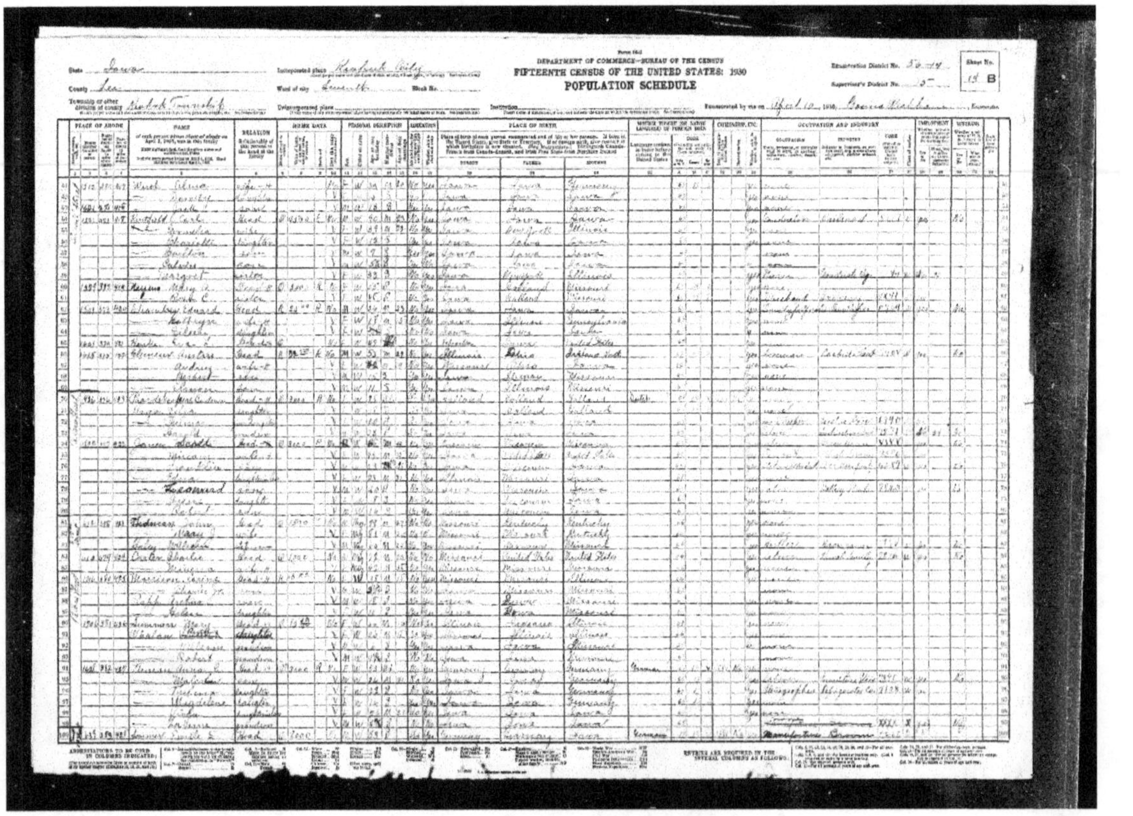

DEPARTMENT OF COMMERCE—BUREAU OF THE CENSUS
FIFTEENTH CENSUS OF THE UNITED STATES: 1930
POPULATION SCHEDULE

STATE OF IOWA

TO THE SECRETARY OF IOWA STATE BOARD OF HEALTH:

Return of Births in the County of .... L E E ....

NAME OF CHILD	SEX M. F.	DATE OF BIRTH Month Day Year	PLACE OF BIRTH (Town or Township)	MOTHER'S FULL MAIDEN NAME	FATHER'S FULL NAME
Reitz Viola E. M	F	Jan 15 1904	Van Buren Twp	Mable K. South	F. W. Reitz

For the Year Ending .... DECEMBER 31ST, A. D. 1904 ....

Dated ...... Dec 31 1904

I hereby certify that the above Return of Births

is a correct transcript from the records in this office.

.... Clerk District Court

For Genealogical Purposes Only

This is to certify that this is a true and correct reproduction of the original record as recorded in this state, issued under the authority of Chapter 144, Code of Iowa. This copy is not valid unless prepared on engraved border displaying state seal and signature of the Registrar.

THIS COPY NOT VALID UNLESS UNALTERED AND PREPARED ON CERTIFIED SECURITY PAPER

AUG 1 8 2016
DATE ISSUED
S2011054

Terry E. Branstad
GOVERNOR, STATE OF IOWA
Kim Reynolds, Lt. Governor

Melissa R. Bird
DEPUTY STATE REGISTRAR
FORM #588-0328S (Rev. 01/2016)

ANY ALTERATION OR ERASURE VOIDS THIS CERTIFICATE

MARRIAGES.

Viola Emma Marie Reitz
June 13th 1925

Ruth Amelia Alma Reitz
April 24th 1929

Cora Mabel Reitz
November 14th 1929

Elsie Matilda Reitz
September 14th 1937

Fred Wm. Reitz — Oct. 14, 1939

Ruth Amelia Alma — Dec. 23, 1939

Fern Irene Reitz — Aug. 23, 1940

Willa Eileen Reitz — June 12, 1946

Fifth Generation Malcolm LaVerne Tieman Timeline
1920-2011

	Tieman Family 1920-2020				
Year	Rulers	World History	U.S. History	Science/Technology	Art
1920	Mussolini - Italy 1922	Hague Court 1920	18th Ammend. No Alcohol		James Joyce
	Pres. C. Coolidge 1925	Spain Dictatorship	19th Ammend. Women Vote		T.S. Eliot
		Stalin Expands Russia			Disney 1st Cartoon 1924
	Pres. Herbert Hoover 1929		Stock Market Crash 1929		Surrealism 1924
1930	Pres. F. D. Roosevelt 1933	World War II 1939	New Deal 1933	Plastics 1937	Hitchcock
	Edward VIII - Eng. 1936				
	George VI - Eng. 1936				
	Hitler - Germany 1933	Spain Civil War	Social Security 1935		Faulkner
1940	Pres. Roosevelt & Truman 1945	United Nations 1945	Marshall Plan 1947	Radar 1940	Hemmingway
	Pres. Harry S. Truman 1949	A-Bomb of Japan 1945		Transistor 1948	Sartre
	Gandhi Assass. 1948	NATO 1949			Jazz
		India Freedom 1947			
1950	Charles de Gaulle France 1958	Korean War 1950	Asian Migration	Sputnik - 1957	Abstract Expressionism
	Elizabeth II - Eng. 1952	Argentine Military 1955	Blacks Boycott Buses 1955	H Bomb 1951	
			School Segregation 1955	DNA 1953	
	Pres. D. Eisenhower 1953		Alaska 1959		
	Khrushchev - Russia		Hawaii 1959		
1960	Pres. Kennedy & Johnson 1961/63	Vietnam War 1964	Peace Corps 1961	Laser 1960	Pop Art
	Pres. L. Johnson 1965	Brazil Military 1964	Civil Rights Move. 1960-65		Bob Dylan
	Pres. Richard Nixon 1969		Kennedy Assass. 1963		Beatles
	Brezhnev - Russia 1964		Anti War Dem. 1965-70		1968 Movie 2001
				US - Moon Landing 1969	
			Hippies 1966-69		
1970	Juan Carlos - Sp. 1975		Many Cultures Migration	Personal Computer 1978	Post Modern
	Pres. Nixon & Ford 1973/74		War Powers Act 1973	Viking I & II on Mars	Solzhenitsyn
	Pres. Jimmy Carter 1977		Nixon Resigns 1973-74		Star Wars 1977
			Wounded Knee 1973		Punk Rock
			Feminism 1970's		
1980	Pres. Ronald Reagan 1981	Berlin Wall Down 1989	War on Drugs 1980's	CD, VCR & Cable	Rap
	Pres. George Bush 1989			Ozone Hole 1987	
1990	Pres. W. Clinton 1993	Gulf War 1991	Welfare Reform 1996	World Wide Web 1993	
		Soviet Union Breakup 1991	Land on Mars 1997		
		Cold War Over	Inter. Space Station 1998		
		Germany United 1990	Longest Robust Economy 1997		
2000	Pres. G. W. Bush 2001	War on Terror 9/11/2001		Animals Cloned 2000	
				Drones Fight War 2004	
	Pres. B. Obama 2009		Global Recession Crisis 2008/9		
2010	Philip VI - Sp. 2014		Affordable Care Act 2010		David Fincher

(Left vertical note spanning 1950–1970 rows: LaVerne Tieman Born 1926 - Married 1944 - Died 2011)

Compiled by: Michael Tieman, September 2017

Fifth Generation
Malcolm LaVerne Tieman 1926-2011

MALCOLM LAVERNE TIEMAN was born on 20 Feb 1926 in Keokuk, Lee, Iowa, USA, died on 5 Jan 2011 in Stow, Summit, Ohio, USA at age 84, and was buried on 8 Jan 2011 in Hillside Memorial Park Cemetary - Akron, Summit, OH, USA. Malcolm married **Doris Earline MORRILL** on 30 Dec 1944 in Kahoka, Clark, Missouri, USA. Doris was born on 12 Nov 1924 in Nevada, Story, Iowa, USA, died on 9 Mar 2003 in Akron, Summit, Ohio, USA at age 78, and was buried on 13 Mar 2003 in Hillside Memorial Park Cemetary - Akron, Summit, OH, USA.

Doris & LaVerne Tieman 1944?

I'm 82 years young I was born Malcolm LaVerne Tieman of the parents of Malcolm Sommer Tieman and Viola Marie Reitz Tieman on Feb 20, 1926 at St. Joseph Hospital in Lee County, Keokuk Iowa.

I weighed 13 lbs. at birth. When I was 3 years old I came down with polio which I don't remember. My dad took me to Dr. Northup a friend of the family and I was given a complete body massage for one hour a day 7 days a week. It cost my parents $1 a day which in those depression days would be like $100 a day in this day. In those days there was no health insurance available. The only deformity I have is my left thumb is crooked and left arm smaller than my right arm. But luckily, I can use my hand.

Keokuk was named after Chief Keokuk of the Sioux Indian Tribe which settled there.

The Mississippi river is a mile wide and I used to swim & fish in the summertime. When I was 6 years old my grandfather, Don Morrill and I would fish by the dam about 500 ft. from the closed spillway and catch catfish and perch. It was great sport. Don would clean them and had a delicious dinner. (Some confusion here as Don was not his grandfather, but his father-in-law, could he have meant his grandfather Fred Reitz?).

Every summer I would spend the summers at my grandfather's farm in Kahoka, MO. an hour drive south of Keokuk. I fed pigs also rode on back of pigs and young calves - didn't stay on long but was fun. Also learned to hunt small game and got to be a good shot - my uncles Fred and Floyd Hewitt taught me how to shoot.

Beverly was born 3/15/47 Richard was stillborn 1/28/48.

In 1941 USA declared war on Japan Dec 7, 1941. I was drafted in the Army which I was a senior in High School. I graduated on June 6, 1944 from Keokuk Senior High and was in service on June 30, 1944 in Fort Dodge, Iowa. I was sent to Fort Leonardwood, MO. for army basic training for 6 weeks. I was then sent to Buckley Field in Denver, CO. for 6 weeks of gunnery school. We had to take apart and reassemble a 50cal. machine gun blind folded in 3 minutes.

While in high school I met your mother Doris Earline Morrill - fell in love with her and we got married on Dec. 30, 1944 in Kahoka, MO by justice of peace. Don & Alta, Dee's parents drove us in a blinding snow storm - it was so bad Don had to look out the window, so he could see out that night. Of course, my mother was crushed because I was only 18 & Dee was 20 - Dad was for us.

Dee was a Registered Nurse just graduating from nurses training of 3 years in1945; she was only the second student in Iowa's history to score 98 on her state board test.

On Christmas Eve 1945 I was in a convoy going through Paris France in a severe thunderstorm. It was cold, 38, we had no canopy over our heads - we were wet and hungry. We arrived in the Black Forest where we slept in tents - got food and dry clothes & boots. Stayed 2 days, then we went to a small village called Furstenfeldbrook which is south of Munich - helped guard SS troops with the Polish guards - who broke open barrels of denatured alcohol and of course died within minutes. Horrible site to see. Then I was shipped to a supply depot out of Munich and stayed till I was sent home in June of 1946. I had an honorable discharge from the 9th Air Force as a Staff Sgt.

Your mother met me in Chicago where we stayed at the Waldorf Astoria for a week. We saw Liberachie play piano before he became famous.

Came back to Keokuk - your mom had rented an upstairs apt. on 16th & Main St. I went to work for J.C. Penney Co. Walked 16 blocks to work one-way 2x a day. We had a little fan - it was really hot - your mom worked at St. Joseph Hospital.

Beverly was born March 15th, 1947 - at St. Joseph Hospital.

I earned a yearly membership at the YMCA by working in the summer teaching boys ages 6 to14 years how to swim in the winter on Saturday I coached a boy's basketball team same ages with another coach while in the 9th to 12th grade at Keokuk High.

I also worked at J.C. Penney as stock boy and marked merchandise after school and all-day Saturdays. Mr. J.C. Penney visited our store in 1948 - he drove himself from Missouri to Keokuk which was a 2hr. drive - on that Father's Day he worked on the floor with the men selling merchandise - I had the pleasure of working next to him - He could call you by your first name after only hearing it once - a remarkable man and mind - He had 3 sons who he made to work for a living as he never gave them any allowance - he remarked you learn more by doing than have someone support you.

Michael was born Aug. 20, 1950.

When Beverly was 4 years old - she would take her chair & coloring book and crayons and sit on the corner and color. Grandma Alta lived across the corner from her - none dare touch her, our Caesar, G. Alta's red cocker spaniel would take them in a minute. The neighbors and friends of ours could talk to her but don't touch. Crazy - but that's the way it was.

Beverly went to school at Garfield School and then I was transferred to Freeport, Illinois, next to Wisc. boarder, where we lived between 4-5 years- then we moved to Elgin, Illinois -with Penney's.

Every year Freeport did a presentation of the Lincoln & Douglas debate - everyone in the city of 25,000 dressed in costumes of that era - this lasted one week - and on Sat. had a big parade of horses & oxen pulling covered wagons - bands & clowns - a big day for Freeport - these were fun times.

Connie was born in Freeport in August 5, 1958.

It was so cold in Elgin, Ill. -20degrees below zero and 5 - 6 feet of snow from Nov. til April - we had red flags on our car antennas, so we could see who was turning the corners. Snow plows kept the main streets open all winter - thank

God for that. Beverly & Michael walked 4 blocks to school, snow drifts so high we could not see them when they were walking.

In Akron, Ohio, Beverly put snow on Michael's face and froze his cheeks. Mom spanked her little butt and she never did it again - It took years before his cheeks healed up.

Beverly graduated from Buchtel High School in Akron - when I quit Penney's and joined Buckeye Mart in Columbus.

Moved from Columbus to Akron where I managed stores for Scotts 5-10. 1962 and'63. Every year in Aug. the city had movie star celebrities come in for the Soap Box Derby race - the one Beverly & Michael was Hoss, Little Joe and Loren Green - they stopped in front of Scotts and I got their autographs but they got lost over the years.

We moved from Columbus where Michael graduated from high school and started art school.

To Mass. with Ben Franklin stores and back to Akron a second time to Ellet where I worked for Prudential Insurance 15 years until 1991.

When Beverly was 18 she went to nursing school at City Hospital in Akron for 3 years then graduated as a registered nurse. She met Bill Starr while in nurses training. He had a red convertible which Connie liked to ride in. Bill was at college in Youngstown where he graduated as a structural engineer. They were married for 23 years, had Nicole & Amy she then got divorced - Bill met another woman. Bill worked at Kodak in Rochester NY till he retired at age 55. He now lives 1 1/2 hours from Dallas. Beverly & Bill lived in Texas once before 1976-1982 - kids were little - 4-5 years old. Mom and I went down there for Xmas a couple of times.

I retired on April 1st, 1991 from Prudential Insurance Company - after 15 years' service - I enjoyed every minute of it.

Mom and I bought a house in Akron and lived there 20 years in Ellet, suburb of Akron where Connie graduated from High School. We sold home and rented an apt. in Cuyahoga Falls across from golf course - when your mom passed away on 3/9/03.

I moved to Danbury Retirement Home on April 22, 2008.

*The years since mom died have been too painful for Dad to write about here. Yet he kept a daily diary from when mom died until 8 months before he died- Dad died Jan 5, 2011. -Michael Tieman-

Memories: Daughter, Beverly Dianne Tieman Starr, 2009

Mom and Dad met in high school when he was a sophomore and she was a senior. According to dad, mom's friend, Faye Peters, introduced them. Mom worked as a nurse for decades, paying for our first TV and automatic washer and dryer. She got 98 out of 100 on her nursing Iowa State Board Exam. She worked at a hospital as a floor nurse where ever we moved to until her knees started bothering her with arthritis.

Dad graduated from Keokuk High School in early June 1944 and was drafted for the 9th Air Force Army Air Corps at the end of the month. He left for basic training in Ft. Dodge, Iowa and then on to Ft. Leonard Wood, MO. for more training. (My grandson Jacob was born there in 1997 when his father was stationed there). Dad was then sent to Buckley Field in Denver, CO for gunnery school where he trained to become a B17 gunner. He was young, gullible and skinny enough to fit into the gunner's bubble he always said. They practiced dropping flour "bombs" into the Grand Canyon before going overseas. When the crew was sent out at night to learn how to navigate over water (the Gulf of Mexico) they got lost in the dark and couldn't find their way back to base until dawn. The navigator was sent back to school after that even though he was not a rookie. Dad was also trained as a tail gunner on a B29 getting ready to go to Japan, but Japan surrendered first.

It's a wonder the military even took him because of his crippled left thumb he has as a result of having polio as a toddler. He was about 3 and was paralyzed on his left side. Daily massage for a year let him recover all of his function except that thumb, but he still could hold onto the B17 machine gun.

He and mom got married Dec. 30, 1944 in a snowstorm in Kahoka, MO by a justice of the peace. Grandma Alta and Grandpa Don drove them there and dad's mother was not happy about it. Dad was 18 and mom had just turned 20 in Nov.

They were together for 2 weeks Gulfport, Mississippi 1945 before he shipped overseas, and she studied for her state boards. There was an incident while they were there of him almost being allowed onto a city bus. It was summertime, he had a deep tan, and the driver thought he was a black man with a white woman. When he proved he was a soldier, the driver let them onto the bus.

He said that on Christmas Eve 1945 he was in Munich and helped guard SS troops along with the Polish guards for a while. He was then shipped to a supply depot outside of Munich and discharged June 1946 as a Staff Sgt. Mom wanted him to go to college on the GI bill, but instead he returned to Penney's as a salesman in shoes and men's clothing. He told me not taking advantage of the college bill is his biggest regret.

He joined the Blue Lodge Masons in Keokuk in 1948 year and became a 32nd degree Mason in the 1960s in Akron joining the Tadmor Shriners. He drove kids and their parents to Cleveland Clinic for their appointments at the burn hospital when he first retired in 1991.

Mom and Dad had a belated honeymoon in Chicago at the Waldorf Astoria for a week after he returned from the war. They saw Liberace play piano in the Palmer Room when he was just a piano player.

They rented an upstairs apt. on 16th and Main when they got back where he started working for J.C. Penney, walking 16 blocks to work one way. Mom was still working at St. Joseph Hospital. like she did while he was gone.

I was born 9 months later, and they moved to the house on Timea St. Many years later, when I was a young adult, mom told me that they had had a stillborn boy on 1/28/48, 10 months after I was born. They named him Richard LaVerne after his best friend in high school, Richard Dunlavey. The baby was 13# and perfectly formed but strangled on the cord. If they had done more C sections in those days the result may have been different. I found his birth date in my baby book and nothing more. Michael has a copy of the obituary where they misspelled his name. Dad to this day still does not talk about him.

When I was very small I was awakened one night from a sound sleep hearing and seeing my dad being taken out of the house in an ambulance. I was scared but didn't leave my room, just hid behind the door. I think he had pneumonia and he wasn't away too long.

Dad had a vegetable garden behind the house when I was little. He always liked growing flowers outside when he had time. He liked to draw and sketched lambs and ducks on my baby quilt and summer dresses that mom would then embroider. He likes to collect Waterford crystal, lighthouses, and has always loved the water. He was a swimming teacher at the YMCA when I was very little, but Michael and I never learned to swim. By the time we were old enough to learn, dad was working long hours in the retail business. Dad loves the ocean and lakes.

Michael lives on the Pacific coast and I like to paint seascapes. Michael and I still to this day do not like to get into the water. As an adult I was upended by an ocean wave in Hawaii and drenched while sitting on a rock in Bermuda, so am not at all fond of oceans. Even though Dad and I are both Pisces, he is the true water sign and I am the "watching from the porch" water sign.

Dad hunted rabbits and squirrels for us to eat with Floyd when I was really little. There wasn't a lot of money and even later, the day before pay day we would have waffles for dinner because that was all we had. We kids thought it was fun, having breakfast for dinner. Some of the things mom served us from time to time made me skip dinner; ham hocks and navy beans, liver and onions (one of Connie's all-time favorites) and dad's favorite and the absolute worst… stuffed beef heart. The smell of these things made it impossible to eat. They must have been cheap.

A tornado went down across the street from us one night, Freeport Ill., and a big tree fell across the driveway putting a huge tree limb through our parents' bedroom window. I don't remember this, but Michael does and dad confirmed his memory.

While we lived in Akron, dad worked for Scotts 5-10 downtown and the Soap Box Derby was (and is still) held there every summer. There was always a parade of current TV stars and in 1962 it was Little Joe, Hoss, Pa, and Adam Cartwright from "Bonanza". We watched from the upstairs office in the Scotts store. The next year the celebrities were John Russell from "Lawman", comedian Paul Lynde, and Paul Anka (who interested me the most)!

Dad had had a heart attack when he was in his early 40's from an enlarged "athlete's" heart he acquired from running track in high school. Much later he has had a pacemaker implanted 3 times for the same reason. In the middle 1990's he was diagnosed with Chronic Lymphatic Leukemia. Thelma also had this for many years. I remember dad smoking a pipe with cherry tobacco until I my girls were little. It always smelled so wonderful.

On July 29, 2008 my dear, kind, smart sister Connie Sue lost her 6-year battle with breast cancer. She had all the radiation and chemo a human can have, and it still took her. It was the day before her 25th wedding anniversary and a week before her 50th birthday. Dad is incredibly sad and depressed. He said he was done when he lost you, "his rock". I can't imagine losing a wife of 50 years and then your youngest child of 50 years. No man should have to endure that.

Map of Migration - Malcolm LaVerne Tieman

Illinois - Late 20c.

The post-World War II era was a time of industrial modification for the production of consumer goods. Even though meat-packing companies began to move away from Chicago and East Saint Louis, in part because of obsolete physical plants, Illinois farms were being mechanized and upgraded for increased output. The use of hybrid seed, chemical fertilizer, herbicides, and insecticides resulted in larger crop yields. Post-World War II Illinois experienced rapid population growth. The rising number of school-age children brought public school reform, rural school consolidations, and huge suburban educational plants. Migration streams of blacks from the South, Hispanics from Mexico and Puerto Rico, and whites from Appalachia reshaped neighborhoods in Chicago, its suburbs, and other large Illinois cities.

As of the census of 2000, Illinois currently has the 6th largest population of the 50 U.S. states. Chicago, in terms of population, is the third largest city in the country.

Freeport is the county seat and largest city of Stephenson County, Illinois. The population was 25,638 at the 2010 census, and the mayor of Freeport is James Gitz, elected in 2013. Freeport is known for hosting the second Lincoln-Douglas debate of 1858, and as "Pretzel City, USA", named after the heritage of its Germanic settlers in the 1850s and the Billerbeck Bakery pretzel company that started as a result of their arrival. Freeport is home to the oldest Carnegie Library in Illinois and one of the first Carnegie Libraries designed by the famous Chicago architectural firm of Patton and Miller.

Elgin is a city in Cook and Kane counties in the northern part of the U.S. state of Illinois. Located roughly 35 mi (56 km) northwest of Chicago, it lies along the Fox River. As of 2013, the city had a total population of 110,145, making it the eighth-largest city in Illinois. Early Elgin achieved fame for the butter and dairy goods it sold to the city of Chicago. Gail Borden established a condensed milk factory here in 1866, and the local library is named in his honor. The dairy industry became less important with the arrival of the Elgin Watch Company. The watch factory employed three generations of Elginites from the late 19th to the mid 20th century, when it was the largest producer of fine watches in the United States (the factory ceased production in 1965 and was torn down in the summer of 1966) and the operator of the largest watchmaking complex in the world. Today, the clocks at Chicago's Union Station still bear the Elgin name.

Ohio - Late 20c.

Both farms and industries in Ohio were hard hit by the Great Depression that began in 1929. In the 1930s the state was wracked by major strikes such as the sit-down strikes in Akron (1935–36) and the so-called Little Steel strike (1937). World War II brought great prosperity to Ohio, but labor strife later resumed, as in the steel strikes of 1949 and 1959. Political unrest also affected the state in the protests of the 1960s and most violently in 1970 when four students were killed by national guardsmen who fired on a group of Vietnam War protesters at Kent State Univ.

Ohio's economy went into massive decline in the 1970s and 80s as the automobile, steel, and coal industries virtually collapsed, causing unemployment to soar. Akron, once world famous as a rubber center, stopped manufacturing rubber products altogether by the mid-1980s. During this period, the state's northern industrial centers were especially hard hit and lost much of their population. Since then, Ohio has concentrated on diversifying its economy, largely through expansion of the service sector. The state became an important center for the health-care industry with the opening of the Cleveland Clinic. Industrial research is also important, with Nela Park near Cleveland and Battelle Memorial Institute in Columbus among the more notable research centers; there are also still important rubber research laboratories in Akron.

Akron is the fifth-largest city in the U.S. state of Ohio and is the county seat of Summit County, the fourth most populous county in the state. The city is located in northeastern Ohio on the western edge of the Glaciated Allegheny Plateau, approximately 39 miles (63 km) south of Lake Erie and was co-founded along the Little Cuyahoga River in 1825 by Simon Perkins and Paul Williams. The name derived from the Greek word "ἄκρον" signifying a summit or high point. Due to Eliakim Crosby founding "North Akron" (Cascade) in 1833, "South" was added to the city's name until the two merged into an incorporated village in 1836. Neighboring settlements Kenmore and Ellet were annexed in 1929. As of the 2015 Census Estimate, the city proper had a total population of 197,542, making Akron the 119th largest city in the United States, and the fifth largest city in Ohio. The Akron, OH Metropolitan Statistical Area (MSA) covers Summit and Portage counties, and in 2010 had a population of 703,200. Akron is also part of the larger Cleveland-Akron-Canton, OH Combined Statistical Area, which in 2013 had a population of 3,501,538, ranking 15th. Creating the first Joint

Economic Development Districts, it did so with Springfield, Coventry, and Copley, also Bath in conjunction with Fairlawn. Residents of Akron are called "Akronites". Akron has had many nicknames, three of which are "Rubber City" "Cross Roads of the Deaf", and "City of Invention".

Akron is known for the rubber, tire, and airship industries among others, including the stoneware, sewer pipe, fishing tackle, farming equipment, mining, match, zipper, and toy industries. With a population increase of 201.8% during the 1910s, it became the nation's fastest-growing city.

Despite the number of rubber workers decreasing by approximately half from 2000–07, Akron's research in polymers gained an international reputation. It now centers the Polymer Valley which consist of 400 polymer-related companies, of which 94 were located in the city itself. Research is focused at the University of Akron which is home to the Goodyear Polymer Center and National Polymer Innovation Center, and first College of Polymer Science and Polymer Engineering. Because of its contributions to the Information Age, *Newsweek's* listed Akron fifth of ten high tech havens in 2001. In 2008 "City of Invention" was added to the seal when the All-America City Award was received for the third time. Some events of the 2014 Gay Games used the city as a venue.

Columbus is the capital and largest city of the U.S. state of Ohio. It is the 15th largest city in the United States, with a population of 850,106 (2015 estimate). It is the core city of the Columbus, OH Metropolitan Statistical Area (MSA), which encompasses a ten-county area. It is Ohio's third largest metropolitan area, behind Cleveland and Cincinnati.The city has a diverse economy based on education, government, insurance, banking, fashion, defense, aviation, food, clothes, logistics, steel, energy, medical research, health care, hospitality, retail, and technology.

Columbus is home to the Battelle Memorial Institute, the world's largest private research and development foundation; Chemical Abstracts Service, the world's largest clearinghouse of chemical information; NetJets, the world's largest fractional ownership jet aircraft fleet; and The Ohio State University, one of the largest universities in the United States. As of 2013, the city has the headquarters of five corporations in the U.S. Fortune 500: Nationwide Mutual Insurance Company, American Electric Power, L Brands, Big Lots, and Cardinal Health. The food service corporations Wendy's, Donatos Pizza, Bob Evans, Max & Erma's and White Castle along with nationally known companies Red Roof Inn, Rogue Fitness and Safelite are also based in the Columbus, Ohio metropolitan area.

Massachusetts - Late 20c.

Industry spurted forward again during World War II, and in the postwar era the state continued to develop. Politically, the state again assumed national importance with the 1960 election of Senator John F. Kennedy as the nation's 35th President. In 1974, Michael S. Dukakis, a Democrat, was elected governor. He lost to Edward King in 1978 but won again in 1982 and was reelected in 1986. In 1988 he ran for president, losing to George H. W. Bush. Dukakis decided not to run again for governor.

During the postwar period the decline of textile manufacturing was offset as the electronics industry, attracted by the skilled technicians available in the Boston area, boomed along Route 128. Growth in the computer and electronics sectors, much of it spurred by defense spending, helped Massachusetts prosper during much of the 1980s. At the end of the decade effects of a nationwide recession and the burden of a huge state budget hit Massachusetts hard, but in the 1990s there was a substantial economic recovery, spearheaded by growth in small high-tech companies.

Children:

BEVERLY D. b. 15 Mar 1947 in Keokuk, IA.; m. William James STARR 1 Sep 1968 Akron, Ohio. The marriage ended in divorce.

RICHARD b. 28 Jan 1948 Keokuk, Iowa; d. 28 Jan 1948 Keokuk, Iowa; b. Oakland Cemetery, Keokuk, Iowa

MICHAEL L. b. 20 Aug 1950 Keokuk, Iowa; baptized 31 Dec 1950 Keokuk, Iowa; m. Nancy Lee MARSHALL 16 Jun 1972 Columbus, Ohio;.Nancy b. 5 Mar 1952 Vancouver, British Columbia, Canada.

CONNIE S. b. 5 Aug 1958 Freeport, Illinois; m. John DROTOS 30 Jul 1983 Akron, Ohio; d. 29 Jul 2008 Akron, Ohio, at age 49; buried on 2 Aug 2008 Stow, Ohio. The cause of her death was Breast Cancer.

1. LaVerne date unknown

2. LaVerne (front row 2nd from right), and his B-17 crew photo1944-45

Doris & LaVerne Tieman 1944?

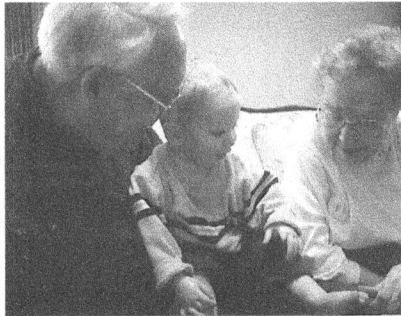

2000 - LaVerne & Doris Tieman with great-grandson Riley Erwin

Tieman Family 1961 - Akron, Ohio
Michael, Beverly, Connie, LaVerne, Doris

1992 LaVerne Tieman Family
Doris, LaVerne
Connie, Michael, Beverly

LaVerne & Doris, Nancy, Heather & Katie Tieman

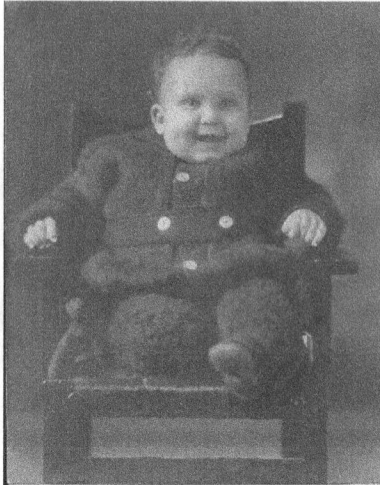

LaVerne Tieman 1926

LaVerne & Doris Tieman The Palmer House - Empire Room, Chicago 1952

Tieman - Malcolm LaVerne
1944 Graduation ?

LaVerne Tieman &
Margaret McLaughlin
1937

LaVerne & Doris Tieman
1946

LaVerne Tieman 3rd grade class
Garfield School 1935

LaVerne & mother Viola Tieman

LaVerne Tieman B-17 Bomber , his home away from home WWII

LaVerne Tieman
Dec. 20, 1944
KAAF, Kingnian AZ.

TIEMAN- MALCOLM LAVERNE WITH FAMILY 1961
BEVERLY, DORIS (WIFE), MICHAEL & CONNIE

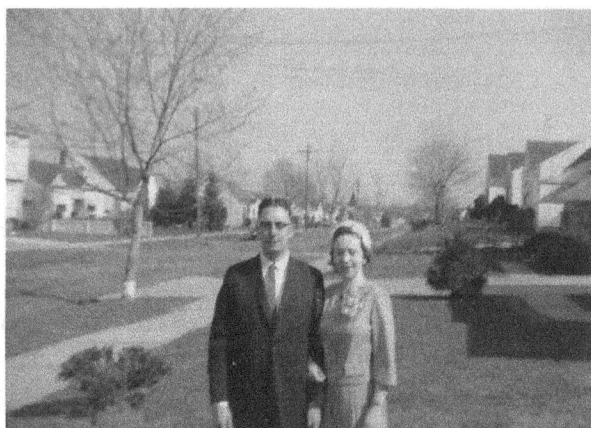

LaVerne & Doris Tieman, 1962

Doris & LaVerne Tieman
Gulfport, Miss. 1945

3. Doris and LaVerne Tieman date unknown

Sixth Generation Michael LaVerne Tieman Timeline 1950 -

		Tieman Family 1950-2016				
Year		Rulers	World History	U.S. History	Science/Technology	Art
1950	Michael Tieman Born 1950 - Married 1972	Charles de Gaulle France 1958	Korean War 1950	Asian Migration	Sputnik - 1957	Abstract Expressionism
		Elizabeth II - Eng. 1952	Argentine Military 1955	Blacks Boycott Buses 1955	H Bomb 1951	
				School Segregation 1955	DNA 1953	
		Pres. D. Eisenhower 1953		Alaska 1959		
		Khrushchev - Russia		Hawaii 1959		
1960		Pres. Kennedy & Johnson 1961/63	Vietnam War 1964	Peace Corps 1961	Laser 1960	Pop Art
		Pres. L. Johnson 1965	Brazil Military 1964	Civil Rights Move. 1960-65		Bob Dylan
		Pres. Richard Nixon 1969		Kennedy Assass. 1963		Beatles
		Brezhnev - Russia 1964		Anti War Dem. 1965-70		1968 Movie *2001*
					US -Moon Landing 1969	
				Hippies 1966-69		
1970		Juan Carlos- Sp. 1975		Many Cultures Migration	Personal Computer 1978	Post Modern
		Pres. Nixon & Ford 1973/74		War Powers Act 1973	Viking I & II on Mars	Solzhenitsyn
		Pres. Jimmy Carter 1977		Nixon Resigns 1973-74		*Star Wars 1977*
				Wounded Knee 1973		Punk Rock
				Feminism 1970's		
1980		Pres. Ronald Reagan 1981	Berlin Wall Down 1989	War on Drugs 1980's	CD, VCR & Cable	Rap
		Pres. George Bush 1989			Ozone Hole 1987	
1990		Pres. W. Clinton 1993	Gulf War 1991	Welfare Reform 1996	World Wide Web 1993	
			Soviet Union Breakup 1991	Land on Mars 1997		
			Cold War Over	Inter. Space Station 1998		
			Germany United 1990	Longest Robust Economy 1997		
2000		Pres. G. W. Bush 2001	War on Terror 9/11/2001		Animals Cloned 2000	
					Drones Fight War 2004	
		Pres. B. Obama 2009		Global Recession Crisis 2008/9		
2010		Philip VI - Sp. 2014		Affordable Care Act 2010		David Fincher

Sixth Generation
Michael LaVerne Tieman 1950 -

MICHAEL LAVERNE TIEMAN was born on 20 Aug 1950 in Keokuk, Lee, Iowa, USA and was baptized on 31 Dec 1950 in Keokuk, Lee, Iowa, USA. Michael married **Nancy Lee MARSHALL** on 16 Jun 1972 in Columbus, Franklin, Ohio, USA.Nancy was born on 5 Mar 1952 in Vancouver, British Columbia, Canada.

This then is me. I was going to tell my "life story", but my sister Beverly has written a pretty good one, and it is an accurate it as older sisters are never wrong. My memories therefore will follow hers.

Memories: Sister, Beverly Tieman Starr, 2009

My brother, Michael La Verne, was born Aug. 20, 1950 in Keokuk, Iowa and according to the stories our mother told, he had his days and nights mixed up until he was about 6 mos. old when he slept through the night. He had a lot of curls and looks like dad. He couldn't say my name and called me "Bebe" which is what I have my grandkids call me.

I mostly remember having to always take him with me growing up no matter where I went. I'm sure he loved going to my friends' house and watch us play! I vowed if I ever had kids they wouldn't have to go everywhere together like we did. The time I rubbed his face in the snow and he got frostbite on his cheeks it was because I was mad at mom for making me take him to the library with me. Since she worked nights, she napped in the daytime and I suppose it was more convenient for her if he was with me. I picked on him a lot as long as he was littler than me ("point to your head and say your initials") Once he got taller I didn't do it as often!

He called himself "the Ketchup Kid" and ate ketchup sandwiches sometimes…ick. Probably while he was wearing his twin gun holsters and the coon skin Davy Crockett cap!

Michael and I spent many Saturdays with Great-grandma, Maggie and Thelma and we learned how to make the yummy cinnamon/sugar coffee cake on the big black wood stove in their kitchen. It would rise overnight and be baked for Sunday breakfast the next morning. They made soap from lye and left-over soap scraps and they had the prettiest china and vases in their dining room.

I mostly remember what the little white house and neighborhood looked like from the years Michael and I returned and spent summers with Grandma (NaNaw) and Don Morrill after we had moved away.

Our first train ride alone was from Elgin to Keokuk in 1959. We were told NOT to get off of the train for any reason until we arrived. Along the way, the train hit a stalled car sitting on the tracks. Michael decided he needed to see what was going on and got off with the engineer. I let him go, because I was told not to leave. No one was hurt, and the engineer brought Michael back to his seat and of course I couldn't wait to tell on him! Probably was the highlight of my summer.

We had our first TV in 1954. Michael watched "Howdy Doody" and "Daniel Boone" and we watched "Capt. Kangaroo". Michael had a coon skin cap like Daniel Boone that he wore everywhere, even to bed until it had a life (and smell) of its own. He loved his double holster Roy Rogers six shooters and we watched "Hopalong Cassidy" and "the Rifleman". When we wanted "color" on our TV we put a blue sky and green grass plastic across the screen, so we could watch "Bonanza". Very high tech. Westerns were popular and "Gunsmoke" was all that Grandpa Don would watch.

Michael and I walked 3 or 4 blocks to Blackhawk School where my best friend was Sylvia Sieferman. Lehman's lived across the street from the school and her little brother was Michael's friend.

A tornado went down across the street from us one night in Freeport Illinois, and a big tree fell across the driveway putting a huge tree limb through our parents' bedroom window. I don't remember this, but Michael does and dad confirmed his memory.

Grandpa Don had given gave Michael a yellow tom cat that they named Nicky (St. Nicholas) at Christmas. He lived to be a was a very old cat with more than 9 lives fighting all the time, scarred, chewed up, bringing home dead mice and live baby rabbits to show us. He brought a baby rabbit into the house once and let it go. Mom caught it and put it in a shoe box on top of the floor register to keep it warm. She gave it a baby bottle of milk every few hours. It lived until the night she worked, and dad wouldn't get up every 2 hrs to feed it. Nicky never looked at it again once it was in the house. Once he brought in the live mouse and it ran under the upright piano she and Michael had to corner it and catch it. After that she never let Nicky in the door again without having him open his mouth to be sure there wasn't a tail hanging out of it. We had him a long time (over 10 years) and we took him on our many moves as dad got transferred to a new town every 3 years.

We went to Coleman Elementary school in Elgin, Illinois and had a very long cold walk (20 below zero) where the snow banks were so high at the intersections that cars had red flags on their antenna to be seen. Girls were not allowed to wear pants to school, so I wore slacks under my dress and took them off and on to walk to and from home. The school sat way back from the road across a big field and a long sidewalk that had no cover from the snow, nor freezing wind, nor rain. It seemed like it went on forever.

We took family vacations to Chicago to the Brookfield Zoo in 1959 and Springfield, Ill in 1960. We went to the Wisconsin Dells and saw the Indian pageantry one summer. 1961 was our first trip to Niagara Falls NY and Canada. Michael and Dad went to the Cave of the Winds and mom, dad and Connie went on the "Maid of the Mist" boat tour leaving Michael and I on the Canadian side with the car. He and I still wonder what we would have done in Canada, with a car and no parents if the boat sank?

Grandma Alta died in June and in July Maggie and Thelma took Michael and I on my "pre-high school graduation" trip to Colorado. We drove out there in their 1959 gray Plymouth at about 40 MPH. When it was Thelma's turn to drive, Maggie would watch the speedometer and often lean up over the back seat and tell her to slow down. Thelma became "deaf" during most of this back seat driving. I don't remember how many days it must have taken us to get there at that speed on 2 lane roads, but I do remember the corn fields in Iowa and the wheat fields in Kansas that never ended. My brain goes numb now just thinking about it.

We stayed overnight at Estes State Park on the Continental Divide where there was still snow on the ground and we made snowballs. We took a bus ride around the area and saw tufted black squirrels and a black bear beside the road.

We also went to the Garden of the Gods Amphitheater where Maggie bemoaned the fact she would miss the Beatles performing there later in the summer. She was crazy about the Beatles and liked the play/movie "Jesus Christ Superstar" music.

We spent time in downtown Denver but missed Pike's Peak because the car wouldn't have made it up there! It was a memorable trip with them and I know we all had fun.

Dad had already been transferred to Zanesville, OH with Buckeye Mart, but the 3 of us stayed in Akron in order for me to finish school. We all joined him in Zanesville where Michael went to high school one month before Buckeye Mart transferred dad to Columbus, Ohio.

May 4, 1970 was the Kent State Ohio Riot and shooting of 2 students on campus by the Ohio National Guard. They were protesting President Nixon invading Cambodia in the ongoing Vietnam War. Kent was close to Youngstown where we had lived so we were alarmed at what happened. The war protests had escalated around the country. I found out decades later that Michael had taken part in some of them.

August 1971 Michael was coming to Rochester from Columbus, and Mom and Dad and Connie were coming from MA. for his 21st birthday and we were all in a car accident. Mom and I were hurt the worst and were in the hospital for a while. She saved Amy by pushing her in between the seats when the car was coming at us. Connie and Amy were taken care of by our friends. Dad, Michael and Bill sort of looked after each other.

June 16, 1972 Michael married Nancy Marshall in Columbus, OH. They had met at Buckeye Mart where they both worked for Dad. They moved to Vancouver, British Columbia in 1973 where he started an art design business.

Michael and Nancy had Heather in 1976 and Kate in 1979 and they were in the United States again but still up in the Northwest in Washington state and then Oregon. He worked on the Expo '86 while doing advertising and tried his hand at graphic design.

On July 29, 2008 my dear, kind, smart sister Connie Sue lost her 6-year battle with breast cancer. She had all the radiation and chemo a human can have, and it still took her. It was the day before her 25th wedding anniversary and a week before her 50th birthday.

She had told us in Feb. that there was nothing more they could do for her and she had 6 months.

Michael and I decided it was important to have a family reunion in Dallas in March while she was still able to travel. He and Nancy came from Oregon, Connie, John and dad came from Ohio, and she was able to be with us and her dear nieces and great niece and nephew and to meet Blake. She adored the little kids and was always a special aunt to Amy and Nicole. We laughed, played games, ate good food, and hugged and loved each other a lot. She enjoyed the spring flowers at the Dallas Arboretum and I polished her nails and trimmed her hair and we played Scrabble. She kept saying it was the sister things we never got to do before.

She never cried even when those of us around her were. Hugging everyone goodbye at the airport was one of the hardest things I've ever done; knowing it was a final goodbye. We all suddenly knew what it meant to want more time together

Michael had silver bracelets made for each of us with "Love Never Fails" on the outside and our initials on the inside. I had them made for Amy and Nicole and we all wear them when we feel especially close to Connie.

She went on hospice in April and they kept her comfortable and active up until a week before she suddenly declined. It was just the 6 months. I was lucky enough to get to Ohio from Dallas in time to spend her last 12 hrs. with her. She was unconscious, but the experts say the person knows we were there loving them to the end.

Michael was en route from Oregon, and he had to hear my phone message when he changed planes in Chicago that she was gone. I felt terrible leaving him that message he would receive all alone.

Connie took one last breath, two tears rolled down her face, and she was at peace. Dad was holding her hand, and John and I were in the room with them.

Michael has been dealing with his grief in an artistic way. He said you came to him in a dream on your birthday and inspired him to do a sculpture. He named her "Courage" which is such a loving and accurate tribute to you. He hopes there will be many of her in public places and that she can give people a connection and comfort. John has purchased the first one for the cancer center in Akron in your memory and there will be a book telling the journey of "Courage". You would be so proud; but then you guided him to do this.

I went to Cannon Beach, OR for the first time in the 30+years that Michael and Nancy have lived on the west coast to the first public showing of the sculpture as it was started. John and I will return May 1, 2009 to see the unveiling of the finished piece and send her on her journey for you.

Just A Few Memories Not Covered By Beverly.

Working seemed to be a big part of life. From ages 13-16 I worked part-time to fund my "art" habit. Being an artist was frowned upon in my house, so I had to work to pay for supplies and classes and eventually my college education. I remember my first supplies were a sketchbook and a pencil and I would fill five pages a day. Now, over fifty years later I still strive to do that as my first passion was and still is drawing.

At first my jobs were odd jobs around the neighborhood, then progressed to contracting my weekends to a number of elderly couples taking care of their lawns and doing the odd jobs around their house they couldn't do anymore.

According to Social Security my first "real job" was when I was 16 and I worked as a stock boy in several retail stores evenings and weekends and full-time in the summer. High-school in Columbus, Ohio I worked nights full time as a fry cook at Burger Chef. My shift was 4pm - midnight, and then I spent an hour cleaning up the grill and mopping the floors. When done at around 1am, I walked home and went to bed. Somehow, I always finished my homework, which was good enough to get mostly B's.

After graduation, I worked two full time jobs in the summer, selling cameras at Buckeye Mart, (it helped that dad was the store manager), and as an art director at Kersker Advertising. Days were spent at the ad agency, and nights and weekends selling cameras. The money went to pay for college as my parents did not approve of wasting my time in Art School, so they did not pay. I did live at home for three years out of the four and a half, and they paid for my rent the last few years when they moved from Columbus, so I am grateful for that.

It seemed this working two jobs set the way I was to work the rest of my life. During college I was lucky to always work at an ad agency full time, but to pay tuition I had to supplement my income by working other really weird jobs ... like one summer after working at the agency I would also work late afternoon or night shifts at a company that made stove doors. My job was - when the painted doors came out of the oven that baked on the paint, I would stand at the oven and with a small brush knock off the paint on the corners of the doors. That is so the doors would close properly. Talk about a hot boring job, but it paid very well.

What was interesting about this period in my career was that I would go to work at the agency as an art director from 6-10am, go to my college classes to learn to be an art director (weird huh?) until 3pm, then back to the agency until 6 then to my Buckeye Mart job until 9. Weekends were full retail days Sat. and Sun. Good scheduling and employers that were flexible were important, and it worked for years, go figure.

After college and until I retired from the business I would always work full time at an ad agency (and there were many as agencies did not keep creative people for more than a few years back then), and work on freelance design jobs at night. Always with the approval of the agencies, as sometimes they set me up with the clients and I would work with them until their budgets became large enough that they became agency clients. It worked out well for all concerned.

With Nancy working as well, we always had food on the table, a roof over our heads, and clothes. We were also fortunate to be able to pay for our kid's college education with no strings attached as to what they wanted to study.

My parents did better for their family then their parents, I was able to do better for my family then my parents, and it looks like my children are doing better than Nancy and I did for them. The American dream is still alive and strong.

Summers As A kid

A few weeks each summer, when Don had to work when Beverly and I were there, Don would take me to work with him. These were special to me because he was a typesetter at the local newspaper, The Daily Gate City in Keokuk Iowa. I was five - eleven and he would take me to his station and put me on a stool, so I could reach the counter and help him set type for that day's newspaper.

At that time, type was set by hand, each letter, one at a time. I would stand on my tip toes in my younger years, so I could reach the California Job Case (collectors now buy the empty cases and hang them on the wall). The case was a large wooden drawer, one drawer for each type style, (font), and it would be sectioned off into compartments, each compartment would contain metal slugs, each compartment was a single letter. I had to learn the position of each letter in the case, because the typesetter's job was to set the story in metal type as fast as possible. I can still remember how Don's hands would fly over the case, picking up the letters and placing them in the metal chase, building the story character by character, line by line until the story was completed. Did I say that the type was set upside down and backwards? That was so that when it was printed, it came out right. Don had a great vocabulary and could spell any word given to him, because the typesetter also had to proof read the story. Throughout my 40 plus years carrer in advertising, I proofread everything by reading it upside down and backwards and taught others to do the same.

One year Don and Alta came to spend Christmas with us and brought me my own Case complete with metal type, a chase, typesetting rulers, spacers and carriers with ink and a tapping block. I could and did print my own papers over the years. How cool is that?

Unfortunately, we moved alot, and to move this case and type, I put the slugs into their own envelope and sealed them and put them into a metal wastepaper basket. Then I waited as the movers came to pick up our belongings. There was always one smart ass mover who saw the basket with envelopes in it and would come along arms full of other boxes and go to pick uo the basket with one hand. And fall down. The basket never moved. It had to have at least 50lbs. of metal in the basket. I know, I was a pill, but it was funny.

After several moves, mom made me get rid of the whole setup rather than move it again. I was heartbroken. Can you imagine how much that whole setup would sell for now? And the memories, I bet I could still set type by hand, a little slower maybe, but I still got it.

There would be other days when Don and I would go fishing on the Mississippi river. Now, this was the summer, in Iowa, on the river during the heat of the day, and I was sitting on the rocks on the bank of the river. The temps were in the triple digits, with 100% humidity. Don would take me to a favorite spot. Don and I would climb down the rocks to the river and fish for catfish.

And there is a science to fishing for catfish. I used a casting reel filled with 50lb. test line, a two-foot-long 35lb. test leader with a 2oz. lead sinker and a treble hook. The hook is baited with a special "very stinky" paste. Normally you just wrap the hook with a ball of the paste, but the Mississippi is fast with strong currents which easily take off the bait, so us "locals" had a trick, we would put a kernel of Green Giant Nibblets Corn on each hook before we put on the paste. It held the paste on the hooks longer and if the paste came off, we could still fish for carp with the corn. In the next paragraph, I will explain the politics of fishing the Mississippi river. Anyhow, come lunch time we would go back to the car, I would have cold hot dogs and a warm Pepsi, Don would have a cold beer. Hummmmm. After lunch I would go back fishing and Don would stay in the car and drink and listen to the radio. At about 3ish, we would pack up and go home. Always with fish. We then had one more stop to make, two if we caught carp.

Here are the politics of fishing the Mississippi river from when I fished it from 1954-61. If you were white, you fished on the rocks on the steep river banks by the dam spillway. And, you fished for catfish, which could weigh as much as 300lbs. If you were black, you fished farther downstream, and you fished for carp, considered a trash fish. If Don and I caught a carp, we were to stop off downstream to where the n****** were and trade our carp for a catfish if they had one. If they didn't have any, we just gave them our carp. A white man never ate carp.

The stop Don and I always did after fishing was to go into town to the Moose lodge and sit at the bar. I would sit on the bar stool and order my usual from the bartender, a bottle of cold Pepsi and a chocolate Hershey bar. Don's order was a can of Blatz beer, or two. The bartender was the most happy, carefree man that everyone liked as a friend. As long as he was in his place, behind the bar serving white folks. Yes, Leroy was black. A small man, with stark white hair and when he smiled he had some yellow teeth, and the bloodiest gums. His smile was all teeth and gums from ear to ear.

Back to the way of the world in Iowa on the Mississippi river in the 50's and 60's. Leroy was everyone's friend when he was in his place behind the bar. When Don and I would pass Leroy, or any other blacks, on the streets of Keokuk, we never spoke, and as we came near them, they would get off the sidewalk and walk in the gutter until we were past. I did not know anything else as I was under 11.

When my dad was a kid in Keokuk, he would sneak away from his block, and go play with the little black boys. His mom would find him and beat him all the way home. The next day he would do the same, as did she.

Later in life I remembered all of this and did what I could to right these wrongs.

December 1, 1969 First Draft Lottery Since 1942

This was the US military draft lottery to see what your chances were of being drafted and sent to Viet Nam. All men born in 1944 - 1950 were in the lottery. Needless to say, that was me. I can still recall that lottery night. I was working at a retail store, Buckeye Mart in Columbus Ohio., Dad was the manager of the store, and when it came time for the lottery draw 366 blue capsules with a birthdate on it were put in a roll cage and spun. All of the young men/boys who worked in the store with me were huddled around the TV displays as the lottery was televised live.

It is hard to describe those minutes as we watched, waiting to hear our destiny, holding your breath as the hand went into the cage, the knot in your stomach, the tightness in the chest, standing there with the boys you have been working with and know. If the next number was not your birthdate, you breathed a quick sigh of relief, and then held your breath as they drew the next number. The first 125 numbers were to be drafted immediately. As the lottery continued, I saw my co-workers/friends stiffen as their number was drawn, close their teary eyes and quietly walk out of the store, I never saw any of them again. After the first 125 were drawn, the few of us left, had hope. Then my birthdate was drawn, #344 out of 366. I was relieved, elated, happy, sad, all of the emotions washed over me like a tidal wave.

For the first time since the first number was drawn, I became aware of someone standing behind me. I looked around and it was dad. With tears in his eyes, he smiled, turned around and walked away, back to work. We never spoke of it, but to this day I still wonder what would have happened if my number would have been the first ones drawn? If I had decided to escape the draft and go to Canada, instead of serving, would this man, my father, who lied about his polio, handicap so he could fight in WWII and proud to have served, would he understand and support my decision?

As a side note, in Dec. 1971 before Nancy and I were married, I received a "Greetings" draft notice to report for military service. It seems that in their books I had lost my student deferment and had to stand the draft. The problem was, I was still a student in college. Now at this time in the war, most college professors would do almost anything to help you keep your student deferment to stay out of Nam, so I was at a loss as to why I lost mine.

Nancy and I went down to the Selective Service offices to speak to someone, hoping to clear up the mistake. We got a very nice older woman and when she looked into it, they had made a mistake and I was still deferred as a student.

But... here it comes; I had an option of keeping my deferment or give it up and stand the draft. I thought I am not crazy; no way am I standing the draft.

Then the lady behind the desk said she had a son and would tell him to stand the draft and here was the reason. It was December and because of the way the original law was written and for this year only, if I stood the draft it would only be until the end of the year, less than 30 days away. Then if my number was not called, I would get a 1H deferment - Registrant not currently subject to processing for induction. She pointed out that I was in the Ohio State University draft pool and they had never called numbers over 125 and mine was 344.

So, I signed away my student deferment and stood the draft until the end of the month. But, neither Nancy nor I got much sleep in Dec., but what a New Year's Eve party we had. After that year, the law was changed so you had to stand the draft for 12 full months; I skated on that one let me tell you,

I loved it when I got my new draft card with the 1H status in Jan., but I still had a draft card burning when I no longer became eligible for military service, at age 35.

May 6, 1970 - The Ohio State Campus Riots - Columbus newspaper article:

"Acting on a recommendation by Ohio Gov. James A Rhodes, Ohio State University closed its doors in mid-quarter on May 6, 1970. The 45,000 students on the riot-racked Columbus campus were told to leave the university by noon the next day.

In the spring of 1970, women were demanding equal rights, blacks were pressing for equal representation, and young people were calling for an end to the Vietnam War. Put these issues on a college campus and combine them with an overwhelmed OSU administration, confused by the wants of a younger generation, and you've got yourself a riot. In early May, riots raged on more than 100 U.S. campuses, as students protested the escalation of the Vietnam War into Cambodia.

At Kent State University, an ROTC building was torched. On May 3, Gov. Rhodes called the demonstrators "the worst type of people we harbor in America" and ordered the Ohio National Guard to restore order at Kent State. Guardsmen killed four people the next day.

Kent State immediately closed, but Ohio State remained open. Amid chants of "Shut it down," protesting OSU students blocked entrances to several buildings on May 5 but dispersed after Guardsmen forced them away.

On May 6, protesters mobbed Ohio State President Novice G. Fawcett's campus home and the school's administration building. Troops with rifles and bayonets drove them back to the Oval. Shortly before 3 p.m., a fire broke out at Hayes Hall, where, according to some reports, protesters threw stones at firefighters.

Fearing what he called "further disruptions and violence," Fawcett said at 5:30 p.m., "I am closing the university until further notice." More than 80 colleges across the country closed that day in the face of growing protests over the war and the Kent State killings.

Ohio State reopened on May 19. In a letter to parents and students, Fawcett wrote: "In the days ahead we will work toward improved student-faculty-administration relationships.""

This Is What I Saw Firsthand As A Student Photographer Covering The OSU Riots:

I must confess this was not my first protest march, and the marches of the previous month of April at OSU and other Ohio university campuses were bloody and tension filled,

The initial reason for the march this day was to protest the unfair treatment of blacks, women, and of course the war, especially the bombing of Cambodia. The campus, city and state police were very undisciplined at that time. Some of the National Guard, however, made honest attempts to curb the violence. In at least one instance that I observed, National Guard officers who tried to calm things down were chastised by their superiors.

I was in a crowd of people, taking photos, not the entire crowd was students by the way, when all of a sudden there was a rush of National Guard in front of me and tear gas cans being thrown. I can still smell the acrid odor of tear gas. Confusion followed and somehow, I was pushed forward into the arms of a National Guard soldier. I had my Nikon in front of my face at the time and I suppose his natural reaction was to push it. Unfortunately, by doing so he broke my nose and camera.

I was with my friend Dale and he grabbed me, and we had to break into a dead run to avoid being trampled by a large group of students charging down a side street from the Oval. They were also being forced back by tear gas and armed police.

Our only thought now was escape. They had closed the campus, so we could not get out. I lived off-campus, quite a distance from campus, but fortunately Dale had an apartment on campus, just a few streets away. Like everyone else we had no idea what was going to happen next, so we ran from alley to alley, street to street to safety, away from the gas.

Dale and I waited in his apartment with all the curtains closed until night. I had to get off campus and back to the safety of home.

This is what a scared, bloodied twenty-year-old does in a riot when reason fails.

We snuck out of Dale's safe apartment into the dark night. No, it was not a dark stormy night like in books, but it was dark. We snuck from alley to alley listening to the noise and chatter from the police radios, trying to stay clear of them.

My last memory of that day was as we were almost free, slowly sneaking around; I turned into the last alley to freedom and came face to face with a young National Guard soldier holding his rifle with bayonet in my face. We both froze. I don't know who was more scared, him or me. Here he was in a faintly lit alley, facing two kids, and me with blood down the front of my shirt from my nose. You know what they say about time stopping and you see flashbacks of your life? Nope. Time did stop though, for how long I don't know. Was his gun loaded like at Kent state? Then in that moment, the young man dropped his gun from my face, turned around and walked out of the alley. I don't recall the rest, but I did find my car and got home safely.

That was my "oh shit, what if" moment, hopefully never to be repeated.

Every now and again I wonder what happened to that young man. Did he end up in Nam? Did he survive to tell his version of the Ohio State riots to his kids and grandkids?

And I thank God for people who have a moment of reason, when the rest of the world is going to hell around them.

Here is a sidebar to these riots. I had met Nancy the month before this, and her father was the head of the endodontics school at Ohio State. During the closure of the school, the professors at OSU had fire watch at the school at night, just in case anything happened. Neither Nancy nor I ever told her father that I was on the other side of the barricades during that time.

June 12, 1972 - I Survived My Honeymoon!

Yes, your wedding day is meant to be special and memorable, as is your honeymoon. You should remember it fondly as you grow old. It should not be a survival class where your life is in danger and you are escaping death, not once, but three times. Fortunately for us our honeymoon was only a long weekend.

Since both Nancy and I were still in school, I was doing summer school classes to finish up my BFA, we had to be married on a Friday and our honeymoon was a room at a state park resort Fri night/Sat/Sun/Mon then back to school.

It all started to go south on us when my best friend and Best Man in my wedding, Dale, decided to trick out my car, a '66 Cuda. Fill it with popcorn and cheese on the muffler as well as balloons and tin cans. When I heard about the plans, I decided to hide the car a couple blocks away and we could make our escape from there.

Escaping Death #1: Dale followed us in his VW bug as we ran to the car and started to drive away. He drove like a crazy man driving straight at us, trying to catch us, and finally trying to run us off the road several times until I could get around him and escape. I have no idea how many trees and cars we narrowly missed. He was a maniac.

Escaping Death #2: Driving the narrow country roads at night on our way to the state park. Nancy and I were coming around a curve and out jumped a deer. I steered left and we just missed her, it was so close we found deer tail hair in the passenger side mirror.

Escaping Death #3: I confess I cannot swim. Many times in my life I tried, even took swimming lessons once as a young tike. I had a scar in the middle of my chest for many years where a lifeguard at Boy Scout camp pushed a metal pole into me to save me from what he thought was drowning. He hit me so hard he succeeded in taking my breath away and I sank like a rock in the pool.

Not to digress, Nancy on the other hand swims like a fish. So, here we are at the resort, out in the lake, close to shore and I am out only as far as I can touch bottom. When my new bride comes up to me and tells me it is ok to come out a bit farther with her. I am young and in love and of course out I go to my wife. And down I drop under water struggling to live. Nancy does grab me and pulls me to where I can again touch bottom. Seems she was treading water but thought I was tall enough to touch bottom. My question was if you are treading water how can you tell how far away the bottom is?

We survived our honeymoon and have now been married over 44 years. Who knew?

And Now I Pass The Torch.

I will now let my wife and daughters and our grandkids tell their stories and hopefully I am in a lot of them. Let me just say that in Nancy and my 44 years together, we have had our joys and sorrows like every family.

The sorrows of almost losing our daughters in a car accident when Heather was in High school; losing both Nancy's parents and mine; the death of my younger sister to cancer; the death of some of our friends; three times we lost almost everything we had because of business and life's bad rolls, but we fought back and, in the end, succeeded.

The joys keep coming every day, but include for me; Nancy as my friend, sole mate and wife; our kids Heather and Katie as we watched them grow up and are now wives and mothers with their own family; our son in laws Phillip and Sam and grandkids Riley, Jack, Connor, Alexis and Owen and us being part of their lives; our being able to retire and travel and see the world and the beauty it holds; and for me, being an artist and capturing the celebration of life in my work.

Our family stories will continue, and hopefully will be not only passed down verbally but also written down so that our descendants will know us better and see they are made up of all of us who came before.

My hope is that someone in our family will take an interest in all of this genealogy and will pick up this history of the Tieman-Marshall Family and carry on, adding new members and filling in the gaps of the older ones.

Marquis Who's Who In The West (23rd Edition):

Tieman, Michael LaVerne, graphic design executive; b. Keokuk, Iowa, Aug 20, 1950; s. Malcolm LaVerne and Doris Earline (Morrill) T.; m. Nancy Lee Marshall, June 16, 1972; children: Heather Anne, Katherine Jane. BFA, Columbus Coll. Art and Design, 1972. Art dir. Kersker Advt., Columbus, Ohio. 1969-72: graphic designer The Studio, Inc., Columbus, 1972-74; sr. art dir. Cockfield & Brown Advt., Vancouver, B.C., Can., 1974-75; ptnr., graphic designer Designers West. Ltd., Vancouver. 1975-78; owner, graphic designer Tieman & Friends, North Vancouver. 1978-86; ptnr., art dir. Printpac Mktg., Ltd., Richmond, B.C., 1978-81; sr. art dir. McKim Advt., Ltd., Vancouver, 1981-84; sr. graphic designer EXPO 86, Vancouver 1984-86; exec. graphic designer Gilchrist & Assoocs., Inc., Portland, Oreg., 1986-. Recipient First Pl. Presentation Folders Award Lithographers & Printing House Craftsmen, 1990. Cert. of Merit Award Printing Industries Am., 1988, First Pl. Ann. Report award Internat. Fedn. Advt. Agys. 1985, PRSA, 1987; named World's Best 30 Second Comedy Spot, Hollywood Radio & TV Soc., 1981. Mem. Nat. Geog. Soc., Am. Inst. Graphic Artists, The Smithsonian Assoc. (Nat.) New England Hist. Geneal.Soc., Trout Unlimited. Friends of the Zoo. Avocations: painting, photography, fly-fishing, reading, computer graphics. Home: 1426 Greentree Cir., Lake Oswego, OR 97034 Office: Gilchrist & Assoc. 815 SE 2nd Ste 300 Portland, OR 97204 503-243-1030.

Places Lived:

1950-55 - Keokuk, Iowa, USA; 1955-58 - Freeport, Illinois, USA; 1958-60 - Elgin, Illinois, USA; 1960-65 - Akron, Ohio, USA; 1965-65 - Zanesville, Ohio, USA; 1965-73 - Columbus, Ohio, USA; 1973-86 - North Vancouver, British Columbia, Canada; 1986-96 - Lake Oswego, Oregon, USA; 1996-2002 - Camas, Washington, USA; 2002-15 - Cannon Beach, Oregon, USA, 2015-present - Beaverton, Oregon, USA

Places Visited:

1988 - Hong Kong, Tokyo, Japan(airport); 1998 - Hong Kong, Shenzhen, China, Seoul, Korea (airport); 2000 - London, England, Paris, France; 2011 -Tuscany area of Italy including Pisa, Rome, Florence, Cinque Terre, Carara, Munich, Germany(airport); 2012- California car trip; Napa Valley and vineyards, San Francisco; 2013 - France; Paris, Avignon, many hill towns of Provence area, Nice. Italy; five towns of Cinque Terre, Siena, many small towns in Tuscany.; 2014- National Parks car trip Utah/Arizona; Zion, Grand Canyon, Bryce, Arches, Canyonlands; 2015 - MA -Boston, (Our homestead in Kittery, Eliot, N. Berwick Maine), Portsmouth, Glouster, Salem, Plymouth, Provincetown, Lexington, Concord, Providence RI. 2016 - Italy for a month, first week with our two daughters; Rome, Pisa, five towns of Cinque Terre, Florence, Venice, many small towns in Tuscany.

Immigrated to Canada in 1973 with wife, Nancy and returned to US in 1986 with Nancy and two children, Heather and Katherine.

Ad Agency Professional Summary:

A seasoned professional with 40 plus years' experience in and solid understanding of strategic marketing and communications as a graphic designer/art director. Demonstrated ability to select, train and retain self-motivated, highly creative employees. Skilled in branding and marketing strategy, creation and execution of packaging, advertising, collateral, direct marketing, multimedia, environmental and interactive design, web site design and coding experience.

Accomplishments - Creative Director: - provide inspiration and motivation - insist on high quality standards - help make the company a positive, challenging place to work - provide mentorship - solutions provider - know and understand strategy and good creative - help the team develop smart solutions that are exciting and successful and that are on target and strategy - develop budgets and schedules...and meet them - work with production managers to seek the most effective solutions - keep current with technology, and help educate the team - strategy and marketing planning and concept development to insure a consistently excellent product brand and corporate image - media strategy, research and development of media plans.

Graphic Designer / Art Director: - concepts - branding - design - graphics - exhibits - packaging - environmental and industrial graphics - print and TV advertising - art direction - marketing strategies - scheduling and production supervision - supervision of teams of writers, designers and production coordinators, art directed photographers and illustrators. - Focused on bringing the first Tripwire Intrusion Detection software product to market, including: corporate and product branding, product strategy, positioning, and lead generation programs. Co. was sold in 2011 when my stock was bought back. - Designed initial web site, collateral, packaging, national ads, tradeshow booths, and international sales materials for Intrusion.com. -Supervised the completion of art/programming and bringing to market the first full CD/Internet virtual game "Piggyland" in 1998. -Designed original Wendy's hamburger chain logo and sign, in store marketing/menus/collateral and interior designs of stores 1971.

Professional Experience - MT Studios, Portland OR, Camas WA, & Cannon Beach, OR,   1993 - 2007   Owner; The Bernhardt Agency, Portland, OR,   1999 - 2001 Partner/V.P. Marketing/Creative Director; Tripwire Security Systems, Portland, OR,   1997-1999 Vice President Marketing ; Online Interactive Network Corporation, Portland, OR, 1997-1999 President ; Internet World Broadcasting Corp. Portland, OR,   1995-1997 VP/CD; Gilchrist & Associates, Inc., Portland, OR,   1986-1995 Co-Creative Director   ; The 1986 World Exposition, Vancouver, Canada,   1984-1986 Sr. Graphic Designer ; McKim Advertising, Ltd., Vancouver, Canada,   1981-1984 Sr. Art Director   ; Tieman & Friends, Ltd., Vancouver, Canada,   1976-1981 CEO/ CD; Cockfield & Brown, Vancouver, Canada, 1973-1976 Sr. Art Director

Education - Bachelor of Fine Arts in Advertising Design, 1972 Columbus College of Art & Design, Columbus, Ohio

Artists Gallerie 2002:

Michael started his own gallery/studio with wife Nancy in April 2002, Artists Gallerie, LLC. The gallery was opened in Cannon Beach, Oregon and represented twelve national and international artists, but after five years the falling economy forced it to close. The company continues as an Internet based company selling the paintings and sculptures of Michael throughout the world.

About Michael Tieman the painter/sculptor/writer

As Michael Tieman sees it, "The role of an artist from the dawn of time has been as a visual storyteller. The stories my paintings and sculptures tell are ones of confidence, strength, passion, playful sophistication and the celebration of life."

Tieman has sketched and painted since childhood and has spent almost four decades as a working artist, both as a graphic designer and a fine artist. Following the encouragement of a friend and gallery owner, Michael recently expanded his talents into sculptures cast in bronze. Tieman's sculptures are unique in that they are a combination of traditional figurative sculpture and his Impressionistic painting style. "I create my bronze sculpture as a three-dimensional painting; texture is the impasto brushstroke, color is the play of light and shadows across the surfaces, and detail is the free style movement of the impressionist style. My ladies have a face with a chiseled jaw and high cheekbones, producing great shadows, and the athletic body and proud confidence of an Amazon warrior."

Sculpture "Courage"
Donated to Summa Health System's Cancer Clinic in Akron, Ohio:

On July 29, 2009 in Akron, Ohio, "Courage" a 36" tall bronze sculpture standing in tribute to those who have, who are, and who will fight Cancer is being donated to the new Summa Health System's Jean B. and Milton N. Cooper Cancer Center, Akron City Hospital, Akron, Ohio.

"Courage" is a limited-edition bronze and is the creation of Pacific Northwest sculptor and painter Michael Tieman. Cancer has hit home hard with Michael as his older sister Beverly Starr is a 13-year survivor of breast cancer, but his younger sister Connie Sue Drotos recently lost her battle with the disease.

The first 36" sculpture "Courage" in the limited edition has been purchased by Connie's husband of 25 years, John Drotos, and he is dedicating it to the Cancer clinic where Connie had treatments for six years. With the purchase of "Courage" there is also a cash donation of $5000 which goes to the Cancer Support Services department of the Cancer Center. Connie's family will be present at the dedication ceremonies in Akron July 29th and will include; husband John Drotos, her father LaVerne Tieman, sister Beverly Starr, brother Michael Tieman and his wife Nancy.

"Courage is dedicated to the women in my family who have battled breast cancer; my mother-in-law Jan Marshall (Muzzy), my aunt Pat Wetzel, my sister Beverly Starr, and my younger sister Connie Sue Drotos, who after a courageous six-year battle with breast Cancer died on July 29, 2008." - Michael Tieman

The Dream

"In July of 2008, after a courageous six-year battle with breast cancer, my younger sister died, one week shy of her 50th birthday and the day before her 25th wedding anniversary," says Tieman. "Since then I have had the same re-occurring dream. I am on a scaffold built around a piece of white marble 15' tall, and I am carving a figure titled "Courage" - she has a bald head wrapped in cloth, piercing eyes, a firm jaw, taunt body and feet apart yet firmly planted. The people battling cancer have an inner strength and courage as they not only face an uncertain future, but they also have to take their treatments knowing it will make them feel worse. Week after week they look forward to this pain in the hope that eventually it will be gone. There is a look of courage in their eyes I cannot describe with words, it's not entirely defiant (Cancer will not win), but with grace with a quiet determination. That is the courage I need to capture.

In the dream I can only sense the figure; all I can really see is the head. I am carving with a chisel and hammer, no power tools, and I can see my scarred swollen hands and feel the pain in them as I continuously strike the chisel. Yet, there are many unanswered questions; why is the stone exactly 15' tall, why can't I see the entire figure? I am carving the stone by looking at a maquette of the piece but how do I know it is exactly 36" tall since I can only see the head?

The Promise

"People who saw me building the clay sculpture "Courage" November 8th and 9th during my demo at the 2008 Stormy Weather Arts Festival expressed a need for the piece to be seen and touched ... now", says Tieman." So, I am casting "Courage" in a limited-edition bronze available in three sizes, 9' high heroic size, 36" high and 18" high maquettes. With up to half of the sale price being donated directly to a local hospital or Cancer center's Cancer Support Services, the daily support and comfort services for those who come to these facilities to battle Cancer. The book "The Building of Courage" (published by Michael Tieman Publishing), which originally was to be made to accompany each sculpture will now be published in a larger edition for people who want the book, so they can be connected to "Courage". Because of the requests from survivors, Michael has also cast the butterfly necklace on "Courage" in silver and is being sold to raise funds for Cancer Support Services.

"Courage" Butterfly Necklace

"Butterflies were a favorite of my sister Connie; she said they brought her peace, freedom and hope. At the cemetery after her internment ceremony, her husband John who brought several Mylar butterfly balloons, walked to the little lake alone and released the butterflies as he had promised her. We silently watched as the wind suddenly came up and the butterflies took flight.

Slowly they rose into the air and maneuvered themselves up and around the clouds, staying in sight and staying in the clear blue sky. Up and up they drifted, slowly they left our sight and sailed to the heavens. So of course, I had to have a butterfly on 'Courage'."

Books Written, Designed, and or Published By Michael Tieman Publishing:

Behind the Bronze - My Sculpture- (paperback) Author, artist: Michael Tieman
Behind the Paint - New England 2015- (paperback) Author, artist: Michael Tieman
Behind the Paint - National Parks 2014- (paperback) Author, artist: Michael Tieman
Behind the Paint - France & Italy 2013 - (paperback) Author, artist: Michael Tieman
Behind the Paint - Italy 2011 - (paperback) Author, artist: Michael Tieman
The Building of "Courage" - (hardcover and paperback) Author: Michael Tieman
The Poet - (hardcover) Author: David Sweet
My Glengarry - (hardcover) Author: Dr. F. James Marshall

1/31/2016

Today found sources from the NEHS and Mayflower publications proving "SOURCES" that my father's mother's mother (SOUTH) is a direct line to the Fuller and Lathrop families that came over on the Mayflower in 1620. I also have a copy of the Mayflower Descendants Application approved for a Fuller, proving our lineage.

Map Of Migration - Michael LaVerne Tieman

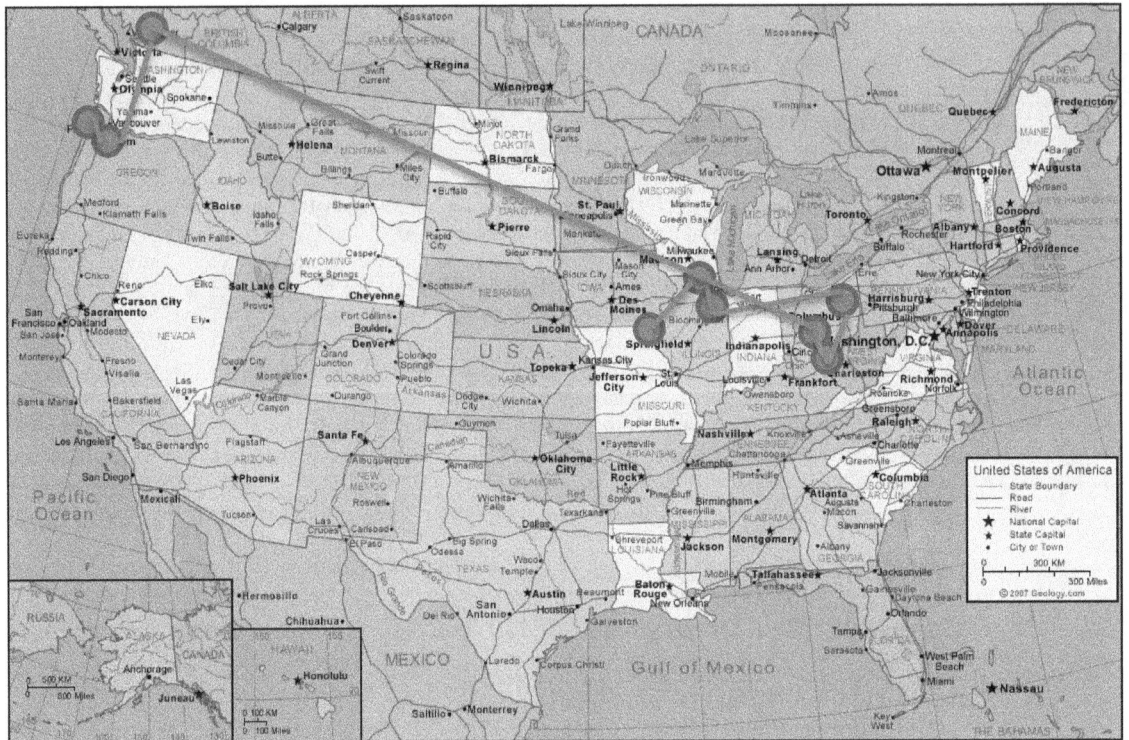

Canada is a country in the northern half of North America. Its ten provinces and three territories extend from the Atlantic to the Pacific and northward into the Arctic Ocean, covering 9.98 million square kilometres (3.85 million square miles), making it the world's second-largest country by total area and the fourth-largest country by land area. Canada's border with the United States is the world's longest land border. The majority of the country has a cold or severely cold winter climate, but southerly areas are warm in summer. Canada is sparsely populated; the majority of its land territory being dominated by forest and tundra and the Rocky Mountains. About four-fifths of the country's population of 36 million people is urbanized and live near the southern border. Its capital is Ottawa, its largest metropolis is Toronto; other major urban areas include Montreal, Vancouver, Calgary, Edmonton, Quebec City, Winnipeg and Hamilton.

North Vancouver is a waterfront municipality on the north shore of Burrard Inlet, directly across from Vancouver, British Columbia. It is the smallest of the three North Shore municipalities and the most urbanized as well. Although it has significant industry of its own, including shipping, chemical production, and film production, the city is usually considered to be a suburb of Vancouver. The city is served by the Royal Canadian Mounted Police, British Columbia Ambulance Service, and the North Vancouver City Fire Department.

Camas is a city in Clark County, Washington, with a population of 19,355 at the 2010 census. Officially incorporated on June 18, 1906, the city is named after the camas lily, a plant with an onion-like bulb prized by Native Americans. At the west end of downtown Camas is a large Georgia-Pacific paper-mill from which the high school teams get their name "the Papermakers". Accordingly, the city is about 20 miles east (upwind) from Portland, Oregon. Historically, the commercial base of the city was almost solely the paper mill; however, the diversity of industries has been enhanced considerably in recent years by the influx of several white-collar, high-tech companies including Hewlett-Packard, Sharp Microelectronics, Linear Technology, WaferTech and Underwriters Labs. Annual events include the summer "Camas Days", as well as other festivals and celebrations.

Portland is the largest city in the U.S. state of Oregon and the seat of Multnomah County. It is located in the Willamette Valley region of the Pacific Northwest, at the confluence of the Willamette and Columbia Rivers. The city covers 145 square miles (380 square kilometers) and had an estimated population of 632,309 in 2015, making it the 26th most populous city in the United States. Approximately 2,389,228 people live in the Portland metropolitan statistical area (MSA), the 23rd most populous MSA in the United States. Its Combined Statistical Area (CSA) ranks 17th with a population of 3,022,178. Roughly 60% of Oregon's population resides within the Portland metropolitan area.

In the 1990s, the technology industry began to emerge in Portland, specifically with the establishment of companies like Intel, which brought more than $10 billion in investments in 1995 alone. After the year 2000, Portland experienced significant growth, with a population rise of over 90,000 between the years 2000 and 2014. The city's increased presence within the cultural lexicon has established it a popular city for young people, and it was second only to Louisville, Kentucky as one of the cities to attract and retain the highest number of college-educated people in the United States. Between 2001 and 2012, Portland's gross domestic product per person grew fifty percent, more than any other city in the country.

Beaverton is a city in Washington County, in the U.S. state of Oregon. The city center is 7 miles (11 km) west of downtown Portland in the Tualatin River Valley. As of the 2010 census, the population is 89,803. This makes it the second-largest city in the county and Oregon's sixth-largest city.

In 2010, Beaverton was named by *Money* magazine as one of the 100 "best places to live", among smaller cities in the country. Along with Hillsboro, Beaverton is one of the economic centers for Washington County, home to numerous corporations in a variety of industries.

According to *Oregon Geographic Names*, Beaverton got its name because of the settlement's proximity to a large body of water resulting from beaver dams.

The area of Tualatin Valley which became Beaverton was originally the home of a Native American tribe known as the *Atfalati*, which settlers mispronounced as *Tualatin*. The Atfalati population dwindled in the latter part of the 18th century, and the prosperous tribe was no longer dominant in the area by the 19th century when settlers arrived.

The **United States (U.S.)**, officially the **United States of America (USA)**, and commonly referred to as **America**, is a federal republic composed of 50 states, a federal district, five major self-governing territories, and various possessions. Forty-eight of the fifty states and the federal district are contiguous and located in North America between Canada and Mexico. The state of Alaska is in the far northwestern corner of North America, with a land border to the east with Canada and separated by the Bering Strait from Russia. The state of Hawaii is an archipelago in the mid-Pacific. The territories are scattered about the Pacific Ocean and the Caribbean Sea. Nine-time zones are covered. The geography, climate and wildlife of the country are extremely diverse.

Children:

HEATHER A. b.17 May 1976 North Vancouver, British Columbia, Canada; baptized 1976 North Vancouver, British Columbia, Canada; m. Phillip ERWIN 22 Jun 1996 Lake Oswego, Clackamas, Oregon.

KATHERINE J b. 25 Jun 1979 North Vancouver, British Columbia, Canada. m. Shawn Schulberg 4 Nov 2000 Portland, Oregon; marriage ended in divorce; next m. Samuel Patrick 25 Jul 2009 Portland, Oregon.

4. Michael & Beverly with cat Niki and dog Caesar1956?

5. Nancy Marshall and Michael

on Nancy's prom night 1970

Beverly, Michael & Connie Tieman - 1958

1981 - Michael Tieman Family
Katie, Michael, Nancy, Heather

Christmas 2004 - Michael & Nancy Tieman in front of their art gallery.
in Cannon Beach Oregon

8. Our grandkids 2014

9. Michael, newest member
of SAR Color Guard in
uniform made by Nancy.
2016

7. Tieman Family 2016, Heather,
Nancy, Michael, Katie.

6. Michael's PR photo 2016

10. Nancy & Michael, Paris
2013

Tieman, Michael - 1956 Union School Class
Photo. Michael is in front of teacher Miss Miller.

Michael Tieman Graduation High School 1968

Caesar, Beverly & Michael Tieman 1952?

Michael Tieman, Pat Wetzel, Beverly Tieman

Michael Tieman, Septemb

TIEMAN- MICHAEL, SUMMER 1951

MICHAEL & NANCY TIEMAN
VIOLA & MALCOLM TIEMAN 1973

Dad's retirement party - 1991
Connie Drotos, LaVerne Tieman, Doris Tieman
Beverly Starr, Michael Tieman

Nancy & Michael, LaVerne & Doris Tieman

Ohio 1972- Doris, LaVerne, Connie
Nancy & Michael Tieman

12. Nancy's Graduation 1973
from Dental Hygeine

11. Nancy at National Park
2014

1953? - front - Willa Reitz Wester, Mabel Reitz,
Beverly & Michael Tieman
back - Malcolm Tieman, Elsie Reitz Hewitt, Viola Reitz
Tieman, Lyle Wester

Funeral for Doris Tieman March 2003.
Back: Sarah Drotos, John Drotos, Katie Connor and Nancy Tieman, Heather &
Riley Erwin, Pat Wetzel, Nicole Starr, Wally Wetzel, Amy Starr Front: Doris'
kids & husband Michael & LaVerne Tieman, Connie Drotos, Beverly Starr

Seventh Generation Timeline 1976 -

			Tieman Family 1970-2016				
Year			Rulers	World History	U.S. History	Science/Technology	Art
1970			Juan Carlos- Sp. 1975		Many Cultures Migration	Personal Computer 1978	Post Modern
			Pres. Nixon & Ford 1973/74		War Powers Act 1973	Viking I & II on Mars	Solzhenitsyn
			Pres. Jimmy Carter 1977		Nixon Resigns 1973-74		Star Wars 1977
					Wounded Knee 1973		Punk Rock
					Feminism 1970's		
1980	Heather Tieman Born 1976 - Married 1996	Katherine Tieman Born 1979 - Married 2000 and 2009	Pres. Ronald Reagan 1981	Berlin Wall Down 1989	War on Drugs 1980's	CD, VCR & Cable	Rap
			Pres. George Bush 1989			Ozone Hole 1987	
1990			Pres. W. Clinton 1993	Gulf War 1991	Welfare Reform 1996	World Wide Web 1993	
				Soviet Union Breakup 1991	Land on Mars 1997		
				Cold War Over	Inter. Space Station 1998		
				Germany United 1990	Longest Robust Economy 1997		
2000			Pres. G. W. Bush 2001	War on Terror 9/11/2001		Animals Cloned 2000	
						Drones Fight War 2004	
			Pres. B. Obama 2009		Global Recession Crisis 2008/9		
2010			Philip VI - Sp. 2014		Affordable Care Act 2010		David Fincher

Seventh Generation 1976 -

These are Nancy and my two beautiful daughters, Heather Anne and Katherine Jane. Both of the girls were born in North Vancouver, Canada, which being born in Canada to a parent who was a U.S. citizen, they were dual-citizens. That is until they became adults, and both dropped their Canadian citizenship to become U.S. citizens.

HEATHER ANNE TIEMAN was born on 17 May 1976 in North Vancouver, British Columbia, Canada and was baptized in 1976 in North Vancouver, British Columbia, Canada. Heather married **Phillip ERWIN** on 22 Jun 1996 in Lake Oswego, Clackamas, Oregon, USA. Phillip was born on 30 May 1971 in Boise, Ada, Idaho, USA.

Children: Riley J., Jackson D.

KATHERINE JANE TIEMAN was born on 25 Jun 1979 in North Vancouver, British Columbia, Canada. Katherine married **Shawn SCHULBERG** on 4 Nov 2000 in Portland, Clackamas, Oregon, USA. The marriage ended in divorce. Children: Connor S. Katherine next married **Samuel Patrick** on 25 Jul 2009 in Portland, Clackamas, Oregon, USA. Samuel was born on 16 Sep 1975 in T'ai-Pei, Taiwan.

Children: Alexis J., Owen R.

2004

15. Katie, Michael & Heather 2016

13. Heather & Katie 1986

14. My Girls- Heather & Katie with Nancy 1981?

1994 - Katie Tieman

1990 - Heather Tieman 8th grade grad.

1982 Heather & Katie Tieman

1984 at Granville Market, Vancouver B.C.
Katie & Heather Tieman

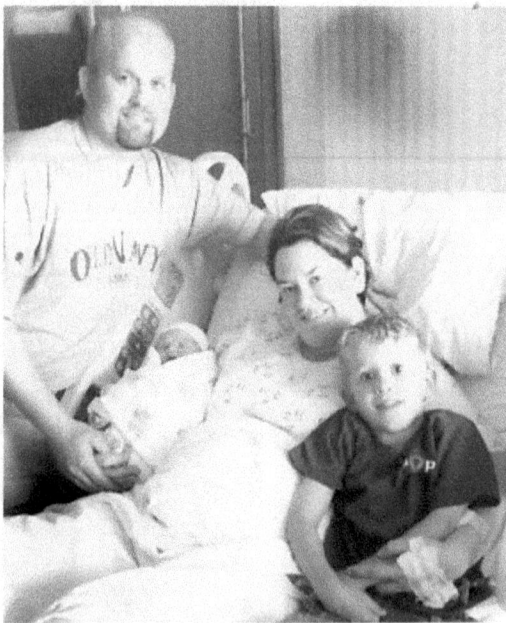

26 July 2005 Jackson Davis Erwin is born
Phillip, Jackson, Heather, Riley

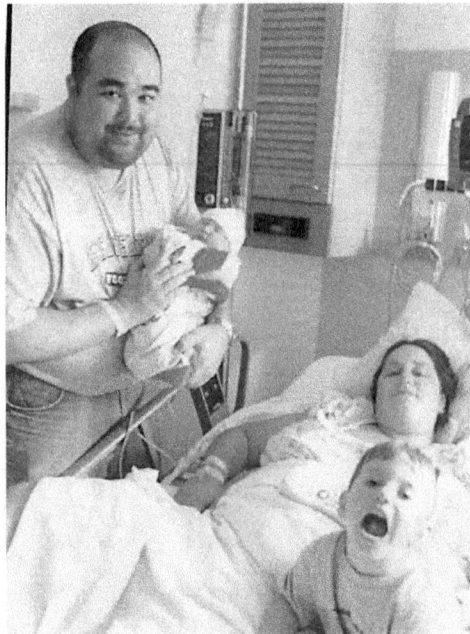

12 Nov. 2006 Alexis Woodward-Tieman is born
Sam, Alexis, Katie & Connor

2003 - Playing at the beach with Nana.
Katie Tieman, Riley Erwin, Nancy (Nana) Tieman, Connor Tieman, Heather Erwin

1987 - Heather & Katie Tieman

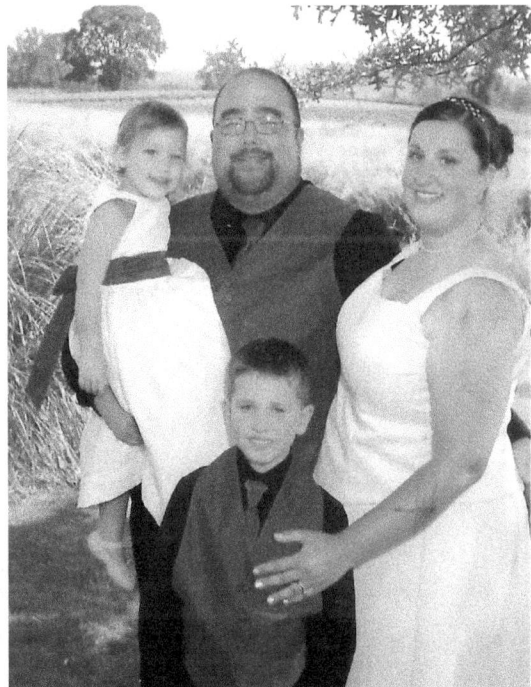

2010 Sam Woodward &
Katie Tieman's wedding
Alexis, Connor, Sam & Katie

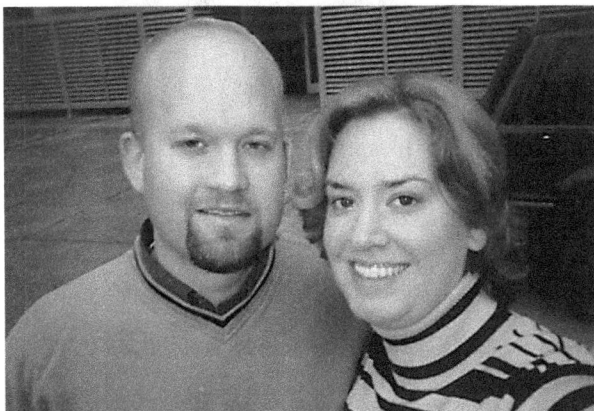

2002 Phillip & Heather Erwin

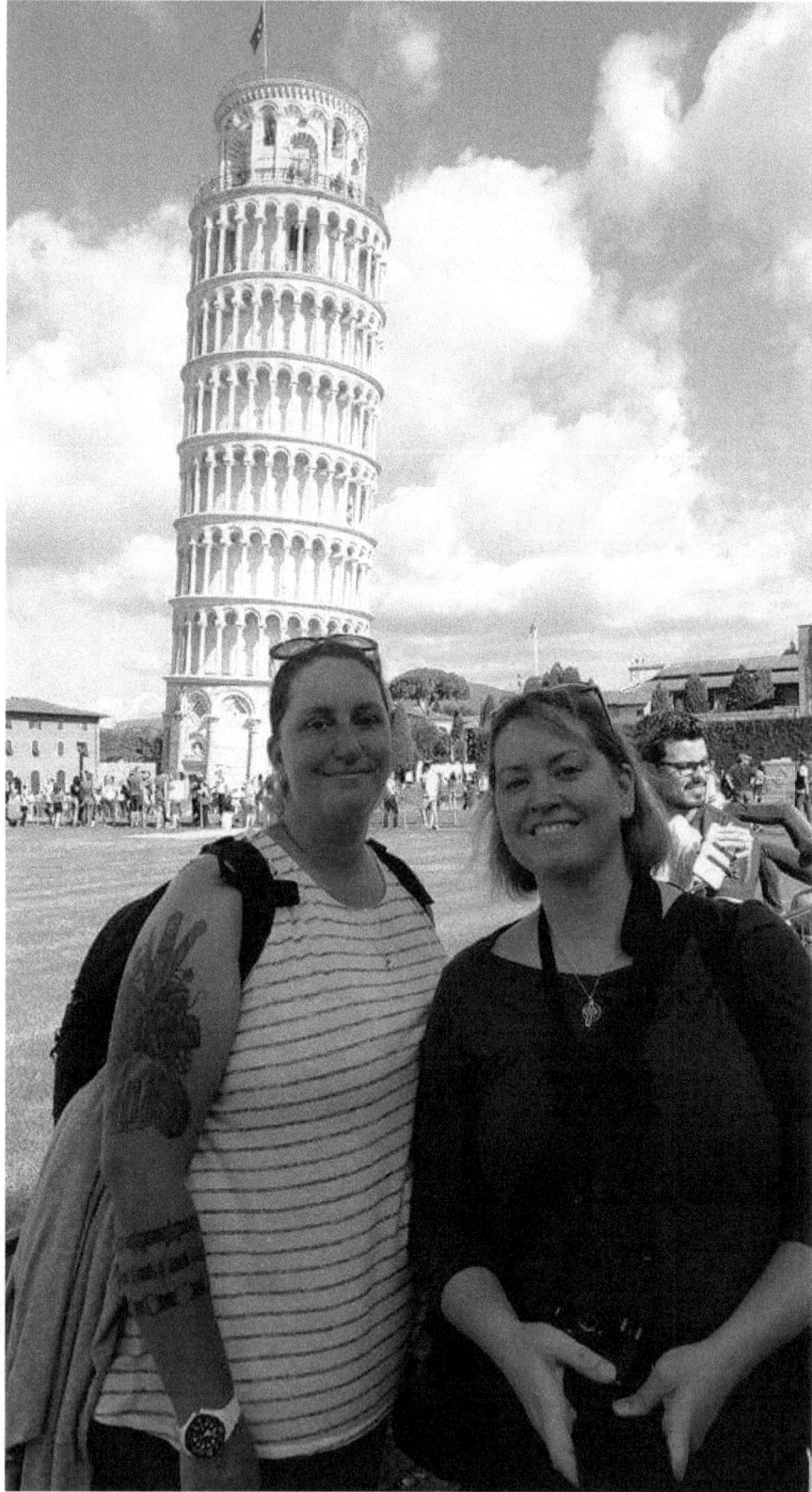

16. Katie & Heather in Pisa, Italy 2016

Eighth Generation Timeline 1999 -

Tieman Family 1990-2016

Year	Births	Rulers	World History	U.S. History	Science/Technology	Art
1990		Pres. W. Clinton 1993	Gulf War 1991	Welfare Reform 1996	World Wide Web 1993	
			Soviet Union Breakup 1991	Land on Mars 1997		
			Cold War Over	Inter. Space Station 1998		
			Germany United 1990	Longest Robust Economy 1997		
2000		Pres. G. W. Bush 2001	War on Terror 9/11/2001		Animals Cloned 2000	
					Drones Fight War 2004	
		Pres. B. Obama 2009		Global Recession Crisis 2008/9		
2010		Philip VI - Sp. 2014		Affordable Care Act 2010		David Fincher

Births (left rotated columns): Riley Erwin Born 1999; Connor Tieman Born 2002; Jack Erwin Born 2005; Alexis Tieman-Woodward Born 2006; Owen Tieman-Woodward Born 2010

Eighth Generation 1999 -

Here are our five grandchildren. Wow, how quickly they have grown up.

RILEY JAMES ERWIN was born on 27 Sep 1999 in Portland, Clackamas, Oregon, USA and was baptized in 2000 in Portland, Clackamas, Oregon, USA.

JACKSON DAVIS ERWIN was born on 26 Jul 2005 in Portland, Clackamas, Oregon, USA and was baptized in Oct 2005 in Portland, Clackamas, Oregon, USA.

2006 Jack and Riley Erwin at the beach visiting Nana & Papa

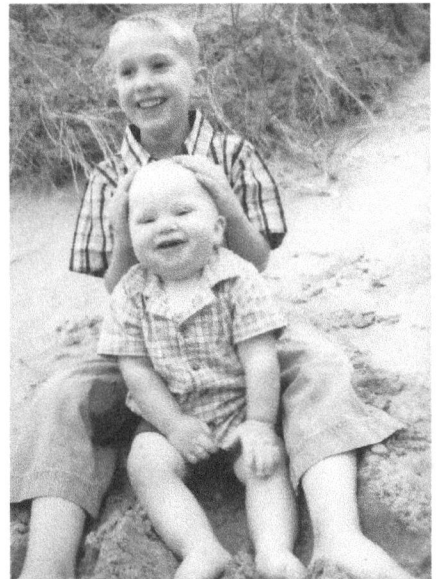

2006 at the beach Riley & Jack (front) Erwin

2007 - Jack & Riley Erwin

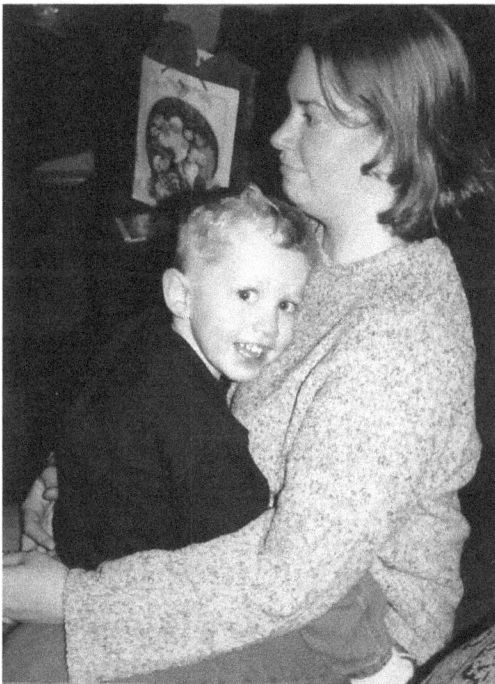

Dec 2002 - Riley & Heather Erwin

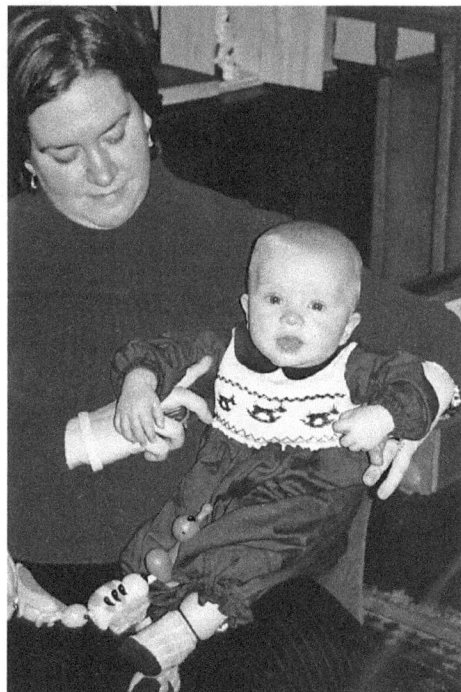

Jan 2006 - Heather & son Jack Erwin

17. RJ, Heather, Jack & Phillip Erwin 2016

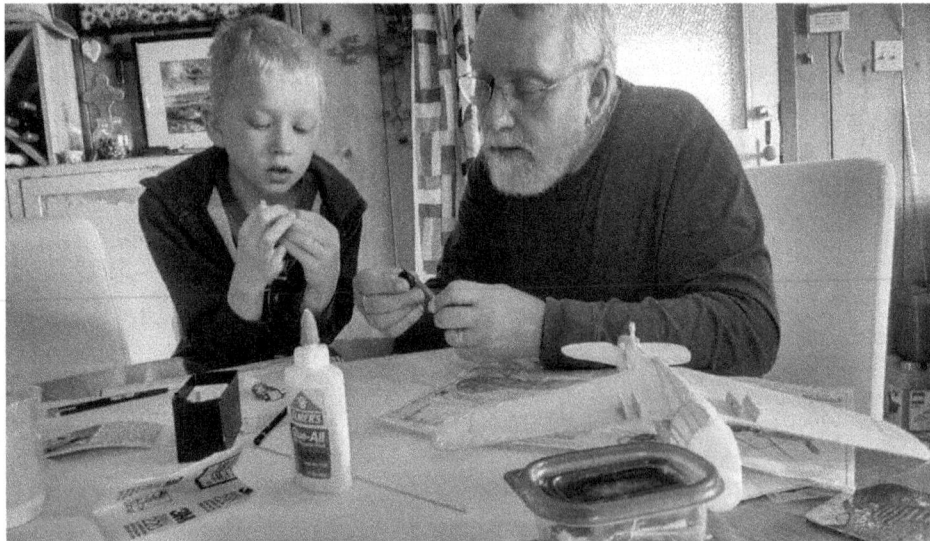

18. Jack and Papa (Michael) on a building project at the beach house 2015

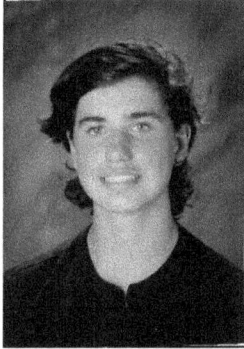

CONNOR SHAMAS TIEMAN was born on 28 Oct 2002 in Portland, Clackamas, Oregon, USA.

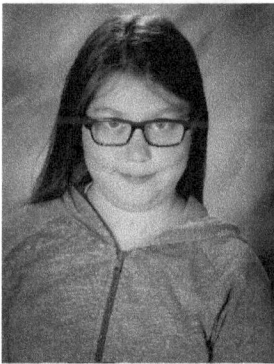

ALEXIS JEAN TIEMAN-WOODWARD was born on 12 Nov 2006 in Portland, Clackamas, Oregon, USA.

OWEN RICHARD TIEMAN-WOODWARD was born on 18 Feb 2010 in Portland, Clackamas, Oregon, USA.

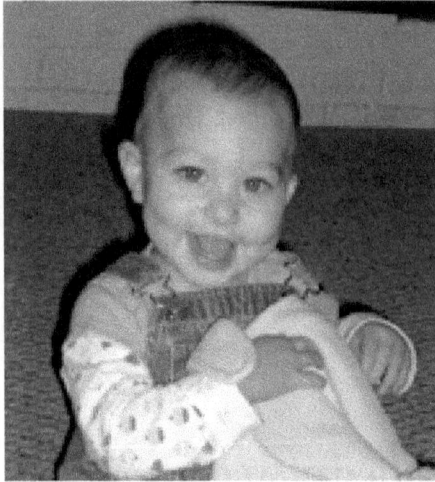

23. Alexis age 1

22. Connor age?

21. Alexis at her passion, 2016

20. Owen at soccer 2016

19Connor (far left) with football team 2014-15

24 The Lacross team Alexis, Connor and Owen (top), 2016

Genealogy Summary - Tieman

1-Georg Wilhelm TIEMANN [846], [1,2,3,4,5,6,7,8, 9,10,11,12 ,13,14] son of **TIEMANN** [4365], was born in 1791 in Lengerich, Steinfurt, Nordrhein-Westfalen, Germany, died in Oct 1869 in Benton Township, Des Moines, Iowa, USA at age 78, and was buried in Benton Township, Des Moines, Iowa, USA.

General Notes: **Prussian Passport G.W. Tiemann 1833** - English Translation of German Passport:

Kings Prussian State

Passport issued to farmer G.W. Thiemann with his wife and eight-year-old son To North America.

There are no civil or military obligations against them, never been in trouble and they are free to come and go.

The Passport must be shown in any state or town in which they stay over 24 hours and should be given police protection if necessary.

Given in Munster the 18th of March One thousand eight hundred thirty-three.

Religion-Evangelical, Age-41 years, Height -5'2", Hair-dark (black), Forehead-flat, Eyebrows-black, Eyes-Green Nose-average, Mouth-big, Beard-black, Chin-round, Face-oval, Complexion-healthy, Stature-short, Characteristics-none

Signature Tiemann

Stamp of taxes of some kind

"History of William Tiemann Family from the Latty Church of Christ Centennial Book 1853-1953" (excerpt)

G. William Tiemann was born in 1792 in Germany as was his wife, Sophia, who was born in 1797. They had one son named William. He was born in Tecklenberg, Munster, Germany May 2, 1825.

The family came to this country in March 1833. They stopped in Virginia before going to Burlington where they resided until they moved to a farm on the Irish Ridge Road, Benton Township, to make their home. The trip took six months by covered wagon.

They were good neighbors and one of the pioneer families who organized the German Evangelical Zion Church of Benton Township in 1853. The church was built near-by on the Irish Ridge Road.

Both William and his wife died in 1869, he was 77 and she was 72. They were buried in the church cemetery. The son William survived.

History of Early America

Early America used the rivers and waterways for much of its travel and transportation. Roads were worse than poor. Even Benjamin Franklin in his "Poor Richards Almanac" complained about the pot holes and hog wallows in Philadelphia. No road beyond the cities, was more than a pair of worn tracks through open land, usually with grass growing up in the center. The traveler was lucky if it was smooth, bad weather from storms or the thawing of spring would leave deep ruts, which dried into shaking and jarring of the steel- rimmed wagon. The roads of necessity wound around the huge forest trees, and the roots of such would lay huge bumps across the road. Trees were cut, to open the road, and the stumps left standing in the road. Ravines, gullies, streams and rivers meant a descent to the bottom, and a climb out on the far bank, if not worse. But America still moved west.

Land travel was slow, seldom over 10 miles a day, often half that. It was considered that the children would easily keep up, walking nearby, and in the process find much to keep themselves entertained. (Nowhere like today's problems taking children in a long automobile trip.) The team of horses might travel a little faster, but long distance was with the ox team, which traveled even slower than a walk, but could keep going, with less food, long after the horses would quit. The normal trip took days and often months.

There was considerable travel and communication among kin in distant communities. People who had to "go back home" for any reason, hand carried messages from all the neighbors, to their different families and friends. A "letter" from home was normal - at least once or twice a year, even though home was in eastern Pennsylvania, and the family might live in Ohio, Indiana, Illinois or even Iowa. A "letter" normally consisted of a single sheet of paper, written on both sides, except for that part which, after folding, would carry the address, like an envelope. Paper was not cheap or readily available, and the "letter" still existent is off times very interesting.

1870 Census Mortality - William Tieman

Persons who Died during the Year ending 1st of June 1870 in Yellow Springs, Des Moines, Iowa Name: William Tieman, Gender: male, Race: white, Marital Status: widowed, Place of Birth: Prussia, Age 75, Month of Death: Oct, Cause of Death: Disease of the Kidney, Line 28, Archive Collection: T1156

"German Marriages, 1558-1929" Georg Wilhelm Tiemann, 1817

Groom's Name: Georg Wilhelm Tiemann; Groom's Age: 26; Bride's Name: Sophia Katherine Koenig; Bride's Age: 24; Marriage Place: Evangelic, Lengerich, Westfalen, Prussia; Indexing Project (Batch) Number: M95279-4; System Origin: Germany-ODM; Source File Number: 526392

US & Canada Passenger and Immigration Lists Index 1500's - 1900's

Name: Georg W. Tiemann; Arrival Year: 1833; Arrival Place: America; Family Members: Family; Source Publication Code: 5861; Primary Immigrant: Tiemann, Georg W Annotation: Westphalian emigrants in the 19th century: emigration from the government district of Muenster, part 1. From state archives in Munster and in Detmold, West Germany. The lists cover pp.57-389 with 6,453 numbered entries. Of 4,100 persons who emigrated. Page 59 - MUELLER, FRIEDRICH. "Westfaelische Auswanderer im 19, Jahrhundert-Auswanderung aus dem Regierungsbezik Munster, Part 1. 1803-1850." In Beitraege zur westfaelischen Familienforschung, vols 22-24 (1964-1966) pp. 7-484.

"Beitraege zur westfaelischen Familienforschung", Band 22-24, Verlag Aschendorf Muenster. Nr.46: Georg W. Tiemann, from Lengerich, emigrated with Family 1833 to Nordamerika.

Evangelische Kirche von Westfalen Parish Records, 1817 Parish Weddings, 1791 Baptisms. Letter from the parish. (my translation see orig)

"Here are 2 copies of the church records of the Evangelical Church in the nearby communities of Lengerich and Lienen. Unfortunately, it is everything I was able to find.

From the enclosed entry of marriage can be seen that Georg Wilhelm Tiemann had to be born in 1791 in Lengerich. It is noted that he was at age of 26, so farmers/farm owner was born on the property where they live.

I saw through the baptism in the years 1785-1795. There has been no single boy Tiemann born in this period there and baptized, also, no boy of a different family name with the name Georg Wilhelm. Because he owns a farm, he had to be, if he has inherited the farm from his father, born there also.

So, I can only assume that the parents came to Lengerich after his birth. But from where? Do you have any data about the children of the couple?

Three sons are baptized in Lengerich: Ernst Jacob Henrich 21-11-1819, Heinrich Wilhelm 16-5-1822, and Henrich Rudolf 8-8-1830. Where and when did at least one of them marry? Maybe you can find notes on the death of his parents from the marriage certificate. I was not able to find any death entries in Lengerich.

Catherarina Sophia agrees with the age at marriage with no date of birth, but that happens often at that time. It is also the only baptism in Lienen that comes into question."   -Johann Miezer-

History of the area

Lengerich is a town in the district of Steinfurt, in North Rhine-Westphalia, Germany. It is situated on the southern slope of the Teutoburg Forest, approx. 15 km south-west of Osnabrück and 30 km north-east of Münster.

Lienen is a municipality in the district of Steinfurt, in North Rhine-Westphalia, Germany. It is situated approximately 15 km south-east of Osnabrück and 30 km north-east of Münster.

Noted events in his life were:

• He worked as a Farmer.
• He was German Evangelical.
• He immigrated on 18 Mar 1833 to USA.

Georg married **Sophia Katharina KOENIG** [847][1,2,4,7,11,13,14,15,16] [MRIN: 276], daughter of _____ **KOENIG** [4366], on 8 Aug 1817 in Evangelisch, Lengerich, Westfalen, Prussia. Sophia was born in 1793 in Lienen, Prussia, died in 1869 in Benton Township, Des Moines, Iowa, USA at age 76, and was buried in Benton Township, Des Moines, Iowa, USA.

Noted events in her life were:

• She was German Evangelical.
• She immigrated in May 1833 to USA.

2-Wilhelm H. TIEMANN [788][1,2,5,7,8,9,10,13,15,17,18,19,20,21,22,23,24,25,26,27,28] was born on 2 May 1822 in Tecklenburg, Westfalen, Germany, was baptized on 16 May 1822 in Lengerich, Westfalen, Germany, died on 11 May 1906 in Benton Township, Des Moines, Iowa, USA at age 84, and was buried in Benton Township, Des Moines, Iowa, USA.

General Notes: **Date of birth and baptism dates do not match up:**

Date of Birth in his father's passport from Prussia state he was eight in 1833, his tombstone and the Latty Church Centennial Booklet below say he was born May 2, 1825, BUT the 1880 US Census puts him at 54 (b.1826) and the Germany Births and Baptism records state he was baptised in 1822.

"History of William Tiemann Family - Latty United Church of Christ Centennial Booklet 1853-1953" (partial)

On February 13, 1859 William was married to Louise Rethemeier, who was born November 30, 1839 in Minden, Germany. They were married in the German Evan. Zion Church, Benton Township. The Pastor was Jakob Schmeiser. The couple were worthy and highly respected pioneers of this county. The couple had nine children, all born in Benton, Twp.

Mr. Tiemann died May 11, 1906 at his home. "Mr. Tiemann spent fully seventy of his eighty years in Des Moines County, his family having come here from Virginia seventy years ago. They lived in the city for about ten years and then moved to the farm near Latty which remained the family home and eventually became the property of the deceased. The old gentleman and his kind wife had many friends in the city and county and their home was famed far and wide for its genuine open-handed hospitality." The quote is from the obituary which was in the Burlington paper. He is buried in the church cemetery, Latty.

Louise Tiemann died Jan. 5, 1917, at the home of a daughter, Magdalene, in Burlington. She is buried in the Latty Cemetery. One daughter, Sarah, born Oct 27, 1863 died April 13, 1865.

The surviving Tiemann children and their families: John H. was born May 15, 1860 and died Aug 19, 1939. He married Wilhelmina Gaiser of Burlington. She was born Aug. 28, 1870 and died April 21, 1952. They had four children: Chester, Wesley, Margaret and Esther. They lived in Burlington.

Mary K. was born Nov. 27, 1861 and died June 22, 1947. She married Henry Gerdom of Burlington. He was born in Nettlestedt, Germany, July 23, 1856 and died Aug. 1, 1935. He was a young man when he came to this country. They had seven children: Norman, Alvine, Albert, Bertha, Selma, Helen and Florence. Their home was in Burlington.

Caroline M. was born Dec. 21, 1865, died Oct 26, 1946. She married Fred Duermeyer of Burlington. He was born in Mittengen, Germany, Feb. 25, 1857 and died Oct. 7, 1938. He was nine years old when he came to this country. He had two children, Margaret and Caroline. They lived in Burlington.

Henry H. born March 16, 1868 and died Aug 19, 1924. He married Anna Sommer of Keokuk who was born May 1, 1876 and died June 15, 1962. She was born in Dresden, Germany and arrived in America in July 1881. They had three children: Malcolm S., Thelma and Magdalene. They lived in Keokuk.

Magdalene C. was born April 29, 1870 and died Feb. 17, 1955. She married Fred Wuellner of Burlington. He was born March 2, 1860 in Minden, Westphalia, Germany and came to this country and Des Moines County in 1871. He died Sep. 17, 1936. They had six children: Frank, Matilda, Alvin, Mildred, Reuben and Paul (twins). They lived in Burlington.

E. William was born June 10, 1873 and died March 10, 1914. He married Anna Kampmeier, born March 7, 1876, and died Oct. 13, 1969. They had one son Arthur (died in a railroad accident when quite young). William remained on the family farm.

H. Samul was born Jan. 5, 1876 and died April 2, 1930. He married Ida Zachmeyer. There were eight children: Walter, Ruth, Helen, Warren, Laura, Richard, Armeda, and Cecil. They lived in Latty.

Louise E. was born April 24, 1881 and died March 21, 1939. She married Chris Schmidt who was born on a farm north of Burlington. He was born Nov. 1, 1875 and died Oct. 17, 1937. They had four children: Frieda, Raymond, Frances and Viola. They lived on a fam near Yarmouth.

About the Latty Church. In 1853 and earlier, German immigrants had been purchasing farms from the Irish owners along the Irish Ridge Road. Two pastors held services among the families. On Aug. 28, 1853 the German Evangelical Church of Benton Township was organized. Rev. Jakob Schmeiser, living at Steeple Church, which had been organized several years previously, served both churches.

Land was purchased and in Dec. 1854 a brick church was dedicated. The William Tiemann family was one of the early members. In 1866 the railroad was built thru the community and gradually the name of the station (Latty) was applied to the church. In 1867 more land was bought and a small brick parsonage was built, but a larger one was built in 1895. In 1903 it was agreed to build a new frame church. May 24, two months after the last service in the brick church, the new church was dedicated. Pastor Schmeiser, the first pastor, was on the program. **William Tiemann** was the only one of the original members present.

Samuel Tiemann was organist for the church for a number of years. On Sept. 13, 1903, the 50th anniversary of the church was celebrated.

Some remodeling and improvements were begun in 1948, and in 1952 the interior was remodeled and decorated, and the church rededicated in Sept. Today the Church is known as the Latty United Church of Christ, and they have an active membership. Most of the information is from the Centennial Booklet 1853-1953.

Marriage Certificate:

This Certifies that Mr. William Tieman and Miss Luise Rethemeier were solemnly united by me in the Holy Bonds of Matrimony at the Germ. Ev. Lions Church in Benton Township, Iowa on the 13th day of February in the year of our Lord One Thousand Eight Hundred and Fifty-nine conformably to the Ordinance of God, and the Laws of the State.

In Presence of Henry Brand and Christine Rethemeier Signed Jakob Schmeiser Evang. Pastor

1880 U.S. Census Page #4, Supervisor's District #1, Enumeration District #104. Benton Township, Des Moines Co. Iowa June 5, 1880. Lines 13-21;

Dwelling #33, Family #33, Teiman, Wm, white, male, 54, married, farmer, checked months unemployed, Birthplace: person- Prussia, father - Prussia, mother- Prussia. Louisa, white, female, 40, wife, married, keepinghouse, Birthplace: person- Prussia, father - Prussia, mother- Prussia. John, white, male, 20, son, single,railroad hand, checked months unemployed, Birthplace: person-Iowa, father - Prussia, mother- Prussia. Mary, white, female,18, daughter, single, no occupation marked, Birthplace: person- Iowa, father - Prussia, mother-Prussia. Caroline, white, female, 14, daughter, single, At Home, attended school, Birthplace: person- Iowa, father - Prussia, mother- Prussia. Henry, white, male,12, son, single, at home, attended school, Birthplace: person- Iowa, father - Prussia, mother- Prussia. Magdalina, white, female, 10, daughter, single, at home, attended school, Birthplace: person- Iowa, father - Prussia, mother-Prussia. Wm, white, male, 7, son, single, at home, Birthplace: person- Iowa, father - Prussia, mother- Prussia. Samuel, white, male, 4, son, single, at home, Birthplace: person- Iowa, father - Prussia, mother- Prussia.

William H. Tieman Gravestone (Can't read this line) Willaim H. Tieman, Born May 2 1825, Died May 11, 1906 (Can't read next two lines) Louise His Wife, Born Nov. 30, 1839, Died Jan 5, 1917 (Can't read next two lines)

"Germany, Births and Baptisms, 1558-1898"
Name: Heinrich Wilhelm Tiemann, Gender: Male, Baptism/Christening Date: 16 May 1822, Baptism/Christening Place: Evangelisch, Lengerich, Westfalen, Prussia, Father's Name: Georg Wilhelm Tiemann, Mother's Name: Catharina Sophia Koenig, Indexing Project (Batch) #: C95277-9, System Origin: Germany-ODM, Source File#: 526387

Burlington Hawkeye Newspaper
William Tiemann Dead - Worthy Pioneer Had Lived Here Fully Seventy Years - Is Survived by a Large Number of Descendants Another of the worthy and highly respected pioneers of this county has gone to his well-earned rest. William Tiemann passed away yesterday morning at 6 o'clock at his residence near Latty. Deceased was a native of Germany, but had spent fully seventy of his eighty years in this country, his family having come here from Virginia seventy years ago. They lived in the city for about ten years and then they removed to the farm near Latty, which remained the family home and eventually became the property of the deceased, and he never left it for any considerable time and who never dreamed of parting with it. He was honest, industrious and economical and henced prospered. He was fortunate in more than one sense of the word, for until a week ago he enjoyed that priceless possession almost perfect health. The old gentleman and his good wife had very many friends in the city and country and their home was famed far and wide for a genuine open-handed hospitality. They really found pleasure in entertaining their friends. William Tiemann is survived by the following relatives: The good wife and eight children; John, Henry, William and Samuel Tiemann, Mrs. Henry Gerdom, Mrs. F.J. Duermeyer, Mrs. Fred Wuellner and Mrs. Chris Schmidt all of whom except Henry who is a resident of Keokuk, live in this city or county. There are twenty grandchildren and one great-grandchild. The funeral will be held from the residence near Latty at 2p.m. Sunday. There will be a service at the Evangelical church at Latty.

Tecklenburg History (details below, see complete text in actual document)

Tecklenburg is a town in the district of Steinfurt, in North Rhine-Westphalia, Germany Location of Tecklenburg within Steinfurt district Coordinates: 52°1310N 7°4845ECoordinates: 52°1310N 7°4845E Country Germany State, North Rhine-Westphalia Admin. region, Münster District, Steinfurt Geography It is located at the foothills of the Teutoburg Forest, southwest of Osnabrück.

History In the 12th century the county of Tecklenburg emerged in the region that is now called the "Tecklenburger Land" in the western foothills of the Teutoburg Forest. It was annexed by the neighbouring county of Bentheim in 1263, and Tecklenburg still had a count until the 19th century. Even today, some local descendents of the Bentheim / Tecklenburg families are sometimes considered as aristocrats. Much like many other European aristocrats, their family can be traced back to Charlemagne (800's) or is linked with the blood lines of old European royal families (e.g. in the case of the Bentheim-Tecklenburg there is a link with the House of Orange - the Dutch royal family).

Tecklenburg has retained some of its medieval townscape to date. Main sites include the ruined castle (now serving as open air theatre during the Summer) and the Stadtkirche (the main, old church) including tombs of the dukes of Tecklenburg and others prominent in the history of the county and city.

Burg Tecklenburg is a castle ruin in Tecklenburg, used today as an outdoor theatre. The castle was built around 1250. Anna von Tecklenburg-Schwerin made a lot of construction changes. Around 1700 the castle was old and the bricks were used for other buildings in Tecklenburg. Only a ruin was the result.

Westphalia History

Westphalia within the federal state of North Rhine-Westphalia bordering on Northern Rhineland in the west and Lippe in the northeast Westphalia or Westfalia (German: Westfalen pronounced [vÉ›stfalÉ™n], Westphalian: Waästfaln) is a region in Germany, centred on the cities of Arnsberg, Bielefeld, Osnabrück, Dortmund, Minden, and Münster.

Westphalia is roughly the region in between the rivers Rhine and Weser, located both north and south of the Ruhr River. No exact definition of borders can be given, because the name "Westphalia" was applied to several different entities in history. For this reason, specifications of area and population differ greatly. They range between 16,000 and 22,000 km2 (6,200 and 8,500 sq mi) in land area, and between 4.3 million and 8 million inhabitants. There is, however, a general consensus that Münster Bielefeld and Dortmund are part of Westphalia. In principle the term "Westphalia" contrasts with the much less used term "Eastphalia", which covers roughly the area of modern Saxony-Anhalt towards the historic region of Brunswick or Braunschweig.

A linguistic definition of Westphalia (see Westphalian language) includes the former Prussian Province of Westphalia (except Siegen-Wittgenstein), Lippe, the region around Osnabrück and the greater area of the Emsland. Present-day common use, however, often restricts the notion to the present part of North Rhine-Westphalia.

Westphalia is known for the 1648 Peace of Westphalia which ended the Thirty Years' War, as the two treaties were signed in Münster and Osnabrück.

The traditional symbol of Westphalia is a white horse on a red field (the Westfalenpferd or Sachsenross), representing the Saxons. This image has been used in the coats of arms of Prussian Westphalia and the modern state of North Rhine-Westphalia. The white horse is also the traditional symbol of neighboring

Lower Saxony. Composed in Iserlohn in 1886 by Emil Rittershaus, the "Westfalenlied" is an unofficial anthem of Westphalia.

Around 1 A.D. there were numerous incursions through Westphalia and perhaps even some permanent Roman or Romanized settlements. The Battle of Teutoburg Forest took place near Osnabrück (as mentioned, it is disputed whether this is in Westphalia) and some of the tribes who fought at this battle came from the area of Westphalia.

Ratification of the Peace of Westphalia of 1648 in Münster by Gerard Terborch (1617-1681) Along with Eastphalia and Engern, Westphalia (Westfalahi) was originally a district of the Duchy of Saxony. In 1180 Westphalia was elevated to the rank of a duchy by Emperor Barbarossa. The Duchy of Westphalia comprised only a small area south of the Lippe River.

Modern Westphalia was part of the Lower Rhenish-Westphalian Circle of the Holy Roman Empire, which comprised territories of Lower Lorraine, Frisia and parts of the former Duchy of Saxony.

As a result of the Protestant Reformation, there is no dominant religion in Westphalia.

Parts of Westphalia came under Brandenburg-Prussian control during the 17th and 18th centuries, but most of it remained divided duchies and other feudal areas of power. The Peace of Westphalia of 1648, signed in Münster and Osnabrück, ended the Thirty Years' War. The concept of nation-state sovereignty resulting from the treaty became known as "Westphalian sovereignty".

After the defeat of the Prussian Army by the French at the Battle of Jena-Auerstedt, the Treaty of Tilsit in 1807 made the Westphalian territories part of the Kingdom of Westphalia from 1807-13. It was founded by Napoleon and was a French vassal state. This state only shared the name with the historical region; it contained only a relatively small part of Westphalia, consisting instead mostly of Hessian and Eastphalian regions.

After the Congress of Vienna, the Kingdom of Prussia received a large amount of territory in the Westphalian region and created the province of Westphalia in 1815. The northernmost portions of the former kingdom, including the town of Osnabrück, had become part of the states of Hanover and Oldenburg.

In the Prussian law code of 1794, marriage between noble males and middle-class females was forbidden without a government dispensation. In cities, sumptuary legislation designated what dress different urban groups should wear so as to keep them separate. Even without government regulation, however, different social groups remained easily distinguished everywhere in Europe by the distinctive, traditional clothes they wore. (see German Costumes in attached Media)

The local villages in which they dwelt remained the centers of peasants, social lives. Villages, especially in western Europe, maintained public order, provided poor relief, a village church, and sometimes a schoolmaster, collected taxes for the central government, maintained roads and bridges, and established common procedures for sowing, ploughing, and harvesting crops. But villages were often dominated by richer peasants and proved highly resistant to innovations, such as new crops and agricultural practices.

The diet of the peasants in the eighteenth century did not vary much from that of the Middle Ages. Dark bread, made of roughly ground wheat and rye flour, remained the basic staple. It was quite nourishing and high in vitamins, minerals, and even proteins since the bran and germ were not ground out. Peasants drank water, wine, and beer and ate soups and gruel made of grains and vegetables.

Especially popular were peas and beans, eaten fresh in summer but dried and used in soups and stews in winter. The new foods of the eighteenth century, potatoes and American corn, added important elements to the peasant diet. Of course, when harvests were bad, hunger and famine became the peasants' lot in life, making them even more susceptible to the ravages of disease.

Noted events in his life were:

• He worked as a Farmer.
• He was baptized on 16 May 1822 in Evangelisch, Lengerich, Westfalen, Prussia.
• He immigrated in May 1833 to USA.

Wilhelm married **Luise (Louisa) RETHEMEIER** [789][2,15,17,18,19,20,22,25,29] [MRIN: 272], daughter of _____ **RETHEMEIER** [790], on 13 Feb 1859 in Benton Township, Des Moines, Iowa, USA. Luise was born on 30 Nov 1839 in Minden, Westphalia, Germany, died on 5 Jan 1917 in Burlington, Des Moines County, Iowa, USA at age 77, and was buried in Benton Township, Des Moines, Iowa, USA.

3-**Johann Heinrich TIEMANN [840]**[2,15,17,22] was born on 15 May 1860 in Benton Township, Des Moines, Iowa, USA and died on 19 Aug 1939 at age 79.

Johann married **Wilhelmina GAISER** [841][2,30] [MRIN: 292], daughter of _____ **GAISER** [4608]. Wilhelmina was born on 28 Aug 1870 and died on 21 Apr 1952 in Burlington, Kane, Illinois, USA at age 81.

4-**Chester TIEMANN [845]**.[2]

4-**Wesley TIEMANN [844]**.[2]

4-**Margaret TIEMANN [843]**.[2]

4-**Esther TIEMANN [842]**.[2]

3-**Maria Karoline TIEMANN [825]**[2,15,17,22,30,31,32] was born on 27 Nov 1861 in Benton Township, Des Moines, Iowa, USA and died on 22 Jun 1947 in Burlington, Kane, Illinois, USA at age 85.

Maria married **Henry J. GERDOM** [824][2,30,32] [MRIN: 286], son of
_____ **GERDOM** [4607], on 31 Mar 1887. Henry was born on 23 Jul
1856 in Nettlestedt, Germany and died on 1 Aug 1935 in Burlington, Kane,
Illinois, USA at age 79.

4-Florence GERDOM [835].[2,32]

Florence married **-- DEIRKUPP** [834] [MRIN: 290], son of
_____ **DEIRKUPP** [4611].

5-Janet DEIRKUPP [836].

4-Alvine GERDOM [833].[2]

Alvine married **Frank G. NEBIKER** [832] [MRIN: 289], son of _____
NEBIKER [4617].

4-Bertha GERDOM [831].[2,32]

Bertha married **Otto S. DAUM** [830] [MRIN: 288], son of _____
DAUM [4618].

4-Helen GERDOM [829].[2,32]

Helen married **John KLAPPMEIER** [828] [MRIN: 287], son of _____
KLAPPMEIER [4619].

4-Albert F. GERDOM [827].[2,32]

4-Norman GERDOM [826].[2,32]

4-Selma GERDOM [838][2,32,33,34] was born on 26 Oct 1895 in Burlington, Kane,
Illinois, USA and died on 17 May 1935 in Burlington, Kane, Illinois, USA at age
39. The cause of her death was Drowning in Mississippi River.

General Notes: **0000-1** Selma Gerdom Obit
   Mrs. Rentzsch Rites Tuesday - Body of Burlington Woman is Found After
Search of Nine Days Services will be held Tuesday afternoon for Mrs. Selma
Rentzsch, 39, widely known Burlington nurse, whose body was found in the
Mississippi river just below the railroad bridge Saturday evening after she had
been missing nine days. (article continues see media)

T500-2
Correspondence from Thelma Tieman in a letter dated 1989

Selma Gerdom Rentzsch was our cousin. Her mother, Mary Gerdom was my father's sister. (She told her mother she was going to do something different that day, so she must have planned her death). Two of her sisters were nurses Alvina and Florence - Alvina has a daughter in New York who has a position in nursing in New York State. Florence worked in nursing until the day she died at age 92.

Noted events in her life were:

• She worked as a Nurse.

Selma married **Arthur RENTZSCH** [837] [MRIN: 291], son of _____ **RENTZSCH** [4616], in 1917 in Chicago, Cook, Illinois, USA. Arthur died in 1920.

5-Arthur RENTZSCH Jr. [839].

3-Karoline Sarah TIEMANN [823][2,17,22,30,31] was born on 27 Oct 1863 in Benton Township, Des Moines, Iowa, USA and died on 13 Apr 1865 at age 1.

3-Karoline Maria TIEMANN [819][2,15,17,22,34] was born on 21 Dec 1865 in Benton Township, Des Moines, Iowa, USA and died on 26 Oct 1946 at age 80.

General Notes: **Correspondence from Thelma Tieman in a letter dated 1989** "A childless widow when she married Fred. He had lost 2 wives in death and his 2 daughters were very young (2&4) when he married Karoline. They had a wonderful family life; the girls took care of their stepmother as though she was their natural mother."

Karoline married **Fred DUERMEYER** [818][2,34] [MRIN: 284], son of _____ _____ and _____ _____, on 24 Jan 1889. Fred was born on 25 Feb 1857 in Mittengen, Germany and died on 7 Oct 1938 in Burlington, Kane, Illinois, USA at age 81.

4-Margaret DUERMEYER [822].[2]

4-Caroline DUERMEYER [821].[2]

Karoline next married -- **KLEIN** [820] [MRIN: 285], son of _____ **KLEIN** [4610].

3-Heinrich Herman TIEMAN [771][2,15,17,19,22,34,35,36,37,38,39,40,41,42,43,44] was born on 16 Mar 1868 in Benton Township, Des Moines, Iowa, USA, died on 19 Aug 1924 in Keokuk, Lee, Iowa, USA at age 56, and was buried on 21 Aug 1924 in Keokuk, Lee Co., IA.

General Notes: This was my great-grandfather whom I never knew and whom was never spoken of by his wife,

Anna and her daughters. The reason finally came out in a conversation I had with his daughter Maggie before her sister Thelma died in 1997. It seems that her father, Henry, went mad and they put him in the asylum and was considered dead by the family. An illness that carried down to his daughter Maggie. Back in the early and mid 1900's the only diagnosis they had was "mad" and they were stuck away in an asylum. The family of course did not talk about those shut away as there was shame attached. My family it seems was no different. Poor Maggie had to live not only with the sigma of her father's illness, but her own as well.

In the late 1990's the diagnosis was bi-polar 2 and with it medication allowing people with it to live a normal life.

Another story my sister Beverly heard, was that he had syphilis and was hospitalized, but again never talked about. Either way, how sad that my great grandfather "disappeared" and we never knew about him.

"History of William Tiemann Family - Latty United Church of Christ Centennial Booklet 1853-1953" (exerpt)
Henry H. born March 16, 1868 and died Aug 19, 1924. He married Anna Sommer of Keokuk who was born May 1, 1876 and died June 15, 1962. She was born in Dresden, Germany and arrived in America in July 1881. They had three children: Malcolm S., Thelma and Magdalene. They lived in Keokuk.

T500-2 Correspondence from Thelma Tieman 1989 Favorite saying of her father, Henry..." Kleine kinder, kleine sorgen; grosse kinder, grosse sorgen" (small children small problems; big children big problems) Henry lost parts of all fingers left hand in a saw mill accident a few days before he was married. A carpenter, he was able to hold a nail between thumb and little finger. He built the little house his family lived in at 1628 Palean in Keokuk in the early 1900's. *That house was still in the family until Maggie died in 2007.

T500-12 1880 U.S. Census Page #4, Supervisor's District #1, Enumeration District #104. Benton Township, Des Moines Co. Iowa June 5, 1880. Lines 13-21; Dwelling #33, Family #33, Teiman, Wm, white, male, 54, married, farmer, checked months unemployed, Birthplace: person- Prussia, father - Prussia, mother- Prussia. Louisa, white, female, 40, wife, married, keepinghouse, Birthplace: person- Prussia, father - Prussia, mother- Prussia. John, white, male, 20, son, single,railroad hand, checked months unemployed, Birthplace: person-Iowa, father - Prussia, mother- Prussia. Mary, white, female,18, daughter, single, no occupation marked, Birthplace: person- Iowa, father - Prussia, mother-Prussia. Caroline, white, female, 14, daughter, single, At Home, attended school, Birthplace: person- Iowa, father - Prussia, mother- Prussia. Henry, white, male,12, son, single, at home, attended school, Birthplace: person- Iowa, father - Prussia, mother- Prussia. Magdalina, white, female, 10, daughter, single, at home, attended school, Birthplace: person- Iowa, father - Prussia, mother-Prussia. Wm, white, male, 7, son, single, at home, Birthplace: person- Iowa, father - Prussia, mother- Prussia. Samuel, white, male, 4, son, single, at home, Birthplace: person- Iowa, father - Prussia, mother- Prussia.

T500-62 Daily Gate City Newspaper Obit Henry H. Tieman of 1628 Palean street, died today at 1am at Mt. Pleasant, Iowa. He has been seriously ill since May of this year. Harry Herman Tieman was born in Latty, Iowa near Burlington, on March 16, 1868, and had made his home in Keokuk for the past twenty-five years. On November 20, 1902, he was united in marriage to Miss Anna Sommer, who survives her husband with three children, Malcolm, Thelma and Magdalene, all living at home. He is also survived by two brothers and four sisters, John Tieman, Sam Tieman, Mrs. Fred Duermeyer, Mrs. Henry Gerdom, and Mrs. Fred Wuellner, all of Burlington, and Mrs. Chris Schmidt of Morning Sun, Iowa, and a number of nieces and nephews. Mr. Tieman was a member of St. Paul's Evangelical church, of the Modern Woodmen of America and the Carpenter's Union. The funeral will be held from St. Paul's Evangelical church Thursday afternoon at 3 o"clock.

Noted events in his life were:

• He worked as a Carpenter.
• He was St. Paul United Church of Christ.

Heinrich married **Anna Ernestine SOMMER** [772] [2,19,36,37,38,39,40,41,42,43,45,46,47,48,49,50,51,52,53,54,55,56,57,58] [MRIN: 255], daughter of **Ernst Clemens SOMMER** [773] [23,36,40,45,47,58,59,60,61,62,63,64,65,66] and **Anna Rosamonde KUNZE** [774], [2,23,36,40,45,47,52,54,58,60,63,64,65,66,67] on 20 Nov 1902 in Keokuk, Lee, Iowa, USA. Anna was born on 1 May 1876 in Dresden, Saxony, Germany, died on 15 Jun 1962 in Keokuk, Lee, Iowa, USA at age 86, and was buried in Keokuk, Lee, Iowa, USA.

Noted events in her life were:

• She was St. Paul United Church of Christ.

4-Malcolm Sommer TIEMAN [716] [2,22,36,37,41,42,51,57,67,68,69,70,71,72,73,74,75,76,77,78,79] was born on 26 Sep 1903 in Keokuk, Lee, Iowa, USA, died on 16 Sep 1974 in Keokuk, Lee, Iowa, USA at age 70, and was buried in Keokuk, Lee, Iowa, USA.

General Notes: **Memories: Grand-Daughter, Beverly Dianne Tieman Starr, 2009**

On very hot summer nights in Iowa on the river with nothing but maybe a small fan at home, we would take a ride along the river road with all the car windows down to cool off. Or sleep in the front yard on blankets when the house got too hot. There must have been mosquitoes the size of aircraft carriers! We lived near a Dairy Queen and in the summer had ice cream cones and Caesar always got one too.

PaPa and Grandma Tieman would take either Michael or I on rides on the river road to try to cool off. They never took us both at the same time and that always upset my mother. Our grandparents Viola (Rietz) (01/15/04-03/22/95) and Malcolm (09/26/03-09/16/74) Tieman also lived in Keokuk in an upstairs apartment on Franklin Street. They were Christian Scientists although my grandmother had to take insulin for her diabetes (the religion doesn't believe any medicine in necessary). She worked at Swift's meat packing plant for a few years before my dad was born and he was an electrician at the Hoopinger's plant.

He sure never taught his craft to dad. The man was known for always using a hammer to fix everything. I saw him change a flood light bulb once with the hammer. It was stuck so he just "gave it a little tap". It took forever to get all the glass up and the rest of the bulb out of the socket. Mom always said dad kept repairmen in business trying to "fix" something around the house.

Grandma made the best yeast donuts from scratch and I used her recipe for years.

They were both very quiet and dad was an only child. I don't remember too much about them. They would never have Michael and I over there at the same time and that was really upsetting to our mother. The women didn't get along very well. Grandma did come twice to see us in NY with Maggie and Thelma when Amy and Nicole were little after PaPa died.

Grand-Son, Michael Tieman

Like Beverly, I do not have many memories of Papa and Viola. Papa was an electrician and loved to putter at home on small projects. He was a about 6', and thin, a very quiet, gentle man and died of a heart attack after repainting the interior of their home. Viola was a Christian Scientist (so I suppose Papa was too), a large lady also close to 6', (large boned from farmer stock), loved to cook. Several years after Papa died, she went to a nursing home in MO. close to her family.

T500-64 - Obit - Daily Gate City Newspaper

Malcolm Sommer Tieman, 70, 1023 Palean, died at 3:05 pm Monday at Graham hospital. Born Sept. 26, 1903 in Keokuk, he was the son of Henry H. and Anna Sommer Tieman, and was a lifelong resident of Keokuk. He was first employed by the Standard Four Tire Co. then by its succeding companies. He retired from Sheller-Globe in 1968. He married Viola Reitz, June 13, 1925 in Keokuk. He was a member of the First Church of Christian Scientist and served as an usher. Mr. Tieman is survived by his wife: one son, Malcolm L. of Akron, Ohio; three grandchildren; two great grandchildren; two sisters, Thelma Tieman of Keokuk and Magdalene Tieman of Keokuk and other relatives. The funeral will be held at 2pm Thursday at the DeJong Funeral Home with Reader Mrs. Paul DeVries officiating. Internment will be in Oakland Cemetery. Visitation will begin at 2pm Wednesday.

Noted events in his life were:

• He worked as an Electrician, Sheller-Globe.

Malcolm married **Viola Emma Marie REITZ** [1382] 41,51,57,70,71,75,76,78,80,81,82,83,84,85,86,87,88,89 [MRIN: 13], daughter of **Frederick William REITZ** [1237] 41,83,84,85,90,91,92,93,94,95,96,97,98 and **Mabel Kansas SOUTH** [1378], 41,77,83, 84,85,90,92,93,98,99,100,101,102,103,104,105,106,107 on 13 Jun 1925 in Keokuk, Lee, Iowa, USA. Viola was born on 15 Jan 1904 in

Van Buran Twp., Lee County, Iowa, USA,[108] died on 22 Mar 1995 in Columbia, Boone, Missouri, USA at age 91, and was buried on 27 Mar 1995 in Keokuk, Lee, Iowa, USA.

5-Malcolm Laverne TIEMAN [26] [41,51,57,67,71,74, 76,78,82,109,110,111,112,113,114,115] was born on 20 Feb 1926 in Keokuk, Lee, Iowa, USA, died on 5 Jan 2011 in Stow, Summit, Ohio, USA at age 84, and was buried on 8 Jan 2011 in Hillside Memorial Park Cemetary - Akron, Summit, OH, USA. The cause of his death was Congestive Heart Failure. Another name for Malcolm was Went by LaVerne or Verne.

General Notes: **Memories**: Daughter, Beverly Dianne Tieman Starr, 2009

Mom and Dad met in high school when he was a sophomore and she was a senior. According to dad, mom's friend, Faye Peters, introduced them. Mom worked as a nurse for decades, paying for our first TV and automatic washer and dryer. She got a 98 out of 100 on her nursing Iowa State Board Exam. She worked at a hospital as a floor nurse where ever we moved to until her knees started bothering her with arthritis.

Dad graduated from Keokuk High School in early June 1944 and was drafted for the 9th Air Force Army Air Corps at the end of the month. He left for basic training in Ft. Dodge, Iowa and then on to Ft. Leonardwood, MO. for more training. (Jacob was born there in 1997 when his father was stationed there). Dad was then sent to Buckley Field in Denver, CO for gunnery school where he trained to become a B17 gunner. He was young, gullible and skinny enough to fit into the gunner's bubble he always said. They practiced dropping flour "bombs" into the Grand Canyon before going overseas. When the crew was sent out at night to learn how to navigate over water (the Gulf of Mexico) they got lost in the dark and couldn't find their way back to base until dawn. The navigator was sent back to school after that even though he was not a rookie. Dad was also trained as a tail gunner on a B29 getting ready to go to Japan, but Japan surrendered first.

It's a wonder the military even took him because of his crippled left thumb he has as a result of having polio as a toddler. He was about 3 and was paralyzed on his left side. Daily massage for a year let him recover all of his function except that thumb, but he still could hold onto the B17 machine gun.

He and mom got married Dec. 30, 1944 in a snowstorm in Kahoka, MO by a justice of the peace. Grandma Alta and Grandpa Don drove them there and dad's mother was not happy about it. Dad was 18 and mom had just turned 20 in Nov.

They were together for 2 weeks Gulfport, Mississippi 1945 before he shipped overseas, and she studied for her state boards. There was an incident while they were there of him almost being allowed onto a city bus. It was summertime, he had a deep tan, and the driver thought he was a black man with a white woman. When he proved he was a soldier, the driver let them onto the bus.

He said that on Christmas Eve 1945 he was in Munich and helped guard SS troops along with the Polish guards for awhile. He was then shipped to a supply depot outside of Munich and discharged June 1946 as a Staff Sgt. Mom wanted him to go to college on the GI bill, but instead he returned to Penney's as a salesman in shoes and men's clothing. He told me not taking advantage of the college bill is his biggest regret.

He joined the Blue Lodge Masons in Keokuk in 1948 year and became a 32nd degree Mason in the 1960s in Akron joining the Tadmor Shriners. He drove kids and their parents to Cleveland Clinic for their appointments at the burn hospital when he first retired in 1991.

Mom and Dad had a belated honeymoon in Chicago at the Waldorf Astoria for a week after he returned from the war. They saw Liberace play piano in the Palmer Room when he was just a piano player.

They rented an upstairs apt. on 16th and Main when they got back where he started working for J.C. Penney, walking 16 blocks to work one way. Mom was still working at St. Joseph Hospital like she did while he was gone.

I was born 9 months later, and they moved to the house on Timea St. Many years later, when I was a young adult, mom told me that they had had a stillborn boy on 1/28/48, 10 months after I was born. They named him Richard LaVerne after his best friend in high school, Richard Dunlavey. The baby was 13# and perfectly formed but strangled on the cord. If they had done more C sections in those days the result may have been different. I found his birth date in my baby book and nothing more. Michael has a copy of the obituary where they misspelled his name. Dad to this day still does not talk about him.

When I was very small I was awakened one night from a sound sleep hearing and seeing my dad being taken out of the house in an ambulance. I was scared but didn't leave my room, just hid behind the door. I think he had pneumonia and he wasn't away too long.

Dad had a vegetable garden behind the house when I was little. He always liked growing flowers outside when he had time. He liked to draw and sketched lambs and ducks on my baby quilt and summer dresses that mom would then embroider. He likes to collect Waterford crystal, lighthouses, and has always loved the water. He was a swimming teacher at the YMCA when I was very little, but Michael and I never learned to swim. By the time we were old enough to learn, dad was working long hours in the retail business. Dad loves the ocean and lakes.

Michael lives on the Pacific coast and I like to paint seascapes. Michael and I still to this day do not like to get into the water. As an adult I was upended by an ocean wave in Hawaii and drenched while sitting on a rock in Bermuda, so am not at all fond of oceans. Even though Dad and I are both Pisces, he is the true water sign and I am the "watching from the porch" water sign.

Dad hunted rabbits and squirrels for us to eat with Floyd when I was really little. There wasn't a lot of money and even later, the day before pay day we would have waffles for dinner because that was all we had. We kids thought it was fun, having breakfast for dinner. Some of the things mom served us from time to time made me skip dinner. Ham hocks and navy beans, liver and onions (one of Connie's all-time favorites) and dad's favorite and the absolute worst... stuffed beef heart. The smell of these things made it impossible to eat. They must have been cheap.

A tornado went down across the street from us one night, Freeport Ill., and a big tree fell across the driveway putting a huge tree limb through our parents' bedroom window. I don't remember this, but Michael does and dad confirmed his memory.

While we lived in Akron, dad worked for Scotts 5-10 downtown and the Soap Box Derby was (and is still) held there every summer. There was always a parade of current TV stars and in 1962 it was Little Joe, Hoss, Pa, and Adam Cartwright from "Bonanza". We watched from the upstairs office in the Scotts store. The next year the celebrities were John Russell from "Lawman", comedian Paul Lynde, and Paul Anka (who interested me the most)!

Dad had had a heart attack when he was in his early 40's from an enlarged "athlete's" heart he acquired from running track in high school. Much later he has had a pacemaker implanted 3 times for the same reason. In the middle 1990's he was diagnosed with Chronic Lymphatic Leukemia. Thelma also had this for many years. I remember dad smoking a pipe with cherry tobacco until I my girls were little. It always smelled so wonderful.

On July 29, 2008 my dear, kind, smart sister Connie Sue lost her 6-year battle with breast cancer. She had all the radiation and chemo a human can have, and it still took her. It was the day before her 25th wedding anniversary and a week before her 50th birthday. Dad is incredibly sad and depressed. He said he was done when he lost you, "his rock". I can't imagine losing a wife of 50 years and then your youngest child of 50 years. No man should have to endure that.

MSgt., US Army Air Corps. WWII Started work at J.C. Penney in Keokuk, Iowa. Retired as a Prudential Insurance Agent. Freemason 3rd degree and 32nd degree and Shriner.

T500-20

I'm 82 years young I was born Malcolm LaVerne Tieman of the parents of Malcolm Sommer Tieman and Viola Marie Reitz Tieman on Feb 20, 1926 at St. Joseph Hospital in Lee County, Keokuk Iowa .

I weighed 13 lbs. at birth. When I was 3 years old I came down with polio which I don't remember. My dad took me to Dr. Northup a friend of the family and I was given a complete body massage for one hour a day 7 days a week. It cost my parents $1 a day which in those depression days would be like $100 a day in this day. In those days there was no health insurance available. The only deformity I have is my left thumb is crooked and left arm smaller than my right arm. But luckily, I can use my hand.

Keokuk was named after Chief Keokuk of the Sioux Indian Tribe which settled there.

The Mississippi river is a mile wide and I used to swim & fish in the summertime. When I was 6 years old my grandfather, Don Morrill and I would fish by the dam about 500 ft. from the closed spillway and catch catfish and perch. It was great sport. Don would clean them and had a delicious dinner. (Some confusion here as Don was not his grandfather, but his father-in-law, could he have meant his grandfather Fred Reitz?)

Every summer I would spend the summers at my grandfather's farm in Kahoka, MO. a hour drive south of Keokuk. I fed pigs also rode on back of pigs and young calves - didn't stay on long but was fun. Also learned to hunt small game and got to be a good shot - my uncles Fred and Floyd Hewitt taught me how to shoot.

Beverly was born 3/15/47 Richard was stillborn 1/28/48

In 1941 USA declared war on Japan Dec 7, 1941. I was drafted in the Army which I was a senior in High School. I graduated on June 6, 1944 from Keokuk Senior High and was in service on June 30, 1944 in Fort Dodge, Iowa . I was sent to Fort Leonardwood, MO. for army basic training for 6 weeks. I was then sent to Buckley Field in Denver, CO. for 6 weeks of gunnery school. We had to take apart and reassemble a 50cal. machine gun blind folded in 3 minutes.

While in high school I met your mother Doris Earline Morrill - fell in love with her and we got married on Dec. 30, 1944 in Kahoka, MO by justice of peace. Don & Alta, Dee 's parents drove us in a blinding snow storm - it was so bad Don had to look out the window, so he could see out that night. Of course, my mother was crushed because I was only 18 & Dee was 20 - Dad was for us.

Dee was a Registered Nurse just graduating from nurses training of 3 years in1945, she was only the second student in Iowa 's history to score 98 on her state board test.

On Christmas Eve 1945 I was in a convoy going through Paris France in a severe thunderstorm. It was cold, 38, we had no canopy over our heads - we were wet and hungry. We arrived in the Black Forest where we slept in tents - got food and dry clothes & boots. Stayed 2 days. Then we went to a small village called Furstenfeldbrook which is south of Munich - helped guard SS troops with the Polish guards - who broke open barrels of denatured alcohol and of course died within minutes. Horrible site to see. Then I was shipped to a supply depot out of Munich and stayed till I was sent home in June of 1946. I had an honorable discharge from the 9th Air Force as a Staff Sgt.

Your mother met me in Chicago where we stayed at the Waldorf Astoria for a week. Saw Liberachie play piano before before he became famous.

Came back to Keokuk - your mom had rented an upstairs apt. on 16th & Main St. I went to work for J.C. Penney Co. Walked 16 blocks to work one-way 2x a day. We had a little fan - it was really hot - your mom worked at St. Joseph Hospital.

Beverly was born March 15th, 1947 - at St. Joseph Hospital.

I earned a yearly membership at the YMCA by working in the summer teaching boys ages 6 to14 years how to swim in the winter on Saturday I coached a boy's basketball team same ages with another coach while in the 9th to 12th grade at Keokuk High.

I also worked at J.C. Penney as stock boy and marked merchandise after school and all-day Saturdays. Mr. J.C. Penney visited our store in 1948 - he drove himself from Missouri to Keokuk which was a 2hr. drive - on that Father's Day he worked on the floor with the men selling merchandise - I had the pleasure of working next to him - He could call you by your first name after only hearing it once - a remarkable man and mind - He had 3 sons who he made to work for a living as he never gave them any allowance - he remarked you learn more by doing than have someone support you.

Michael was born Aug. 20, 1950

When Beverly was 4 years old - she would take her chair & coloring book and crayons and sit on the corner and color. Grandma Alta lived across the corner from her - none dare touch her, our Caesar, G. Alta's red cocker spaniel would take them in a minute. The neighbors and friends of ours could talk to her but don't touch. Crazy - but that's the way it was.

Beverly went to school at GARFIELD SCHOOL and then I was transferred to Freeport, Illinois , next to Wisc. boarder, where we lived between 4-5 years- then we moved to Elgin, Illinois -with Penney's.

Every year Freeport did a presentation of the Lincoln & Douglas debate - everyone in the city of 25,000 dressed in costumes of that era - this lasted one week - and on Sat. had a big parade of horses & oxen pulling covered wagons - bands & clowns - a big day for Freeport - these were fun times.

Connie was born in Freeport in August 5, 1958.

It was so cold in Elgin, Ill. -20degrees below zero and 5 - 6 feet of snow from Nov. til April - we had red flags on our car antennas, so we could see who was turning the corners. Snow plows kept the main streets open all winter - thank God for that. Beverly & Michael walked 4 blocks to school, snow drifts so high we could not see them when they were walking.

In Akron, Ohio, Beverly put snow on Michael's face and froze his cheeks. Mom spanked her little butt and she never did it again - It took years before his cheeks healed up.

Beverly graduated from Buchtel High School in Akron - when I quit Penney's and joined Buckeye Mart in Columbus.

Moved from Columbus to Akron where I managed stores for Scotts 5-10. 1962 and'63. Every year in Aug. the city had movie star celebrities come in for the Soap Box Derby race - the one Beverly & Michael was Hoss, Little Joe and Loren Green - they stopped in front of Scotts and I got their autographs, but they got lost over the years.

We moved from Columbus where Michael graduated from high school and started art school.

To Mass. with Ben Franklin stores and back to Akron a second time to Ellet where I worked for Prudential Insurance 15 years until 1991.

When Beverly was 18 she went to nursing school at City Hospital in Akron for 3 years then graduated as a registered nurse. She met Bill Starr while in nurses training. He had a red convertible which Connie liked to ride in. Bill was at college in Youngstown where he graduated as a structural engineer. They were married for 23 years, had Nicole & Amy she then got divorced - Bill met another woman. Bill worked at Kodak in Rochester NY till he retired at age 55. He now lives 1 1/2 hours from Dallas. Beverly & Bill lived in Texas once before 1976-1982 - kids were little - 4-5 years old. Mom and I went down there for Xmas a couple of times.

I retired on April 1st, 1991 from Prudential Insurance Company - after 15 years service - I enjoyed every minute of it.

Mom and I bought a house in Akron and lived there 20 years in Ellet, suburb of Akron where Connie graduated from High School. We sold home and rented an apt. in Cuyahoga Falls across from golf course - when your mom passed away on 3/9/03.

I moved to Danbury Retirement Home on April 22, 2008.

*11/6/09 - The years since mom died have been too painful for Dad to write about here. Yet he kept a daily diary from when mom died until 8 months before he died- Dad died Jan 5, 2011. -Michael Tieman-

Noted events in his life were:

• He was a member of 32nd Degree Mason and Shriner.
• He worked as a J.C. Penney Mgr. and Prudential Insurance Agent.
• He was Methodist.
• Malcolm served in the military between 1944 and 1946 in USA, Germany: WWII, Army Air Corps, B17 belly gunner, trained as B29 tail gunner.[109]
• EDUC: Keokuk High School, in Jun 1944, in Keokuk, Lee County, Iowa, USA.

Malcolm married **Doris Earline MORRILL** [27] [19,41,67,71,82,113,116,117,118,119,120,121,122,123,124] [MRIN: 2], daughter of **Donald Reginald MORRILL** [28][19,30,41,70,119,120,122,125,126,127,128,129,130,131,132,133,134] and **Alta Arvilla VINSON** [29],[41,70,119,120,121,127,131,132,134,135,136,137,138,139] on 30 Dec 1944 in Kahoka, Clark, Missouri, USA. Doris was born on 12 Nov 1924 in Nevada, Story, Iowa, USA, died on 9 Mar 2003 in Akron, Summit, Ohio, USA at age 78, and was buried on 13 Mar 2003 in Hillside Memorial Park Cemetary - Akron, Summit, OH, USA.

Noted events in her life were:

• Cause of Death: Pneumonia.
• She worked as a RN.
• She was Methodist.
• She had a residence in Keokuk, Iowa.[124]
• Doris served in the military on 10 Mar 1944.[124]
• She was educated at RN in 1945 in Keokuk, Lee, Iowa, USA.

6-Beverly Dianne TIEMAN [893][41,70,71,82,140,141] was born on 15 Mar 1947 in Keokuk, Lee, Iowa, USA.

General Notes: Beverly's Story

I was born Saturday, March 15, 1947 8:16 pm (the "Ides of March") at 9 # 5 oz. in Keokuk, IA. the first child of Doris Earline (Morrill) Tieman (11/12/24-03/09/03) and Malcolm LaVerne Tieman.(02/20/26-). My mother said the weather that day did a little of everything; rain, snow, sun and every birthday afterwards has had unpredictable weather, especially all the years I lived north of the Mason Dixon line.

Mom said my name was supposed to be Katherine, with black, curly hair and blue eyes like my dad. When I got here and was bald and blue eyed they didn't know what to name me. My grandpa Don visited Mom in the hospital and took her a box of blue stationary. On the side it said, "for the best get Beverly" and they liked the name. My middle name was always to be Dianne but my dad wanted the 2 "n"s so it would be different.

The 75.8 million of us born in my generation are labeled the "Baby Boomers" after WWII from 1946-1964.

We lived in a little white rented house at 1511 Timea St. a block from my grandparents, Alta and Donald Morrill (NaNaw and Grandpa Don). Dad worked at J.C. Penney in the shoe department and my mother was an RN labor and delivery nurse who worked nights at St. Joseph Hospital where she trained. Mom was a good cook who taught me how to can fruit and vegetables, sew clothes, knit and do embroidery. She had all the housewife traits and also worked at the hospital. Little did I know that was to be my future.

I was baptized on Mother's Day at Trinity Methodist Church May 1947. I still have the baby locket from Aunt Pat and gold ring from Great Aunt Elsie and Uncle Floyd Hewitt and the big black and white piggy bank from my mom's friend that were christening gifts. I keep the ring and locket on a gold charm bracelet now. My favorite toys as a little girl were Mr. Bear, Caesar, Lulu, books and any kind of baby doll According to my baby book and the stories mom told, I never crawled, just scooted around the house with one leg tucked under me and walked when I was a year old. I did run over her beloved cat Razz (Razzmataz) by reaching over to pet him from my walker and he didn't survive. Another time I brought her a very flat cat from our alley that had been run over a few times for her to fix because she was a nurse. Cats have always attracted me!

My mother's middle name (Earline) was a bone of contention between my grandparents as "Earl" had been the name of an old boyfriend of my grandmother according to the story mom told. Grandma wrote it on the birth certificate without my grandfather knowing until later. My dad always called mom "Dee" or "Honey" as he never liked Doris.

Mom belonged to the Eastern Star, the Methodist Church, usually a garden club where ever we were living; she loved to read, sing, play the piano and grow African violets. I took piano lessons during grade school because she liked it and I ended up enjoying it too. She sang and danced in minstrel shows in nurses' training and she and dad liked to Jitterbug when they were dating.

She liked jewelry; any kind; Eisenberg brooches that were costume jewelry and later on, real pearls, diamonds and rubies. She collected bells and Waterford crystal and Spode Christmas china, and always wore hats for church. I have never liked wearing hats except the pillbox popular in the 60's thanks to Jackie Kennedy's popularity.

Mom sewed a lot of my formals for Rainbow Girls and school dances and designed and sewed my wedding gown and pillbox veil. She made poodle skirts in the "60s for me and 2 friends. It impressed me that she could put newspapers over the couch, make a pattern and have new slipcovers by dinnertime. It was a talent I didn't inherit; I always had to buy a pattern.

Mom and Dad met in high school when he was a sophomore and she was a senior. According to dad, mom's friend, Faye Peters, introduced them.

Mom worked as a nurse for decades, paying for our first TV and automatic washer and dryer. She got a 98 out of 100 on her nursing Iowa State Board Exam. She worked at a hospital as a floor nurse where ever we moved to until her knees started bothering her with arthritis.

Dad graduated from Keokuk High School in early June 1944 and was drafted for the 9th Air Force Army Air Corps at the end of the month. He left for basic training in Ft. Dodge, Iowa and then on to Ft. Leonardwood, MO. for more training.(Jacob was born there in 1997 when his father was stationed there). Dad was then sent to Buckley Field in Denver, CO for gunnery school where he trained to become a B17 gunner. He was young, gullible and skinny enough to fit into the gunner's bubble he always said. They practiced dropping flour "bombs" into the Grand Canyon before going overseas. When the crew was sent out at night to learn how to navigate over water (the Gulf of Mexico) they got lost in the dark and couldn't find their way back to base until dawn. The navigator was sent back to school after that even though he was not a rookie. Dad was also trained as a tail gunner on a B29 getting ready to go to Japan, but Japan surrendered first.

It's a wonder the military even took him because of his crippled left thumb he has as a result of having polio as a toddler. He was about 3 and was paralyzed on his left side. Daily massage for a year let him recover all of his function except that thumb, but he still could hold onto the B17 machine gun.

He and mom got married Dec. 30, 1944 in a snowstorm in Kahoka, MO by a justice of the peace. Grandma Alta and Grandpa Don drove them there and dad's mother was not happy about it. Dad was 18 and mom had just turned 20 in Nov.

They were together for 2 weeks Gulfport, Mississippi 1945 before he shipped overseas, and she studied for her state boards. There was an incident while they were there of him almost being allowed onto a city bus. It was summertime, he had a deep tan, and the driver thought he was a black man with a white woman. When he proved he was a soldier, the driver let them onto the bus.

He said that on Christmas Eve 1945 he was in Munich and helped guard SS troops along with the Polish guards for awhile. He was then shipped to a supply depot outside of Munich and discharged June 1946 as a Staff Sgt.

Mom wanted him to go to college on the GI bill, but instead he returned to Penney's as a salesman in shoes and men's clothing. He told me not taking advantage of the college bill is his biggest regret.

He joined the Blue Lodge Masons in Keokuk in 1948 year and became a 32nd degree Mason in the 1960s in Akron joining the Tadmor Shriners. He drove kids and their parents to Cleveland Clinic for their appointments at the burn hospital when he first retired in 1991.

Mom and Dad had a belated honeymoon in Chicago at the Waldorf Astoria for a week after he returned from the war. They saw Liberace play piano in the Palmer Room when he was just a piano player. They rented an upstairs apt. on 16th and Main when they got back where he started working for J.C. Penney, walking 16 blocks to work one way. Mom was still working at St. Joseph Hospital like she did while he was gone. I was born 9 months later, and they moved to the house on Timea St.

Many years later, when I was a young adult, mom told me that they had had a stillborn boy on 1/28/48, 10 months after I was born. They named him Richard LaVerne after his best friend in high school, Richard Dunlavey. The baby was 13# and perfectly formed but strangled on the cord. If they had done more C sections in those days the result may have been different. I found his birth date in my baby book and nothing more. Michael has a copy of the obituary where they misspelled his name. Dad to this day still does not talk about him.

When I was very small I was awakened one night from a sound sleep hearing and seeing my dad being taken out of the house in an ambulance. I was scared but didn't leave my room, just hid behind the door. I think he had pneumonia and he wasn't away too long. He had pneumonia a few times later on when I was older too. I had a bad habit for many years sleep walking and talking. Sometimes mom said I would end up in the bathtub or try to get outside in the summertime and not wake up. They would just walk me back to bed and I had no memory of it. I had a couple of sleepwalking episodes as an adult when I was under stress.

Monday was laundry day and it took all day with the wringer washer and hanging the clothes outside on the line and always keeping one eye on the weather in case they had to be taken down quickly. These were the "good old days"? I still love the smell of sheets that were hung outside to dry and the smell of newly mown grass.

There was a the black cocker spaniel that lived across the street from us on Timea different from the red spaniel, Caesar, that lived with NaNaw and Grandpa

Don. He actually belonged to my Aunt Pat while she was in high school, but Caesar appointed himself my guard dog and was usually with me. We shared his dog food and he helped me learn to walk holding onto him according to the stories my mother told.

He never let anyone come near me if he was "on guard" and when I would take my little chair and coloring book and crayons to the corner to wait for NaNaw, he wouldn't let my own grandfather near me. There was a huge tree on that corner with a hole in the roots that my red chair just fit into. My mother would call NaNaw on the phone and then hang up when she answered because when grandma looked out that window she could see me and come and help me across the street. I was around 3 or 4 then.

Caesar and I both got in trouble one time when I went for a long walk down a busy street to look for someone to play with. He knew better than I did it was wrong. I finally found a little girl to play with and he went home and got my mother. I was up on a porch playing with this little girl when mom and the dog arrived. I got in trouble all the way home and Caesar was the hero. Tattle tale. He lived in and patrolled his neighborhood for 11 years. No leash laws then so he was the boss.

On very hot summer nights in Iowa on the river with nothing but maybe a small fan at home, we would take a ride along the river road with all the car windows down to cool off. Or sleep in the front yard on blankets when the house got too hot. There must have been mosquitoes the size of aircraft carriers! We lived near a Dairy Queen and in the summer had ice cream cones and Caesar always got one too. PaPa and Grandma Tieman would take either Michael or I on rides on the river road to try to cool off. They never took us both at the same time and that always upset my mother. Dad didn't have a car for years (his first was a 1955 turquoise and white Chevy Belair) and he took the bus or walked everywhere.

One story my mom told and retold about me when I was very little was how I got in trouble with Aunt Pat. I was at NaNaw's house, Pat was at work and I got into her room. She had just bought a cedar chest as she was engaged to Wally Wetzel who was in Korea. I spilled a whole bottle of perfume on the top of the hope chest and didn't tell anyone. When Pat got home later of course the finish was ruined and I got my one and only spanking from her. Pat is 7 years younger than mom, so she took me with her and her high school friends when I was little. Mom and Pat always said I just sat and listened and then told everything that was said later when I got home.

Dad had a vegetable garden behind the house when I was little. He always liked growing flowers outside when he had time. He liked to draw and sketched lambs and ducks on my baby quilt and summer dresses that mom would then embroider. He likes to collect Waterford crystal, lighthouses, and has always loved the water. He was a swimming teacher at the YMCA when I was very little, but Michael and I never learned to swim. By the time we were old enough to learn, dad was working long hours in the retail business. Dad loves the ocean and lakes. Michael lives on the Pacific coast and I like to paint seascapes. Michael and I still to this day do not like to get into the water. As an adult I was upended by an ocean wave in Hawaii and drenched while sitting on a rock in Bermuda, so am not at all fond of oceans. Even though Dad and I are both Pisces, he is the true water sign and I am the "watching from the porch" water sign.

My brother, Michael La Verne, was born Aug. 20, 1950 and according to the stories our mother told, he had his days and nights mixed up until he was about 6 mos. old when he slept through the night. He had a lot of curls and looks like dad. He couldn't say my name and called me "Bebe" which is what I have my grandkids call me.

I mostly remember having to always take him with me growing up no matter where I went. I'm sure he loved going to my friends' house and watch us play! I vowed if I ever had kids they wouldn't have to go everywhere together like we did. The time I rubbed his face in the snow and he got frostbite on his cheeks it was because I was mad at mom for making me take him to the library with me. Since she worked nights, she napped in the daytime and I suppose it was more convenient for her if he was with me. I picked on him a lot as long as he was littler than me ("point to your head and say your initials") Once he got taller I didn't do it as often!

He called himself "the Ketchup Kid" and ate ketchup sandwiches sometimes…ick. Probably while he was wearing his twin gun holsters and the coon skin Davy Crockett cap!

Our grandparents Viola (Rietz) (01/15/04-03/22/95) and Malcolm (09/26/03-09/16/74) Tieman also lived in Keokuk in an upstairs apartment on Franklin Street. They were Christian Scientists although my grandmother had to take insulin for her diabetes (the religion doesn't believe any medicine in necessary). She worked at Swift's meat packing plant for a few years before my dad was born and he was an electrician at the Hoopinger's plant. He sure never taught his craft to dad. The man was known for always using a hammer to fix everything. I saw him change a flood light bulb once with the hammer. It was stuck so he just "gave it a little tap". It took forever to get all the glass up and the rest of the bulb out of the socket. Mom always said dad kept repairmen in business trying to "fix" something around the house.

Grandma made the best yeast donuts from scratch and I used her recipe for years. They were both very quiet and dad was an only child. I don't remember too much about them. They would never have Michael and I over there at the same time and that was really upsetting to our mother. The women didn't get along very well.

Grandma did come twice to see us in NY with Maggie and Thelma when Amy and Nicole were little after PaPa died.

Christmas was always a very special holiday for us and Michael and I couldn't contain ourselves waiting for Christmas morning after Santa came. Mom was the worst of us and we all were usually up by 4 or 4:30 am opening gifts. A tradition I carried on with my kids, but Michael made his family wait until after breakfast. That's just wrong!

Some of the best gifts Santa brought me over the years were a doll buggy, Pamper the lamb, a Kodak Brownie camera, ice skates, a hair dryer (I always had curlers in or a wild Toni perm done at home that I hated) a record player. Grandma Alta got me a transistor radio one year that was the best!

Our Great Aunts Maggie (11/28/12-6/02/07) and Thelma (09/12/07-09/18/97) Tieman lived with my Great Grandmother Anna (Sommer) Tieman (5/01/1876-06/15/63) near us at 1628 Palean St. I remember Great Grandma's beautiful long white hair that Maggie did up in a braided coiled bun for her. She sure looked like the German housewife then! (Great Grandma was born in Dresden, Germany). In nice weather Maggie would wash the hair and Great Grandma would sit in the backyard in the sun and Maggie would brush and brush it until it was almost dry and then she would braid it up for the week.

Michael and I spent many Saturdays with them and we learned how to make the yummy cinnamon/sugar coffee cake on the big black wood stove in their kitchen. It would rise overnight and be baked for Sunday breakfast the next morning. They made soap from lye and left-over soap scraps and they had the prettiest china and vases in their dining room. Years later I got the Havilland china Thelma collected over the years and still cherish it and use it.

Their upstairs ceiling also slanted and that's where Maggie and Thelma had their bedrooms. The highlight of the house was the powder room off of the kitchen for Great Grandma as her room was downstairs. No one had powder a room in those days!

The house was built by Henry Tieman who was a carpenter by trade. The day before his wedding to Anna, he accidentally sliced off 3 fingers of his left hand with a circular saw. He was still able to build the house and work as a carpenter, but for an unnamed reason he was sent to an institution where he later died in his 50's. Thelma had to quit school as a teenager and become the breadwinner.

Their backyard was surrounded with flower and vegetable beds and we spent many lazy summer days in the shade or in the coolness of the house with the window shades down keeping out the heat. Maggie's hobby was photography and she took black and white portrait poses of us all the time.

Great Grandma's tradition for her May 1st birthday was to have breakfast on the screened porch no matter what the weather. There were many May Days that we wore our winter coats and mittens for breakfast in Iowa!

We made May baskets with flowers for her and her neighbors and hung them on their front doors as a surprise. Michael and I "borrowed" whatever flowers in gardens we could find to do this.

The worst part of their house was the cellar. There was a trap door in the floor of the screen porch off the kitchen and when it was lifted up the cellar steps went down to the washer and dryer (eventually) and where their canned goods were stored. It had a dirt floor and was always creepy to me. They had a wringer washer on that porch before the electric appliances and Michael and I hung clothes from the clothesline like we did at home.

Great Grandma had a brother Emil and a sister Myrtle Wilson that lived in Keokuk. Maggie or Thelma would take Michael and I to visit them from time to time and they spooked me. Emil owned a broom factory and it was dark inside and smelled funny. It had several sets of stairs up to the next level. He always wore bib overalls and seemed to silently just appear from nowhere. It was like a scary movie set (and I didn't even know what that was then). I thought for years that the line in the Lord's Prayer we said in church every Sunday was "and deliver us from Emil". He also made homemade wine from his vineyards across the street from the broom factory. Mom would give a little of his wine if we had a cough that wouldn't go away. Dad said Emil sold the vineyards to Thelma and Maggie after he retired.

Myrtle was a widow that always spoke in a whisper, was very, very thin, always had her window shades drawn and always wore cotton hose with garters. She had run a florist with her husband when he was alive. We would just sit and be bored while Maggie or Thelma talked to her and then leave. They usually took her food of some kind, so they must have been looking after her.

She also had a brother, George, who lived in California for years. Maggie went out there to live with him when she went to college for 2 years at UCLA.

Neither Thelma nor Maggie ever married, and they worked as secretaries at Electro Metals Co. their entire career. Thelma was executive secretary to the president of the company. They traveled to Mexico and Europe a couple of times and were very frugal, having grown up in the depression and loosing their father at a young age.

I remember Thelma having a boyfriend at one time. He was around for quite a while, but I remember mom saying that Maggie and their mom "ran him off" because they needed her to take care of them. Who knows what the true story was?

Great Grandma died June 1962 at the age of 86. I have her wedding china from Bavaria, her engagement pocket watch engraved and dated 1901 from Henry (Maggie's note says she did not like rings). I also have the twin size quilt she made and left for me for my high school graduation. Amy has her monogrammed silverware.

I mostly remember what the little white house and neighborhood looked like from the years Michael and I returned and spent summers with Grandma (NaNaw) and Don Morrill after we had moved away. Our first train ride alone was from Elgin to Keokuk in 1959. We were told NOT to get off of the train for any reason until we arrived. Along the way, the train hit a stalled car sitting on the tracks. Michael decided he needed to see what was going on and got off with the engineer. I let him go, because I was told not to leave. No one was hurt and the engineer brought Michael back to his seat and of course I couldn't wait to tell on him! Probably was the highlight of my summer.

My good friend Cindy Roth lived across and down the street from NaNaw and although she was a couple of years older than me, we played together in the summers on my Grandma's front porch. It was shady and cool, had a porch swing all the way across and had high walls we could sit behind and not be seen from the street.

I would go down the block and sit on my side of the street and call Cindy's name until either she or her mother came to their door and said if she could play or not. I wasn't allowed to cross the street.... but why didn't I use the phone? Who knows? We played with our dolls and several summers we had teddy bears with bendable joints that we dressed in doll clothes. We played with tons of paper dolls; just girl stuff. We would walk up the hill on Grandma's corner to the "little store" and get a Fudgesicle or popsicle once in a while. It was a big deal to be allowed to go alone.

Cindy and I are still in touch with annual Christmas cards. She's a retired school teacher and never married.

Grandma Alta (NaNaw) (04/11/05-07/24/64) was an elevator operator in at the 1st National Bank and my grandfather Don (02/14/01-05/13/78) was a linotype printer for the "Daily Gate City"newspaper.

** (Don's family line (Morrill (Morrell) went back to the Mayflower. His sister, May Crette #540203 and her daughter, Coralee Reynolds, are members of the DAR (Daughters of the American Revolution). We all could join if we wanted to. We are related to the Maine branch of the Quakers; who were landowners, senators, lawyers, a state supreme court justice and the wife of Charles Hamiln, V.P. to Abraham Lincoln. He was also related to Joseph Smith, founder of the Church Latter Day Saints when they split off from the Quakers and Mormons and stayed in Nauvoo, Ill. Michael has done fantastic, extensive genealogy research for decades.) **

Grandma had the best laugh. She was maybe 5' tall, round and wore a size 4 shoe and loved her soap operas. I started watching "As the World Turns" with her and still watch it today.

I can still see her sitting in the big chair in her living room, watching TV, sometimes drinking a beer, and laughing and laughing at something funny. She had a lot of friends that would drop by the house on the spur of the moment. Mom said that drove her crazy when she was growing up because she never knew how many people were in the house when she got up every day as a kid. I thought it was neat and Grandma was a fun person. She raised canaries and parakeets (at different times) and her dining room window was always full of birds and African violets. I have never liked birds except OUTSIDE of my window, but I do still try to grow violets.

Mom always said she liked to go to a funny movie with both dad and grandma and listen to them laugh out loud.

Grandma let me ride the elevator with her sometimes when she worked when I visited in the summer. We went to play bingo at the Elks Lodge on Friday nights and she usually won a lot of the games. I remember being amazed at how many cards she played at one time. It looked like a table full to me as a kid. Grandpa Don belonged to the Moose Lodge and took Michael there where he mostly remembers drinking homemade root beer.

She died of a heart attack at the age of 56 when I was a junior in high school. I was working at my first job as a checkout clerk at Scott's in Akron when my dad called to tell me the news. Grandma had been sick a week and mom and Connie were already in Iowa with her. It was a long ride back to the funeral and I still think of her and her laugh.

Grandpa Don spent his evenings sitting in the kitchen in the back of the house in the dark, listening to the ball games (St. Louis Cardinals especially) on the radio, drinking his Blatz beer and smoking Lucky Strikes. He worked hard all day in the print shop in the cold and heat setting type and liked to relax with radio baseball, fishing with Michael on the Mississippi river, and growing vegetables and flowers in his yard. He loved to fish and once brought home a HUGE snapping turtle…alive….and then tried to kill it on the picnic table in the backyard with Michael and I watching. I used to like eating fried turtle until that display. Don also raised rabbits to eat when my mom was little. He told her not to name them but being a kid, she did. When the rabbits ended up on the dinner table she couldn't eat them.

Dad hunted rabbits and squirrels for us to eat with Floyd when I was really little. There wasn't a lot of money and even later, the day before pay day we would have waffles for dinner because that was all we had. We kids thought it was fun, having breakfast for dinner. Some of the things mom served us from time to time made me skip dinner. Ham hocks and navy beans, liver and onions (one of Connie's all-time favorites) and dad's favorite and the absolute worst… stuffed beef heart. The smell of these things made it impossible to eat. They must have been cheap.

One of funniest things that happened was one summer Michael and I were sitting in the kitchen with Grandpa Don and all of a sudden in the next room the claw foot bathtub fell through the ceiling. It didn't fall all the way to the floor of the dining room, but the dust was tremendous, and we kids were panicked. Grandpa Don never moved from the kitchen table. He said, "nothing we can do about it till the dust settles so just sit down and wait". I don't remember how my grandmother reacted when she got home from work. Probably pretty much the same way she did when the beets in the pressure cooker exploded on her kitchen ceiling! Exciting things happened there.

Their house too had a slanted ceiling upstairs over the bathtub. Hard to get in and out if you were over 4-foot-tall without hitting your head! They also had a dirt floor cellar, but you went into it from the outside of the house. It wasn't as creepy to me as Tieman's, but then I didn't have to sit at a table over a trap door over it either and I was only down there maybe once. Don made root beer sometimes and mom used to talk about the time the bottles weren't sealed right and there were explosions of root beer, one bottle at a time.

There was a small apt. attached to the back of the house, and according to dad, Grandma's mother, Lottie Vinson lived there for many years into her 90s. The lady I remember living there was "Bertie Mae".

Grandpa Don died May 13, 1978 at the age of 77 at the Retired Printer's home in Colorado Springs after a second stroke.

When I was 7 we moved across town in Keokuk to a little brick house at 517 Morgan Street. I changed schools from Wells Carey to Garfield. We had a dog Rusty, Caesar's son, a beautiful little red cocker. The people next door to us had 6 kids and we played with them a lot. The dining room table in their house was incredible.... always piled high with clean laundry and that's where all the kids found their clothes to wear. Mrs. Neyens and mom were friends and Michael had a crush on Ruthie. My friend was Rita and they went to a Catholic school, so we only saw them at home after school. Unfortunately, Rusty was not with us long because he ran out into the street and got hit by a car in front of the house.

We had our first TV in 1954. Michael watched "Howdy Doody" and "Daniel Boone" and we watched "Capt. Kangaroo". Michael had a coon skin cap like Daniel Boone that he wore everywhere, even to bed until it had a life (and smell) of its own. He loved his double holster Roy Rogers six shooters and we watched "Hopalong Cassidy" and "the Rifleman". When we wanted "color" on our TV we put a blue sky and green grass plastic across the screen, so we could watch "Bonanza". Very high tech. Westerns were popular and "Gunsmoke" was all that Grandpa Don would watch.

Freeport, Illinois Oct. 1955- Dec.15, 1958

When I was 8 Dad got a promotion from Penney's to floor manager and this was our first long distance move. 1103 Carroll St. was a gray house with a enclosed back porch. Mr. and Mrs. Bordner were landlords who they lived upstairs. The house sat on a lot that made you walk up steps to get to the house itself. One summer mom canned sauerkraut and set the jars on the back porch to cool. Some of the lids weren't sealed tightly and they exploded kraut and glass all over the porch. The smell must have been tremendous, as well as the clean up.

Michael and I walked 3 or 4 blocks to Blackhawk School where my best friends were Sylvia Sieferman, Marjorie Lehman and Cheryl Frye. Lehman's lived across the street from the school and her little brother was also my brother's friend. I taught myself one weekend to ride Michael's bike because I never had one of my own. Guess it was a boy thing.

A tornado went down across the street from us one night, and a big tree fell across the driveway putting a huge tree limb through our parents' bedroom window. I don't remember this, but Michael does, and dad confirmed his memory.

Grandpa Don had given gave Michael a yellow tom cat that they named Nicky (St. Nicholas) at Christmas. He lived to be a was a very old cat with more than 9 lives fighting all the time, scarred, chewed up, bringing home dead mice and live baby rabbits to show us. He brought a baby rabbit into the house once and let it go. Mom caught it and put it in a shoe box on top of the floor register to keep it warm. She gave it a baby bottle of milk every few hours. It lived until the night she worked, and dad wouldn't get up every 2 hrs to feed it. Nicky never looked at it again once it was in the house. Once he brought in the live mouse and it ran under the upright piano she and Michael had to corner it and catch it. After that she never let Nicky in the door again without having him open his mouth to be sure there wasn't a tail hanging out of it.

Nicky even survived having his tail amputated for cancer. Mom had said she thought he was mostly embarrassed and he wouldn't go out of the house for weeks afterwards. We had him a long time (over 10 years) and we took him on our many moves as dad got transferred to a new town every 2 year.

I roller skated all the time. I went up and down the hill at the end of our street and got had my first broken arm from skating. Actually, I was just standing on wet grass waiting for my friend and slipped and fell forward. When I went home crying, in pain, mom was sewing and thought I wasn't hurt very badly. She told me to just go run cold water on it. A while later she realized I was still crying and running water over it so we walked to the doctor for x-rays and it was broken.

 I also learned to ice skate while we lived here, but my ankles weren't too strong, and I wasn't very successful. I was better off roller skating with the key hanging around my neck for constant skate adjustments.

I joined Girl Scouts there for several years and had my one and only camping experience. The Scouts had a day camp for a week and up until that time I had never before been hotter, dirtier, more bored and downright miserable. I shudder to think how bad it would have been if I couldn't have gotten on a bus at the end of the day and go home for a bath and bed. From then on, my idea of a camping out and roughing it is a suite at a nice hotel.

Constance Sue was born Aug. 5, 1958 and was a total surprise. Mom thought she had the flu for months before seeing a doctor and finding out she was pregnant. (I was 11 ½ yrs. older than her and Connie was 11 1/2 yrs. older than Amy.) I was so excited when I was told the news and I couldn't wait to tell my friend Sylvia. I was so disappointed when I said, "guess what?" and she said, 'Your mom's going to have a baby". Did everyone know but me? I was crushed.

Connie Sue had dark curly hair and we thought she looked like dad. She adored Michael as he was 8 yrs. older and we all spoiled her rotten. Mom said it was like living a rerun and whatever Connie did, it had been done before. She loved her Felix the cat, any kind of dog, her panda bear and her dolls. She was especially crazy about the TV show "Surfside Six" and wore the Capri pants and striped tee shirt like Troy Donahue all the time when she was around 2.

She became afraid of sleeping in her crib very early on, so we had to share a room and in one house, the bed, so she could sleep. She was in kindergarten when I left home for nurses' training, so we really didn't grow up together.

Mom finally learned to drive a car after Connie was born as she needed to get back and forth to work and the town was bigger and not that easy to get around by bus or walking like she was used to.

All the times we moved, we always took the upright piano and round dining room table with us and it was repainted in every house. I know they were both gray one time, and black another. We had some very wild wallpaper and carpets sometimes because the houses were always rented, but our furniture I remember the most vividly. Sometimes dad was allowed to paint a room or two, but he NEVER would move or cover up anything. We had a toaster that was like a rainbow with all the kitchen colors from various houses on it. Our black cocker,

Jet, in Columbus ended up with a yellow nose and butt as dad constantly pushed him out of the way instead of putting him outside while he painted that kitchen.

Dad was transferred again Dec.15, 1958 to Elgin, Illinois near Chicago when I was in 6th grade. Connie was 4 mos. old and the house we moved to was so cold on moving day that she got pneumonia. Mom had to find a pediatrician right away practically before the movers left. We lived at 360 Congdon Street in a house that none of us really remember any inside details about. It was yellow and had an enclosed front porch. Michael and I remember there was a dog next door and that our driveway was higher than the neighbors'. I remember the dog was a Boston bulldog and he remembers it was a boxer. Dad also said it was a boxer, so now I've been wrong at least once.

We went to Coleman Elementary school and had a very long cold walk (20 below zero) where the snow banks were so high at the intersections that cars had red flags on their antenna to be seen. Girls were not allowed to wear pants to school, so I wore slacks under my dress and took them off and on to walk to and from home. The school sat way back from the road across a big field and a long sidewalk that had no cover from the snow, nor freezing wind, nor rain. It seemed like it went on forever. I went to Larsen Jr. high 7th and half of 8th grade before Dad was transferred to Akron, Ohio in Feb. 1960, and I went to Perkins Jr. High there.

We lived at 1140 Orlando Street and that is where Mom and Dad met and became lifelong friends with Grace and Ken Broggini. I babysat for their 3 kids and young Gracie and Connie became friends later on as adults. This house had a finished attic and Connie and I shared the attic bedroom.

We moved to another house in Akron at 445 Storer Ave. when I started 9th grade at Buchtel High School in 1962 and I actually stayed there long enough to graduate in 1965. For the first time Connie and I had our own rooms. Zip codes were just starting to be used in 1960 for the mail and the Akron zip code was 20. I had kept postcards from friends over the years and that is how I "remember" this!

While we lived in Akron, dad worked for Scotts 5-10 downtown and the Soap Box Derby was (and is still) held there every summer. There was always a parade of current TV stars and in 1962 it was Little Joe, Hoss, Pa, and Adam Cartwright from "Bonanza". We watched from the upstairs office in the Scotts store. The next year the celebrities were John Russell from "Lawman", comedian Paul Lynde, and Paul Anka (who interested me the most)!

Christmas in Akron always included the trip downtown at night to see the window displays in Polsky's and O'Neil's department stores. They always had a theme and were animated and beautiful. People would line up on the street and around the block, standing in the cold waiting for a turn to see them (just like in "The Christmas Story" movie).

I met Betty Mueller (Gill) and Lois Emery in junior high and we did everything together. Betty married her high school sweetheart, Ray, and still lives in the Akron area. We still write and email and get together if I am in Akron. She and I discovered Chinese food at the Sheraton Hotel across the street from the Scotts store. We never had tasted it before and it became our great discovery. We catch up on our kids and grandkids and assorted cats throughout the years.

Lois married in our senior year and her husband died at 18 of pneumonia and left her with a little girl. Betty and I have lost contact with her over the years. Lois's older brother was killed by a sniper in Vietnam and thankfully that is the only military funeral I have ever attended. Some of my classmates died there too over the years.

I pretty well in school but started having trouble with math in 6th grade "finds story problems difficult" said the teachers. Then there was algebra and geometry. Never could understand why I had to learn how to put a triangle inside a circle as a nurse and to this day I have never had to. I even had a tutor outside school for geometry and the teacher knew I tried and felt sorry for me a passed me with a D in high school. My checkbook still remains a mystery to me.

My best courses were English, science, chemistry, biology, psychology and I got through the required 4 yrs of Latin for nursing. Latin, do they still teach that dead language? I forgot to mention geography…. let's just skip talking about that one. Loved American history and even took extra courses at Texas Grayson College when the kids were little because it was so interesting to me.

I belonged to the Rainbow Girls organization in Akron that is a part of the Eastern Star. For several years I was recording secretary and we had a lot of formal dances with the Demolays which the young men's part of the Masons was. There I met my fist serious boyfriend Bob. He was a year older than me and my mother didn't like him, and Connie made fun of him after listening to her talk about him. We dated for a about year and he took me to my junior prom right after he joined the Navy. My friends were impressed that he wore his uniform to the dance. We kept in touch for only a short while after he left town.

I went to Friday night football games (go Griffins) with Betty and Lois and worked part time at the Scotts store riding the bus downtown to and from work. We had great slumber parties in Betty's finished basement and teasing her next-door neighbor boy and his friends that we went to school with.

I got my learner's permit (several times when it expired) with mom teaching to drive the white 1959 Chevy with the fins out to here. I didn't get my drivers license until I was 21 because after my parents moved to Columbus and I was in nurses' training and no one had a car.

My worst habit growing up was biting my nails. They were awful, and I didn't quit until I was in high school. Now I like the acrylic nails because they are such low maintenance and always look good.

Ricky Nelson was my "teenage idol" a term coined about him in the popular "Teen" magazine. He was in the TV show every week; "The Nelsons" with his family and I loved his "dreamy" looks and his songs. I saw him perform live in Rochester at a dinner club in 1975 with his Stone Canyon Band after he had lost a lot of popularity after the Beatles "invaded" America. He had long shaggy hair; so different from his younger days, but he was still "dreamy". He died in a plane crash on his way to Dallas New Year's Eve 1985. Ricky and Elvis; dying too young. Maybe teen idols are not meant to grow old.

I didn't really discover Elvis until later years after he was gone. I was just a few years too young at his heyday I guess to be caught up in it, but I like listening to his music now.

I also liked Bobby Vinton and Bobbie Darin at the time. I watched "Bandstand" when my mother wasn't paying attention. She was not a fan. I never could dance or carry a beat, so I always liked watching the show. My deepest desire in my next life would be to come back as a graceful dancer…or a male cat if I don't have to be human again.

We took family vacations to Chicago to the Brookfield Zoo in 1959 and Springfield, Ill in 1960. We went to the Wisconsin Dells and saw the Indian pageantry one summer. 1961 was our first trip to Niagara Falls NY and Canada.

Michael and Dad went to the Cave of the Winds and mom, dad and Connie went on the "Maid of the Mist" boat tour leaving Michael and I on the Canadian side with the car. He and I still wonder what we would have done in Canada, with a car and no parents if the boat sank?

We also went to Ft. Erie in Canada and saw the flower clock and botanical gardens. When I lived in upstate NY many years later, we went to the "Falls" and Niagara On the Lake pretty often because it is so beautiful and close by.

We always drove in the car on vacation and to Iowa to visit and I always got motion sick in the back seat. One trip when we moved mom told the story of me making Michael and the cat sick in the back seat and the car never smelled the same. To this day, I do not like to travel in any way, shape or form and can't tolerate the back seat for very long. I have been in movies where they used hand held cameras and it makes me nauseous.

My first plane trip was in 1965 as a graduation gift from Aunt Pat and Grandpa Don and they took me back to Iowa for a visit. I found it confining and impossible that the plane could stay up in the air. I have been on many planes since and some out of the country, but I still don't enjoy it.

The 60's were all about bee hive hairdos, poodle skirts and saddle shoes; shirtwaist dresses, crinolines under skirts, and wearing white gloves and hats to church every Sunday. We walked everywhere or rode the bus alone and played outside all over the neighborhood day and night without a worry. Neighbors looked after each others' kids and we always felt safe. My children were lucky enough to have this privilege too, but not my grandchildren. It's a different world now, and not always better.

The 60's were also about violence. Vietnam, Civil Rights, the KKK, and assassinations of the nation's leaders President Kennedy, Robert Kennedy and the Rev.Martin Luther King.Jr. Drugs were making the news more often; marijuana, LSD, Haight Ashbury, communes, hippies, and us 'Boomers" were never going to get old!

In 1963 while I was a sophomore is high school President John Kennedy was assassinated in Dallas. I was sitting in study hall in Akron after lunch and they announced it over the loud speaker and shortly afterwards they sent us home. We all sat around the TV for days, crying and watching all the burial proceedings and then the assassination of Lee Harvey Oswald by Jack Ruby. Mom and I saw that as it happened on TV. That was really the first time the news started continual coverage of any event that I can remember. Before this the only 3 network stations went off the air at midnight.   The violence of it seemed so surreal because we had been so isolated from the ongoing Vietnam War (1959-April 1975). We only saw heavily edited news tapes a couple of days or weeks old from there and it was a long time before we ever saw he body bags coming home and heard about the killing of Vietnamese civilians. Some of the information took years to come out. Over 58.000 Americans were killed and 2,300 MIA in the Vietnam War that we badly lost trying to fight Communism and the Soviet Union (Russia).

In the current War in Iraq and Afghanistan in 2008 over 4200 Americans have been killed and more have been maimed from roadside bombs and once again, the media ignores the body bags. Both are unpopular wars and the outcome of Middle East is still in question. We still have troops in South Korea since the 1950 "conflict".

1964…

Freedom Summer in Mississippi and civil rights riots, bombings and kidnappings in the south and women's rights marches. I thought I had forgotten most of this, but after reading "Boomers" by Tom Brokow, I do remember all that took place.

Grandma Alta died in June and in July Maggie and Thelma took Michael and I on my "pre-high school graduation" trip to Colorado. We drove out there in their 1959 gray Plymouth at about 40 MPH. When it was Thelma's turn to drive, Maggie would watch the speedometer and often lean up over the back seat and tell her to slow down. Thelma became "deaf" during most of this back seat driving. I don't remember how many days it must have taken us to get there at that speed on 2 lane roads, but I do remember the corn fields in Iowa and the wheat fields in Kansas that never ended. My brain goes numb now just thinking about it.

Part of our trip we met and stayed with Mrs. Beck in Evergreen, CO. She had worked for our dad in Akron. She and her husband had retired there, and it was way up in the mountains with no one around them. It was beautiful. I loved driving along the roads beside the Colorado River running along beside us.

We stayed overnight at Estes State Park on the Continental Divide where there was still snow on the ground and we made snowballs. We took a bus ride around the area and saw tufted black squirrels and a black bear beside the road.

We also went to the Garden of the Gods Amphitheater where Maggie bemoaned the fact she would miss the Beatles performing there later in the summer. She was crazy about the Beatles (not my favorite) and liked the play/movie "Jesus Christ Superstar" music.

Colorado Springs was beautiful, and the Air Force Academy and Cathedral were fantastic.

We spent time in downtown Denver but missed Pike's Peak because the car wouldn't have made it up there! It was a memorable trip with them and I know we all had fun.

In 1964 Connie got a black and white puppy that we named Cindy. She was very neurotic and wouldn't go out in the dark. Mom always had to have the porch light on for her when she went outside at night, and the dog never left the circle of light. We had to give her away to someone in the country after awhile because she was so nervous and jumpy that she had started nipping at Michael and his friends when they played over.

In June 1965 I graduated from Buchtel High School and had been accepted into nurses' training at Akron City Hospital.

My classmate Terry Caston took me to the senior prom and he was a lot of fun. He always made me laugh but was very full of himself. I practiced my sarcasm on him and he thought I was funny. We walked everywhere. My house was halfway between the high school and his house, so he always stopped by to pick me up before school every day and walk me home. He was tall with dark hair and eyes. He became an Akron police officer after we graduated but died of cancer before our 10th reunion leaving behind a wife and child. He was a nice guy.

Dad had already been transferred to Zanesville, OH with Buckeye Mart 6mos. before I graduated, but the 3 of us stayed in Akron in order for me to finish school. We all joined him in Zanesville where I spent the summer waiting to return to Akron to go to nurses' training and Michael went to high school one month before Buckeye Mart transferred dad to Columbus, Ohio. Zanesville's claim to fame was the "Y" bridge over the river which we lived near. I only remember the house was brick and I was counting the days until I left for Akron.

Mom's physical problems started while we were in Akron waiting to join dad. She had her first bouts with what later turned out to Crohn's disease and the arthritis in her knees was worsening form all those years walking on hospital floors.

Dad had had a heart attack when he was in his early 40's from an enlarged "athlete's" heart he acquired from running track in high school. Much later he has had a pacemaker implanted 3 times for the same reason. In the middle 1990's he was diagnosed with Chronic Lymphatic Leukemia. Thelma also had this for many years.

He and mom quit smoking after his heart attack and it's one habit I didn't pick up although I tried twice. The first time I was about 13 or so and because mom and dad smoked, I took some of her cigarettes and tried it in my room with the windows open. Of course, mom caught me pretty quickly as her cigarettes were missing and she made me sit in the kitchen in the breakfast nook and smoke an entire pack until I was sick as a dog.

I remember dad smoking a pipe with cherry tobacco until I my girls were little. It always smelled so wonderful.

1965-1968 Akron, Ohio

After I graduated from Buchtel High School in May, I went to Akron City Hospital for nurses' training at 31 Arch Street. It was a 3-year diploma program which meant you became a Registered Nurse when you passed the state board exams but did not get a bachelor's degree. The 4 yr degree programs were not popular at the time and now the diploma schools are gone. I planned on going into the Air Force as a nurse first lieutenant after graduation.

In the 3-year program, we went to Akron University the first year for the required classes as well as taking the nursing courses in the clinical classroom. It was a year-round program, no summer nor holiday vacations. We trained and worked at the hospital learning procedures on real patients, not plastic mannequins like students do today. They had charity wards full of patients that were our practice subjects. Of course, we always had an instructor with us and some of them were very intimidating.

We wore white starched uniforms, white hose and shoes and our student caps were winged and plain white. When we became juniors, our caps got one black stripe, and as seniors 2 black stripes. Caps are unique to the school you attended across the country, everyone with a different style. Our graduate caps are round, organdy with a white trim that look like soufflé cups. For many years as I moved around and worked in different hospitals it was fun seeing all the different caps in a hospital cafeteria. Caps and uniforms became obsolete in the 1980's and it is a sad thing to not be able to wear the pride of the profession. Now everyone wears scrubs of different colors and you can't tell by looking if the person is a janitor, a doctor, or a nurse.

We lived in a 5-story dormitory across the street from the hospital. In bad weather or if we worked the night shift, we went back and forth in a locked tunnel under the street. Many times, we were still getting dressed as we passed through the tunnel if we overslept.

There were double and single rooms and my first roommate was Jackie Show in room 511. She was from also Akron and had a long-time boyfriend Jerry. We started with 100 girls from all over Ohio and 50 graduated. They told us at the beginning only half would make it for one reason or another, and they were right.

Our room had 2 twin beds, 2 desks, a sink and mirror, 2 closets and cold linoleum floors. We were allowed to put things on the walls if we didn't use nails. Each floor had a phone booth, a bathroom with showers, a TV in the "study lounge" and the laundry room was in the basement. The phone could not be used after 10 PM and all calls went through the switchboard downstairs. Whoever was near the phone when it rang, answered it and then screamed the name of who the call was for down the hall.

We did our own personal laundry, but the hospital did our uniforms and there was a housecleaning person that gave us fresh bed linen each week and dusted the floors if they were visible!

The dorm had a house mother at the front desk that everyone had to check in with coming and going. We had a sign in book and curfews of 10 PM on weekdays and 12 PM on weekends. We had to write a note if we spent the weekend away. No men were allowed above the first floor and there was a common living room downstairs where we could meet with visitors. I don't now of anyone that used it. Parents were allowed upstairs at designated times, like moving in and out days and certain weekends.

The house mother also did room checks every night. She sometimes looked in every room, and sometimes not. We had to be in our own rooms and if we weren't we got detention. Three detentions in one year and you were expelled. We got very clever in being in someone's closet while she checked rooms and fast enough to get to our own in time for the check. Since we didn't have phones, someone kept track of the elevator and what floor it was on after 10 pm so we knew where she was.

When we went to Akron U, we had to walk back and forth for classes. Since the hospital cafeteria food was "free" (included in our tuition) we would walk the 2 miles back and forth if we didn't have money to go to the student union on campus and had classes in both morning and afternoon. It was a very fast walk some days, but it kept us in shape for floor duty. Wish I had known then that all that walking was good for me.

I would go to Columbus once a month or so by Greyhound bus to visit my family or for a short holiday.

As juniors we were no longer at the university, just worked in the hospital and took clinical classes. During this year we dissected a cat in biology class. Mine was pregnant and the most interesting in the class. The rumor was that these cats were road kill, but they weren't flat nor mangled so we never believed it. The anatomy of a cat is similar enough to human is why we had them in the lab.

As the junior year ended, we became team leaders for our assigned floor and learned to manage staff and give the medications. By then we could work extra on the weekends and get paid $1.95/hour as a student nurse. I worked a lot of Saturdays for spending money. Other than makeup and personal products, there wasn't a lot of things we had to buy since most of our time was spent in uniform and food was provided during certain hours if we wanted it, and if it was edible.

We had a rotation of 2 weeks in ICU working nights (I hated night shift), 2 weeks in the burn unit, a month in surgery, a few weeks on the cardiac floor, a month in OB/GYN and newborn nursery, 3 months going to Cleveland to the State Psychiatric Facility every day by cab, 3 months living at the Children's hospital, and the majority of the time on medical-surgical floors.

At the psych facility they put students on the safer wards and we spent our time in the day room playing pool with the patients. One time one of them grabbed me around the neck and threatened me, but the other patients talked him into letting me go before the staff got there. I was a pretty good pool player after 3 months of daily practice.

By the time the outside rotations started, Jackie was assigned to go to Children's Hospital first. She was a great roommate and is still a good friend. She pretty much taught me about sex because she had the boyfriend and I knew very little about it. She secretly married Jerry in our senior year as it was not allowed and was very pregnant by the time of our graduation. Everyone helped her hide it as much as possible, so she wouldn't be expelled. She had the baby 2 days after we wrote our state boards. She didn't pass them and had to retake them later. She failed the OB/GYN section and then became a labor and delivery nurse! Jerry was sent to Vietnam with the Air Force as a fighter pilot and when he came back, they were stationed in Okinawa for years as he taught pilots to fly F15s. When they returned to the U.S. they had 2 daughters and Jackie retired from nursing. Jerry got his 20 years in the Air Force then became a pilot for Southwest Airlines and is now retired twice. I first saw her again in San Antonio in the late 70's when we were all in Texas with our husbands and children. They have 5 grandchildren.

After Jackie left, I was transferred to a new room; a suite…it had a bedroom, a study room and its own bathroom. Noreen Wilson became my new roommate. She is one of my closest friends. She was from Warren about an hour away from Akron. Dot Matusky, Pat Phillips, Saundra Harrison, and Barb Himes were all part of our group. Barb is the only one I have lost track of over the years.

Noreen is always so funny and upbeat. She didn't like to study or do the term papers until the night before they were due, and it drove her nuts that mine were done and I went to bed. I still see her with the swimming cap with the holes in it with hair pulled out, so she could streak her blonde hair white, and the calamine lotion all over her face to dry out her blemishes. When I was bored, and she was trying to study I liked to annoy her by walking all over the beds and the furniture. She still reminds me of that when I see her.

Noreen and I shared a pack of Marlboros for a month or more because it was cool, and "everyone" was doing it. We soon gave it up and played Canasta day and night instead.

In our senior year we found a dog wandering on the street. It was a mangy, brown, hungry, scared little thing and we decided to sneak it into the dorm. There was a back door in the dorm that was open during certain hours and then of course we had to get it past the house mother and upstairs to our room. Somehow, we managed that, and we named him Sir Osis (cirrhosis) because he was so pitiful. We snuck food to him from the cafeteria and took him up to the tar roof to use as his bathroom. He was the nicest little dog and never barked or called any attention to himself. When someone knocked on the door he hid under the bed until he knew it was a friend and he could come out. On the day the housekeeper came we put him in someone else's room. We had him for a month or longer and then got nervous that he would be found, and we would be expelled right before graduation. One of the other girls said her parents would take him if we could get him out of the dorm. So, some of our friends kept the house mother busy at the desk and blocked her view from the elevator and we walked him right out the front door.

As upperclassmen we thought it was our duty to harass the new students coming in. We would put saran wrap under the toilet seats or Vaseline their door knobs and then call out that they had a phone call and they couldn't get out of their room. They also had clothes and towels disappear when they were in the shower and their room was down the hall.

One night we thought we would be all grown up and went out and bought some liquor. You only had to be 18 in Ohio then. Noreen stopped drinking beer early in the evening but after I had had some whiskey, Saundra and I finished all the sloe gin. During the night while Noreen was asleep, I got very sick all over the bathroom. It was red everywhere and looked like someone had been butchered. I just went to bed. Noreen was the first one up the next morning to go to work and she freaked out at the mess. By the time I had cleaned it up and got on the elevator to go to work, I really reeked. Somehow, I made it through the day without being tossed out and I have never had that much to drink again. It just wasn't that much fun. Sort of like the smoking experiment.

One weekend when Noreen took me to Warren we went to the Belvedere Club with some of her friends to dance. By the end of the evening and a lime vodka or two, a guy came up and asked me to dance. He offered to take Noreen and I and 2 others home in his blue Rambler station wagon. He told me his name, but it was noisy in the club and I didn't hear him. The next day, Noreen and I are sitting on her front stoop reading the paper and the Rambler pulls into her driveway. I asked her if she knew who it was, and she said it's the guy that took us home last night. Bill Starr reintroduced himself and after we all talked for awhile he asked me to go to the drive-in movie with him. The next day he took 4 of us back to Akron to the dorm and we started dating long distance on Sundays.

He would drive up to Akron and we would go to church in the morning, to Red Barn for our meal of the day, and then to a drive-in, or Goodyear Park, according to how much money we had. He went full time to Youngstown University studying civil engineering, worked part time, and lived at home. One day he came around the corner to the dorm in a 1965 Ford Fairlane convertible red, with a white top. He worked hard and saved for that car and no one was allowed to get fingerprints on it. He carried a rag to wipe it off for the longest time. Connie loved that car almost as much as he did. She made him take her 2 blocks to the store with the top down so her friends could see her when we visited Columbus.

I rotated to Children's Hospital across town and we lived in an old house that had been turned into a dorm. Gwen Walluchi became my roommate. We had fun, but worked opposite shifts, so we didn't see a lot of each other. She was the oldest of 11 children; at least until her mom had #12 while Gwen was having her #1 a few years after graduation. Gwen never worked as a nurse after graduation. She married and moved to California and raised 9 kids of her own and has as many grandchildren. We still exchange Christmas cards.

Children's Hospital had patients from all over the state and had some very unusual cases. There was one case of a chromosome malfunction and the poor child looked like a fox. It didn't live long and that was a blessing. I felt so bad for the parents.

The first person that I ever saw die was a young boy and I was the only one with him at the time. I decided right then, pediatrics was not for me. Kids get too sick too fast and the parents are usually impossible because of their fear and grief. I admire the nurses that can do it, but I found through the years adults who can tell you what hurts are much easier to deal with.

While I was at Children's one night, we all decided I needed my ears pierced. So, using an ice cube, a sterile syringe, and a potato, Gwen pierced my ears. No one was allowed to wear jewelry on duty, so I had to put boiled (sterile??) pieces of nylon in the holes during the day under my hair to keep the holes open and put earrings in at night. Needless to say, I got a raging infection and to this day get itchy earlobes if I wear any kind of clip on earring. The holes closed quickly after the antibiotics took hold. It made me allergic to nickel, so I can't wear cheap jewelry anywhere on my body...only the good stuff. My mother's only comment, "Just what you needed, more holes in your head". No sympathy there.

The infection resulted in an allergy to nickel, so I get hives if I wear cheap jewelry. Thus, my love of aquamarines, tanzanite, diamonds, yellow and white gold.

Bill and I were still dating and had been back and forth to each others' parents over time and June 1967 "on a dark and stormy night" at Goodyear Park in the car, he asked me to marry him. He had cut newspapers into very small pieces and buried the ring in it in the box. When he took me back to the dorm, I ran yelling all the way up the staircase "hey you guys, I'm engaged! He had picked out the ring himself and worked as a janitor at night at the high school to pay for it.

When I rotated out of Children's, I got a room to myself. It was sort of nice after the years of roommates... starting with Connie! I got a fish for company. It was a black mollie that kept jumping out of the bowl. Crazy fish. It survived longer than it probably should have.

Noreen went to Children's and Jackie lived in another dorm, but I was with Dot and Saundra again, so it was ok. We got really bored one weekend and decided to fly a kite out of my window since it faced the back of the dorm and we could climb out on the little roof over the offices. All went well until someone from the hospital spied the kite and called the dorm. We barely got it hidden and in our own rooms by the time the house mother got to our floor. No one knew what she was talking about, so the next weekend the entire dorm was on detention and no one was allowed to leave. No one ever told, so they couldn't give us a personal detention. Boredom does get one into a lot of trouble at times.

Noreen married Tim Ashley who was a lineman stringing electric cable in Vietnam. After he was drenched in Agent Orange several times he was discharged, and they still live in the Akron area. As a result of the Orange, Tim has lost a lot of the feeling in his hands and legs and had to quit his job as an electrician. They had one Mongoloid child and the other 2 have behavior disorders. Noreen worked in surgery and doctor's offices over the years but has had fibromyalgia for many years and is pretty crippled from it. She is such a dear person and has had such a hard life. They have 2 granddaughters.

Dot married John Felber and has one son currently in the Navy. They still live in the Akron area. She was a surgical nurse for over 30 years and is now retired due to poor health.

Saundra married Bill Sanderson, has one son and lives in Florida. She is a cardiac Nurse Practitioner.

We all graduated in May 1968 and 4 of us stayed in Columbus with my family to take our 3-day state boards exams. I moved home to finish the wedding plans for Sept. 1st and for mom to make my wedding gown. We waited for the board results until at the end of the summer. I worked at Methodist Hospital in ICU evenings, and mom worked at the same hospital as a private duty night nurse. I got my driver's license and we shared her Chevy Valiant to get back and forth to work. I could do anything legally by the end of the summer; drive, work as an RN and had my marriage license.

By the time they moved to Columbus, OH, mom did private duty nights at the Methodist Hospital because there was less walking involved. She once had pro golfer Jack Nickalaus's father as a patient there. After I graduated from nurses' training in May 1968 and while waiting for my state board results, I worked at the same hospital on the 3-11 shift in ICU and we shared her car.

June 5, 1968 Robert Kennedy United States Senator and brother of John Kennedy was assassinated in Los Angeles. He was campaigning in the California primaries for the Democratic nomination for President. Sirhan Sirhan, a Palestinian immigrant was caught on tape shooting him. He's still in prison as of 2008. Ted Kennedy, an older brother, became a long-time senator, but never ran for President. He said his family couldn't take another assassination. The Kennedy's are Catholic and were pursued for their religion.

Sept. 1, 1968 Bill and I were married at the First Methodist Church in Akron. Betty was my matron of honor and Cindy and Connie were my bridesmaids. We honeymooned at the Poconos in PA and moved to Youngstown, so he could finish his last 6 months of college in structural engineering. I worked as an RN evening shift on a cancer unit for $5/hr. We lived in an upstairs apt. over a 3-car garage on Crandall Ave. that belonged to the man Bill worked for part time. It had a kitchen/living room, bedroom and bathroom with a slanted ceiling over the bathtub and we thought it was cute. We paid $80 a month and it was furnished except for the TV we added. We lived there until he graduated from Youngstown and took a job offer from Kodak in Rochester, NY in March 1969.

1969-

When we moved to NY, we lived in a furnished basement apt. in a house at 1066 Cooper Rd. that had a gorgeous yard overlooking Irondequoit Creek. It had the same amount of rooms as Crandall Ave. but no bathtub. The bathroom had been added from a closet right inside the front door. The shower drains, and curtain were between the toilet and sink. Cozy when the shower curtain wrapped around you when you got wet and soapy. By that time, I knew I was pregnant and we had started looking for somewhere bigger to move to as it had been a 4-month lease.

We were so happy about having a baby! I sewed my own maternity clothes to save money and knitted blankets, sweaters and booties for the baby. I wasn't working so had plenty of time to get ready. We hoped for a girl this first time but didn't know for sure what the baby was. All the things I made were yellow or pale green or white just to be safe.

While we lived there we watched Neil Armstong walk on the moon on July 20, 1969. We stayed up all night watching the moon landing and this moment in history. It was exciting and surreal.

Bill and I started friendships with people he was meeting at Kodak. Birgit and Ernie Hafner became best friends and we essentially raised our families together. They were originally from Germany, then Long Island as children and then to college and Rochester. Ernie was an electrical engineer and Birgit was an executive secretary at RIT University until she retired. Bryan and Pam were Amy and Nicole's friends for years. They now all live in San Diego and there are 3 grandchildren.

Pat and Mike Trost, Joann and Bill Esch, Linda and Ed Dzackowick, Pat and Bob Zampi all were part of the group. The men played poker once a month, some bowled on Kodak teams, played golf and we would all get together for birthdays and holidays and dinners in between with all our new babies. Bill E. and Ed D. sadly passed away at an early age. We girls did better staying in touch through the years, deaths, marital changes and job transfers than the guys did.

In Aug.1969 we moved to brand new apartments on Spencerport Rd. It was a downstairs apt. that was half underground and had 2 bedrooms, an eat in kitchen, bath, living room and central air conditioning. The laundry room was out in the hall and we bought blue Early American furniture on lay away. It was closer to Hafners, so we saw each other a lot.

I made a few friends in the apts. while I was waiting for the baby to be born. No sonograms in those days to tell you what it was, so we had picked out Amy Christine and Jeffrey William as the names we would use. Christine was a very popular name, and I really liked it, so held that in play for a middle name if it was a girl. We took Lamaze classes that were all the rage back then and of course breast feeding was the only way to go.

Nov. 20, 1969 Amy Christine Starr was born at Highland Hospital 2 ½ weeks late weighing in at 8#. She was beautiful and perfect of course. My parents and Connie came up for Thanksgiving and the turkey was bigger than Amy! She had a full head of dark hair and was a very content and easy baby. She slept through the night in about 6 wks after I added a bedtime cereal to her routine along with the bottle. I always breast fed, and bottle fed her at the same time, so the transition was easy for us.

She was the first grandchild on both sides of the family and both the Starrs and Tiemans were very proud of her. They all came to Rochester a lot and we went to Ohio just as often to see each other. In Dec.we drove to Ohio in snowstorms just to be with everyone for Amy's first Christmas when she was barely a month old. She traveled like a trooper in the car bed that sat on the back seat and slept wherever she was put down. We made many snowy, blizzard trips along route I90 from NY to Ohio throughout the years with the girls without car seats and seat belts. Now it sounds scary and dangerous.

I had embroidered the nursery curtains with Dumbo faces and we got her a yellow crib with lambs on it and a dresser we painted yellow. A black rocking chair was a gift from Tiemans and we used the card table for a bathing/changing table. Amy, Nicole and Jacob all used the crib and I still use the dresser. Amy's Aunt Connie was just over 11 yrs, old and she embroidered her fist baby quilt for the crib. She was so proud she finished it in time.

We had the best time with her growing up. We all shared lots of laughs and silly games and hugs and kisses. Her face always showed what she was feeling, just like mine did. She was outgoing, self confident, exuberant and very serious at times.

By the time Amy was 3, I missed working as a nurse, so I worked for a nursing temp agency at Genesse Hospital floating on med-surg floors. It was great working 2 Sundays a month and being myself while Amy was at home with her daddy.

May 4, 1970 was the Kent State Ohio Riot and shooting of 2 students on campus by the Ohio National Guard. They were protesting President Nixon invading Cambodia in the ongoing Vietnam War. Kent was close to Youngstown where we had lived so we were alarmed at what happened. The war protests had escalated around the country. I found out decades later that Michael had taken part in some of them.

Bill and I went to Bermuda on vacation while Amy went to Massassachutes so Tiemans could spoil her for a week. They had been transferred there from Columbus, OH. Grandma and Aunt Connie had a ball with her.

August 1971 Michael was coming to Rochester from Columbus, and Mom and Dad and Connie were coming from MA. for his 21st birthday and we were all in a car accident. Mom and I were hurt the worst and were in the hospital for awhile. I had surgery on my face and she had a broken pelvis. She saved Amy by pushing her in between the seats when the car was coming at us. Connie and Amy were taken care of by our friends, Bev and Ed Huber. Dad, Michael and Bill sort of looked after each other. Thelma came from Iowa after everyone else left to help until I was getting around and seeing better.

I needed to get the sight in my left eye back to normal, so Thelma had me make a Christmas tree skirt with felt cutouts and lots of breads and sequins sewn on. It helped my double vision improve and it became a tradition of me making tree skirts for family and friends for years to come.

Thelma was so cute with Amy. She had never been around children and a 2-yr. old is a challenge at best. She took Amy up to the nearby plaza one day in the stroller and as they checked out, the cashier asked Thelma if she was going to pay for the deodorant in the stroller. It seems Amy had put two cans down beside her as they went down an aisle. Thelma thought that was so funny when she told us.

June 16, 1972 Michael married Nancy Marshall in Columbus, OH. They had met at Buckeye Mart where they both worked for Dad. They moved to Vancouver, British Columbia in 1973 where he started an art design business.

We wanted another child and when I became pregnant again the baby was due in August 1973. In the fall of 1972 we had decided to build a house in Greece NY at the opposite end of town from where the apt. was. It was closer to Kodak and in a new area surrounded by woods. We chose a colonial 4-bedroom design with a wooded area in the back and it was to be finished before the baby arrived. It was a great white house with black shutters and I had them paint the front door red.

In June Connie came to NY after she got out of school to help me move into the new house at 214 Applecreek Lane and help keep Amy busy. Connie was 11 ½ the same age span as she and I. We were so happy to be pregnant again and Amy was thrilled to find out she was having a baby sister.... she KN EW it was a girl and wouldn't consider anything else. We hoped she was right for our sake. No sonograms were done in those days unless there was a problem, so the sex of a baby was unknown until the arrival. I still think that is best; like a surprise gift at Christmas.

It was so hot that summer and I was so pregnant, I spent most of the time in the downstairs playroom that had a room air conditioner or our bedroom that also had one. Connie and Amy had a grand time and they played a lot in the empty blue dining room. I had ordered raspberry plush carpeting, but it hadn't arrived yet. My friend Beverly Huber had that carpet throughout her entire house and I loved it. It was installed while I was in the hospital having Nicole and Amy sat on the stairs and watched them put it in.

August 19, 1973 Nicole Renee Starr arrived at Highland Hospital in Rochester, NY weighing in at 9 #. She was beautiful, very quiet and observant in the delivery room. She had big blue eyes and medium brown hair and we all adored her. Fathers still were not allowed in the delivery room and we still used the

Lamaze method of childbirth and it took almost 24 hours for her to arrive. She started out feet first and had to get turned around to get the job done.

Amy was thrilled beyond words that she had a sister. She couldn't wait for us to get home, so she could see her. Amy had moved out of the crib and into her "big girl" 4 poster canopy bed in her pink room when we moved into the house, so she was ready.

Nicole's nursery was painted pale green and I had made Disney curtains for the windows. I was into ceramics by that time, taking classes with Birgit, so Nicole also had a lamp that I made her and animals and a clown for her dresser and shelves.

Bonnie and Jim Shirmer were our friends next door and they had 6 kids. Christine was Amy's age but none of them were as young as Nicole. We spent many summer evenings in our backyard in the screen house talking and watching the kids play. Bonnie passed away in 2008 of cancer.

Amy had been going 3 mornings a week to nursery school with Scottie Trost over the last year before Nicole was born, but by Sept. 1973 she was heading off to kindergarten on the school bus. She had to walk a few driveways down the block to get onto the bus, and she did NOT want me to go with her. She was still 4 in Sept. but very grown up she thought. She was just gone in the mornings and didn't want go back the second day. She thought she had learned everything!

By the time Nicole got to kindergarten, she didn't want to go back the second day because she didn't like to stand and wait in lines. They both went back.

I was still working part time at the hospital and we had a lot of friends in the neighborhood as we were all stay at home moms. Barb Williams and I became friends and her little boy Eric played with Amy. Nicole didn't have a lot of kids her age there, but we moved to Texas when she was 2 ½. Amy was her main playmate and they enjoyed each other a lot. Amy was always the "teacher"; she had baby Nicole set up in front of a chalk board more times than I can remember teaching her letters or numbers or something she thought Nicole should know. Maybe that's why Nicole could read at 4 ½!

July 1974 President Nixon had to resign for bugging the Democratic National Committee at the Watergate Hotel and destroying incriminating tapes. The Vietnam War was still going on until April 1975.

March 1976 Bill was transferred to Dallas, Tx with Kodak. I hated leaving my friends, my house and being so far from family, but we had to go for the job. The same reason we moved so much when I was a kid.

We bought a brick ranch house at 2905 Sewanee Dr. in Plano, Texas and I got a Sunday job at Plano General Hospital. The hospital only had 200 beds and stood out in a field surrounded by nothing. Plano at the time was only 25,000 people being the suburb farthest north of Dallas. There was one main highway down to Dallas, and I spent all of my time in Plano. We bought a blue Marquis for me and for the first time I had my own car. Plano now has over 260,000 people and the hospital is a huge medical center taking up several blocks.

Mary Ellen Cummings and her family moved in across the street from us the same week from Fargo, N. Dakota and she was my lifesaver. She had moved many times to many places and knew the ropes. We learned Plano together and Amy and Peggy became best friends. She liked a lot of the things I did, sewing, gardening, crafts and we had fun together. When they put in a backyard pool, Amy and Nicole had to take swimming lessons at the "Y", so they could swim in it. They loved swimming and took to it like fish and are still so good at it.

They got transferred to Santa Barbara about a year before we went back to Rochester, but we kept in touch. She was a such a fun, outgoing person and it hit me hard when she died of Alzheimers at the age of 59.

While we lived in Texas we visited San Antonio, Austin, Houston and Waco. We saw the Alamo, San Antonio River Walk and Dallas zoo. We visited the Waco Texas Ranger Museum and the state capital in Austin. We toured the NASA space museum in Houston and went to a rodeo in Mesquite. We went to a couple of State Fairs in Dallas and went to the book depository where Oswald assassinated President Kennedy. There is a museum there now. We went to the Byron Nelson golf classic and saw Lee Trevino and Arnold Palmer.

Linda James who lived next door to us on Sewanee Dr. became a good friend of mine and we still meet for lunch now and then. She was one of the few Texans that actually spoke to us and didn't consider us Yankees (a dirty word in the 80's in Texas).

Amy went to school as Jackson Elementary and Nicole was almost 3 when we moved in. I volunteered in the school library and Nicole took ballet lessons and Amy took jazzercise classes a few years. I tried to make roses grow like I did in NY and the heat killed them. I tried to get used to being housebound in the summer because of the heat instead of the winter instead of the snow. It was hot, hot, hot.

Friends and family came to Plano to visit us during the 6 years we lived there, but only made the mistake of coming in the summer once. It was over 100 degrees when the Hafners and Eschs came the first time and it was too hot to do anything. Tiemans and Starrs usually came during Easter or Christmas when the weather was much more pleasant. Great Grandma Annabell Starr came down a couple of times with Gummy and PaPa and had a great time shopping the mall and going to the botanical gardens. Connie always liked making cookies or dyeing Easter eggs with the girls and Grandma always had a newly knitted sweater or poncho for Amy and Nicole. She knitted all the time in order to keep her arthritic fingers mobile.

Michael and Nancy had Heather in 1976 and Kate in 1979 and they were in the United States again but still up in the Northwest in Washington state and then Oregon. He worked on the Expo '86 while doing advertising and tried his hand at graphic design.

Connie had graduated from high school and gone to work at a bank. She took night courses that they paid for while she lived at home and eventually became an audit supervisor. She was at the bank 30 years. She met John Drotos in 1982 at a young adults meeting at church and they were married in Akron July 29, 1983. He had a daughter, Sarah, from him first marriage and she was the cutest little blonde! She has the same birthday as Nicole, only 5 years younger.

In the 1980s Mom got interested in hand sewing quilts for us. She sat on the front porch at the quilting loom for years in Akron making her kids and grandkids quilts even after her hip replacement. She made Nicole a purple and pink "Tumbling Blocks" quilt, Amy a lavender and white State Flower embroidered quilt and me a green "Lone Star" quilt when we moved to Texas. She later made other ones for the girls' weddings. Connie always made any new baby in the family an embroidered crib quilt, so the quilting tradition continued for years.

In 1981 I took the girls one day to the humane society and we picked out a cat. I named her Sweetums, because that was her personality and she was with me 23 years. She was petite a little tabby cat with a half black nose who raised Amy,

Nicole and Jacob and was a great companion for me when everyone had left home.

I always felt out of place in Texas. Some people I met were openly hostile because I was from NY. I missed my friends, didn't like the heat nor the food, and sometimes couldn't understand people when they talked. At times I felt like I was in a foreign country. I missed the change of seasons, especially the crisp, leafy smell and sights of fall. I tried to adapt by making new friends, having the school and hospital jobs, and planting what survived the summer heat. The summer of 1980 when it was over 110 for the month of June about did me in. The air conditioner stopped because the condenser froze from never shutting off and in 1981 the foundation of the house cracked from corner to corner from the drought and the clay ground shifting.

I started having IBS symptoms in 1976 and was hospitalized twice for it in the 1980's. Probably stress related the doctor said and it still flares up when I am nervous. I tried taking sulfa as a preventive but became allergic to it. I was afraid it would turn into Crohn's disease like mom, but it hasn't.

My marriage started to deteriorate while we were in Texas. I was miserable, and he found someone to make him feel better. Bill was transferred back to Rochester by Kodak in March 1982 and I hoped that would help us get back on track. I was so happy to leave Texas and he wasn't. It took 10 more years and yet one other person to finally end it.

We bought a 2-story colonial house at 12 Foxbourne Rd in Penfield, NY that had 4 bedrooms, an in-ground pool (in NY!), family, living, and dining room and upstairs laundry room. I loved the ½ acre lot and had all the flower gardens I could manage.

The best part of "going home" were our neighbors, Dee and Marsh Guntrum. They became surrogate grandparents to the girls and we all loved them dearly. Even after they retired and went to Hilton Head, Bill and I visited them there. They returned to Rochester to be near family in the 90's and Dee was so special to me. She died in May 2008 of breast cancer she had for 24 years on and off, and I miss her like my second mother.

The girls thrived in their new schools and I went back with the nursing temporary agency and this time worked at Strong Memorial Hospital a couple of Sundays a month. Amy was in 8th grade at Bay Trail Jr. High and Nicole was in 4th grade at Harris Hill Elementary and once again, I volunteered at the school library. I also worked part time at Penfield Public Library 2 days a week typing up overdue notices.

I was back with my old friends, made new ones, and was near enough to Ohio again to drive there or have family come visit us more than once a year. We all went to Disney World in 1983 and had a good time. Nicole was 9 and said she doesn't remember the trip except Epcot Center that was half built. Amy was 12 and remembers it better. Especially "It's a Small World" and Nicole riding it over and over.

Bill and I went to Hawaii and drove up the East coast to Bar Harbor Maine trying to recapture our marriage. Amy and Nicole stayed with Guntrums and were wild about the Fluffernutter sandwiches Dee let them have anytime they wanted.
The trips were fun, and we saw beautiful places, but the trust was gone, and the damage was done. Counseling didn't help because only I wanted it to work.

Nicole was 9 when she started having seizures; the first one in Guntrum's driveway. She was on medication until college and thankfully they stopped, and she has been fine ever since without medication. It was very scary for a while until the medication started working for her.

Nicole was in the band in high school and took xylophone and drum lessons from the Eastman School of Music in Rochester. She had a natural talent and it was very easy for her.

In 1986 I started working at the Penfield Library full time and was part of converting the old paper cataloging system to a new computer system. I was part of the beta training and went to other libraries with my friend, Sandy Newport, to train them. I was secretary to the library board for many years and had to learn to use Microsoft Word for the first time for the minutes. I liked the computers because it was logical, and the same action caused the same reaction. I am best learning one system inside and out; and not good at looking around to figure it out like Amy and Nicole are.

Amy graduated from Penfield High School in 1985 and got her associate degree at Paul Smith's College in Saranac Lake, NY. There she met Bryan Stewart and they fell in love. He went to the Army to Panama during the Noriega takeover and she went to Illinois to work for Red Roof Inn while he was gone. They got married in 1990 when he returned, and they moved to Ft. Collins, Colorado where he was stationed. I visited them there in 1991 and Colorado was as beautiful as I remembered. We went to Pike's Peak on this trip and to an old mining town to gamble. It's still one of Amy's favorite places on earth.

Nicole had then graduated from Penfield High School in 1989 and started her 4-yr. degree course in theater at Suny New Paltz NY. She made good friends there and loved the independence of being away.

Bill and I separated in Feb. 1991 after Nicole left for college and were divorced Oct. 1992.

I sold the house on Foxbourne and moved into a new condo at 49 Lenora Lane in Webster. I had been working full time at the Penfield Public Library from 1986-1991, but I needed more money, so I went back to nursing full time. I found a job in home care community nursing as I didn't want to return to a hospital. Home care was like Nursing 101 and I loved the flexibility of being able to give time to the patients that needed it the most. I learned that I COULD read a map (I was always told I couldn't) and learned that I was not afraid in the ghetto in the summer and most people are helpful and trust you if you are there to help them. It helped me regain some confidence I had lost over the years.

It was a good choice and it has given me a lot of opportunities to change what job I did and stay with the same agency. I still worked part time at either the Penfield or Webster library just because I liked the work and the people there.

One of my best friends from the library is Pat Gough (her daughter Kate and Nicole went to school together). We are still in touch via email and phone calls all the time and occasionally I go back to NY to visit.

My friend Joann remarried after Bill Esch died, and she and her new husband Dick introduced me in 1993 to Ron Fulmer. We hit it off and had a great time for many years going to movies, on a Norwegian cruise during Hurricane Roxanne in 1995 (we only landed in Jamaica), Canandiagua, Niagara Falls, Toronto, and Napels, NY. We got to know each other's families well and he was kind and always made me laugh. I helped him through his heart problems and quitting smoking and he helped me through my breast cancer surgery in 1998. We knew our relationship would not last forever, but we parted on good terms and I'm glad he's happy playing golf and retired in NY near his family.

Nicole had graduated from college and moved to NYC. I visited her there for a fantastic long weekend in 1996 seeing all the sights in New York. We went to the top of the World Trade tower, Battery Park, South Street Seaport, saw the bulls on Wall Street, cruised Manhattan on the Circle Line boat; rode the subway from the top to the bottom of Manhattan; saw "Beauty and the Beast on Broadway; and went to Central Park. We a ball! She had a cute little walk up apt. she shared with Christine and it was perfect for her and her cat, Gramps. It is a great city to visit and she lived there 6 years.

Nicole and I went to Panama together in 1991 to see Amy and Bryan where he was stationed after Colorado. It was a very interesting experience being out of the United States for a couple of weeks. It was beautiful there with the rolling green hills and standing on side of the Panama Canal was extraordinary. We saw the QE II going through the locks there. It was also very weird being the American and being the minority. The shops had armed guards outside the doors, the windows all had bars and there were beaches and places Americans were not allowed to go because of safety concerns. We went downtown to shop the markets in the daytime and out to dinner downtown one night. The beaches were beautiful, but the difference from the very rich in the mansions to the very poor in the shacks was so evident. The military was the only middle class the country had. I wonder what it's like now that the United States has left Panama?

My first grandchild, Jacob Bryan Stewart, was born May 21, 1997 in Ft. LenardWood MO. to Amy and Bryan. He was just the cutest thing with his big brown eyes and curly hair and happy grin. I was there for his birth and returned to visit there his first Christmas. He already had a couple of teeth and had started this bad habit of growing up too fast!

I had been diagnosed with breast cancer the day before I went to Missouri and Feb.7, 1998 I had a mastectomy. Ron, Brigit, my mom and dad were with me and helped me a lot.

Amy and Jake surprised me with a visit from MO. while I was recovering, and we planned his first birthday and christening party to be held in Akron in May so everyone could come. The party and christening were a fun time, but we did not know that Amy's marriage was almost over.
She and Jacob came home to Rochester in 1999 when she divorced. Amy had been miserable in the Army and like Bill, Bryan turned to someone else and that ended the marriage.

Nicole had gone out to drive the UHaul truck back to NY with Amy and Jacob and their belongings. They moved in with Bill for a year until she found a job and apt. and had Jacob in day care.

I started taking oil painting lessons at a local art studio in Webster using the Bob Ross painting method. I painted for years and sold a lot of them to people at work and at a craft show. It was a of fun and I hope I improved as I went along. (I don't want Michael's professional artist opinion) I met some nice people in the classes and became close to the instructor.

Nicole got tired of bartending in NYC and had found a job with a dot.com computer company. She called to tell me they were asking her to transfer to Dallas and what did I think? I told her to go for it because she wanted a change from NYC and the ice and cold, so she went. She had only been there a few months and the company was one of many that went out of business. After unemployment, she was back to bartending, but in a warmer climate. She got her first car there (she didn't need one in NYC) and met Kyle Metcalf while tending bar.

Sept. 11, 2001. I was at work in the office at Genesee Region Home Care and one of the nurses on the road called to tell me she heard on her car radio that the World Trade Center in NYC had been attacked. We all went to a TV in the lunch room to watch in horror as world went insane. A commercial jet had been flown into one of the buildings and it was on fire. In half an hour there was a report of another plane flying into the second building and they were starting to collapse. A third plane had hit the Pentagon and there was another that the passengers crashed into a field in order to avoid hitting the White House.

My first thought was that I was so glad Nicole no longer lived there. We had been to the top of the Trade Center and she often ate a meal there while she was working. In the end, the hijackers taking credit were the Talaban, almost 3000 people died as the towers fell, and the US declared on Afghanistan and Iraq. Police, firefighters, and rescue workers were among the dead. It was a surreal as we saw it all happen over and over on TV and felt the anguish of people lost for no reason other than hate.

In 1992 I missed having a cat, so I got a new calico and named her Callie. She was with me 2 yrs. until I gave her to Connie on my way to Texas. She was a good replacement for her beloved black lab, Baer, and Scooter (Amy's cat she had giver to her) that had passed away.

Nicole and Kyle were married in May 2002 and have since blessed me with 2 more fantastic grandchildren, gorgeous Jessica Renee in 2003 and adorable Blake Andrew in 2007.

Mom passed away March 9, 2003 in Akron before she saw beautiful Jessica. We were all so excited and looking forward to having a new girl in the family. She had been working on a gift for the baby shower and Aunt Connie was finishing a crib quilt.

Connie had been diagnosed with breast cancer in Oct. 2002 and had one radiation treatment left when mom died. Dad still says that Connie's cancer was very hard for mom to come to terms with and that made her sicker.

Mom had been chronically ill with Crohn's and congestive heart failure for decades and her body finally gave out. She told us she was just tired and wanted to go see her mother and refused life support. We agreed with her and let her go. I miss her every day and still want to pick up the phone and call her with news from time to time. Dad was devastated but also relieved I think that her suffering was over. He took terrific care of her for many years from his second retirement from Prudential Life in 1991 until she passed away.

On May 29, 2004 dad, Connie and John traveled to Washington, D.C. for the dedication of the WW II Memorial built between the Lincoln Memorial and the Washington Monument. Amy had registered her Grandpa to be among the16 million WWI veteran honorees with their names placed within the memorial and on the web site www.wwiimemorial.com

Amy got tired of shoveling snow in NY and didn't want to miss out on knowing her new niece in Dallas, so she quit a job she loved and her friends at the YMCA and she and Jacob moved south. She found a job at Penney's corporate office in Plano and Jacob started school at Vaughn Elementary in Allen. Nicole had found them an apt. not far from her and they moved in July 2004.

I didn't want to stay in NY alone without my sweet Jake so I found a job with VNA in Dallas, sold my condo and moved to Texas.... where I swore I would NEVER go again. Never say Never. It's more crowded and hotter but it's a good trade to be able to go to see the grandkids in a recital, or Boy Scout awards ceremony, or see a TaeKwando competition. I can baby sit and have them stay overnight. I love to color in their coloring books, teach them to paint and plant flowers and hug and kiss them any time I want. They are so smart and funny and some of the things they say are a riot. Especially if they don't know it's funny. I keep an ongoing journal for each of them as they grow up so all the little things they do and say are remembered. It includes some of their mothers' fears and prideful moments too. I hope they all (kids and grandkids) know how much I love them. They just grow up too fast and I don't want to miss any of it.

Amy and Nicole have become incredible mothers of very diverse children. There are pieces of each of them in their children of course, and the interesting part for me is to see a behavior or personality quirk repeated. I wrote Amy and Nicole a special note in 1996 I call "My daughters and me" for Mother's Day because I am so proud of them. I may have to work on a new piece to include what I see they mean to their children.

I haven't found a class nor the interest to do any painting since I have moved here. I work from home for VNA doing Medicare coding as I write this and am happy not to be commuting with all of the Dallas motorists twice a day.

I still read a lot and exchange books with the girls as we find something we like to share. I think one reason I like to read so much is because of all the moving around we did. I can always escape in a book and be someone else or be somewhere else and it is comforting to me. I have always liked to make crafts, paint and sew to have something pretty at the end of the day after all the years of nursing and seeing people in pain

I've really enjoyed teaching Jacob and Jessica to paint and do craft projects for gifts and am always amazed at their imagination and different perception of what I see in a painting. "The Eye of the Beholder" is never truer than sitting with them and watching them create something from nothing more than their imaginations.

I loved sewing clothes for me, Amy and Nicole and their dolls. Dance recitals and costumes were a favorite of mine; even when Nicole came home from college on a weekend with shiny green material and an idea for a mermaid costume needed by Sunday afternoon. I got it finished by working on it almost until her ride picked her up.

In later years I made Jacob an adorable dinosaur costume, a bear costume he only would wear for one picture to be taken. I made Jessica a baby pea pod costume for her fist Halloween. When I moved to Texas I made Jessica curtains for her room and knitted her stuffed dog a scarf and hat to keep him warm. He is a Siberian Husky in Texas, but that's what Jessica wanted.

I have made new friends this time in Texas; Glynda, Kuniko, Becky, Bev Childs and gotten reacquainted with Linda James. I still miss my NY friends a lot as they had become my family over the 30 years I lived there. They too have moved on; Hafners now live in San Diego and 2 of my friends have passed away so the NY group is diminished.

On July 29, 2008 my dear, kind, smart sister Connie Sue lost her 6-year battle with breast cancer. She had all the radiation and chemo a human can have, and it still took her. It was the day before her 25th wedding anniversary and a week before her 50th birthday.

She had told us in Feb. that there was nothing more they could do for her and she had 6 months.

Michael and I decided it was important to have a family reunion in Dallas in March while she was still able to travel. He and Nancy came from Oregon,

Connie, John and dad came from Ohio, and she was able to be with us and her dear nieces and great niece and nephew and to meet Blake. She adored the little kids and was always a special aunt to Amy and Nicole. We laughed, played games, ate good food, and hugged and loved each other a lot. She enjoyed the spring flowers at the Dallas Arboretum and I polished her nails and trimmed her hair and we played Scrabble. She kept saying it was the sister things we never got to do before.

She never cried even when those of us around her were. Hugging everyone goodbye at the airport was one of the hardest things I've ever done; knowing it was a final goodby. We all suddenly knew what it meant to want more time together

Michael had silver bracelets made for each of us with "love never fails" on the outside and our initials on the inside. I had them made for Amy and Nicole and we all wear them when we feel especially close to Connie.

She went on hospice in April and they kept her comfortable and active up until a week before she suddenly declined. It was just the 6 months. I was lucky enough to get to Ohio from Dallas in time to spend her last 12 hrs. with her. She was unconscious, but the experts say the person knows we were there loving them to the end.

Michael was en route from Oregon, and he had to hear my phone message when he changed planes in Chicago that she was gone. I felt terrible leaving him that message he would receive all alone.

Connie took one last breath, two tears rolled down her face, and she was at peace. Dad was holding her hand, and John and I were in the room with them.

Connie:

You were so brave and optimistic and supportive of the rest of us. The end came while I was there for which I am grateful. I had already grieved all the while you were sick and the tears I shed now are of relief from your pain and struggle. In time, I hope peace will replace my heartache. I miss you every day and see you in every butterfly.

We were far apart in years and always in miles because I never lived near you after I left for nurses' training. Our lives too were different as I had children and grandchildren and you had a career. I married young and divorced after 23 years and you married at 25 and lived with John Drotos, the love of your life for 25 years. You loved his daughter, Sarah, as your own. Sadly, we did share the experience of having breast cancer, but yours was more aggressive.

John is lost without you and tries his best to keep busy and get involved in new things. It has only been 5 months since you left as I write this, so our pain is still fresh. He has been down to Texas to visit all of us and get hugs he badly needed, and we are happy to provide. Sarah is getting married this year and that would have made you so happy.

John says he will always be married to you and he visits you often at the cemetery. You were lucky to find a man to love you like that. Some of us never will.

Dad is incredibly sad and depressed. He said he was done when he lost you, "his rock". I can't imagine losing a wife of 50 years and then your youngest child of 50 years. No man should have to endure that.

Michael has been dealing with his grief in an artistic way. He said you came to him in a dream on your birthday and inspired him to do a sculpture. He named her "Courage" which is such a loving and accurate tribute to you. He hopes there will be many of her in public places and that she can give people a connection and comfort. John has purchased the first one for the cancer center in Akron in your memory and there will be a book telling the journey of "Courage". You would be so proud; but then you guided him to do this.

I went to Cannon Beach, OR for the first time in the 30+years that Michael and Nancy have lived on the west coast to the first public showing of the sculpture as it was started. John and I will return May 1, 2009 to see the unveiling of the finished piece and send her on her journey for you.

It's a fitting place for the debut. Cannon Beach is lush, peaceful, full of wildlife, sunsets, and hope.

January 20, 2009 the 44th president of the United States was sworn in. Barack Obama is a black man and Sarah Palin ran on the opposing Republican ticket as Vice President. It feels like century is stepping into it's own. Blacks and women; the struggle I was witness to from the 60's on that began decades before me. Quite a triumph for the United States.

The new president has a lot to deal with: a recession than began last October, wars in Afghanistan and Iraq and the rising cost of health care for 24 million uninsured Americans. The threat of terrorists is still here, and the concern for assassination of a black president is obvious.

Random thoughts;

I had started my Hummel collection with the first one I received in high school from Broggini's and many were gifs to me in the years after that. I also bought some and now have 78. Amy and Nicole already have favorites picked out that they plan on inheriting.

Over the years my taste in music has changed a lot. I went from Ricky, Bobby, the Beach Boys, Johnny Mathis and Elvsis to Frankie Vallie and the 4 Season, the Platters (Bill's influence) to Tom Petty and the Eagles (Ron's influence) to Toby Keith and Josh Turner (Amy's influence) and finding Lou Rawls, Norah Jones, Michael Buble and Il Divo on my own. I still listen to some of those old favorites from time to time.

I did get a chance to see Frankie Vallie and the Platters live in college, and later as a Grandma I saw Toby Keith in concert. A long time in between.

I have many faults, but my worst is not forgiving someone who has hurt me or my child.

My vanity is my fingernails. After I stopped biting them as a teenager, I have always liked them long and pretty and have had acrylic nails since 1996. They always look good.

I cry at everything…. kindness, cuteness, bravery, sadness, movies and songs. The one that always puts me away is Tim McGraw's "Please remember me".

My feelings are easily hurt, and I usually cannot tell someone that they have done it.

I used to have pretty eyes and long legs. Now I have osteoporosis, hyperthyroid (thinning hair and lashes) and have always fought my weight changes.

I have regrets and have moments of "shoulda, woulda, coulda". I regret that my marriage failed because I loved him.

I take pride in my family and having good friends.

I like cats, mysteries, roses, lilacs, peonies, and violets. I am dedicated to buying new shoes, the color blue and the fine art of sarcasm. I am pulled into the first snow, fall leaves, mountains, thunderstorms, fresh baked bread and chocolate cake (no icing).

I abhor liars, cheats, people that act stupid on purpose, slapstick and coconut. I'm not wild about dogs, lilies or beer.

Sometimes what we care about the most gets all used and goes away never to return.

So, while we have it, it's best to love it and care for it; fix it when it's broken and try to heal it when it's sick. This is true for a marriage, children with a bad report card, aging parents, grandparents and pets. We keep them because they are worth it, because we are worth it. Some things we keep, like a best friend that moved away or a classmate we grew up with. There are some things that make life important, like people we know who are special, the laughter and hug from a child, and we keep them close.

Hold on to what is good even if it's a handful of earth.
Hold on to what you believe even if it's not popular.
Hold on to what you must do even if it's a long way from here.
Hold on to my hand even when I have gone away.

The best sound in the world is a child's laugh.

Noted events in her life were:

• She worked as a RN, Libraian.
• She was Methodist.

Beverly married **William James STARR** [892][19,41,82,142] [MRIN: 309], son of **James Edward STARR** [894][41,142] and **Aloma Dolores SLOAN** [895],[41,142] on 1 Sep 1968 in Akron, Summit, Ohio, USA. The marriage ended in divorce. William was born on 16 May 1946 in Cowanshannock, Armstrong, Pennsylvania, USA.

Noted events in his life were:

• He worked as a Civil Engineer (Kodak).
• He was Protestant.

March 2008 - John Drotos with niece Amy Starr

7-Amy Christine STARR [916][19,41,70,82,142] was born on 20 Nov 1969 in Rochester, Monroe, New York, USA.

Noted events in her life were:

• She worked as an Exec. Secretery - JC Penney in 2010 in Stewart, Rusk, Texas, USA.

Amy married **Bryan Keith STEWART** [915][70] [MRIN: 323], son of **Russell STEWART** [917][30] and **Elaine**

_____ [918],[30] on 3 Nov 1990. The marriage ended in divorce. Bryan was born on 18 Aug 1969 in Boiceville, Ulster, New York, USA.

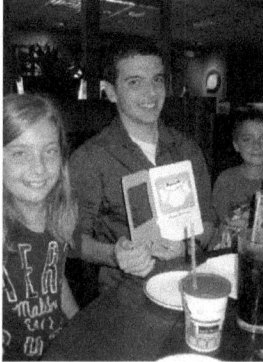

8-**Jacob Bryan STEWART [1022]**[70] was born in 1997 in Ft. Lenoardwood, MO

May 2002 - Wedding of Nicole (Starr) Metcalf here with nephew Jake Stewart

7-**Nicole Renee STARR [914]**[70,82,143] was born on 19 Aug 1973 in Rochester, Monroe, New York, USA.

Noted events in her life were:

• She worked as an Actress in New York City.

Nicole married **Kyle A. METCALF** [3087][143] [MRIN: 322], son of _____ **METCALF** [4623], on 4 May 2002 in Akron, Summit, Ohio, USA. The marriage ended in divorce in 2014. Kyle was born in 1966.

8-**Jessica METCALF [3088]** was born on 16 Jun 2003 in Texas, USA.

8-**Blake METCALF [3217]**[144] was born on 19 Feb 2007 in Allen, Collin, Texas, USA.

6-Richard Laverne TIEMAN [891][70,145,146] was born on 28 Jan 1948 in Keokuk, Lee, Iowa, USA, died on 28 Jan 1948 in Keokuk, Lee, Iowa, USA, and was buried in Oakland Cemetery, Keokuk, Lee, Iowa.

General Notes: T500-4 Obit

Richard LaVerne Tieman Funeral services for Richard LaVerne Tieman, son of M. LaVerne and Doris Morrill Tieman, 1511 Timea St. born Wednesday morning, were held today in Oakland cemetery.

The Rev. Paul McDade conducted services. Surviving are Mr. & Mrs. Tieman, his parents, one sister, Beverly Dianne Tieman, and his grandparents, Mr. & Mrs. Malcolm Tieman and Mr. & Mrs. Don Morrill, all of Keokuk.

Great-grandparents Mrs. Marion Morrill of Peoria, Ill., Mrs. Mabel Reitz of Bethel, Mo., and Mrs. Anna Tieman of Keokuk also survive.

6-Michael LaVerne TIEMAN [1][71,82,147,148,149,150,151,152,153,154,155,156,157,158,159] was born on 20 Aug 1950 in Keokuk, Lee, Iowa, USA[147] and was baptized on 31 Dec 1950 in Keokuk, Lee, Iowa, USA. Other names for Michael are MT, Papa.

General Notes: **How it all started:**

My quest for Nancy and my history, or roots, began innocently enough, Christmas, 1982.

Nancy's grandmother, Dede, gave us a book for Christmas titled The History of Our Family. A book of empty pages with headings like: Our Children, Husband's Parents' Family and Where Our Ancestors Have Lived. As Nancy and I started to fill it out, we found that we knew almost nothing of our family from before our great-grandparents, and my family whenI asked, would tell me nothing.

I am an artist, and artists are a curious lot by nature and we love knowledge. So, there it is, I was hooked.

First, my quest was who were my great-grandparents and where did they come from? All I knew was that they came from Prussia in the early 1800's and that because they were of German descent living in the U.S. during two great wars, the past was never talked about. I then took it upon myself to try and fill in the blanks. First, I talked to my parents, and great aunts, as no one else would tell me squat. I began to fill in names of ancestors, and some questionable dates. As time went on, I spent many hours in the archives and library of the Mormon Church. I was lucky that we lived in cities that had local libraries of the main church.

Back then, I had to search actual books and newspapers and hundreds of rolls of film, searching out our ancestors and records of birth and census' and maybe even a parish record. It took a long time back then in the 80's, and money as I had to order the loan of papers and actual records and books from the Mormon Church archives in Salt Lake City. Which I could only look at in their library. Anything I wanted copies of, I had to pay to copy and get their permission. Their genealogical library is extensive, the largest in the world, and in the case of Prussia, they had the only info as most of it was destroyed in the wars.

My list of ancestors started to become impressive. Then I asked, "Who were these people?" I started to collect stories from our relatives about the families.

Oh, the stories I heard when the family finally decided to share. Some info turned out accurate as I researched, others, not so much. Like all families we were descended from kings and leading scholars and vice presidents and famous inventors. Or, so the stories went on that were handed down.

Then with the stories, I became interested in the towns and farms and countries our ancestors came from. What was Millom, England like in the 1600's when Nancy's ancestors lived there? So, I looked into the town histories, and when was Prussia a country, country histories, and maps of the periods when our ancestors lived. Plot maps where I actually found our famiy names. Curious more, what did my ancestors wear and eat in the 18th century on their farms and what did they grow? What church did they attend and why were there no birth record in a particular period of the 1600's but there were baptism records instead? How did my family name change from Thiemann to Tiemann to Tieman?

Because of that book and asking who was the greatgrandfaher I never knew, this project has now over 4200 people in our two families, over 1500 source documents dating back to the 1600's (some originals pre-19th century), and a collection of over 2000 original photos some dating back to the beginning of photography.

I hope you enjoy reading and searching this project of mine, this labor of love.

When my friends have asked my why I do this, why am I so interested in the past, that only the future is important? I ask them to tell me about their grandparents, and half way through their memories, they begin to understand that their stories and memories of their families might die with them, and that I never had any.

-Michael Tieman, 10 Mar. 2015-

Memories:
Sister, Beverly Dianne Tieman Starr, 2009

My brother, Michael La Verne, was born Aug. 20, 1950 and according to the stories our mother told, he had his days and nights mixed up until he was about 6 mos. old when he slept through the night. He had a lot of curls and looks like dad. He couldn't say my name and called me "Bebe" which is what I have my grandkids call me.

I mostly remember having to always take him with me growing up no matter where I went. I'm sure he loved going to my friends' house and watch us play! I vowed if I ever had kids they wouldn't have to go everywhere together like we did. The time I rubbed his face in the snow and he got frostbite on his cheeks it was because I was mad at mom for making me take him to the library with me. Since she worked nights, she napped in the daytime and I suppose it was more convenient for her if he was with me. I picked on him a lot as long as he was littler than me ("point to your head and say your initials") Once he got taller I didn't do it as often!

He called himself "the Ketchup Kid" and ate ketchup sandwiches sometimes…ick. Probably while he was wearing his twin gun holsters and the coon skin Davy Crockett cap!

Our Great Aunts Maggie (11/28/12-6/02/07) and Thelma (09/12/07-09/18/97) Tieman lived with my Great Grandmother Anna (Sommer) Tieman (5/01/1876-06/15/63) near us at 1628 Palean St. I remember Great Grandma's beautiful long white hair that Maggie did up in a braided coiled bun for her. She sure looked like the German housewife then! (Great Grandma was born in Dresden, Germany). In nice weather Maggie would wash the hair and Great Grandma would sit in the backyard in the sun and Maggie would brush and brush it until it was almost dry and then she would braid it up for the week.

Michael and I spent many Saturdays with them and we learned how to make the yummy cinnamon/sugar coffee cake on the big black wood stove in their kitchen. It would rise overnight and be baked for Sunday breakfast the next morning. They made soap from lye and left-over soap scraps and they had the prettiest china and vases in their dining room. Years later I got the Havilland china Thelma collected over the years and still cherish it and use it.

I mostly remember what the little white house and neighborhood looked like from the years Michael and I returned and spent summers with Grandma (NaNaw) and Don Morrill after we had moved away. Our first train ride alone was from Elgin to Keokuk in 1959. We were told NOT to get off of the train for any reason until we arrived. Along the way, the train hit a stalled car sitting on the tracks. Michael decided he needed to see what was going on and got off with the engineer. I let him go, because I was told not to leave. No one was hurt, and the engineer brought Michael back to his seat and of course I couldn't wait to tell on him! Probably was the highlight of my summer.

We had our first TV in 1954. Michael watched "Howdy Doody" and "Daniel Boone" and we watched "Capt. Kangaroo". Michael had a coon skin cap like Daniel Boone that he wore everywhere, even to bed until it had a life (and smell) of its own. He loved his double holster Roy Rogers six shooters and we watched "Hopalong Cassidy" and "the Rifleman". When we wanted "color" on our TV we put a blue sky and green grass plastic across the screen, so we could watch "Bonanza". Very high tech. Westerns were popular and "Gunsmoke" was all that Grandpa Don would watch.

Michael and I walked 3 or 4 blocks to Blackhawk School where my best friends were Sylvia Sieferman, Marjorie Lehman and Cheryl Frye. Lehman's lived across the street from the school and her little brother was also my brother's friend. I taught myself one weekend to ride Michael's bike because I never had one of my own. Guess it was a boy thing.

A tornado went down across the street from us one night, and a big tree fell across the driveway putting a huge tree limb through our parents' bedroom window. I don't remember this, but Michael does, and dad confirmed his memory.

Grandpa Don had given gave Michael a yellow tom cat that they named Nicky (St. Nicholas) at Christmas. He lived to be a was a very old cat with more than 9 lives fighting all the time, scarred, chewed up, bringing home dead mice and live baby rabbits to show us. He brought a baby rabbit into the house once and let it go. Mom caught it and put it in a shoe box on top of the floor register to keep it warm. She gave it a baby bottle of milk every few hours. It lived until the night she worked, and dad wouldn't get up every 2 hrs to feed it. Nicky never looked at it again once it was in the house. Once he brought in the live mouse and it ran under the upright piano she and Michael had to corner it and catch it. After that she never let Nicky in the door again without having him open his mouth to be sure there wasn't a tail hanging out of it.

Nicky even survived having his tail amputated for cancer. Mom had said she thought he was mostly embarrassed and he wouldn't go out of the house for weeks afterwards. We had him a long time (over 10 years) and we took him on our many moves as dad got transferred to a new town every 2 year.

Dad was transferred again Dec.15, 1958 to Elgin, Illinois near Chicago when I was in 6th grade. Connie was 4 mos. old and the house we moved to was so cold on moving day that she got pneumonia. Mom had to find a pediatrician right away practically before the movers left. We lived at 360 Congdon Street in a house that none of us really remember any inside details about. It was yellow and had an enclosed front porch. Michael and I remember there was a dog next door and that our driveway was higher than the neighbors'. I remember the dog was a Boston bulldog and he remembers it was a boxer. Dad also said it was a boxer, so now I've been wrong at least once.

We went to Coleman Elementary school and had a very long cold walk (20 below zero) where the snow banks were so high at the intersections that cars had red flags on their antenna to be seen. Girls were not allowed to wear pants to school, so I wore slacks under my dress and took them off and on to walk to and from home. The school sat way back from the road across a big field and a long sidewalk that had no cover from the snow, nor freezing wind, nor rain. It seemed like it went on forever. I went to Larsen Jr. high 7th and half of 8th grade before Dad was transferred to Akron, Ohio in Feb. 1960, and I went to Perkins Jr. High there.

We took family vacations to Chicago to the Brookfield Zoo in 1959 and Springfield, Ill in 1960. We went to the Wisconsin Dells and saw the Indian pageantry one summer. 1961 was our first trip to Niagara Falls NY and Canada. Michael and Dad went to the Cave of the Winds and mom, dad and Connie went on the "Maid of the Mist" boat tour leaving Michael and I on the Canadian side with the car. He and I still wonder what we would have done in Canada, with a car and no parents if the boat sank?

Grandma Alta died in June and in July Maggie and Thelma took Michael and I on my "pre-high school graduation" trip to Colorado. We drove out there in their 1959 gray Plymouth at about 40 MPH. When it was Thelma's turn to drive, Maggie would watch the speedometer and often lean up over the back seat and tell her to slow down. Thelma became "deaf" during most of this back seat driving. I don't remember how many days it must have taken us to get there at that speed on 2 lane roads, but I do remember the corn fields in Iowa and the wheat fields in Kansas that never ended. My brain goes numb now just thinking about it.

Part of our trip we met and stayed with Mrs. Beck in Evergreen, CO. She had worked for our dad in Akron. She and her husband had retired there, and it was way up in the mountains with no one around them. It was beautiful. I loved driving along the roads beside the Colorado River running along beside us.

We stayed overnight at Estes State Park on the Continental Divide where there was still snow on the ground and we made snowballs. We took a bus ride around the area and saw tufted black squirrels and a black bear beside the road.

We also went to the Garden of the Gods Amphitheater where Maggie bemoaned the fact she would miss the Beatles performing there later in the summer. She was crazy about the Beatles (not my favorite) and liked the play/movie "Jesus Christ Superstar" music.

Colorado Springs was beautiful, and the Air Force Academy and Cathedral were fantastic.

We spent time in downtown Denver but missed Pike's Peak because the car wouldn't have made it up there! It was a memorable trip with them and I know we all had fun.

Dad had already been transferred to Zanesville, OH with Buckeye Mart 6mos. before I graduated, but the 3 of us stayed in Akron in order for me to finish school. We all joined him in Zanesville where I spent the summer waiting to return to Akron to go to nurses' training and Michael went to high school one month before Buckeye Mart transferred dad to Columbus, Ohio. Zanesville's claim to fame was the "Y" bridge over the river which we lived near. I only remember the house was brick and I was counting the days until I left for Akron.

May 4, 1970 was the Kent State Ohio Riot and shooting of 2 students on campus by the Ohio National Guard. They were protesting President Nixon invading Cambodia in the ongoing Vietnam War. Kent was close to Youngstown where we had lived so we were alarmed at what happened. The war protests had escalated around the country. I found out decades later that Michael had taken part in some of them.

August 1971 Michael was coming to Rochester from Columbus, and Mom and Dad and Connie were coming from MA. for his 21st birthday and we were all in a car accident. Mom and I were hurt the worst and were in the hospital for awhile. I had surgery on my face and she had a broken pelvis. She saved Amy by pushing her in between the seats when the car was coming at us. Connie and Amy were taken care of by our friends, Bev and Ed Huber. Dad, Michael and Bill sort of looked after each other.

June 16, 1972 Michael married Nancy Marshall in Columbus, OH. They had met at Buckeye Mart where they both worked for Dad. They moved to Vancouver, British Columbia in 1973 where he started an art design business.

Michael and Nancy had Heather in 1976 and Kate in 1979 and they were in the United States again but still up in the Northwest in Washington state and then Oregon. He worked on the Expo '86 while doing advertising and tried his hand at graphic design.

On July 29, 2008 my dear, kind, smart sister Connie Sue lost her 6-year battle with breast cancer. She had all the radiation and chemo a human can have, and it still took her. It was the day before her 25th wedding anniversary and a week before her 50th birthday.

She had told us in Feb. that there was nothing more they could do for her and she had 6 months.

Michael and I decided it was important to have a family reunion in Dallas in March while she was still able to travel. He and Nancy came from Oregon, Connie, John and dad came from Ohio, and she was able to be with us and her dear nieces and great niece and nephew and to meet Blake. She adored the little kids and was always a special aunt to Amy and Nicole. We laughed, played games, ate good food, and hugged and loved each other a lot. She enjoyed the spring flowers at the Dallas Arboretum and I polished her nails and trimmed her hair and we played Scrabble. She kept saying it was the sister things we never got to do before.

She never cried even when those of us around her were. Hugging everyone goodbye at the airport was one of the hardest things I've ever done; knowing it was a final goodby. We all suddenly knew what it meant to want more time together

Michael had silver bracelets made for each of us with "love never fails" on the outside and our initials on the inside. I had them made for Amy and Nicole and we all wear them when we feel especially close to Connie.

She went on hospice in April and they kept her comfortable and active up until a week before she suddenly declined. It was just the 6 months. I was lucky enough to get to Ohio from Dallas in time to spend her last 12 hrs. with her. She was unconscious, but the experts say the person knows we were there loving them to the end.

Michael was en route from Oregon, and he had to hear my phone message when he changed planes in Chicago that she was gone. I felt terrible leaving him that message he would receive all alone.

Connie took one last breath, two tears rolled down her face, and she was at peace. Dad was holding her hand, and John and I were in the room with them.

Michael has been dealing with his grief in an artistic way. He said you came to him in a dream on your birthday and inspired him to do a sculpture. He named her "Courage" which is such a loving and accurate tribute to you. He hopes there will be many of her in public places and that she can give people a connection and comfort. John has purchased the first one for the cancer center in Akron in your memory and there will be a book telling the journey of "Courage". You would be so proud; but then you guided him to do this.

I went to Cannon Beach, OR for the first time in the 30+years that Michael and Nancy have lived on the west coast to the first public showing of the sculpture as it was started. John and I will return May 1, 2009 to see the unveiling of the finished piece and send her on her journey for you.

Michael Tieman, 2014 - Just a few memories from my past not covered by Beverly.

Summers as a kid:

A few weeks each summer, when Don had to work when Beverly and I were there, Don would take me to work with him some days. These were special to me because he was a typesetter at the local newspaper, The Daily Gate City in Keokuk Iowa. I was five - eleven and he would take me to his station and put me on a stool, so I could reach the counter and help him set type for that day's newspaper.

At that time, type was set by hand, each letter, one at a time. I would stand on my tip toes in my younger years, so I could reach the California Job Case (collectors now buy the empty cases and hang them on the wall). The case was a large wooden drawer, one drawer for each type style, (font), and it would be sectioned off into compartments, each compartment would contain metal slugs, each compartment was a single letter. I had to learn the position of each letter in the case, because the typesetter's job was to set the story in metal type as fast as possible. I can still remember how Don's hands would fly over the case, picking up the letters and placing them in the metal chase, building the story character by character, line by line until the story was completed. Did I say that the type was set upside down and backwards? That was so that when it was printed, it came out right. Don had a great vocabulary and could spell any word given to him, because the typesetter also had to proof read the story. Throughout my 40 plus years carrer in advertising, I proofread everything by reading it upside down and backwards and taught others to do the same.

One year Don and Alta came to spend Christmas with us and brought me my own Case complete with metal type, a chase, typesetting rulers, spacers and carriers with ink and a tapping block. I could and did print my own papers over the years. How cool is that?

Unfortunately, we moved alot, and to move this case and type, I put the slugs into their own envelope and sealed them and put them into a metal wastepaper basket. Then I waited as the movers came to pick up our belongings. There was always one smart ass mover who saw the basket with envelopes in it and would come along arms full of other boxes and go to pick uo the basket with one hand.

And fall down. The basket never moving. It had to have at least 50lbs. of metal in the basket. I know, I was a pill, but it was funny.

After several moves, mom made me get rid of the whole setup rather than move it again. I was heartbroken. Can you imagine how much that whole setup would sell for now? And the memories, I bet I could still set type by hand, a little slower maybe, but I still got it.

There would be other days when Don and I would go fishing on the Mississippi river. Now, this was the summer, in Iowa, on the river during the heat of the day, and I was sitting on the rocks on the bank of the river. The temps were in the triple digits, with 100% humidity. Don would take me to a favorite spot. Don and I would climb down the rocks to the river and fish for catfish.

And there is a science to fishing for catfish. I used a casting reel filled with 50lb. test line, a two-foot-long 35lb. test leader with a 2oz. lead sinker and a treble hook. The hook is baited with a special "very stinky" paste. Normally you just wrap the hook with a ball of the paste, but the Mississippi is fast with strong currents which easily take off the bait, so us "locals" had a trick, we would put a kernal of Green Giant Nibblets Corn on each hook before we put on the paste. It held the paste on the hooks longer and if the paste came off, we could still fish for carp with the corn. In the next paragraph, I will explain the politics of fishing the Mississippi river. Anyhow, come lunch time we would go back to the car, I would have cold hot dogs and a warm Pepsi, Don would have a cold beer. Hummmmm. After lunch I would go back fishing and Don would stay in the car and drink and listen to the radio. At about 3ish, we would pack up and go home. Always with fish. We then had one more stop to make, two if we caught carp.

The politics of fishing the Mississippi river from when I fished it from 1954-61. If you were white, you fished on the rocks on the steep river banks by the dam spillway. And, you fished for catfish, which could weigh as much as 300lbs. If you were black, you fished farther downstream, and you fished for carp, considered a trash fish. If Don and I caught a carp, we were to stop off downstream to where the n****** were and trade our carp for a catfish if they had one. If they didn't have any, we just gave them our carp. A white man never ate carp.

The stop Don and I always did after fishing was to go into town to the Moose lodge and sit at the bar. I would sit on the bar stool and order my usual from the bartender, a bottle of cold Pepsi and a chocolate Hershey bar. Don's order was a can of Blatz beer, or two. The bartender was the most happy, carefree man that everyone liked as a friend. As long as he was in his place, behind the bar serving white folks. Yes, Leroy was black. A small man, with stark white hair and when he smiled he had some yellow teeth, and the bloodiest gums. His smile was all teeth and gums from ear to ear.

Back to the way of the world in Iowa on the Mississippi river in the 50's and 60's. Leroy was everyone's friend when he was in his place behind the bar. When Don and I would pass Leroy, or any other blacks, on the streets of Keokuk, we never spoke, and as we came near them, they would get off the sidewalk and walk in the gutter until we were past. I did not know anything else as I was under 11.

When my dad was a kid in Keokuk, he would sneak away from his block, and go play with the little black boys. His mom would find him and beat him all the way home. The next day he would do the same, as did she.

Later in life I remembered all of this and did what I could to right these wrongs.

December 1, 1969 First Draft Lottery since 1942

This was the US military draft lottery to see what your chances were of being drafted and sent to Viet Nam. All men born in 1944 - 1950 were in the lottery. Needless to say, that was me. I can still recall that lottery night. I was working at a retail store, Buckeye Mart in Columbus Ohio., Dad was the manager of the store, and when it came time for the lottery draw 366 blue capsules with a birthdate on it were put in a roll cage and spun. All of the young men/boys who worked in the store with me were huddled around the TV displays as the lottery was televised live.

It is hard to describe those minutes as we watched, waiting to hear our destiny, holding your breath as the hand went into the cage, the knot in your stomach, the tightness in the chest, standing there with the boys you have been working with and know. If the next number was not your birthdate, you breathed a quick sigh of relief, and then held your breath as they drew the next number. The first 125 numbers were to be drafted immediately. As the lottery continued, I saw my co-workers/friends stiffen as their number was drawn, close their teary eyes and quietly walk out of the store, I never saw any of them again. After the first 125 were drawn, the few of us left, had hope. Then my birthdate was drawn, #344 out of 366. I was relieved, elated, happy, sad, all of the emotions washed over me like a tidal wave.

For the first time since the first number was drawn, I became aware of someone standing behind me. I looked around and it was dad. With tears in his eyes, he smiled, turned around and walked away, back to work. We never spoke of it, but to this day I still wonder what would have happened if my number would have been the first ones drawn? If I had decided to escape the draft and go to Canada, instead of serving, would this man, my father, who lied about his polio handicap so he could fight in WWll and proud to have served, would he understand and support my decision?

As a side note, in Dec. 1971 before Nancy and I were married, I received a "Greetings" draft notice to report for military service. It seems that in their books I had lost my student deferment and had to stand the draft. The problem was, I was still a student in college. Now at this time in the war, most college professors would do almost anything to help you keep your student deferment to stay out of Nam, so I was at a loss as to why I lost mine.

Nancy and I went down to the Selective Service offices to speak to someone, hoping to clear up the mistake. We got a very nice older woman and when she looked into it, they had made a mistake and I was still deferred as a student. But... Here it comes; I had an option of keeping my deferment or give it up and stand the draft. I thought I am not crazy; no way am I standing the draft.

Then the lady behind the desk said she had a son and would tell him to stand the draft and here was the reason. It was December and because of the way the original law was written and for this year only, if I stood the draft it would only be until the end of the year, less than 30 days away. Then if my number was not called, I would get a 1H deferment - Registrant not currently subject to processing for induction. She pointed out that I was in the Ohio State University draft pool and they had never called numbers over 125 and mine was 344.

So, I signed away my student deferment and stood the draft until the end of the month. But, neither Nancy nor I got much sleep in Dec., but what a New Year's Eve party we had. After that year, the law was changed so you had to stand the draft for 12 full months, I skated on that one let me tell you,

I loved it when I got my new draft card with the 1H status in Jan., but I still had a draft card burning when I no longer became eligible for military service, at age 35.

May 6, 1970 - The Ohio State Campus Riots - newspaper article

"Acting on a recommendation by Ohio Gov. James A Rhodes, Ohio State University closed its doors in mid-quarter on May 6, 1970. The 45,000 students on the riot-racked Columbus campus were told to leave the university by noon the next day.

In the spring of 1970, women were demanding equal rights, blacks were pressing for equal representation, and young people were calling for an end to the Vietnam War. Put these issues on a college campus and combine them with an overwhelmed OSU administration, confused by the wants of a younger generation, and you've got yourself a riot. In early May, riots raged on more than 100 U.S. campuses, as students protested the escalation of the Vietnam War into Cambodia.

At Kent State University, an ROTC building was torched. On May 3, Gov. Rhodes called the demonstrators "the worst type of people we harbor in America" and ordered the Ohio National Guard to restore order at Kent State. Guardsmen killed four people the next day.

Kent State immediately closed, but Ohio State remained open. Amid chants of "Shut it down," protesting OSU students blocked entrances to several buildings on May 5 but dispersed after Guardsmen forced them away.

On May 6, protesters mobbed Ohio State President Novice G. Fawcett's campus home and the school's administration building. Troops with rifles and bayonets drove them back to the Oval. Shortly before 3 p.m., a fire broke out at Hayes Hall, where, according to some reports, protesters threw stones at firefighters.

Fearing what he called "further disruptions and violence," Fawcett said at 5:30 p.m., "I am closing the university until further notice." More than 80 colleges across the country closed that day in the face of growing protests over the war and the Kent State killings.

Ohio State reopened on May 19. In a letter to parents and students, Fawcett wrote: "In the days ahead we will work toward improved student-faculty-administration relationships."'

This is what I saw firsthand as a student photographer covering the OSU riots:

I must confess this was not my first protest march, and the marches of the previous month of April at OSU and other Ohio university campuses were bloody, and tension filled,

The initial reason for the march this day was to protest the unfair treatment of blacks, women, and of course the war, especially the bombing of Cambodia. The campus, city and state police were very undisciplined at that time. Some of the National Guard, however, made honest attempts to curb the violence. In at least one instance that I observed, National Guard officers who tried to calm things down were chastised by their superiors.

I was in a crowd of people, taking photos, not the entire crowd was students by the way, when all of a sudden there was a rush of National Guard in front of me and tear gas cans being thrown. I can still smell the acrid odor of tear gas. Confusion followed and somehow, I was pushed forward into the arms of a

National Guard soldier. I had my Nikon in front of my face at the time and I suppose his natural reaction was to push it. Unfortunately, by doing so he broke my nose and camera.

I was with my friend Dale and he grabbed me, and we had to break into a dead run to avoid being trampled by a large group of students charging down a side street from the Oval. They were also being forced back by tear gas and armed police.

Our only thought now was escape. They had closed the campus, so we could not get out. I lived off-campus, quite a distance from campus, but fortunately Dale had an apartment on campus, just a few streets away. Like everyone else we had no idea what was going to happen next, so we ran from alley to alley, street to street to safety, away from the gas.

Dale and I waited in his apartment with all the curtains closed until night. I had to get off campus and back to the safety of home.

This is what a scared, bloodied twenty-year-old does in a riot when reason fails.

We snuck out of Dale's safe apartment into the dark night. No, it was not a dark stormy night like in books, but it was dark. We snuck from alley to alley listening to the noise and chatter from the police radios, trying to stay clear of them.

My last memory of that day was as we were almost free, slowly sneaking around; I turned into the last alley to freedom and came face to face with a young National Guard soldier holding his rifle with bayonet in my face. We both froze. I don't know who was more scared, him or me. Here he was in a faintly lit alley, facing two kids, and me with blood down the front of my shirt from my nose. You know what they say about time stopping and you see flashbacks of your life? Nope. Time did stop though, for how long I don't know. Was his gun loaded like at Kent state? Then in that moment, the young man dropped his gun from my face, turned around and walked out of the alley. I don't recall the rest, but I did find my car and got home safely.

That was my "oh shit, what if" moment, hopefully never to be repeated.

Every now and again I wonder what happened to that young man. Did he end up in Nam? Did he survive to tell his version of the Ohio State riots to his kids and grandkids?

And I thank God for people who have a moment of reason, when the rest of the world is going to hell around them.

Here is a sidebar to these riots. I had met Nancy the month before this, and her father was the head of the endodontics school at Ohio State. During the closure of the school, the professors at OSU had fire watch at the school at night, just in case anything happened. Neither Nancy nor I ever told her father that I was on the other side of the barricades during that time.

June 12, 1972 - I survived my honeymoon!

Yes, your wedding day is meant to be special and memorable, as is your honeymoon. You should remember it fondly as you grow old. It should not be a survival class where your life is in danger and you are escaping death, not once, but three times. Fortunately for us our honeymoon was only a long weekend.

Since both Nancy and I were still in school, I was doing summer school classes to finish up my BFA, we had to be married on a Friday and our honeymoon was a room at a state park resort Fri night/Sat/Sun/Mon then back to school.

It all started to go south on us when my best friend and Best Man in my wedding, Dale, decided to trick out my car, a '66 Cuda. Fill it with popcorn and cheese on the muffler as well as balloons and tin cans. When I heard about the plans, I decided to hide the car a couple blocks away and we could make our escape from there.

Escaping Death #1: Dale followed us in his VW bug as we ran to the car and started to drive away. He drove like a crazy man driving straight at us, trying to catch us, and finally trying to run us off the road several times until I could get around him and escape. I have no idea how many trees and cars we narrowly missed. He was a maniac.

Escaping Death #2: Driving the narrow country roads at night on our way to the state park. Nancy and I were coming around a curve and out jumped a deer. I steered left and we just missed her, it was so close we found deer tail hair in the passenger side mirror.

Escaping Death #3: I confess I cannot swim. Many times in my life I tried, even took swimming lessons once as a young tike. I had a scar in the middle of my chest for many years where a lifeguard at Boy Scout camp pushed a metal pole into me to save me from what he thought was drowning. He hit me so hard he succeeded in taking my breath away and I sank like a rock in the pool.

Not to digress, Nancy on the other hand swims like a fish. So, here we are at the resort, out in the lake, close to shore and I am out only as far as I can touch bottom. When my new bride comes up to me and tells me it is ok to come out a bit farther with her. I am young and in love and of course out I go to my wife. And down I drop under water struggling to live. Nancy does grab me and pulls me to where I can again touch bottom. Seems she was treading water but thought I was tall enough to touch bottom. My question was if you are treading water how can you tell how far away the bottom is?

We survived our honeymoon and have now been married 42 years. Who knew?

And now I pass the torch.

I will now let my wife and daughters and our grandkids tell their stories and hopefully I am in alot of them. Let me just say that in Nancy and my 44 years together, we have had our joys and sorrows like every family.

The sorrows of almost losing our daughters in a car accident when Heather was in High school; losing both Nancy's parents and mine; the death of my younger sister to cancer; the death of some of our friends; three times we lost almost everything we had because of business and life's bad rolls, but we fought back and, in the end, succeeded.

The joys keep coming every day, but include for me; Nancy as my friend, sole mate and wife; our kids Heather and Katie as we watched them grow up and are now wives and mothers with their own family; our son in laws Phillip and Sam and grandkids Riley, Jack, Connor, Alexis and Owen and us being part of their lives; our being able to retire and travel and see the world and the beauty it holds; and for me, being an artist and capturing the celebration of life in my work.

Our family stories will continue, and hopefully will be not only passed down verbally but also written down so that our descendants will know us better and see they are made up of all of us who came before.

My hope is that someone in our family will take an interest in all of this genealogy and will pick up this history of the Tieman-Marshall Family and carry on, adding new members and filling in the gaps of the older ones.

Marquis Who's Who In The West (23rd Edition)

Tieman, Michael LaVerne, graphic design executive; b. Keokuk, Iowa, Aug 20, 1950; s. Malcolm LaVerne and Doris Earline (Morrill) T.; m. Nancy Lee Marshall, June 16, 1972; children: Heather Anne, Katherine Jane. BFA, Columbus Coll. Art and Design, 1972. Art dir. Kersker Advt., Columbus, Ohio. 1969-72: graphic designer The Studio, Inc., Columbus, 1972-74; sr. art dir. Cockfield & Brown Advt., Vancouver, B.C., Can., 1974-75; ptnr., graphic designer Designers West. Ltd., Vancouver. 1975-78; owner, graphic designer Tieman & Friends, North Vancouver. 1978-86; ptnr., art dir. Printpac Mktg., Ltd., Richmond, B.C., 1978-81; sr. art dir. McKim Advt., Ltd., Vancouver, 1981-84; sr. graphic designer EXPO 86, Vancouver 1984-86; exec. graphic designer Gilchrist & Assoocs., Inc., Portland, Oreg., 1986-. Recipient First Pl. Presentation Folders award Lithographers & Printing House Craftsmen, 1990. Cert. of Merit Award Printing Industries Am., 1988, First Pl. Ann. Report award Internat. Fedn. Advt. Agys. 1985, PRSA, 1987; named World's Best 30 Second Comedy Spot, Hollywood Radio & TV Soc., 1981. Mem. Nat. Geog. Soc., Am. Inst. Graphic Artists, The Smithsonian Assoc. (Nat.) New England Hist. Geneal.Soc., Trout Unlimited. Friends of the Zoo. Avocations: painting, photography, fly-fishing, reading, computer graphics. Home: 1426 Greentree Cir., Lake Oswego, OR 97034 Office: Gilchrist & Assoc. 815 SE 2nd Ste 300 Portland, OR 97204 503-243-1030.

Places Lived:

1950-55 - Keokuk, Iowa, USA; 1955-58 - Freeport, Illinois, USA; 1958-60 - Elgin, Illinois, USA; 1960-65 - Akron, Ohio, USA; 1965-65 - Zanesville, Ohio, USA; 1965-73 - Columbus, Ohio, USA; 1973-86 - North Vancouver, British Columbia, Canada; 1986-96 - Lake Oswego, Oregon, USA; 1996-2002 - Camas, Washington, USA; 2002-15 - Cannon Beach, Oregon, USA, 2015-present - Beaverton, Oregon, USA

Places Visited:

1988 - Hong Kong, Tokyo, Japan(airport); 1998 - Hong Kong, Shenzhen, China, Seoul, Korea (airport); 2000 - London, England, Paris, France; 2011 -Tuscany area of Italy including Pisa, Rome, Florence, Cinque Terre, Carara, Munich, Germany(airport); 2012- California car trip; Napa Valley and vinyards, San Francisco; 2013 - France; Paris, Avignon, many hilltowns of Provence area, Nice. Italy; five towns of Cinque Terre, Siena, many small towns in Tuscany.; 2014- National Parks car trip Utah/Arizona; Zion, Grand Canyon, Bryce, Arches, Canyonlands; 2015 - MA -Boston, (Our homestead in Kittery, Eliot, N. Berwick Maine), Portsmouth, Glouster, Salem, Plymouth, Provencetown, Lexington, Concord, Providence RI,

Immigrated to Canada in 1973 with wife, Nancy. Returned to US in 1986 with Nancy and two children, Heather and Katherine.

2002 - Michael started his own gallery/studio with wife Nancy in April 2002, Artists Gallerie, LLC. The gallery was opened in Cannon Beach, Oregon and represented twelve national and international artists, but after five years the falling economy forced it to close. The company continues as an Internet based company selling the paintings and sculptures of Michael throughout the world.

Professional Summary (2010) - A seasoned professional with 40 plus years experience in and solid understanding of strategic marketing and communications as a graphic designer/art director. Demonstrated ability to select, train and retain self-motivated, highly creative employees. Skilled in branding and marketing strategy, creation and execution of packaging, advertising, collateral, direct marketing, multimedia, environmental and interactive design, web site design and coding experience.

Accomplishments - Creative Director: - provide inspiration and motivation - insist on high quality standards - help make the company a positive, challenging place to work - provide mentorship - solutions provider - know and understand strategy and good creative - help the team develop smart solutions that are exciting and successful and that are on target and strategy - develop budgets and schedules...and meet them - work with production managers to seek the most effective solutions - keep current with technology, and help educate the team - strategy and marketing planning and concept development to insure a consistently excellent product brand and corporate image - media strategy, research and development of media plans. Graphic Designer / Art Director: - concepts - branding - design - graphics - exhibits - packaging - environmental and industrial graphics - print and TV advertising - art direction - marketing strategies - scheduling and production supervision - supervision of teams of writers, designers and production coordinators, art directed photographers and illustrators.

Computer Skills - PC and Macintosh platforms,

Professional Experience - MT Studios, Portland OR, Camas WA, & Cannon Beach, OR, 1993 - 2007 Owner; The Bernhardt Agency, Portland, OR, 1999 - 2001 Partner/V.P. Marketing/Creative Director; Tripwire Security Systems, Portland, OR, 1997-1999 Vice President Marketing ; Online Interactive Network Corporation, Portland, OR, 1997-1999 President ; Internet World Broadcasting Corp. Portland, OR, 1995-1997 VP/CD; Gilchrist & Associates, Inc., Portland, OR, 1986-1995 Co-Creative Director ; The 1986 World Exposition, Vancouver, Canada, 1984-1986 Sr. Graphic Designer ; McKim Advertising, Ltd., Vancouver, Canada, 1981-1984 Sr. Art Director ; Tieman & Friends, Ltd., Vancouver, Canada, 1976-1981 CEO/ CD; Cockfield & Brown, Vancouver, Canada, 1973-1976 Sr. Art Director

Education - Bachelor of Fine Arts in Advertising Design, 1972 Columbus College of Art & Design, Columbus, Ohio

Professional Accomplishments - Throughout the years I have won numerous international awards for my designs, print and TV ads.-These include: International Federation of Advertising Agencies, Creativity (New York), International Broadcasting Award (Hollywood), One Show (Vancouver), Graphic Designers of Canada, Art Directors Club (Toronto), Art Directors Club

(LA.), Printing Industries of America, Lithographers & Printing House Craftsmen. -Listed in "Sterling's Who's Who" (in the West).

-Focused on bringing the first Tripwire Intrusion Detection software product to market, including: corporate and product branding, product strategy, positioning, and lead generation programs. Co. was sold in 2011 when my stock was bought back.
-Designed initial web site, collateral, packaging, national ads, tradeshow booths, and international sales materials for Intrusion.com.
-Supervised the completion of art/programming and bringing to market the first full CD/Internet virtual game "Piggyland" in 1998.
-Designed original Wendy's hamburger chain logo and sign, in store marketing/menus/collateral and interior designs of stores 1971

About Michael Tieman the painter/sculptor/writer

As Michael Tieman sees it, "The role of an artist from the dawn of time has been as a visual storyteller. The stories my paintings and sculptures tell are ones of confidence, strength, passion, playful sophistication and the celebration of life."

Tieman has sketched and painted since childhood and has spent almost four decades as a working artist, both as a graphic designer and a fine artist. Following the encouragement of a friend and gallery owner, Michael recently expanded his talents into sculptures cast in bronze. Tieman's sculptures are unique in that they are a combination of traditional figurative sculpture and his Impressionistic painting style. "I create my bronze sculpture as a three-dimensional painting; texture is the impasto brushstroke, color is the play of light and shadows across the surfaces, and detail is the free style movement of the impressionist style. My ladies have a face with a chiseled jaw and high cheekbones, producing great shadows, and the athletic body and proud confidence of an Amazon warrior."

Sculpture "Courage" Donated to Summa Health System's Cancer Clinic in Akron, Ohio

On July 29, 2009 in Akron, Ohio, "Courage" a 36" tall bronze sculpture standing in tribute to those who have, who are, and who will fight Cancer is being donated to the new Summa Health System's Jean B. and Milton N. Cooper Cancer Center, Akron City Hospital, Akron, Ohio.

"Courage" is a limited-edition bronze and is the creation of Pacific Northwest sculptor and painter Michael Tieman. Cancer has hit home hard with Michael as his older sister Beverly Starr is a 13-year survivor of breast cancer, but his younger sister Connie Sue Drotos recently lost her battle with the disease.

The first 36" sculpture "Courage" in the limited edition has been purchased by Connie's husband of 25 years, John Drotos, and he is dedicating it to the Cancer clinic where Connie had treatments for six years. With the purchase of "Courage" there is also a cash donation of $5000 which goes to the Cancer Support Services department of the Cancer Center. Connie's family will be present at the dedication ceremonies in Akron July 29th and will include; husband John Drotos, her father LaVerne Tieman, sister Beverly Starr, brother Michael Tieman and his wife Nancy.

"Courage is dedicated to the women in my family who have battled breast cancer; my mother-in-law Jan Marshall (Muzzy), my aunt Pat Wetzel, my sister

Beverly Starr, and my younger sister Connie Sue Drotos, who after a courageous six-year battle with breast Cancer died on July 29, 2008." - Michael Tieman

The Dream

"In July of 2008, after a courageous six-year battle with breast cancer, my younger sister died, one week shy of her 50th birthday and the day before her 25th wedding anniversary," says Tieman. "Since then I have had the same re-occurring dream. I am on a scaffold built around a piece of white marble 15' tall, and I am carving a figure titled "Courage" - she has a bald head wrapped in cloth, piercing eyes, a firm jaw, taunt body and feet apart yet firmly planted. The people battling cancer have an inner strength and courage as they not only face an uncertain future, but they also have to take their treatments knowing it will make them feel worse. Week after week they look forward to this pain in the hope that eventually it will be gone. There is a look of courage in their eyes I cannot describe with words, it's not entirely defiant (Cancer will not win), but with grace with a quiet determination. That is the courage I need to capture.

In the dream I can only sense the figure; all I can really see is the head. I am carving with a chisel and hammer, no power tools, and I can see my scarred swollen hands and feel the pain in them as I continuously strike the chisel. Yet, there are many unanswered questions; why is the stone exactly 15' tall, why can't I see the entire figure? I am carving the stone by looking at a maquette of the piece but how do I know it is exactly 36" tall since I can only see the head?

The Promise

"People who saw me building the clay sculpture "Courage" November 8th and 9th during my demo at the 2008 Stormy Weather Arts Festival expressed a need for the piece to be seen and touched ... now", says Tieman." So I am casting "Courage" in a limited edition bronze available in three sizes, 9' high heroic size, 36" high and 18" high maquettes. With up to half of the sale price being donated directly to a local hospital or Cancer center's Cancer Support Services, the daily support and comfort services for those who come to these facilities to battle Cancer. The book "The Building of Courage" (published by Michael Tieman Publishing), which originally was to be made to accompany each sculpture will now be published in a larger edition for people who want the book, so they can be connected to "Courage". Because of the requests from survivors, Michael has also cast the butterfly necklace on "Courage" in silver and is being sold to raise funds for Cancer Support Services.

"Courage" Butterfly Necklace

"Butterflies were a favorite of my sister Connie; she said they brought her peace, freedom and hope. At the cemetery after her internment ceremony, her husband John who brought several Mylar butterfly balloons, walked to the little lake alone and released the butterflies as he had promised her. We silently watched as the wind suddenly came up and the butterflies took flight.

Slowly they rose into the air and maneuvered themselves up and around the clouds, staying in sight and staying in the clear blue sky. Up and up they drifted, slowly they left our sight and sailed to the heavens. So of course, I had to have a butterfly on 'Courage'."

Books Written, Designed, and or Published By Michael Tieman Publishing:
Behind the Bronze - My Sculpture- (paperback) Author, artist: Michael Tieman

Behind the Paint - New England 2015- (paperback) Author, artist: Michael Tieman

Behind the Paint - National Parks 2014- (paperback) Author, artist: Michael Tieman

Behind the Paint - France & Italy 2013 - (paperback) Author, artist: Michael Tieman

Behind the Paint - Italy 2011 - (paperback) Author, artist: Michael Tieman

The Building of "Courage" - (hardcover and paperback) Author: Michael Tieman

The Poet - (hardcover) Author: David Sweet

My Glengarry - (hardcover) Author: Dr. F. James Marshall

1/31/2016

Today found sources from the NEHS and Mayflower publications proving "SOURCES" that my father's mother's mother (SOUTH) is a direct line to the Fuller and Lathrop families that came over on the Mayflower in 1620. I also have a copy of the Mayflower Descendants Application approved for a Fuller, proving our lineage.

Noted events in his life were:

• He was described as White Male, Blue Eyes, Brown Hair.
• He was Methodist.
• He was educated at Grad. North High School on 20 Jun 1968 in Columbus, Franklin, Ohio, USA.
• He worked as a Graphic Designer/artist between 1969 and 2012 in Ohio/British Columbia/Washington/Oregon.
• He graduated from BFA, Columbus College of Art & Design on 20 Jun 1972 in Columbus, Franklin, Ohio, USA.
• He emigrated on 14 Jan 1974 from Vancouver, British Columbia, Canada.
• He immigrated on 20 Aug 1986 to Portland, Clackamas, Oregon, USA.
• He retired on 1 Jan 2014 in Cannon Beach, Clatsop, Oregon, USA.
• He was a member of Sons of the American Revolution Became National Member #196909 on 1 Dec 2015 in Lewis & Clark Chapter, Beaverton, Washington, OR, USA.

Michael married **Nancy Lee MARSHALL** [2] [82,150, 152,155,156,160,161,162,163,164,165,166,167,168,169,170] [MRIN: 1], daughter of **Dr. Frederick James MARSHALL** [2223] [82,152,164,165,171,172,173,174,175,176,177,178,179,180,181] and **Janet Alma ORMANDY** [2224], [82,149,152,164,165,173,176,180,182,183] on 16 Jun 1972 in Columbus, Franklin, Ohio, USA.[150] Nancy was born on 5 Mar 1952 in Vancouver, British Columbia, Canada.[161] Another name for Nancy is Nana.

Noted events in her life were:

• EDUC: BS/MS.
• She was naturalized in Portland, Clackamas, Oregon, USA.[163]

- She was Protestant.
- She was educated at Ohio State - Dental Hygiene Degree in 1973 in Columbus, Franklin, Ohio, USA.
- She worked as a Dental Hygienist/Mental Health Counselor between 1973 and 2011 in Ohio/British Columbia/Washington/Oregon.
- She emigrated on 14 Jan 1974 from Vancouver, British Columbia, Canada.
- She immigrated on 20 Aug 1986 to Portland, Clackamas, Oregon, USA.
- She graduated from Portland State University, BS & MS in 1992 in Portland, Clackamas, Oregon, USA.

7-**Heather Anne TIEMAN [920]**[82,144,152,184,185] was born on 17 May 1976 in North Vancouver, British Columbia, Canada[184] and was baptized in 1976 in North Vancouver, British Columbia, Canada.

Noted events in her life were:

- She was Lutherin.
- She immigrated on 20 Aug 1986 to Portland, Clackamas, Oregon, USA.
- She was educated at Lake Oswego High School in 1994 in Lake Oswego, Clackamas, Oregon, USA.
- She graduated from University of Idaho, BSEd in 1998 in Moscow, Latah, Idaho, USA.
- She was naturalized in 2010 in Portland, Clackamas, Oregon, USA.

Heather married **Phillip ERWIN** [921][152,185,186] [MRIN: 326], son of **Sidney Fred ERWIN** [1024][185] and **Judith Lee BENSCOTER** [1023],[185] on 22 Jun 1996 in Lake Oswego, Clackamas, Oregon, USA. Phillip was born on 30 May 1971 in Boise, Ada, Idaho, USA.

Noted events in his life were:

- EDUC: University of Idaho, BCS.
- He graduated from BS in Moscow, Latah, Idaho, USA.
- He worked as an Oracle, Computer Software Engineer in Portland, Clackamas, Oregon, USA.
- He was Lutherin.
- He was baptized in 1972 in Bruneau, Owyhee, Idaho, USA.

8-Riley James ERWIN [1197][152,185,186] was born on 27 Sep 1999 in Portland, Clackamas, Oregon, USA and was baptized in 2000 in Portland, Clackamas, Oregon, USA.

8-Jackson Davis ERWIN [3091][152,186] was born on 26 Jul 2005 in Portland, Clackamas, Oregon, USA and was baptized in Oct 2005 in Portland, Clackamas, Oregon, USA.

7-Katherine Jane TIEMAN [919][82,144,152,187,188,189,190] was born on 25 Jun 1979 in North Vancouver, British Columbia, Canada.

Noted events in her life were:

• She was baptized on 7 Oct 1979 in Lake Oswego, Clackamas, Oregon, USA.
• She immigrated on 20 Aug 1986 to Portland, Clackamas, Oregon, USA.
• She was educated at Lake Oswego, Clackamas, Oregon, USA in Jun 1997 in Lake Oswego High School.
• EDUC: Portland Stae University &Washington State University, and Western, in 2004, in Portland, Clackamas, Oregon, USA.
• She graduated from Western Culinary Institute - Cordon Bleu in 2004 in Portland, Clackamas, Oregon, USA.
• She worked as an Also Teacher, Kindercare Daycare, Cordon Bleu Pastry Chef in 2004 in Portland, Clackamas, Oregon, USA.

2004

Katherine married **Shawn SCHULBERG** [3015][191] [MRIN: 325], son of _____ **SCHULBERG** [4624], on 4 Nov 2000 in Portland, Clackamas, Oregon, USA. The marriage ended in divorce.

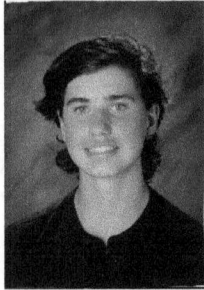

8-**Connor Shamas TIEMAN-WOODWARD [3086]**[152,191] was born on 28 Oct 2002 in Portland, Clackamas, Oregon, USA.

Katherine next married **Samuel Patrick WOODWARD** [3089][82,152,188,189] [MRIN: 1078], son of **Gary Milton WOODWARD** [3189][189,192] and **(Rosa) Yung-Mei KAO** [3190],[189] on 25 Jul 2009 in Portland, Clackamas, Oregon, USA.[188] Samuel was born on 16 Sep 1975 in T'ai-Pei, Taiwan.

8-**Alexis Jean TIEMAN-WOODWARD [3090]**[152,191] was born on 12 Nov 2006 in Portland, Clackamas, Oregon, USA.

8-**Owen Richard TIEMAN-WOODWARD [3268]**[191] was born on 18 Feb 2010 in Portland, Clackamas, Oregon, USA.[191]

6-**Constance Sue TIEMAN [851]**[70,71,82,116,193,194] was born on 5 Aug 1958 in Freeport, Stephenson, Illinois, USA, died on 29 Jul 2008 in Akron, Summit, Ohio, USA at age 49, and was buried on 2 Aug 2008 in Stow, Summit, Ohio, USA. The cause of her death was Breast Cancer.

General Notes: Memories: Sister, Beverly Dianne Tieman Starr, 2009

Constance Sue was born Aug. 5, 1958 and was a total surprise. Mom thought she had the flu for months before seeing a doctor and finding out she was pregnant. (I was 11 ½ yrs. older than her and Connie was 11 1/2 yrs. older than Amy.) I was so excited when I was told the news and I couldn't wait to tell my friend Sylvia. I was so disappointed when I said, "guess what?" and she said, 'Your mom's going to have a baby". Did everyone know but me? I was crushed. Connie Sue had dark curly hair and we thought she looked like dad. She adored Michael as he was 8 yrs. older and we all spoiled her rotten. Mom said it was like living a rerun and whatever Connie did, it had been done before. She loved her Felix the cat, any kind of dog, her panda bear and her dolls. She was especially crazy about the TV show "Surfside Six" and wore the Capri pants and striped tee shirt like Troy Donahue all the time when she was around 2. She became afraid of sleeping in her crib very early on, so we had to share a room and in one house, the bed, so she could sleep. She was in kindergarten when I left home for nurses' training, so we really didn't grow up together. Mom finally learned to drive a car after Connie was born as she needed to get back and forth to work and the town was bigger and not that easy to get around by bus or walking like she was used to. August 1971 Michael was coming to Rochester from Columbus, and Mom and Dad and Connie were coming from MA. for his 21st birthday and we were all in a car accident. Mom and I were hurt the worst and were in the hospital for awhile. I had surgery on my face and she had a broken pelvis. She saved Amy by pushing her in between the seats when the car was coming at us. Connie and Amy were taken care of by our friends, Bev and Ed Huber. Dad, Michael and Bill sort of looked after each other. Thelma came from Iowa after everyone else left to help until I was getting around and seeing better. Connie had graduated from high school and gone to work at a bank. She took night courses that they paid for while she lived at home and eventually became an audit supervisor. She was at the bank 30 years. She met John Drotos in 1982 at a young adults meeting at church and they were married in Akron July 29, 1983. He had a daughter, Sarah, from him first marriage and she was the cutest little blonde! She has the same birthday as Nicole, only 5 years younger. In the 1980s Mom got interested in hand sewing quilts for us. She sat on the front porch at the quilting loom for years in Akron making her kids and grandkids quilts even after her hip replacement. She made Nicole a purple and pink "Tumbling Blocks" quilt, Amy a lavender and white State Flower embroidered quilt and me a green "Lone Star" quilt when we moved to Texas. She later made other ones for the girls' weddings. Connie always made any new baby in the family an embroidered crib quilt, so the quilting tradition continued for years. Connie had been diagnosed with breast cancer in Oct. 2002 and had one radiation treatment left when mom died. Dad still says that Connie's cancer was very hard for mom to come to terms with and that made her sicker. On May 29, 2004 dad, Connie and John traveled to Washington, D.C. for the dedication of the WW II Memorial built between the Lincoln Memorial and the Washington Monument. Amy had registered her Grandpa to be among the16 million WWI veteran honorees with their names placed within the memorial and on the web site www.wwiimemorial.com On July 29, 2008 my dear, kind, smart sister Connie Sue lost her 6-year battle with breast cancer. She had all the radiation and chemo a human can have, and it still took her. It was the day before her 25th wedding anniversary and a week before her 50th birthday. She had told us in Feb. that there was nothing more they could do for her and she had 6 months. Michael and I decided it was important to have a family reunion in Dallas in March while she was still able to travel. He and Nancy came from Oregon, Connie, John and dad came from Ohio, and she was able to be with us and her dear nieces and great niece and nephew and to meet Blake. She adored the little kids and was always a special aunt to Amy and Nicole. We laughed, played games, ate good food, and hugged and loved each other a lot. She enjoyed the spring flowers at the Dallas Arboretum and I polished her nails and trimmed her hair and we played Scrabble. She kept saying it was the sister things we never got to do before. She never cried even when those of us around her were. Hugging everyone goodbye at the airport was one of the hardest things I've ever done; knowing it was a final goodby. We all suddenly knew what it meant to want more time together Michael had silver bracelets made for each of us with "love never fails" on the outside and our initials on the inside. I had them made for Amy and Nicole and we all wear them when we feel especially close to Connie. She went on hospice in April and they kept her comfortable and active up until a week before she suddenly declined. It was just the 6 months. I was lucky enough to get to Ohio from Dallas in time to spend her last 12 hrs. with her. She was unconscious, but the experts say the person knows we were there loving them to the end. Michael was en route from Oregon, and he had to hear my phone message when he changed planes in Chicago that she was gone. I felt terrible leaving him that message he would receive all alone. Connie took one last breath, two tears rolled down her face, and she was at peace. Dad was holding her hand, and John and I were in the room with them.

Connie: You were so brave and optimistic and supportive of the rest of us. The end came while I was there for which I am grateful. I had already grieved all the while you were sick and the tears I shed now are of relief from your pain and struggle. In time, I hope peace will replace my heartache. I miss you every day and see you in every butterfly. We were far apart in years and always in miles because I never lived near you after I left for nurses' training. Our lives too were different as I had children and grandchildren and you had a career. I married young and divorced after 23 years and you married at 25 and lived with John Drotos, the love of your life for 25 years. You loved his daughter, Sarah, as your own. Sadly, we did share the experience of having breast cancer, but yours was more aggressive. John is lost without you and tries his best to keep busy and get involved in new things. It has only been 5 months since you left as I write this, so our pain is still fresh. He has been down to Texas to visit all of us and get hugs he badly needed, and we are happy to provide. Sarah is getting married this year and that would have made you so happy. John says he will always be married to you and he visits you often at the cemetery. You were lucky to find a man to love you like that. Some of us never will. Dad is incredibly sad and depressed. He said he was done when he lost you, "his rock". I can't imagine losing a wife of 50 years and then your youngest child of 50 years. No man should have to endure that. Michael has been dealing with his grief in an artistic way. He said you came to him in a dream on your birthday and inspired him to do a sculpture. He named her "Courage" which is such a loving and accurate tribute to you. He hopes there will be many of her in public places and that she can give people a connection and comfort. John has purchased the first one for the cancer center in Akron in your memory and there will be a book telling the journey of "Courage". You would be so proud; but then you guided him to do this.

Had three bouts with breast cancer, which finally took her life in 2008.

T500-19
Connie Drotos (Tieman) passed away July 29, 2008 of cancer. Born in Freeport, Il Connie has been a Stow resident since 1990. She graduated from Ellet High School, had an associate degree from the University of Akron, where she was active in the sorority Gamma Beta, and worked at First Merit for 29 years. She was a devoted member of the First United Methodist Church of Akron, UMW, Keystone Class and served on many committees. Connie was the treasurer of the Lighthouse of Hope Mission for several years. Her favorite activity was gardening, and she loved the summer months in Ohio. She and John traveled many miles together exploring Ohio. Connie was preceded in death by her mother, Doris and grandparents. She is survived by by a loving husband John and father Verne, stepdaughter Sarah, sister Beverly of Texas, brother Michael (Nancy) of Oregon, 16 nieces and nephews, 19 great nieces and nephews. Memorial services will be Saturday, August 2 at 11:00 am with receiving of friends from 4:00 - 8:00 pm Friday, August 1 at First United Methodist Church, 263 E. Mill Street, Akron, OH 44308. In lieu of flowers, donations can be made to the First United Methodist Church Free Lunch, American Cancer Society or Lighthouse of Hope Mission.

Noted events in her life were:

• She worked as a Bank Examiner/ Bank Vice President.
• She was Methodist.

Constance married **John DROTOS** [850][193,194,195] [MRIN: 294], son of **Louis DROTOS Jr.** [852][194,195] and **Margaret Elizabeth SIMON** [853],[194,195] on 30 Jul 1983 in Akron, Summit, Ohio, USA. John was born on 27 Mar 1954.

4-Thelma Louisa TIEMAN [849] [2,19,30,36,37,38,40,46,51,57,67,196,197] was born on 12 Sep 1907 in Keokuk, Lee, Iowa, USA, died on 18 Sep 1997 in Keokuk, Lee, Iowa, USA at age 90, and was buried on 22 Sep in Keokuk, Lee, Iowa, USA.

General Notes: Memories: Great Grand-Daughter, Beverly Dianne Tieman Starr, 2009

Our Great Aunts Maggie (11/28/12-6/02/07) and Thelma (09/12/07-09/18/97) Tieman lived with my Great Grandmother Anna (Sommer) Tieman (5/01/1876-06/15/63) near us at 1628 Palean St.

I remember Great Grandma's beautiful long white hair that Maggie did up in a braided coiled bun for her. She sure looked like the German housewife then! (Great Grandma was born in Dresden, Germany). In nice weather Maggie would wash the hair and Great Grandma would sit in the backyard in the sun and Maggie would brush and brush it until it was almost dry and then she would braid it up for the week.

Michael and I spent many Saturdays with them and we learned how to make the yummy cinnamon/sugar coffee cake on the big black wood stove in their kitchen. It would rise overnight and be baked for Sunday breakfast the next morning. They made soap from lye and left-over soap scraps and they had the prettiest china and vases in their dining room. Years later I got the Havilland china Thelma collected over the years and still cherish it and use it.

Their upstairs ceiling also slanted and that's where Maggie and Thelma had their bedrooms. The highlight of the house was the powder room off of the kitchen for Great Grandma as her room was downstairs. No one had powder a room in those days! The house was built by Henry Tieman who was a carpenter by trade. The day before his wedding to Anna, he accidentally sliced off 3 fingers of his left hand with a circular saw. He was still able to build the house and work as a carpenter, but for an unnamed reason he was sent to an institution where he later died in his 50's.

Thelma had to quit school as a teenager and become the breadwinner.

Their backyard was surrounded with flower and vegetable beds and we spent many lazy summer days in the shade or in the coolness of the house with the window shades down keeping out the heat.

Maggie's hobby was photography and she took black and white portrait poses of us all the time.

Great Grandma's tradition for her May 1st birthday was to have breakfast on the screened porch no matter what the weather. There were many May Days that we wore our winter coats and mittens for breakfast in Iowa! We made May baskets with flowers for her and her neighbors and hung them on their front doors as a surprise. Michael and I "borrowed" whatever flowers in gardens we could find to do this. The worst part of their house was the cellar. There was a trap door in the floor of the screen porch off the kitchen and when it was lifted up the cellar steps went down to the washer and dryer (eventually) and where their canned goods were stored. It had a dirt floor and was always creepy to me. They had a wringer washer on that porch before the electric appliances and Michael and I hung clothes from the clothesline like we did at home.

Great Grandma had a brother Emil and a sister Myrtle Wilson that lived in Keokuk. Maggie or Thelma would take Michael and I to visit them from time to time and they spooked me. Emil owned a broom factory and it was dark inside and smelled funny. It had several sets of stairs up to the next level. He always wore bib overalls and seemed to silently just appear from nowhere. It was like a scary movie set (and I didn't even know what that was then). I thought for years that the line in the Lord's Prayer we said in church every Sunday was "and deliver us from Emil". He also made homemade wine from his vineyards across the street from the broom factory. Mom would give a little of his wine if we had a cough that wouldn't go away. Dad said Emil sold the vineyards to Thelma and Maggie after he retired.

Myrtle was a widow that always spoke in a whisper, was very, very thin, always had her window shades drawn and always wore cotton hose with garters. She had run a florist with her husband when he was alive. We would just sit and be bored while Maggie or Thelma talked to her and then leave. They usually took her food of some kind, so they must have been looking after her. She also had a brother, George, who lived in California for years. Maggie went out there to live with him when she went to college for 2 years at UCLA.

Neither Thelma nor Maggie ever married, and they worked as secretaries at Electro Metals Co. their entire career. Thelma was executive secretary to the president of the company. They traveled to Mexico and Europe a couple of times and were very frugal, having grown up in the depression and loosing their father at a young age. I remember Thelma having a boyfriend at one time. He was around for quite a while, but I remember mom saying that Maggie and their mom "ran him off" because they needed her to take care of them. Who knows what the true story was?

Great Grandma died June 1962 at the age of 86. I have her wedding china from Bavaria, her engagement pocket watch engraved and dated 1901 from Henry (Maggie's note says she did not like rings). I also have the twin size quilt she made and left for me for my high school graduation. Amy has her monogrammed silverware. Grandma Alta died in June and in July Maggie and Thelma took Michael and I on my "pre-high school graduation" trip to Colorado. We drove out there in their 1959 gray Plymouth at about 40 MPH. When it was Thelma's turn to drive, Maggie would watch the speedometer and often lean up over the back seat and tell her to slow down. Thelma became "deaf" during most of this back seat driving. I don't remember how many days it must have taken us to get there at that speed on 2 lane roads, but I do remember the corn fields in Iowa and the wheat fields in Kansas that never ended. My brain goes numb now just thinking about it. Part of our trip we met and stayed with Mrs. Beck in Evergreen, CO. She had worked for our dad in Akron. She and her husband had retired there, and it was way up in the mountains with no one around them. It was beautiful. I loved driving along the roads beside the Colorado River running along beside us. We stayed overnight at Estes State Park on the Continental Divide where there was still snow on the ground and we made snowballs. We took a bus ride around the area and saw tufted black squirrels and a black bear beside the road. We also went to the Garden of the Gods Amphitheater where Maggie bemoaned the fact she would miss the Beatles performing there later in the summer. She was crazy about the Beatles (not my favorite) and liked the play/movie "Jesus Christ Superstar" music. Colorado Springs was beautiful, and the Air Force Academy and Cathedral were fantastic. We spent time in downtown Denver but missed Pike's Peak because the car wouldn't have made it up there! It was a memorable trip with them and I know we all had fun.

August 1971 Michael was coming to Rochester from Columbus, and Mom and Dad and Connie were coming from MA. for his 21st birthday and we were all in a car accident. Mom and I were hurt the worst and were in the hospital for awhile. I had surgery on my face and she had a broken pelvis. She saved Amy by pushing her in between the seats when the car was coming at us. Connie and Amy were taken care of by our friends, Bev and Ed Huber. Dad, Michael and Bill sort of looked after each other. Thelma came from Iowa after everyone else left to help until I was getting around and seeing better. I needed to get the sight in my left eye back to normal, so Thelma had me make a Christmas tree skirt with felt cutouts and lots of breads and sequins sewn on. It helped my double vision improve and it became a tradition of me making tree skirts for family and friends for years to come. Thelma was so cute with Amy. She had never been around children and a 2-yr. old is a challenge at best. She took Amy up to the nearby plaza one day in the stroller and as they checked out, the cashier asked Thelma if she was going to pay for the deodorant in the stroller. It seems Amy had put two cans down beside her as they went down an aisle. Thelma thought that was so funny when she told us.

T500-11 Thelma L. Tieman 1907-1997

Thelma Louisa Tieman, 90, of Keokuk, died Thursday, September 18, 1997 at the Keokuk Area Hospital.

She was born September 12, 1907 in Keokuk, IA, the daughter of Henry H. and Anna Sommer Tieman.

She spent her entire life in Keokuk, graduating from Keokuk High School in 1925. She began employment in 1927 Keokuk Electro Metals Company which later merged with Vanadium Corporation from which she retired in October 1967.

She was a life long member of St. Paul United Church of Christ in Keokuk, where she was babtised, confirmed, taught Sunday School and served two terms on the consistory. She also attended Baker Memorial Chapel Sunday afternoon Bible Class until its closure.

Survivors include one sister, Magdalene Tieman of Keokuk, IA., one nephew Malcolm L. Tieman and his wife Doris Morrill Tieman of Cuyahoga Falls, Ohio, one great-nephew, Michael Tieman of Lake Oswego, Oregon, two great-nieces, Beverly Tieman Starr of Webster, NY, and Connie Tieman Drotos, of Stow, Ohio, four great-great nieces, a great-great great nephew and severa; cousins.

She was preceded in death by her parents and one brother, Malcolm.
Memorials may be made to the Lee County American Cancer Society.

Noted events in her life were:

• EDUC: Keokuk High School, 1925.
• She worked as an Exec. Secretery 1927 Keokuk Electro Metals Co. /Oct. 1967.
• She was St. Paul United Church of Christ.

4-Magdalene TIEMAN [848][2,19,30,36,37,46,51,57] was born on 28 Nov 1912 in Keokuk, Lee, Iowa, USA and died on 2 Jun 2007 in Keokuk, Lee, Iowa, USA at age 94.

General Notes: Memories: Great Grand-Daughter, Beverly Dianne Tieman Starr, 2009

Our Great Aunts Maggie (11/28/12-6/02/07) and Thelma (09/12/07-09/18/97) Tieman lived with my Great Grandmother Anna (Sommer) Tieman (5/01/1876-06/15/63) near us at 1628 Palean St.

I remember Great Grandma's beautiful long white hair that Maggie did up in a braided coiled bun for her. She sure looked like the German housewife then! (Great Grandma was born in Dresden, Germany). In nice weather Maggie would wash the hair and Great Grandma would sit in the backyard in the sun and Maggie would brush and brush it until it was almost dry and then she would braid it up for the week.

Michael and I spent many Saturdays with them and we learned how to make the yummy cinnamon/sugar coffee cake on the big black wood stove in their kitchen. It would rise overnight and be baked for Sunday breakfast the next morning. They made soap from lye and left-over soap scraps and they had the prettiest china and vases in their dining room. Years later I got the Havilland china Thelma collected over the years and still cherish it and use it.

Their upstairs ceiling also slanted and that's where Maggie and Thelma had their bedrooms. The highlight of the house was the powder room off of the kitchen for Great Grandma as her room was downstairs. No one had powder a room in those days! The house was built by Henry Tieman who was a carpenter by trade. The day before his wedding to Anna, he accidentally sliced off 3 fingers of his left hand with a circular saw. He was still able to build the house and work as a carpenter, but for an unnamed reason he was sent to an institution where he later died in his 50's.

Thelma had to quit school as a teenager and become the breadwinner.

Their backyard was surrounded with flower and vegetable beds and we spent many lazy summer days in the shade or in the coolness of the house with the window shades down keeping out the heat.

Maggie's hobby was photography and she took black and white portrait poses of us all the time.

Great Grandma's tradition for her May 1st birthday was to have breakfast on the screened porch no matter what the weather. There were many May Days that we wore our winter coats and mittens for breakfast in Iowa! We made May baskets with flowers for her and her neighbors and hung them on their front doors as a surprise. Michael and I "borrowed" whatever flowers in gardens we could find to do this. The worst part of their house was the cellar. There was a trap door in the floor of the screen porch off the kitchen and when it was lifted up the cellar steps went down to the washer and dryer (eventually) and where their canned goods were stored. It had a dirt floor and was always creepy to me. They had a wringer washer on that porch before the electric appliances and Michael and I hung clothes from the clothesline like we did at home.

Great Grandma had a brother Emil and a sister Myrtle Wilson that lived in Keokuk. Maggie or Thelma would take Michael and I to visit them from time to time and they spooked me. Emil owned a broom factory and it was dark inside and smelled funny. It had several sets of stairs up to the next level. He always wore bib overalls and seemed to silently just appear from nowhere. It was like a scary movie set (and I didn't even know what that was then). I thought for years that the line in the Lord's Prayer we said in church every Sunday was "and deliver us from Emil". He also made homemade wine from his vineyards across the street from the broom factory. Mom would give a little of his wine if we had a cough that wouldn't go away. Dad said Emil sold the vineyards to Thelma and Maggie after he retired.

Myrtle was a widow that always spoke in a whisper, was very, very thin, always had her window shades drawn and always wore cotton hose with garters. She had run a florist with her husband when he was alive. We would just sit and be bored while Maggie or Thelma talked to her and then leave. They usually took her food of some kind, so they must have been looking after her. She also had a brother, George, who lived in California for years. Maggie went out there to live with him when she went to college for 2 years at UCLA.

Neither Thelma nor Maggie ever married, and they worked as secretaries at Electro Metals Co. their entire career. Thelma was executive secretary to the president of the company. They traveled to Mexico and Europe a couple of times and were very frugal, having grown up in the depression and loosing their father at a young age. I remember Thelma having a boyfriend at one time. He was around for quite a while, but I remember mom saying that Maggie and their mom "ran him off" because they needed her to take care of them. Who knows what the true story was?

Great Grandma died June 1962 at the age of 86. I have her wedding china from Bavaria, her engagement pocket watch engraved and dated 1901 from Henry (Maggie's note says she did not like rings). I also have the twin size quilt she made and left for me for my high school graduation. Amy has her monogrammed silverware. Grandma Alta died in June and in July Maggie and Thelma took Michael and I on my "pre-high school graduation" trip to Colorado. We drove out there in their 1959 gray Plymouth at about 40 MPH. When it was Thelma's turn to drive, Maggie would watch the speedometer and often lean up over the back seat and tell her to slow down. Thelma became "deaf" during most of this back seat driving. I don't remember how many days it must have taken us to get there at that speed on 2 lane roads, but I do remember the corn fields in Iowa and the wheat fields in Kansas that never ended. My brain goes numb now just thinking about it. Part of our trip we met and stayed with Mrs. Beck in Evergreen, CO. She had worked for our dad in Akron. She and her husband had retired there, and it was way up in the mountains with no one around them. It was beautiful. I loved driving along the roads beside the Colorado River running along beside us. We stayed overnight at Estes State Park on the Continental Divide where there was still snow on the ground and we made snowballs. We took a bus ride around the area and saw tufted black squirrels and a black bear beside the road. We also went to the Garden of the Gods Amphitheater where Maggie bemoaned the fact she would miss the Beatles performing there later in the summer. She was crazy about the Beatles (not my favorite) and liked the play/movie "Jesus Christ Superstar" music. Colorado Springs was beautiful, and the Air Force Academy and Cathedral were fantastic. We spent time in downtown Denver but missed Pike's Peak because the car wouldn't have made it up there! It was a memorable trip with them and I know we all had fun.

August 1971 Michael was coming to Rochester from Columbus, and Mom and Dad and Connie were coming from MA. for his 21st birthday and we were all in a car accident. Mom and I were hurt the worst and were in the hospital for awhile. I had surgery on my face and she had a broken pelvis. She saved Amy by pushing her in between the seats when the car was coming at us. Connie and Amy were taken care of by our friends, Bev and Ed Huber. Dad, Michael and Bill sort of looked after each other. Thelma came from Iowa after everyone else left to help until I was getting around and seeing better. I needed to get the sight in my left eye back to normal, so Thelma had me make a Christmas tree skirt with felt cutouts and lots of breads and sequins sewn on. It helped my double vision improve and it became a tradition of me making tree skirts for family and friends for years to come. Thelma was so cute with Amy. She had never been around children and a 2-yr. old is a challenge at best. She took Amy up to the nearby plaza one day in the stroller and as they checked out, the cashier asked Thelma if she was going to pay for the deodorant in the stroller. It seems Amy had put two cans down beside her as they went down an aisle. Thelma thought that was so funny when she told us.

T500-9

An Important July for the Tiemans July of this year held special significance for Magdalene & Thelma Tieman as it was in July 1881 that their grandparents, Clemens & Rosamonde Sommer and children came to Keokuk from Dresden, Germany. They attended St. Paul Church at that time and this family affiliation has been constant to date. Anna Sommer then age 5 - married Henry Tieman in 1902. They became parents of Malcolm, Thelma and Magdalene.

Noted events in her life were:

- EDUC: Keokuk High School.
- She worked as an Exec Sec.
- She was St. Paul United Church of Christ.

3-**Magdalena Christine "Martha" TIEMANN [802]**[2,15,17,22,34] was born on 29 Apr 1870 in Benton Township, Des Moines, Iowa, USA and died on 17 Feb 1955 in Burlington, Kane, Illinois, USA at age 84.

General Notes: **T500-1** "History of William Tiemann Family"

Magdalene C. was born April 29, 1870 and died Feb. 17, 1955. She married Fred Wuellner of Burlington. He was born March 2, 1860 in Minden, Westphalia, Germany and came to this country and Des Moines County in 1871. He died Sep. 17, 1936. They had six children: Frank, Matilda, Alvin, Mildred, Reuben and Paul (twins). They lived in Burlington.

T500-2

Correspondence from Thelma Tieman in a letter dated 1989

First auto mechanic in Burlington, becoming very prosperous. They built a home on the outskirts of town and in time bought a lot of land adjoining it. As each child was married, he built or bought a home for them. Eventually an airport was built behind Alvins place, and in time sold to airport.

Magdalena married **Fred WUELLNER** [801][2,33,34] [MRIN: 280], son of
_____ **WUELLNER** [4612]. Fred was born on 2 Mar 1860 in Minden,
Westphalia, Germany and died on 17 Sep 1936 at age 76.

4-Frank WUELLNER [814].[2]

4-Matilda WUELLNER [813].[2]

4-Alvin WUELLNER [812].[2]

4-Mildred WUELLNER [806].[2]

General Notes: **T500-2** Correspondence from Thelma Tieman in a letter dated
1989

Herbert and Mildred Wuellner (Jackson ?) have two sons - Glenn teaches in
Rochester, Minnesota and is the only one in the Tieman family I know of who
has a Doctorate. (He and his wife have two sons, both in college. Neal, the other
son, according to his mother, was not a good student. He was a stockman in a
factory in Minneapolis, where they lived. He remained a bachelor, which irked
his mother until the day she died. He wanted to retire at age 45 but Mildred said,
"No you are not going to sit at home all day and watch television." But his father
is very glad to have him at home now that he is a semi-invalid, and Mildred is no
longer with them.

Mildred married **Herbert JACOBSON** [805][34] [MRIN: 281], son of
_____ **JACOBSON** [4620].

5-Glenn JACOBSON [808].[34]

General Notes: T500-2 Correspondence from Thelma Tieman in a letter dated
1989

Herbert and Mildred Wuellner (Jackson ?) have two sons - Glenn teaches in
Rochester, Minnesota and is the only one in the Tieman family I know of who
has a Doctorate. (He and his wife have two sons, both in college. Neal, the other
son, according to his mother, was not a good student. He was a stockman in a
factory in Minneapolis, where they lived. He remained a bachelor, which irked
his mother until the day she died. He wanted to retire at age 45 but Mildred said,
"No you are not going to sit at home all day and watch television." But his father
is very glad to have him at home now that he is a semi-invalid, and Mildred is no
longer with them.

Noted events in his life were:

• EDUC: Phd.
• He worked as a Teacher In Rochester, Minn.

Glenn married _____ **UNKNOWN** [809] [MRIN: 282], daughter of
_____ _____ and _____ _____.

6--- JACOBSON [811].

6---- JACOBSON [810].

5-Neal JACOBSON [807].[34]

General Notes: T500-2 Correspondence from Thelma Tieman in a letter dated
1989

Herbert and Mildred Wuellner (Jackson ?) have two sons - Glenn teaches in
Rochester, Minnesota and is the only one in the Tieman family I know of who
has a Doctorate. (He and his wife have two sons, both in college. Neal, the other
son, according to his mother, was not a good student. He was a stockman in a
factory in Minneapolis, where they lived. He remained a bachelor, which irked
his mother until the day she died. He wanted to retire at age 45 but Mildred said,
"No you are not going to sit at home all day and watch television." But his father
is very glad to have him at home now that he is a semi-invalid, and Mildred is no
longer with them.

Noted events in his life were:

• He worked as a Stockman In Factory.

4-Reuben WUELLNER [804].[2]

Noted events in his life were:

• He worked as a Furrier.

4-Paul WUELLNER [803].[2]

Noted events in his life were:

• He worked as a Telephone Co.

3-Ernst H. Wilhelm TIEMANN [815][2,15,17,22,30,31,198] was born on 10 Jun 1873 in Benton Township, Des Moines, Iowa, USA and died on 10 Mar 1914 at age 40.

General Notes: **T500-1** "History of William Tiemann Family"
     E. William was born June 10, 1873 and died March 10, 1914. He married Anna Kampmeier, born March 7, 1876, and died Oct. 13, 1969. They had one son Arthur (died in a railroad accident when quite young). William remained on the family farm.

Ernst married **Anna KAMPMEIER** [816][2,30,33,34,198] [MRIN: 283], daughter of _____ **KAMPMEIER** [4613]. Anna was born on 7 Mar 1876 and died on 13 Oct 1969 at age 93.

4-Arthur TIEMANN [817][2,34,198] was born in 1905 and died in 1934 at age 29.

General Notes: **T500-2** Thelma Tieman Corresp. 1989
     Arthur was killed in a train when a very young boy. Aunt Anna lived to be 93 (widowed at 39). She said had she been the marrying kind she would still be a widow because all the young men she knew as a girl preceded her in death. When the Tieman family farm was for sale, she bought it and lived on the earnings for many, many years.

3-Ernst H. Samuel TIEMANN [799][2,15,17,22,34,199] was born on 5 Jan 1876 in Benton Township, Des Moines, Iowa, USA and died on 2 Apr 1930 at age 54.

General Notes: **T500-1**
Organist for the Latty Church.

T500-2
Correspondence from Thelma Tieman in a letter dated 1989

Uncle Sam was not able to provide for his family as his wife thought was necessary, so she divorced him and married a well-to-do man, taking all the children with her.

Ernst married **Ida ZACHMEYER** [800][2,33] [MRIN: 279], daughter of _____ **ZACHMEYER** [4614].

4-Walter TIEMANN [3043].[2]

4-Ruth Marie TIEMANN [3044][2,199] was born in 1909 and died in 2002 at age 93.

4-Helen TIEMANN [3045].[2]

4-Warren TIEMANN [3046].[2]

4-Laura TIEMANN [3047].[2]

4-Richard Frederick TIEMANN [3048][2,199] was born in 1916 and died in 1999 at age 83.

4-Edith Armeda TIEMANN [3049][2] was born in 1919 and died in 2008 at age 89.

Edith married _____ **WEYRICK** [3814][199] [MRIN: 1358], son of _____ **WEYRICK** [4621].

4-Cecil Samuel TIEMANN [3050][2,199] was born in 1921 and died in 2003 at age 82.

3-Emilie Louise TIEMANN [794][2,17,22,30,31,34] was born on 24 Apr 1881 in Benton Township, Des Moines, Iowa, USA and died on 21 Mar 1939 at age 57.

Emilie married **Chris SCHMIDT** [793][2,30] [MRIN: 278], son of _____ **SCHMIDT** [4615]. Chris was born on 1 Nov 1875 in Burlington, Kane, Illinois, USA and died on 17 Oct 1937 at age 61.

4-Frieda SCHMIDT [798].[2]

4-Raymond SCHMIDT [797].[2]

4-Frances SCHMIDT [796].[2]

4-Viola SCHMIDT [795].[2,34]

General Notes: **T500-2** Correspondence from Thelma Tieman in a letter dated 1989

Aunt Anna lived to be 93 (widowed at 39). She said had she been the marrying kind she would still be a widow because all the young men she knew as a girl preceded her in death. When the Tieman family farm was for sale, she bought it and lived on the earnings for many, many years.

Shortly before she died she was named heir to $80,000 from a brother but died before settlement. Her share went to a blood niece, Daisy, who was not at all friendly with Aunt Anna, but who was given credit for all the work Viola Schmidt Marshall (Aunt Louisa Tieman Schmidt's daughter) did for her. So, goes the world. Fortunately, Aunt Anna had a joint bank account with Viola and made her executor, so it was some compensation.

Viola married _____ **MARSHALL** [3945] [MRIN: 1396], son of _____ **MARSHALL** [4622

Source Citations

1. T500-10 Prussian Passport G.W. Thiemann 1833.
2. T500-1 "History of William Tiemann Family" (Name: Centennial Booklet 1853-1953;).
3. T500-31 Gravestone_G. William and Sophia, Can't read too degraded.
4. T500-40 "German Marriages, 1558-1929" Georg Wilhelm Tiemann, 1817, Indexing Project (Batch) Number: M95279-4; System Origin: Germany-ODM; Source File Number: 526392.
5. T500-41 W. H. Tieman "Germany, Births and Baptisms, 1558-1898."
6. T500-30 1870 Census Mortality William Teeman, National Archives and Records Administration (NARA); Washington, D.C., Archive Collection: T1156; Archive Roll #: 56; Census Year 1870; Census Location: Yellow Springs, Des Moines, Iowa; Page 296; Line 28.
7. T500-56 G.W. Tiemann - US & Canada Passenger and Immigration Lists Index 1500's - 1900's, MUELLER, FRIEDRICH. "Westfaelische Auswanderer im 19, Jahrhundert-Auswanderung aus dem Regierungsbezik Munster, Part 1.1803-1850." In Beitraege zur westfaelischen Familienforschung, vols22-24 (1964-1966) pp. 7-484.
8. MP-0005 Prussia Map 1440-1866.
9. MP-0004 Tecklenburg, Westfalia, Prussia Map 1790.
10. HY-0003 Tecklenburg, Prussia History.
11. T500-61 Evangelische Kirche von Westfalen Parish Records, 1817 Parish Weddings, 1791 Baptisms.
12. HY-0018 National Road Migration Routes, The National Road, by Philip D. Jordan, Indianapolis: Bobbs-MerrillCo., 1948. 442pp.
13. MP-0012 Lengerich and area, Germany, 2014 -Maps/Photos.
14. T500-57 G.W. Tiemann/Koenig Germany Select Marriages 1558-1929, Ancestry.com. Germany Select Marriages, 1558-1929 [database on-line]. Provo, UT, USA: Ancestry.com Operations, Inc., 2014. Original data: Germany, Marriages, 1558-1929. Salt Lake City, Utah: FamilySearch,2013.
15. T500-12 1880 US Census William Tieman (Name: William Tieman;), Page #4, Supervisor's District #1, Enumeration District #104. BentonTownship, Des Moines Co. Iowa June 5, 1880. Last name was written down as "Teiman" not Tieman or Tiemann
16. T500-31 Gravestone_G. William and Sophia.
17. T500-7 Copy of Tiemann Family Bible.
18. T500-8 William Tieman/Rethemeier Marriage Certificate (Name: photocopy;).
19. T500-3 Tieman/Morrill 1989 (Name: Unknown;).
20. T500-32 Gravestone William H Tieman and Luise.
21. T500-29 1850 New Orleans Pass.List Will Tieman.
22. T500-54 Tieman/Brumm Family line.
23. MP-0007 Prussia Map 1815-1871.
24. MP-0008 Prussia Map 1789.
25. HY-0004 Prussia History.
26. HY-0017 American Occupation of Iowa 1833-1860, Cardinal Goodwin, Mills College.
27. MP-0013 Des Moines County, Iowa-Maps, Geological Maps of Des Moines County, Iowa by Charles R. Keyes,18941894.
28. T500-66 William Tiemann - Obit, The Burlington Hawkeye Newspaper, Saturday, May 12, 1906.
29. HY-0012 Minden, Germany History.
30. M640-1 Crete Family Bible page (Name: Mae Morrill Crete;).
31. M640-3 Biographical Directory of the United States Congress, Anson Peaslee Morrill p 1439 (Name: Unknown;).
32. T500-75 Selma Gerdom Obit (Burlington Gazette; Date: 27 May 1935;), Burlington Gazette 27 May 1935.
33. T500-78 LDS IGI Files (Location: LDS Family History Center, IGI files;).
34. T500-2 Thelma Tieman Corresp. 1989.
35. T500-68 Find a Grave - Heinrich Herman Tieman 1924, database.
36. T500-9 Church Bulletin- St. Paul's Evangelican Church.
37. T500-22 1920 US Census, Malcolm Tieman, 5 Jan.1920, Keokuk, Lee Co., Iowa Sheet #3A. S.D. #1 E.D. #79, Ward7.
38. T500-25 1910 US Census, Henry Tieman.
39. T500-38 Marriage Certificate - Henry & Anna Tieman.
40. S560-11 1910 US Census, C. Sommer.
41. S360-2 Ancestor Chart - Starr (Name: Amy Starr; Date: 1992;).
42. T500-43 1905 Iowa State Census, Malcolm Tieman.
43. T500-52 Henry Tieman County Marriage Certificate.
44. T500-62 Henry H. Tieman Obit, Daily Gate City Newspaper 19 Aug 1924, Keokuk Iowa.
45. S560-19 Dresden, Germany, Births 1876-1902 - Anna Sommer 1876.
46. T500-71 1940 U.S. Census Anna (Sommer) Tieman.
47. S560-1 Corres. from Doris Tieman - Sommer (Date: 1989;).
48. S560-2 Corres. Thelma Tieman - Sommer/Tieman (Date: 23 Mar 1989;).
49. S560-6 Obit- Anna Sommer Tieman (Name: Newspaper;).
50. S560-10 Birth Certificate- Anna Ernestine Sommer (Name: Original 1876;).
51. T500-15 1930 US Census - Malcolm Tieman, April 10, 1930 - Sheet #14B, Enumeration Dist. #56-17,

Supervisor'sDist. #15, Keokuk Township, Lee Co. Iowa.
52. S560-7 Anna Sommer Funeral Service.
53. S560-8/9 Anna & Myrtle Obits.
54. HY-0005 Saxony, Germany - History.
55. HY-0006 Dresden, Saxony, Germany - History.
56. MP-0006 Germany 1871-1918 - Map.
57. T500-24 1930 US Census, LaVerne Tieman.
58. S560-14 1900 US Census - Clemens Sommer.
59. S560-3 Obit- Clemens Sommer.
60. S560-12 E.C. Sommer and family naturalization.
61. HY-0014 Glowitz, Pomeranian, Germany (Now Poland), - History.
62. HY-0007 Pomerania, Germany - History.
63. S560-13 Dresden, Germany, Births, 1876-1902 - Ida Martha (Myrtle) Sommer.
64. S560-15 Dresden Germany Births 1876-1902 - Martha Emma (Myrtle) Sommer.
65. S560-17 Dresden Germany Marriages 1876-1922 - Clemmens Sommer.
66. S560-18 Dresden Germany Births 1876-1902 - Ernst Emil Sommer.
67. T500-42 LaVerne Tieman Marriage Announcement.
68. T500-73 Birth Certificate (Orig), Malcolm Tieman, Iowa.
69. T500-74 Death Certificate (Orig), Malcolm S. Tieman, Iowa death certificate.
70. Source From Doris E. (Morrill) Tieman.
71. T500-20 Verne Tieman life History (Name: Verne Tieman;).
72. T500-26 Social Security Death Index - Malcolm S. Tieman.
73. T500-25 1910 US Census, Henry Tieman, 22 April 1910, Sheet #13A, S.D.#1, E.D.#75, Ward #6(?), Keokuk, LeeCo. Iowa.
74. T500-27 Iowa Births & Christenings Index 1857-1947 - Malcolm Tieman.
75. T500-36 Marriage Certificate - Malcolm & Viola Tieman.
76. T500-44 1940 U.S. Census Malcolm Tieman, April 12, 1940, Sheet #12B, S.D.#1, E.D. 56-17, Keokuk, Lee Co Iowa.3rd Ward.
77. S320-2 South Family Reunion.
78. T500-58 Birth Certificate (Orig) M. LaVerne Tieman, Dept of Vital Statistics, State of Iowa, County of Lee, City of Keokuk, Index # 05C-1451, Registered # 1725.
79. T500-64 Malcolm S. Tieman - Obit, Daily Gate City Newspaper, Keokuk, Iowa, Sept 17, 1974.
80. T500-72 Death Certificate (Orig), Viola Reitz Tieman, Missouri Dept of Heath & Senior Services.
81. R320-36 BirthCertificate (Orig), Viola Reitz.
82. From Individual.
83. R320-2 Corres. from LaVerne Tieman on Rietz Family (Name: 1992;).
84. R320-3 1920 US Census, Fred Wm. Reitz.
85. R320-5 1910 US Census, Fred Wm. Reitz.
86. R320-14 Iowa Births & Christenings Index 1857-1947, Viola Reitz.
87. R320-1 Reitz Letter.
88. R320-19 Reitz Family Bible page of Marriages.
89. T500-47 Viola Tieman Obit.
90. R320-32 1930 U.S. Census Frederick William Reitz.
91. R320-37 Death Certificate (Orig), Fred Wm. Reitz death certificate.
92. *R320-38 Registration Card Fred Wm. Reitz* (N.p.: n.p., n.d.).
93. R320-10 William Family Tree (Name: Sandy Rumsey;).
94. R320-4 1900 US Census, William Reitz.
95. R320-12 WWI Draft Registration Cards 1917-1918, Fred Reitz.
96. R320-13 Missouri State Board of Heath Death Certif, Fred Reitz.
97. R320-16 Portrait & Biographical album of Lee County, Iowa, Henry Reitz.
98. R320-17 Frederick W. Reitz Marriage Certificate.
99. R320-33 1940 U.S. Census Mabel (South) Reitz (N.p.: n.p., n.d.).
100. R320-34 1915 Iowa State Census Collection - Mable (South) Reitz.
101. S320-28 1900 U. S. Census John L. South.
102. Death certificate.
103. R320-39 Deathh Certificate (Orig) Mable (South) Reitz death certificate.
104. S320-25 1883 Iowa Census - John L. South; digital images.
105. R320-6 1880 US Census, John L. South.
106. R320-11 Social Security Death Index, Mable South.
107. R320-20 Mable Reitz Obit.
108. M640-48 1940 United States Federal Census, Don Morrill (Name: Ancestry.com Operations, Inc; Location: Provo, UT, USA; Date: 2012;), Year: 1940; Census Place: Keokuk, Lee, Iowa; Roll: T627_1174; Page:12B; Enumeration District: 56-17. United States of America, Bureau of the Census. Sixteenth Census of the United States, 1940. Washington, D.C.: National Archives and Records Administration, 1940. T627, 4,643 rolls.
109. T500-23 US WWII Army Enlistment Records 1938-1946, LaVerne Tieman.
110. T500-37 WWII Seperation Papers, LaVerne Tieman.
111. T500-46 LaVerne Tieman National Thespian Certif.
112. T500-53 LaVerne Tieman WWll Honoree.
113. T500-50 LaVerne & Doris Tieman Marriage License.

114. T500-59 Death Certificate (Orig), M. LaVerne Tieman, Ohio Dept. of Heath, Vital Statistics, Certificate of Death, Reg.Dist. # 77, Primary Reg. Dist. #7705.
115. T500-60 Military Papers, WWII, M. LaVerne Tieman, Greetings letter (Orig), Report for Induction letter (orig), SpecialOrders #162 (Orig), Honorable Discharge Certif.(Orig).
116. M640-20 Copy of Newspaper Death Notice - Doris E. (Morrill) Tieman (Date: 2003;).
117. M640-40 Doris Morrill Birth Registration.
118. M640-41 Doris Morrill Birth Certificate.
119. M640-47 1930 United States Federal Census, Don Morrill (Name: Ancestry.com Operations Inc; Location: Provo, UT, USA; Date: 2002;). United States of America, Bureau of the Census. Fifteenth Census of the United States, 1930. Washington, D.C.: National Archives and Records Administration, 1930. T626, 2,667 rolls.
120. M640-48 1940 United States Federal Census, Don Morrill (Name: Ancestry.com Operations, Inc; Location: Provo, UT, USA; Date: 2012;). United States of America, Bureau of the Census. Sixteenth Census of the United States, 1940. Washington, D.C.: National Archives and Records Administration, 1940. T627, 4,643 rolls.
121. M640-46 Iowa, State Census Collection, 1836-1925, Don Morrill (Name: Ancestry.com Operations Inc; Location: Provo, UT, USA; Date: 2007;). Microfilm of Iowa State Censuses, 1856, 1885, 1895, 1905, 1915, 1925 as well various special censuses from 1836-1897 obtained from the State Historical Society of Iowa via Heritage Quest.
122. M640-16 Corresp. Doris (Morrill) Tieman (Name: Letter;).
123. T500-67 Doris (Morrill) Tieman Orig Death Certif.
124. M640-143 U.S., World War II Cadet Nursing Corps Card Files, 1942-1948 Doris Morrill (Name: Ancestry.com Operations, Inc; Location: Provo, UT, USA; Date: 2011;), National Archives and Records Administration; Washington, D.C; CadetNurse Corps Files, compiled 1943 - 1948, documenting the period 1942 -1948; Box #: 204.
125. *M640-139 1920 US Census Marion (Walther) Morrill.* (N.p.: n.p., n.d.).
126. M640-33 US Dept. of Veterans Affairs MIRLS Death File 1850-2010, Donald Morrill.
127. M640-37 Morrill Online.
128. M640-46 1925 Iowa Census Don Morrill.
129. M640-53 1910 US Census, Donald Morrill, 1910 US Census District 17, Sheet #14B, Household ID: 253.
130. M640-63 Donald Morrill Obit.
131. P300-7 Moses Parkhurst Family Tree - Davis Tree.
132. M640-98 Marriage License - Don & Alta Morrill.
133. M640-134 Donald R. Morrill Orig. Death Certificate.
134. M640-135 Alta (Vinson) Morrill Orig Death Certificate, Orig Death Certificate - Iowa Certificate of Death, State file#114-64-15650, Keokuk, Lee County, Iowa.
135. V525-2 Alta Vinson Letters.
136. V525-31 Wilson-Jensen-Cook-Richardson Family Tree, Database online.
137. V525-25 1910 U.S. Census - Edward F. Vinson, Sheet #2A 4049, State Iowa, County Lee, Jackson Township, 15 Apr 1910, Sup. Dist #1, Enumer. Dist. #71, 4th Ward.
138. M640-87 Alta Vinson Morrill Obit, Daily Gate City Newspaper, 24 Jul 1964, Keokuk, Iowa.
139. V525-42 Alta Vinson Birth Certificate - Orig.
140. T500-28 Beverly Tieman Bio.
141. T500-65 Beverly Tieman Birth Announcement, Daily Gate City Newspaper, Keokuk, iowa.
142. S360-1 Corres. from Beverly (Tieman) Starr (Date: 1989;).
143. S360-4 Ohio Marriage Index 1970, 1972-2007 Nicole Starr.
144. Source From Nancy L. (Marshall) Tieman.
145. T500-69 Find a Grave - Richard LaVerne Tieman 1948, database.
146. T500-4 Newspaper Obit - Richard Tieman (Name: Daily Gate City Newspaper - Keokuk, Iowa;).
147. T500-13 Copy of State of Iowa Birth Certificate, - Michael L. Tieman (Name: State of Iowa;).
148. T500-14 U.S. Passport - Michael Tieman (Name: US Government;).
149. S530-1 Corres. Smoot Ancestry (Name: unknown;).
150. T500-16 Marriage Certificate Michael Tieman & Nancy Marshall (Name: State of Ohio;).
151. T500-6 Marquis Who's Who In The West 1989- Michael Tieman (Name: 23rd Edition;).
152. M624-10 Marshall Family Chart (Name: Bob Marshall; Date: 2008;).
153. T500-21 Michael Tieman Bio (Name: Michael Tieman;).
154. T500-34 Birth Registration, Michael Tieman.
155. M624-17 Nancy Marshall Wedding Announcement (Name: Newspaper; Location: Columbus, Ohio; Date: 1972;).
156. M624-18 Nancy Marshall Engagement Announcement.
157. T500-35 Canada Immagration, Michael Tieman.
158. HY-0016 Keokuk, Lee Co., Iowa - History.
159. T500-63 Michael L. Tieman Birth Announcement, Daily Gate City Newspaper, Keokuk, Iowa.
160. Source From Janet O. Marshall.
161. M624-5 Copy of Canadian Birth Certificate - Nancy Lee Marshall (Name: British Columbia Division of Vital Statistics; Location: Vancouver, British Columbia, Canada; Date: March 13, 1952;).
162. M624-6 Christening Papers - Nancy Lee Marshall.
163. M624-7 U.S. Passport - Nancy L. (Marshall) Tieman (Date: Issued 25 APR 2008;).
164. M624-3 Corres. Marshall Line (Name: Janet (Ormandy) Marshall;).

165. M624-8 Marshall Ancestry Charts.
166. M624-20 US Certificate of Citizenship -Nancy Marshall (Name: Application # A19 583 620, Certificate # 35294; Date: Issued on 13 FEB 1974, but became a U.S. citizen on date of birth5 MAR 1952;).
167. M624-19 Registration of Live Birth - Nancy Marshall (Name: Dept. of Health & Welfare Division of Vital Statisics Victoria, BC- Certified A True Photographic Print of the Original Registration #52-09-004896; Date: 18 Mar 1952;).
168. M624-16 Certificate of Canadian Citizenship - Nancy Marshall (Name: Nancy Lee Tieman;).
169. M624-24 Nancy Marshall Ohio State Admission.
170. T500-51 Nancy (Marshall) Tieman Portland State Admittance.
171. M624-9 Obit - F. James Marshall (Oregonian Newspaper; Portland, Oregon; 2008;).
172. M624-21 Baptisim Certificate - Frederick James Marshall (Name: St. George's Church, Vancouver, British Columbia, Easter Day 1925;).
173. B600-1 Braun Family Line - 2008, Database online. Connie Braun
174. M624-22, My Glengarry Dr. F. James Marshall (Cannon Beach, OR, Michael Tieman Publishing, 2007).
175. M624-23 Interview with F. James Marshall 1998.
176. M624-38 Source from Geraldine Beverly (Nesbit) Marshall.
177. M624-39 F. James Marshall US Naturalization Papers (Columbus, OH).
178. M624-40 F James Marshall Death Certificate - Orig.
179. M624-41 F James Marshall Cert. of Birth.
180. M624-42 F James and Janet Marshall Marriage Certif.
181. M624-44 F James Marshall WWII Discharge Papers.
182. O653-1 William Lewthwaite Ormandy Family Bible - Original (Name: Original 1872;).
183. M624-43 Janet (Ormandy) Marshall Death Certif (Intercranial Hemorage).
184. T500-17 Copy of Canadian Birth Abroad Certificate - Heather A. Tieman.
185. E300-1 Source From Book from Judy Erwin.
186. Source From Heather A. (Tieman) Erwin.
187. T500-18 Copy of Canadian Birth Abroad Certificate - Katherine J. Tieman.
188. W500-2 Marriage Certificate Sam Woodward/ Katie Tieman.
189. W500-1 Sam Woodward's family tree - Mother's side (Name: Sam's Mother, Rosa; Date: 2008;). Rosa's Chinese family history
190. T500-45 Katie Tieman Baptisim Papers.
191. Source From Katherine J. Tieman.
192. "W500-3 Find a Grave - Gary Woodward Family," database.
193. T500-19 Obituary Akron Beacon Journal, 2008, Connie Tieman.
194. D632-3 Drotos Ancestry Family Tree.
195. D632-1 Corres. from John Drotos (Date: 1989;).
196. T500-70 U.S. Social security Death Index, 1935-2014 Thelma Tieman d. 1997 Social Security Administration, database.
197. T500-11 Memory of Thelma Tieman 1997.
198. T500-33 Gravestone - Ernst Will. H.
199. T500-39 Gravestone - Samuel Tieman

Name Index

Appendix A - Pedigree Charts

Chart no. 1

2 Malcolm Laverne TIEMAN
b. 20 Feb 1926
p. Keokuk, Lee, Iowa, USA
m. 30 Dec 1944
p. Kahoka, Clark, Missouri, USA
d. 5 Jan 2011
p. Stow, Summit, Ohio, USA

4 Malcolm Sommer TIEMAN
b. 26 Sep 1903
p. Keokuk, Lee, Iowa, USA
m. 13 Jun 1925
p. Keokuk, Lee, Iowa, USA
d. 16 Sep 1974
p. Keokuk, Lee, Iowa, USA

8 Heinrich Herman TIEMAN   cont. 2
b. 16 Mar 1868
p. Benton Township, Des Moines, Iowa, USA
m. 20 Nov 1902
p. Keokuk, Lee, Iowa, USA
d. 19 Aug 1924
p. Keokuk, Lee, Iowa, USA

9 Anna Ernestine SOMMER   cont. 3
b. 1 May 1876
p. Dresden, Saxony, Germany
d. 15 Jun 1962
p. Keokuk, Lee, Iowa, USA

5 Viola Emma Marie REITZ
b. 15 Jan 1904
p. Van Buran Twp., Lee County, Iowa, USA
d. 22 Mar 1995
p. Columbia, Boone, Missouri, USA

10 Frederick William REITZ   cont. 4
b. 6 May 1879
p. Lee, Iowa, USA
m. 11 Mar 1903
p. Primrose, Lee County, Iowa
d. 15 Apr 1935
p. Luray, Clark County, Missouri, USA

11 Mabel Kansas SOUTH   cont. 5
b. 14 Aug 1879
p. Kansas, USA
d. 15 Nov 1970
p. Shelbina, Shelby, Missouri, USA

1 Michael LaVerne TIEMAN
b. 20 Aug 1950
p. Keokuk, Lee, Iowa, USA
m. 16 Jun 1972
p. Columbus, Franklin, Ohio, USA
d.
p.
sp. Nancy Lee MARSHALL

6 Donald Reginald MORRILL
b. 14 Feb 1901
p. Nauvoo, Hancock, Illinois, USA
m. 20 Nov 1923
p. Rushville (Clayton?), Schuyler, Illinois
d. 13 May 1978
p. Colorado Springs, El Paso, Colorado, USA

12 Charles Edwin MORRILL   cont. 6
b. 17 Aug 1876
p. Nauvoo, Hancock, Illinois, USA
m. 18 Aug 1897
p.
d. 27 Jan 1949
p. Golden Eagle, Calhoun, Illinois, USA

13 Marion WALTHER   cont. 7
b. 2 Jan 1872
p. Nauvoo, Hancock, Illinois, USA
d. 15 Feb 1955
p. Peoria, Peoria, Illinois, USA

3 Doris Earline MORRILL
b. 12 Nov 1924
p. Nevada, Story, Iowa, USA
d. 9 Mar 2003
p. Akron, Summit, Ohio, USA

7 Alta Arvilla VINSON
b. 11 Apr 1905
p. Keokuk, Lee, Iowa, USA
d. 24 Jul 1964
p. Keokuk, Lee, Iowa, USA

14 Edward Francis "Eddie" VINSON   8
b. 3 Jun 1869
p. Aurora, Dearborn, Indiana, USA
m. 28 Mar 1900
p. Lee County, Iowa, USA
d. 20 Mar 1939
p. Keokuk, Lee, Iowa, USA

15 Lottie Belle PARKHURST   cont. 9
b. 12 Sep 1879
p. Keokuk, Lee, Iowa, USA
d. 30 Jun 1945
p. Keokuk, Lee, Iowa, USA

No. 1 on this chart is the same as no. 8 on chart no. 1

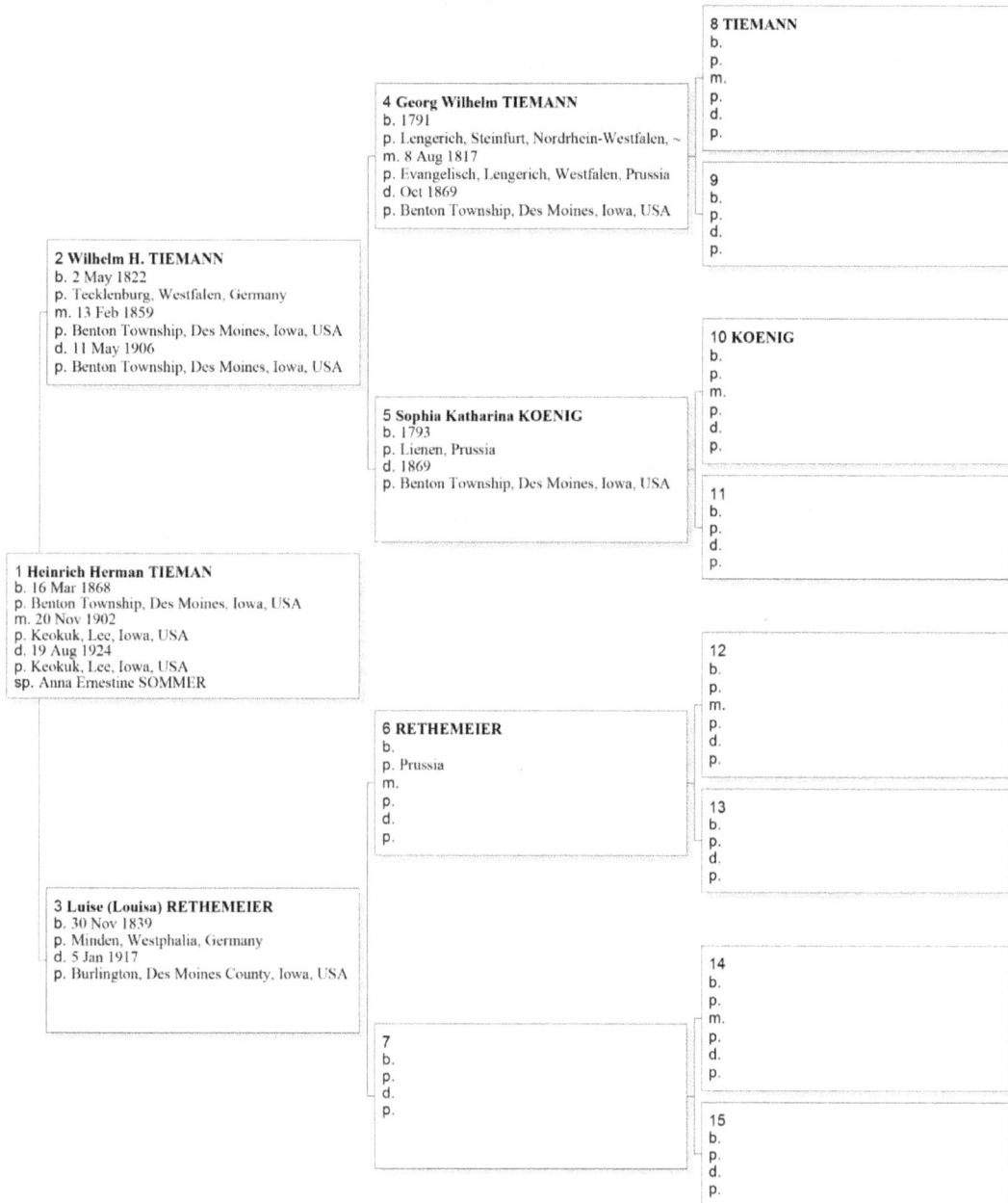

8 TIEMANN
b.
p.
m.
p.
d.
p.

9
b.
p.
d.
p.

4 Georg Wilhelm TIEMANN
b. 1791
p. Lengerich, Steinfurt, Nordrhein-Westfalen, ~
m. 8 Aug 1817
p. Evangelisch, Lengerich, Westfalen, Prussia
d. Oct 1869
p. Benton Township, Des Moines, Iowa, USA

10 KOENIG
b.
p.
m.
p.
d.
p.

11
b.
p.
d.
p.

2 Wilhelm H. TIEMANN
b. 2 May 1822
p. Tecklenburg, Westfalen, Germany
m. 13 Feb 1859
p. Benton Township, Des Moines, Iowa, USA
d. 11 May 1906
p. Benton Township, Des Moines, Iowa, USA

5 Sophia Katharina KOENIG
b. 1793
p. Lienen, Prussia
d. 1869
p. Benton Township, Des Moines, Iowa, USA

1 Heinrich Herman TIEMAN
b. 16 Mar 1868
p. Benton Township, Des Moines, Iowa, USA
m. 20 Nov 1902
p. Keokuk, Lee, Iowa, USA
d. 19 Aug 1924
p. Keokuk, Lee, Iowa, USA
sp. Anna Ernestine SOMMER

12
b.
p.
m.
p.
d.
p.

13
b.
p.
d.
p.

6 RETHEMEIER
b.
p. Prussia
m.
p.
d.
p.

14
b.
p.
m.
p.
d.
p.

15
b.
p.
d.
p.

3 Luise (Louisa) RETHEMEIER
b. 30 Nov 1839
p. Minden, Westphalia, Germany
d. 5 Jan 1917
p. Burlington, Des Moines County, Iowa, USA

7
b.
p.
d.
p.

Descendants of Michael Tieman

1-Michael LaVerne TIEMAN
 born: 20 Aug 1950, Keokuk, Lee, Iowa, USA

+Nancy Lee MARSHALL
born: 5 Mar 1952, Vancouver, British Columbia, Canada
marr: 16 Jun 1972, Columbus, Franklin, Ohio, USA
parents: Dr. Frederick James MARSHALL and Janet Alma ORMANDY

2-Heather Anne TIEMAN
 born: 17 May 1976, North Vancouver, British Columbia, Canada

+Phillip ERWIN
born: 30 May 1971, Boise, Ada, Idaho, USA
marr: 22 Jun 1996, Lake Oswego, Clackamas, Oregon, USA
parents: Sidney Fred ERWIN and Judith Lee BENSCOTER

3-Riley James ERWIN
 born: 27 Sep 1999, Portland, Clackamas, Oregon, USA

3-Jackson Davis ERWIN
 born: 26 Jul 2005, Portland, Clackamas, Oregon, USA

2-Katherine Jane TIEMAN
 born: 25 Jun 1979, North Vancouver, British Columbia, Canada

+Shawn SCHULBERG
born:
marr: 4 Nov 2000, Portland, Clackamas, Oregon, USA
parents: SCHULBERG and Unknown

3-Connor Shamas TIEMAN-WOODWARD
 born: 28 Oct 2002, Portland, Clackamas, Oregon, USA

+Samuel Patrick WOODWARD
born: 16 Sep 1975, T'ai-Pei, Taiwan
marr: 25 Jul 2009, Portland, Clackamas, Oregon, USA
parents: Gary Milton WOODWARD and (Rosa) Yung-Mei KAO

3-Alexis Jean TIEMAN-WOODWARD
 born: 12 Nov 2006, Portland, Clackamas, Oregon, USA

3-Owen Richard TIEMAN-WOODWARD
 born: 18 Feb 2010, Portland, Clackamas, Oregon, USA

Relationship Chart

John Morrell [281] is the 8th great-grandfather of Michael LaVerne Tieman [1]

Common Ancestor

John Morrell [281]
(1640-1723)
Saraih Hodgsden [282]
(1650-1710/1717)
Married Abt 1665 [124]

John Morrell [277]
(1675-Abt 1763)
Hannah Dixon [278]
(1684-1765)
Married 18 Mar or Dec 16 1701 [123]

Peter Morrell (Morrill) [275]
(1709-1801)
Sarah Peaslee [276]
(1709-1780)
Married 27 Oct 1731 [121]

Peaslee Morrill (Morrell) [273]
(1748-1828)
Phoebe Chadbourne [274]
(1749-1782)
Married 14 Jul 1768 [118]

Peaslee Morrill [271]
(1768-1855)
Nancy Macomber [272]
(1782-1859)
Married 28 May 1797 [111]

Milton Maxwell Morrill [255]
(1820-1892)
Amanda M. Hibbard [256]
(1829-1914)
Married 22 Jun 1846 [110]

Milton Lot Morrill [253]
(1848-1938)
Mary Elizabeth Snyder [254]
(1846/1848-1926)
Married 1869 [26]

Relationship Chart

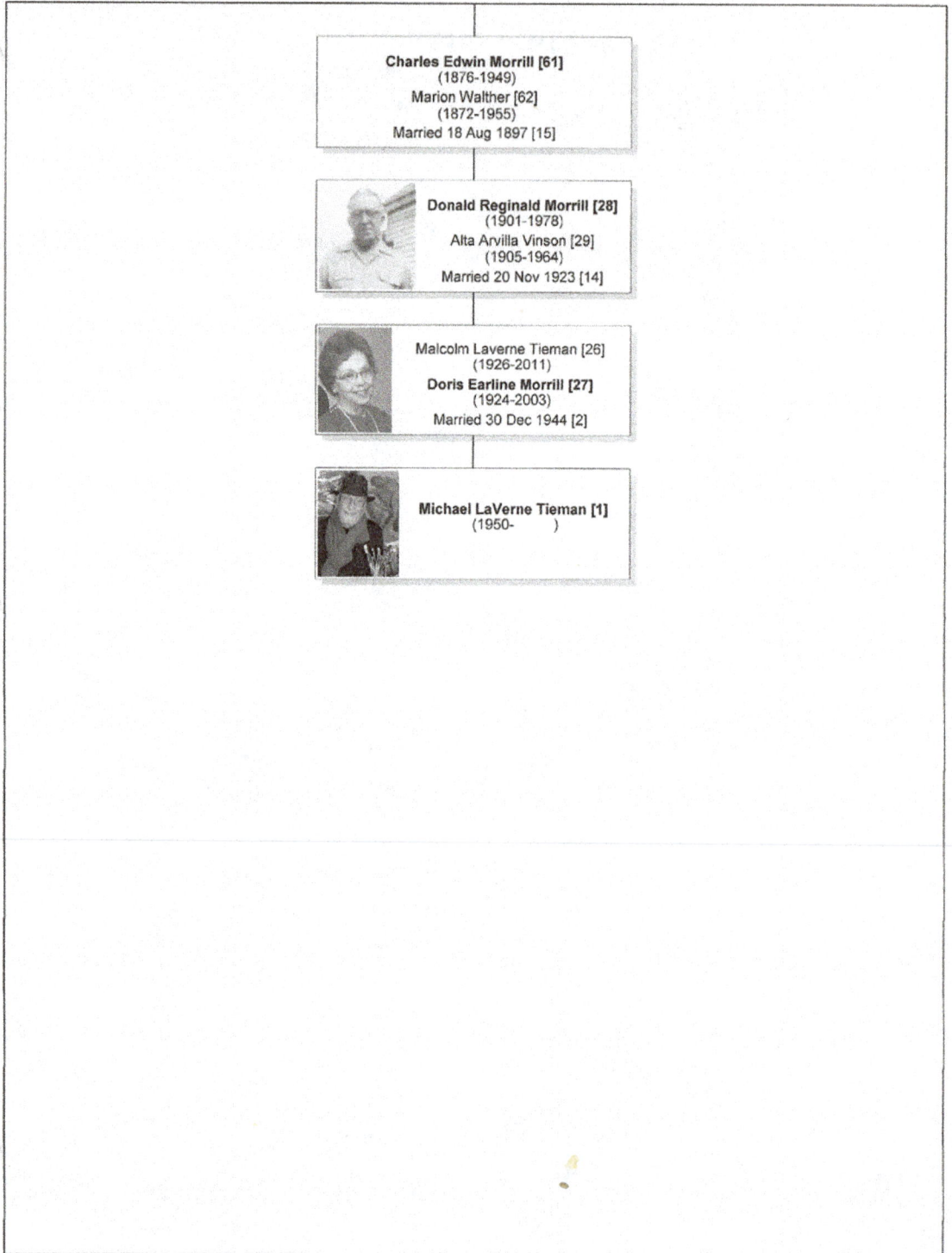

Charles Edwin Morrill [61]
(1876-1949)
Marion Walther [62]
(1872-1955)
Married 18 Aug 1897 [15]

Donald Reginald Morrill [28]
(1901-1978)
Alta Arvilla Vinson [29]
(1905-1964)
Married 20 Nov 1923 [14]

Malcolm Laverne Tieman [26]
(1926-2011)
Doris Earline Morrill [27]
(1924-2003)
Married 30 Dec 1944 [2]

Michael LaVerne Tieman [1]
(1950-   )

Relationship Chart

Robert FULLER [4501] is the 12th great-grandfather of Michael LaVerne Tieman [1]

Common Ancestor

Robert FULLER [4501]
(1539-1614)
Sarah DUNKHORN [4504]
(Abt 1550-1584)
Married 29 Jan 1572 [1582]

Edward FULLER [4487]
(1575-Between 1621/1621)
Ann HOPKINS [4500]
(1581-1621)
Married 1602 [1580]

PASS. on Mayflower

Samuel FULLER [4485]
(1608-1683)
Jane LATHROP [4486]
(1614-1683)
Married 8 Apr 1635 [1579]

Pass. on Mayflower

Nicholas BONHAM [4483]
(1630-1684/1684)
Hannah FULLER [4484]
(1636-After 1686)
Married 1 Jan 1659 [1578]

Daniel LIPPINGTON [4410]
(1659-1694)
Hannah BONHAM [4411]
(1659-1689)
Married [1565]

Thomas South [4408]
(1682-1757)
Dorothy LIPPINGTON [4409]
(1683-1757)
Married 1700 [1564]

Joseph South [734]
(1733-1811)
Sarah GILPIN [735]
(1730-1814)
Married 1757 [259]

Elijah South [721]
(1753-1834)
Rachel HARDUPOE (HARTUPEE)
[731]
(1764-1838)
Married 1784 [258]

Pvt.
Revolutionary War

Relationship Chart

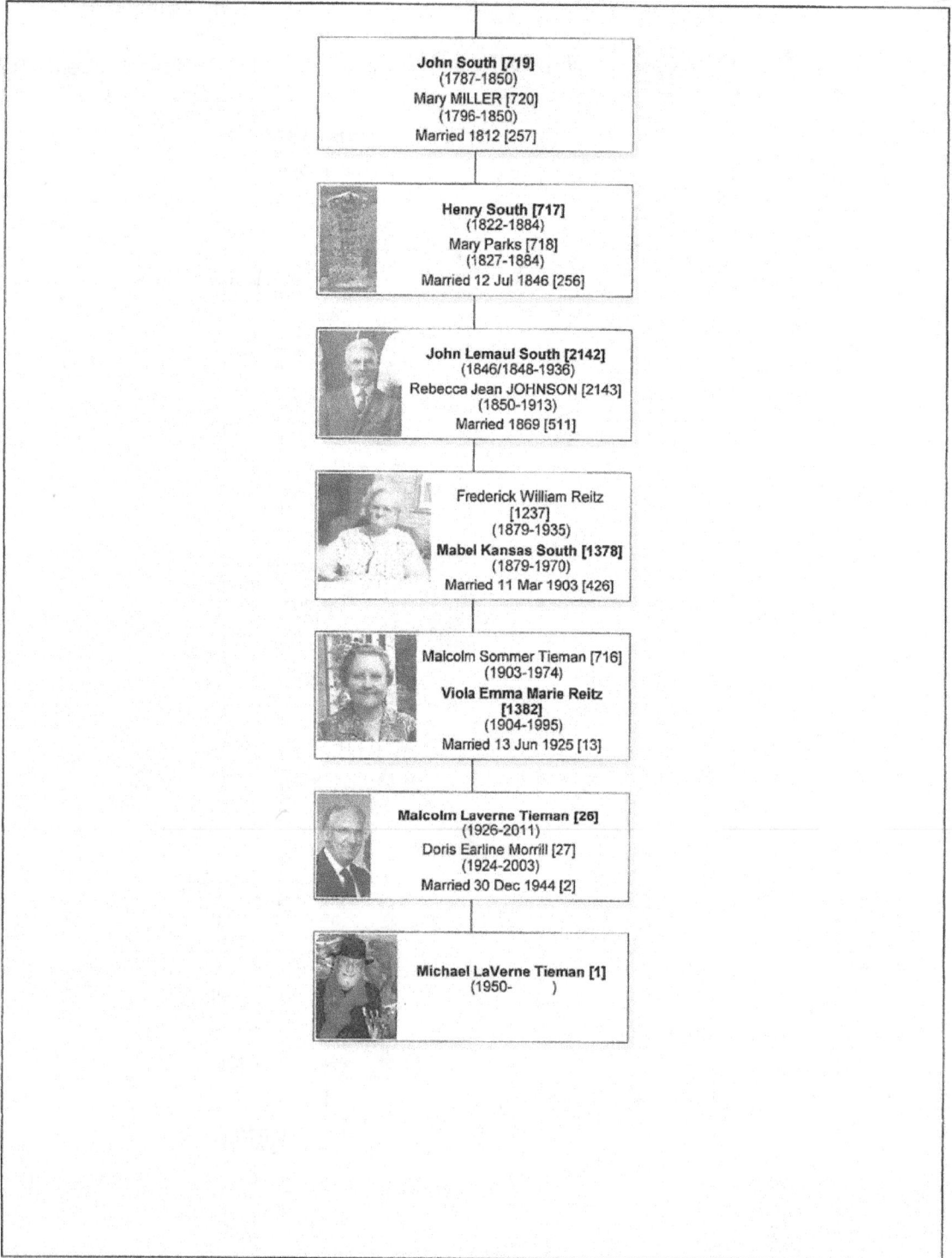

John South [719]
(1787-1850)
Mary MILLER [720]
(1796-1850)
Married 1812 [257]

Henry South [717]
(1822-1884)
Mary Parks [718]
(1827-1884)
Married 12 Jul 1846 [256]

John Lemaul South [2142]
(1846/1848-1936)
Rebecca Jean JOHNSON [2143]
(1850-1913)
Married 1869 [511]

Frederick William Reitz
[1237]
(1879-1935)
Mabel Kansas South [1378]
(1879-1970)
Married 11 Mar 1903 [426]

Malcolm Sommer Tieman [716]
(1903-1974)
Viola Emma Marie Reitz
[1382]
(1904-1995)
Married 13 Jun 1925 [13]

Malcolm Laverne Tieman [26]
(1926-2011)
Doris Earline Morrill [27]
(1924-2003)
Married 30 Dec 1944 [2]

Michael LaVerne Tieman [1]
(1950-   )

Relationship Chart

Moses Parkhurst [3994] is the 4th great-grandfather of Michael LaVerne Tieman [1]

Common Ancestor

PVT.
Revolutionary WAR

Moses Parkhurst [3994]
(1762-1827)
Catherine HUCKER [4154]
(1755-1830)
Married 11 Oct 1787 [1474]

Moses Henry Parkhurst [3961]
(1820-1881)
Mary Elizabeth Jane Armstrong
[3962]
(1827-1874)
Married 7 Sep 1847 [1401]

Moses H. Parkhurst [36]
(1857-1909)
Adeline Bird [37]
(1856-1921)
Married 1876 [18]

Edward Francis "Eddie" Vinson [30]
(1869-1939)
Lottie Belle Parkhurst [31]
(1879-1945)
Married 28 Mar 1900 [16]

Donald Reginald Morrill [28]
(1901-1978)
Alta Arvilla Vinson [29]
(1905-1964)
Married 20 Nov 1923 [14]

Malcolm Laverne Tieman [26]
(1926-2011)
Doris Earline Morrill [27]
(1924-2003)
Married 30 Dec 1944 [2]

Michael LaVerne Tieman [1]
(1950-   )

Appendix B - Maps

2 MAJOR POPULATION MOVEMENTS 1500–1914

Migration originating from:
Europe, Scandinavia and western Russia — Asia — Africa

US MIGRATION ROUTES

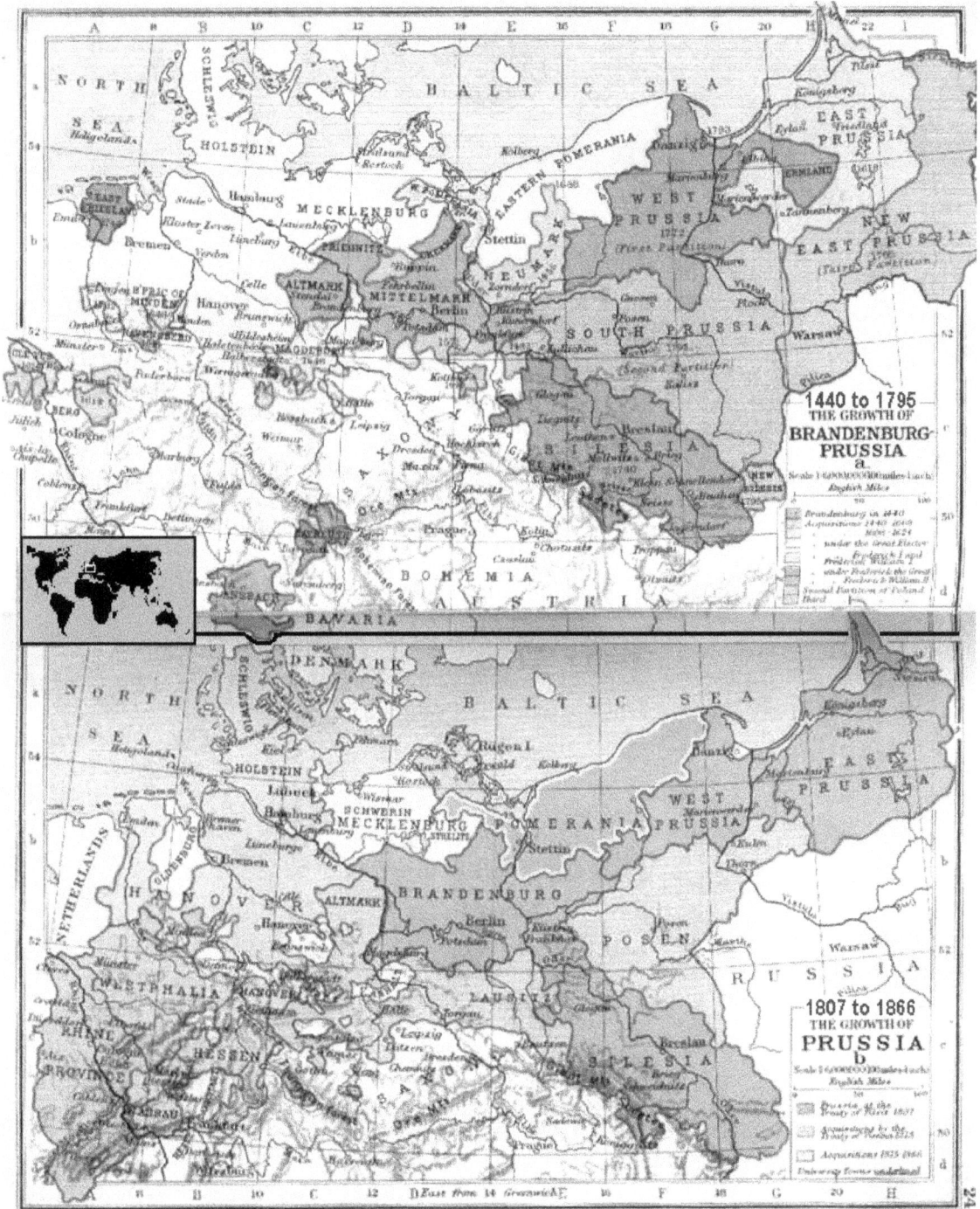

1440 to 1795
THE GROWTH OF
BRANDENBURG-
PRUSSIA
a.

1807 to 1866
THE GROWTH OF
PRUSSIA
b

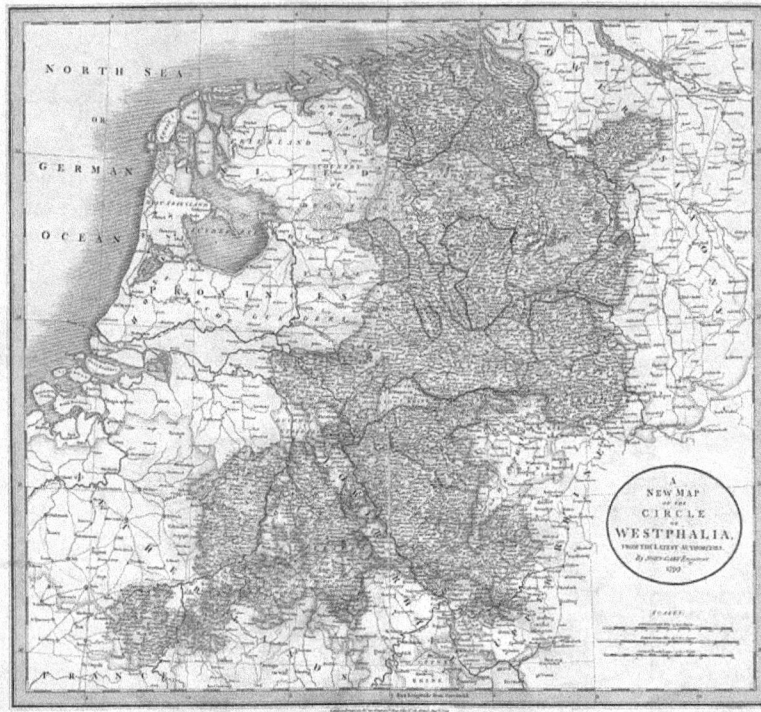

A NEW MAP of the CIRCLE of WESTPHALIA, FROM THE LATEST AUTHORITIES. By John Cary Engraver 1799

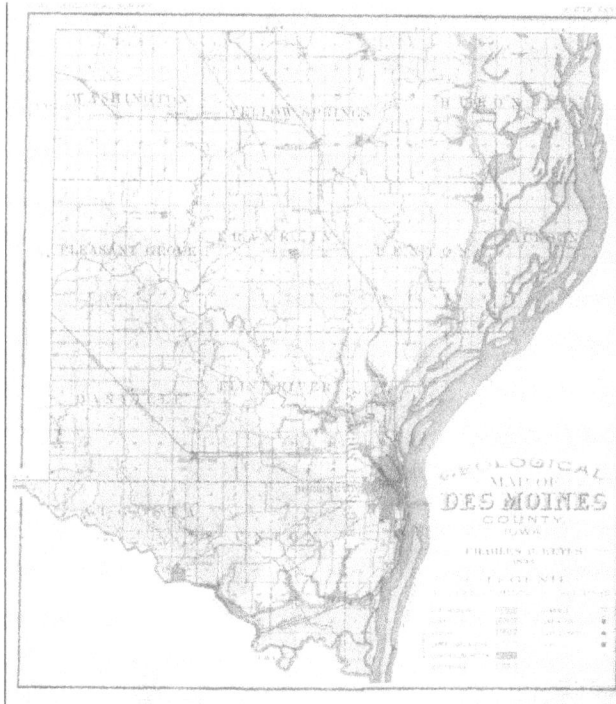

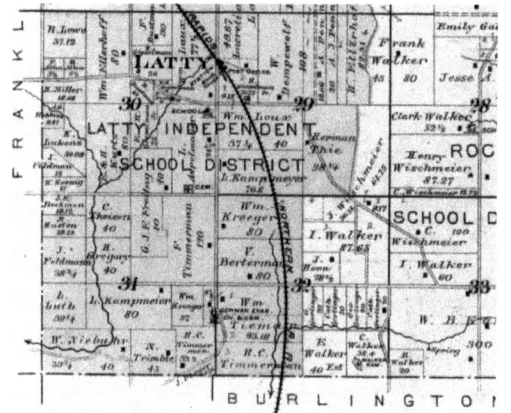

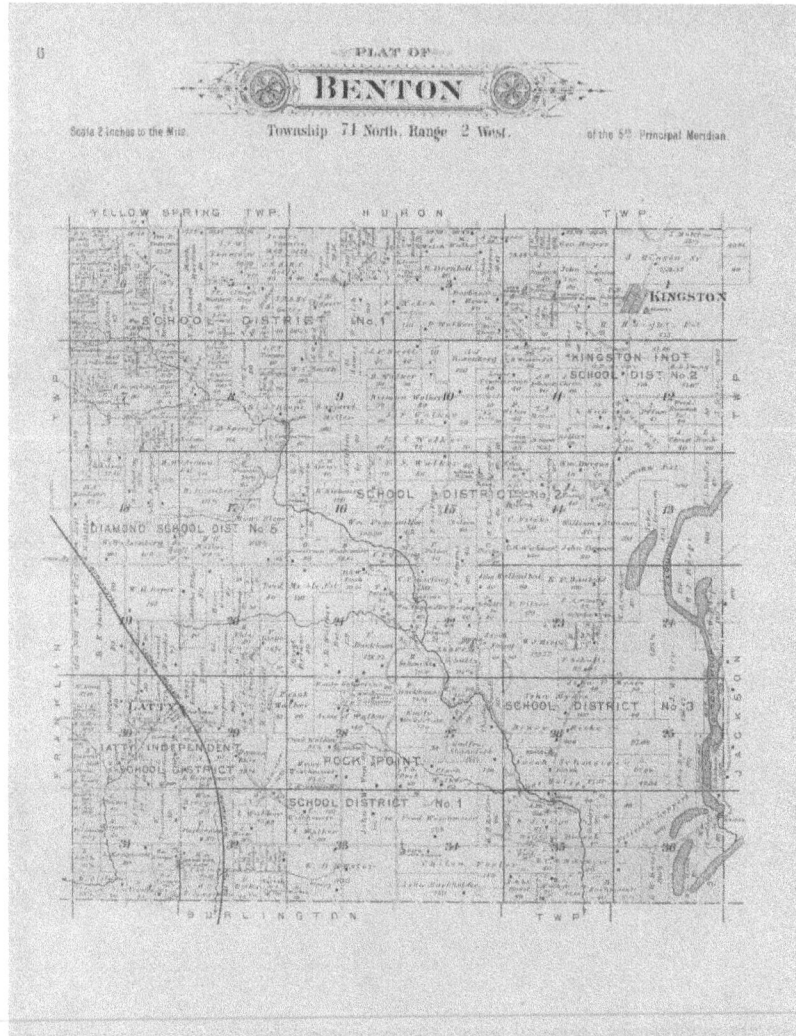

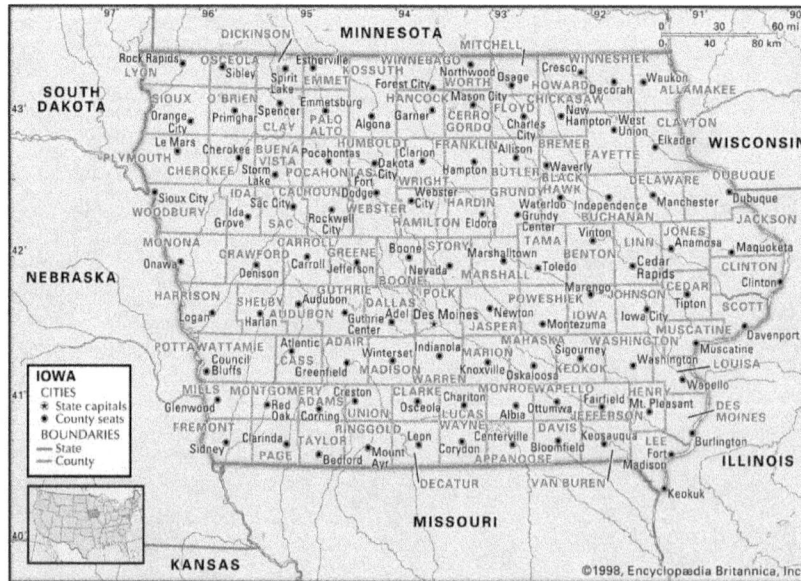

OHIO
State Map

MICHIGAN

CANADA

Lake Erie

INDIANA

PENNSYLVANIA

Bryan
Wauseon
Toledo
Port Clinton
Sandusky
Lorain
Euclid
Painesville
Jefferson
Chardon
Cleveland
Elyria
Parma
Warren
Defiance
Napoleon
Bowling Green
Fremont
Tiffin
Medina
Akron
Youngstown
Ottawa
Findlay
Van Wert
Upper Sandusky
Bucyrus
Ashland
Wooster
Canton
Lisbon
Lima
Kenton
Marion
Mansfield
Carrollton
Wapakoneta
Millersburg
New Philadelphia
Steubenville
Celina
Mount Gilead
Mount Vernon
Coshocton
Cadiz
Sidney
Delaware
Saint Clairsville
Wheeling
Greenville
Marysville
Urbana
Newark
Cambridge
Troy
Springfield
Columbus
Zanesville
Caldwell
Eaton
Dayton
Xenia
Washington Court House
Lancaster
Woodsfield
Middletown
Kettering
Circleville
New Lexington
Lebanon
Wilmington
Marietta
Hamilton
Chillicothe
Athens
Parkersburg
Saint Marys
Cincinnati
Hillsboro
Waverly City
Jackson
Pomeroy
Portsmouth
Maysville
Vanceburg
Greenup
Ironton
Catlettsburg
Huntington

WEST VIRGINIA

KENTUCKY

50 Km
25 Miles

Copyright © 2013 www.mapsofworld.com
(Updated on 20th June, 2013)

LEGEND
Country Boundary
State Boundary
County Boundary
Interstate Highway
State Capital
Major City
Other City

ILLINOIS
State Map

WISCONSIN

Lake Michigan

MICHIGAN

IOWA

INDIANA

MISSOURI

KENTUCKY

Galena
Freeport
Rockford
Woodstock
Waukegan
Belvidere
Arlington Heights
Mount Carroll
Oregon
Elgin
Evanston
Sycamore
Geneva
Cicero
Chicago
Morrison
Dixon
Aurora
Naperville
Yorkville
Joliet
Cambridge
Princeton
Ottawa
Aledo
Morris
Hennepin
Oquawka
Galesburg
Toulon
Lacon
Kankakee
Monmouth
Eureka
Pontiac
Watseka
Peoria
Pekin
Macomb
Lewistown
Bloomington
Paxton
Carthage
Havana
Lincoln
Clinton
Champaign
Danville
Rushville
Mount Sterling
Petersburg
Monticello
Quincy
Virginia
Decatur
Tuscola
Jacksonville
Springfield
Taylorville
Sullivan
Paris
Winchester
Shelbyville
Toledo
Marshall
Carrollton
Carlinville
Hillsboro
Effingham
Robinson
Jerseyville
Newton
Hardin
Vandalia
Edwardsville
Greenville
Olney
Vincennes
East ST. Louis
Salem
Louisville
Lawrenceville
Belleville
Carlyle
Fairfield
Albion
Mount Carmel
Waterloo
Nashville
Mount Vernon
Pinckneyville
Carmi
Chester
Benton
McLeansboro
Murphysboro
Harrisburg
Marion
Shawneetown
Vienna
Elizabethtown
Golconda
Mound City
Metropolis
Cairo
Paducah

50 Km   100 Km
50 Miles

Copyright © 2013 www.mapsofworld.com
(Created on 9th June, 2013)

LEGEND
State Boundary
County Boundary
Interstate Highway
State Capital
Major City

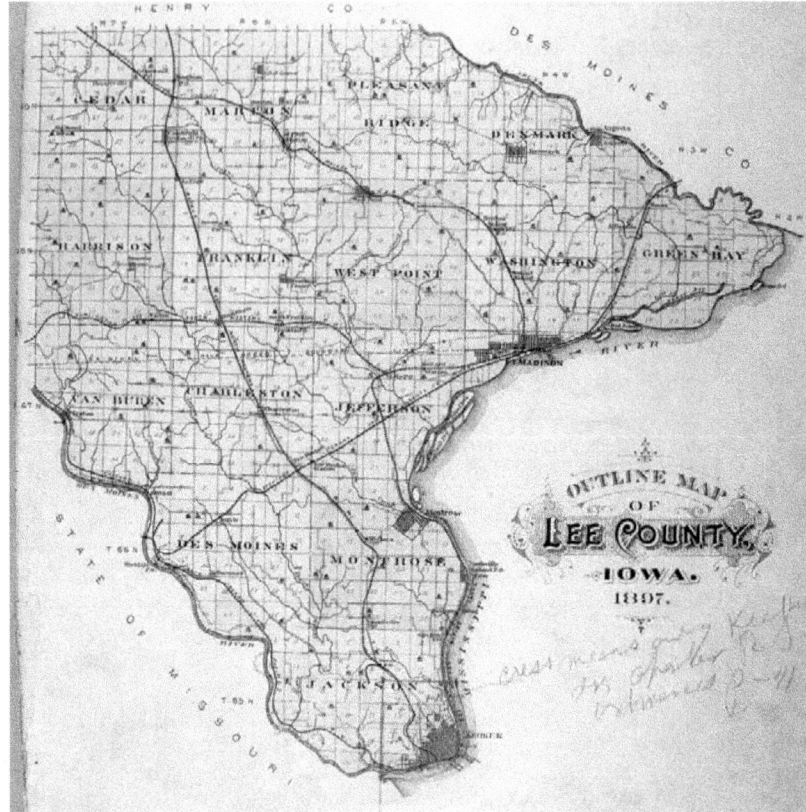

Outline Map of Lee County, Iowa. 1897.

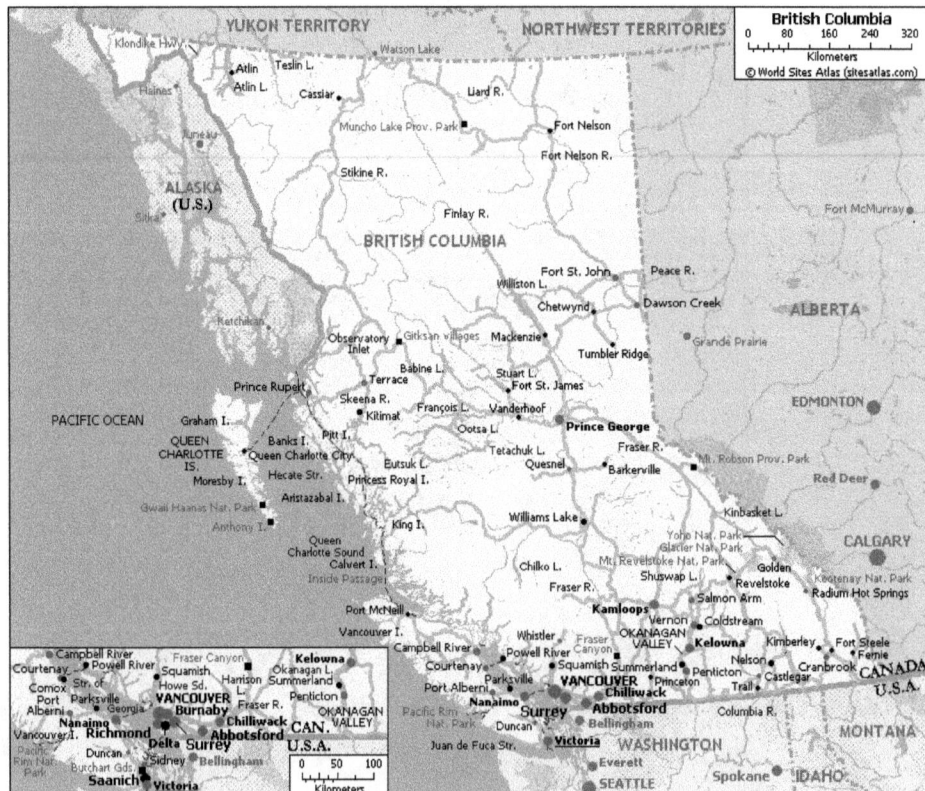

British Columbia

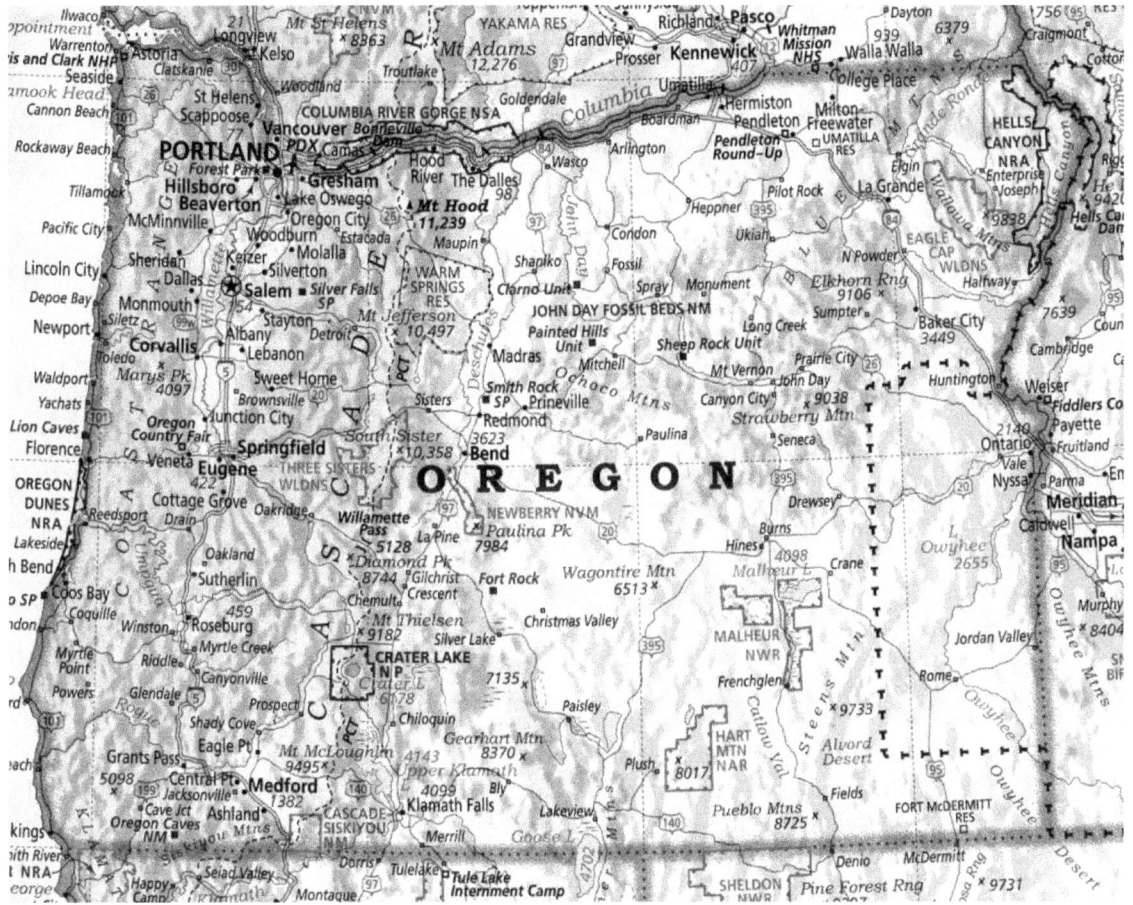

Appendix C - History

1. Migration Routes: The National Road

The National Road, by Philip D. Jordan. Indianapolis: Bobbs-Merrill Co., 1948. 442 pp. Hardcover. Illustrations, photographs, map, source notes.

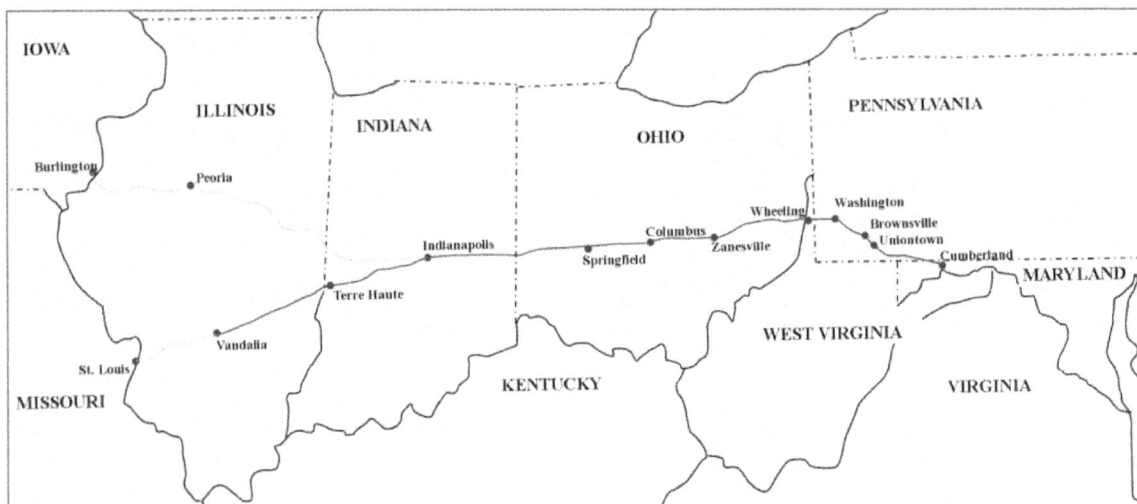

If your ancestors came to Iowa in the 1800s from eastern states, it's possible they traveled the National Road. Extending 600 miles from Cumberland, Maryland, it crossed the states of Pennsylvania, West Virginia, Ohio, Indiana, and Illinois, terminating at Vandalia. The Road served as a major migration route for pioneers heading west in the first half of the 19th century.

The oldest section of the National Road is the original Cumberland Trail blazed by General Braddock during the French and Indian War and is sometimes referred to as the Cumberland Road. The close of the Revolutionary War and the opening of the Northwest Territory for settlement created a wave of migration into western Pennsylvania and Eastern Ohio. In 1797 veteran Col. Ebenezer Zane responded to the needs of these west bound migrants by establishing Zane's Trace, a rough wagon road based on old Indian trails, from Wheeling, (West) Virginia to Maysville, Kentucky.

Ohio's entrance into the Union in 1803 stimulated discussions of how to connect the rapidly developing western frontier with eastern markets. The idea of federally-funded "internal improvements" included the construction of roads using monies raised from the sale of federal lands. The first construction contracts for the National Road were granted in the spring of 1811; the road pushed west in varying degrees over the next forty years, incorporating older trails like the Cumberland Road and Zane's Trace.

Some eastern sections were "macadamized" using crushed rock to create a hard, durable surface, but many western portions were never fully developed. In the 1830s the federal government began turning the Road over to states' control. In 1839 Illinois opened an eighty-nine-mile clay-surfaced section from Indiana to Vandalia, Illinois's former capital. Plans to extend the route to St. Louis never materialized.

The close of the Civil War and renewed railroad expansion marked the decline of the National Road as a major transportation route until the era of the automobile revived interest in a federal highway system. In 1926 the old National Road was incorporated into U.S. Highway 40. Today's Interstate 70 follows much the same route.

Experiencing the Historical Road

Between 1835 and 1865 pioneers headed to Iowa would have had plenty of company as thousands of settlers streamed west over the National Road. My Ohio ancestors probably picked up the route at Zanesville, then traveled west at least as far as Indianapolis. They may have left the main road there and cut across Illinois on lesser-known trails, perhaps through Peoria to Burlington, Iowa. Or they could have traveled all the way to Vandalia then on to St. Louis where they would have found transportation north on the Mississippi River to Keokuk or Burlington. Either way, it would have been an arduous journey.

What would such a journey have been like? It's not easy to picture the past, and it's even more difficult to understand your ancestor's unique experience, especially if they did not leave personal papers. Fortunately, many early travelers of the National Road recorded their impressions and experiences, and author Phillip D. Jordan drew heavily on these original sources in his 1948 book.

Jordan's well-sourced book weaves together the history of the road with first-hand accounts, reminiscences, anecdotes and legends. His words paint pictures of the rough-and-tumble world of frontier life, recreating the lives and personalities of the old Northwest's most colorful characters. Loosely chronological, each chapter explores a facet of life on the National Road: road construction, U.S. mail service, livestock drovers, stagecoach travel, westward migration, inns and taverns, peddlers and entertainers.

Although this book is out of print, it's available at many public libraries and used copies can be found through online vendors. If you want to get a taste of what your ancestor may have experienced in the 19th century as he moved his household west along the roads and trails to Iowa, Jordan's *National Road* will add a new dimension to your understanding of your migrant ancestor's life and times.

American Trail Series

Jordan's book was one of the *American Trail Series* published between 1947 and 1977, the earliest books by Bobbs-Merrill, later volumes published by McGraw Hill. Other titles include *Westward Vision: The Oregon Trail,* by David Lavender (1963); *The Great Wagon Road From Philadelphia to the South*, by Parke Rouse (1973); *The California Trail: An Epic with Many Heroes*, by George R. Stewart (1962). Look for these series titles and others at your local library.

2. Prussia 1800-1850

Frederick William III (reigned 1797–1840), pursued at first a foreign policy of caution and neutrality with respect to France and Napoleon I, and, when at last he went to war in 1806, it was too late to avert catastrophe. Napoleon's overwhelming defeat of the Prussians in the battle of Jena was followed by the rapid collapse of the state.

By the Treaty of Tilsit (1807) the king ceded all his possessions west of the Elbe River and all that had been gained under the Second and Third Partitions of Poland, together with the southern part of what had been gained under the First, so that the monarchy was reduced to Brandenburg, Silesia, the Pomeranian provinces, northern West Prussia (without Danzig [now Gdańsk, Poland]), and East Prussia. Moreover, the state was required to pay an exorbitant contribution to Napoleon's finances and to accept a French occupation of much of its territory.

The backwardness of Prussia was revealed by the disaster of 1806. Administrative, social, and military reforms were clearly overdue, and the king's chief minister, Karl Stein, seized the opportunity to introduce them. His basic idea was to evoke a positive consciousness of solidarity with the state by allowing the citizens to take a more active part in public affairs. This idea underlay the emancipation of the serfs (begun in 1807), the measures for local self-government, and the reshaping of the central government.

Among educated groups, meanwhile, the Napoleonic domination of Europe was provoking an upsurge of national sentiment, which was felt in Prussia no less strongly than in the other German states and was eventually to manifest itself in the War of Liberation (1813–14). The reform of the Prussian army was begun by Gerhard von Scharnhorst, who thus prepared it for the part that it was to play.

At the same time, the Romantic Movement in the intellectual and artistic fields further stimulated patriotism and the cult of liberty, to the service of which it even brought its interpretation of history. The foundation, in 1809, of the Friedrich Wilhelm University in Berlin, with Wilhelm von Humboldt as its chief promoter, affirmed Prussia's spirit in the aftermath of defeat.

Hardenberg adroitly steered Prussia through the difficulties of 1812, when Prussia and Austria, in enforced alliance with France, participated in Napoleon's attack on Russia. Napoleon's retreat from Moscow was the signal for a rising against the French. The Prussian army, with Gebhard Leberecht von Blücher and August Neidhardt von Gneisenau as its leaders, took a major part in the Battle of Leipzig, in the campaign of 1814 in France, and in the Battle of Waterloo in 1815.

The Congress of Vienna (1814–15) did not restore Ostfriesland, Lingen, Hildesheim, Ansbach, or Bayreuth to Prussia, and the latter recovered nothing of its gains under the Third Partition of Poland and regained only Danzig and a few other towns under the Second. But the rest of what Prussia had possessed in 1803 was restored practically entirely by the Congress, with considerable additions of new territory. This new territory comprised (1) areas taken from the kingdom of Saxony, which were merged with older Prussian territories on the west bank of the lower Elbe to form the Prussian province of Saxony; (2) areas west and east of the Rhine River, which were merged with older Prussian territories to form the Prussian Rhine province and the province of Westphalia; and (3) the formerly Swedish part of Vorpommern, with Rügen Island, which was merged with the rest of the Pomeranian territory to form the province of Pomerania, or Pommern. Moreover, by the Peace of Paris (1815), France ceded Saarlouis and Saarbrücken to Prussia, which incorporated them in the Rhine province. Thus, after 1815 Prussia stretched uninterrupted from the Neman River in the east to the Elbe River in the west, and west of the Elbe it possessed large (if discontinuous) territories in western Germany.

With its major territorial axis shifted from eastern Europe to western and central Germany, Prussia was henceforth the only great power with a predominantly German-speaking population. It was thus Austria's potential rival for hegemony in the German Confederation (Deutscher Bund), which the Congress also created.

The reforming impulse flagged after 1815. Frederick William III promised in May 1815 to introduce a constitution but failed to carry out his promise. By contrast, the Prussian educational system remained the best in Europe, the University of Berlin in particular enjoying an unrivaled reputation. The major parts of the kingdom's western provinces, however, had never been Prussian before and, being mainly Roman Catholic, were alien to Prussia in outlook. This often produced a fierce conflict between church and state. The Prussian bureaucracy established a high standard of efficiency and honesty that was at this time unique in Europe. In 1818 a simplified tariff, with moderate customs dues, was introduced for the entire kingdom; and this tariff became the basis for the Zollverein (Customs Union) established in 1834, which by 1852 included all the German states except Austria and Hamburg.

The population of German lands grew from about 20 million in 1750 to 33 million in 1816, and up to 52 million by 1865.

Housing in most of these cities unfortunately lagged far behind population growth, spawning dreadful urban slums. For most of the period, though, almost three-quarters of the population continued to live in communities of under 2,000 people. Infant and child mortality rates remained appallingly high, and illegitimate births rose from 15 percent in the early 19th century to 25 percent by mid-century.

Not until the Napoleonic Wars did the social structure of German states show some sign of change. Prussia had freed its peasantry in 1807, but had then given much of the land to landowners to compensate them for lost labor, leaving many peasants without the means to sustain themselves. Although serfdom was threatened by political liberalism and growing urban centers, it only collapsed fully following the revolutions of 1848.

Urbanization and the Food Industry

Prior to the beginning of the industrial era, European societies, in spite of all their differences, had a number of structural characteristics in common. An absolute majority of the population lived in the countryside and was directly or indirectly employed in agriculture. Additionally, the people – and consequently the economy and culture – were heavily influenced by local factors such as soil composition and the climate. The years around 1800 witnessed fundamental change in a number of areas; this applies in particular to dietary habits.

The potato and liquor, which had become increasingly widespread during the second half of the 18th century, were, to an extent, harbingers of the industrial age. Other harbingers were a strong growth in the economy and in the population.

Workers were drawn to the newly founded factories, resulting in an explosion in the population of the cities. This fundamentally changed daily dietary habits in two regards. Firstly, the density of urban development in the industrial conurbations excluded the possibility of growing one's own food in gardens or on larger plots of land. The agrarian subsistence farming of rural

Europe was now replaced by a modern commercial system of food supply. Secondly, the daily meals changed as a result of the new rhythm of working life. Particularly in the dynamic early phase of industrialization, machines and the attendance clock hardly permitted any time for family meals. Eating on one's own to fend off hunger replaced collective mealtimes.

The habitual food of the individual working-man naturally varies according to his wages. The better-paid workers, especially those in whose families every member is able to earn something, have good food as long as this state of things lasts; meat daily and bacon and cheese for supper. Where wages are less, meat is used only two or three times a week, and the proportion of bread and potatoes increases. Descending gradually, we find the animal food reduced to a small piece of bacon cut up with the potatoes; lower still, even this disappears, and there remain only bread, cheese, porridge, and potatoes, until on the lowest round of the ladder, among the Irish, potatoes form the sole food, As an accompaniment, weak tea, with perhaps a little sugar, milk, or spirits, is universally drunk.

In addition to the demographic changes, the transformative processes of the first half of the 19th century also manifested themselves in an expansion of the range of foods available and the adoption of new foodstuffs. Three main developments can be identified.

Firstly, the proliferation of the cultivation of potatoes resulted in profound change in the daily diet and replaced the early modern system of bread and porridge in many parts of Europe. It took a long time, for example, for the potato to integrate into the cuisine of southern Germany and Austria, which had been dominated by flour-based dishes. In northern Germany, by contrast, the potato replaced bread as an accompaniment to the main dish very quickly. In the Central German Uplands, the potato secured its place in the diet as an ingredient in soups and in the form of mash, which was comparable in texture and consistency to the porridge which had long been a part of the local diet. By the mid-19th century, the perception of the potato as the food of the impoverished classes_ had finally abated, and middle class European cuisine increasingly benefitted from the versatility of the potato.

Secondly, the distilling trade expanded, with the potato and other substances increasingly being used in the distilling process. For example, in Prussia, the amount of liquor distilled doubled between 1820 and 1840.

Thirdly, the extensive cultivation of sugar beet resulted in a dramatic reduction in the price of sugar, which had previously been an expensive imported commodity. It became commonly used among an ever-increasing portion of the population from the second half of the 19th century.

The growing importance of sugar beet during the early 19th century, or more precisely the production of industrially refined sugar, indicates another development which would continue to fundamentally transform nutrition in Europe: Science_ and technology became decisive factors in the production and distribution of food. The most significant innovations after 1850 were the application of technological advances to food (particularly in the area of preservation), the industrially standardized mass production and uniformization of food by means of newly developed machines, and the production of completely new food products, such as margarine, baking powder, artificial honey, and powdered milk.

In tandem with important changes in farming techniques and land usage (such as the use of artificial fertilizers and the development of agricultural machinery) and economic policies facilitating the easier circulation of goods, these developments made it possible for the first time since the Middle Ages to ensure that the broad masses of the European population had a dependable food supply. Whereas around 1800 the work of four peasants had been required to provide sufficient food for one non-agrarian consumer, 100 years later one farmer was able to provide for four consumers. The last large famine that was not caused by war occurred in Europe in 1846/1847.

The continuing expansion of the railway network in Europe_ and of the infrastructure of the retail trade, which further assisted an accelerated and comprehensive supply of basic food requirements, also contributed to the fundamental improvements in the supply of food during the 19th century. In the larger cities, large modern stores emerged to complement the smaller retailers. Intercontinental steam shipping also enabled a diversification of diets even in the rural parts of Europe. Colonial goods, tropical fruits, and imported spices now became part of the diet of broader sections of the population.

3. Westphalia, Prussia

Around 1 A.D. there was numerous incursions through Westphalia and perhaps even some permanent Roman or Romanized settlements. The Battle of Teutoburg Forest took place near Osnabrück (as mentioned, it is disputed whether this is in Westphalia) and some of the Germanic tribes who fought at this battle came from the area of Westphalia. Charlemagne is thought to have spent considerable time in Paderborn and nearby parts. His Saxon Wars also partly took place in what is thought of as Westphalia today. Popular legends link his adversary Widukind to places near Detmold, Bielefeld, Lemgo, Osnabrück and other places in Westphalia. Widukind was buried in Enger, which is also a subject of a legend.

Along with Eastphalia and Engern, Westphalia (Westfalahi) was originally a district of the Duchy of Saxony. In 1180 Westphalia was elevated to the rank of a duchy by Emperor Barbarossa. The Duchy of Westphalia comprised only a small area south of the Lippe River.

Parts of Westphalia came under Brandenburg-Prussian control during the 17th and 18th centuries, but most of it remained divided duchies and other feudal areas of power. The Peace of Westphalia of 1648, signed in Münster and Osnabrück, ended the Thirty Years' War. The concept of nation-state sovereignty resulting from the treaty became known as "Westphalian sovereignty".

As a result of the Protestant Reformation, there is no dominant religion in Westphalia. Roman Catholicism and Lutheranism are on relatively equal footing. Lutheranism is strong in the eastern and northern parts with numerous free churches. Münster and especially Paderborn are thought of as Catholic. Osnabrück is divided almost equally between Catholicism and Protestantism.

After the defeat of the Prussian Army at the Battle of Jena-Auerstedt, the Treaty of Tilsit in 1807 made the Westphalian territories part of the Kingdom of Westphalia from 1807–13. It was founded by Napoleon and was a French vassal state. This state only shared the name with the historical region; it contained only a relatively small part of Westphalia, consisting instead mostly of Hessian and Eastphalian regions.

After the Congress of Vienna, the Kingdom of Prussia received a large amount of territory in the Westphalian region and created the province of Westphalia in 1815.

4. Lengerich, Germany

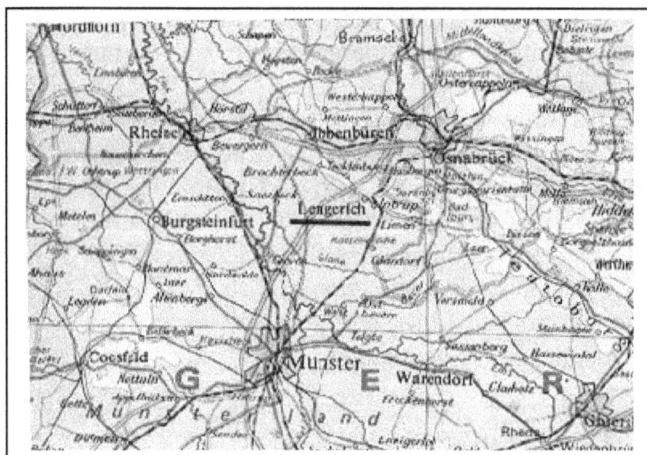

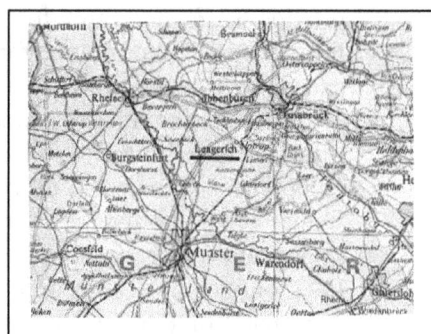

A small town in the district of Steinfurt, in North Rhine-Westphalia, Germany, it is situated on the southern slope of the Teutoburg Forest, approx. 15 km south-west of Osnabrück and 30 km north-east of Münster.

The first written source in which Lengerich is mentioned dates back to 1147. In this first written source the place is referred to as "Liggerkerke". It received its "City Rights" (Stadtrechte) in 1727.

Lengerich has been a small village for long time: in 1591 Lengerich counted 41 houses; in 1728 it counted 150 houses, with altogether 614 inhabitants and in 1821 the village had 1173 inhabitants in the town, and in the surrounding territory there were 4408 inhabitants.

Between 1832 and 1891, however, more than 1000 inhabitants emigrated, most of them to Canada and the USA. Since 1901 a railway passes Lengerich. I n 1927 the town and the surrounding territory were united into one community. From 1816 until 1975 Lengerich belonged to the "Kreis" Tecklenburg, since 1975 it belongs to the "Kreis" Steinfurt.

5. IOWA OFFICIAL REGISTER HISTORY OF IOWA

By Dorothy Schwieder, professor of history, Iowa State University

In the summer of 1673, French explorers Louis Joliet and Father Jacques Marquette traveled down the Mississippi River past the land that was to become the state of Iowa. The two explorers, along with their five crewmen, stepped ashore near where the Iowa river flowed into the Mississippi. It is believed that the 1673 voyage marked the first time that white people visited the region of Iowa. After surveying the surrounding area, the Frenchmen recorded in their journals that Iowa appeared lush, green, and fertile. For the next 300 years, thousands of white settlers would agree with these early visitors: Iowa was indeed lush and green; moreover, its soil was highly productive. In fact, much of the history of the Hawkeye State is inseparably intertwined with its agricultural productivity. Iowa stands today as one of the leading agricultural states in the nation, a fact foreshadowed by the observation of the early French explorers.

Before 1673, however, the region had long been home to many Native Americans. Approximately 17 different Indian tribes had resided here at various times including the Ioway, Sauk, Mesquaki, Sioux, Potawatomi, Oto, and Missouri. The Potawatomi, Oto, and Missouri Indians had sold their land to the federal government by 1830 while the Sauk and Mesquaki remained in the Iowa region until 1845. The Santee Band of the Sioux was the last to negotiate a treaty with the federal government in 1851.

The Sauk and Mesquaki constituted the largest and most powerful tribes in the Upper Mississippi Valley. They had earlier moved from the Michigan region into Wisconsin and by the 1730s, they had relocated in western Illinois. There they established their villages along the Rock and Mississippi Rivers. They lived in their main villages only for a few months each year. At other times, they traveled throughout western Illinois and eastern Iowa hunting, fishing, and gathering food and materials with which to make domestic articles. Every spring, the two tribes traveled northward into Minnesota where they tapped maple trees and made syrup.

In 1829, the federal government informed the two tribes that they must leave their villages in western Illinois and move across the Mississippi River into the Iowa region. The federal government claimed ownership of the Illinois land as a result of the Treaty of 1804. The move was made but not without violence. Chief Black hawk, a highly-respected Sauk leader, protested the move and in 1832 returned to reclaim the Illinois village of Saukenauk. For the next three months, the Illinois militia pursued Black Hawk and his band of approximately 400 Indians northward along the eastern side of the Mississippi River. The Indians surrendered at the Bad Axe River in Wisconsin, their numbers having dwindled to about 200. This encounter is known as the Black Hawk War. As punishment for their resistance, the federal government required the Sauk and Mesquaki to relinquish some of their land in eastern Iowa. This land, known as the Black Hawk Purchase, constituted a strip 50 miles wide lying along the Mississippi River, stretching from the Missouri border to approximately Fayette and Clayton Counties in Northeastern Iowa.

Today, Iowa is still home to one Indian group, the Mesquaki, who reside on the Mesquaki Settlement in Tama County. After most Sauk and Mesquaki members had been removed from the state, some Mesquaki tribal members, along with a few Sauk, returned to hunt and fish in eastern Iowa. The Indians then approached Governor James Grimes with the request that they be allowed to purchase back some of their original land. They collected $735 for their first land purchase and eventually they bought back approximately 3,200 acres.

Iowa's First White Settlers

The first official white settlement in Iowa began in June 1833, in the Black Hawk Purchase. Most of Iowa's first white settlers came from Ohio, Pennsylvania, New York, Indiana, Kentucky, and Virginia. The great majority of newcomers came in family units. Most families had resided in at least one additional state between the time they left their state of birth and the time they arrived in Iowa. Sometimes families had relocated three or four times before they reached Iowa. At the same time, not all settlers remained here; many soon moved on to the Dakotas or other areas in the Great Plains.

Iowa's earliest white settlers soon discovered an environment different from that which they had known back East. Most northeastern and southeastern states were heavily timbered; settlers there had material for building homes, outbuildings, and fences. Moreover, wood also provided ample fuel. Once past the extreme eastern portion of Iowa, settlers quickly discovered that the state was primarily a prairie or tall grass region. Trees grew abundantly in the extreme eastern and southeastern portions, and along rivers and streams, but elsewhere timber was limited.

In most portions of eastern and central Iowa, settlers could find sufficient timber for construction of log cabins, but substitute materials had to be found for fuel and fencing. For fuel, they turned to dried prairie hay, corn cobs, and dried animal droppings. In southern Iowa, early settlers found coal outcroppings along rivers and streams. People moving into northwest Iowa, an area also devoid of trees, constructed sod houses. Some of the early sod house residents wrote in glowing terms about their new quarters, insisting that "soddies" were not only cheap to build but were warm in the winter and cool in the summer. Settlers experimented endlessly with substitute fencing materials. Some residents built stone fences; some constructed dirt ridges; others dug ditches. The most successful fencing material was the osage orange hedge until the 1870s when the invention of barbed wire provided farmers with satisfactory fencing material.

Early settlers recognized other disadvantages of prairie living. Many people complained that the prairie looked bleak and desolate. One woman, newly arrived from New York State, told her husband that she thought she would die without any trees. Emigrants from Europe, particularly the Scandinavian countries, reacted in similar fashion. These newcomers also discovered that the prairies held another disadvantage - one that could be deadly. Prairie fires were common in the tall grass country, often occurring yearly. Diaries of pioneer families provide dramatic accounts of the reactions of early Iowans to prairie fires, often a mixture of fear and awe. When a prairie fire approached, all family members were called out to help keep the flames away. One nineteenth century Iowan wrote that in the fall, people slept "with one eye open" until the first snow fell, indicating that the threat of fire had passed.

Pioneer families faced additional hardships in their early years in Iowa. Constructing a farmstead was hard work in itself. Families not only had to build their homes, but often they had to construct the furniture used. Newcomers were often lonely for friends and relatives. Pioneers frequently contracted communicable diseases such as scarlet fever. Fever and ague, which consisted of alternating fevers and chills, was a constant complaint. Later generations would learn that fever and ague was a form of malaria, but pioneers thought that it was caused by gas emitted from the newly turned sod. Moreover, pioneers had few ways to relieve even common colds or toothaches.

Early life on the Iowa prairie was sometimes made more difficult by the death of family members. Some pioneer women wrote of the heartache caused by the death of a child. One women, Kitturah Belknap, had lost one baby to lung fever. When a second child died, she confided in her diary:

In most portions of eastern and central Iowa, settlers could find sufficient timber for construction of log cabins, but substitute materials had to be found for fuel and fencing. For fuel, they turned to dried prairie hay, corn cobs, and dried animal droppings. In southern Iowa, early settlers found coal outcroppings along rivers and streams. People moving into northwest Iowa, an area also devoid of trees, constructed sod houses. Some of the early sod house residents wrote in glowing terms about their new quarters, insisting that "soddies" were not only cheap to build but were warm in the winter and cool in the summer. Settlers experimented endlessly with substitute fencing materials. Some residents built stone fences; some constructed dirt ridges; others dug ditches. The most successful fencing material was the osage orange hedge until the 1870s when the invention of barbed wire provided farmers with satisfactory fencing material.

Early settlers recognized other disadvantages of prairie living. Many people complained that the prairie looked bleak and desolate. One woman, newly arrived from New York State, told her husband that she thought she would die without any trees. Emigrants from Europe, particularly the Scandinavian countries, reacted in similar fashion. These newcomers also discovered that the prairies held another disadvantage - one that could be deadly. Prairie fires were common in the tall grass country, often occurring yearly. Diaries of pioneer families provide dramatic accounts of the reactions of early Iowans to prairie fires, often a mixture of fear and awe. When a prairie fire approached, all family members were called out to help keep the flames away. One nineteenth century Iowan wrote that in the fall, people slept "with one eye open" until the first snow fell, indicating that the threat of fire had passed.

Pioneer families faced additional hardships in their early years in Iowa. Constructing a farmstead was hard work in itself. Families not only had to build their homes, but often they had to construct the furniture used. Newcomers were often lonely for friends and relatives. Pioneers frequently contracted communicable diseases such as scarlet fever. Fever and ague, which consisted of alternating fevers and chills, was a constant complaint. Later generations would learn that fever and ague was a form of malaria, but pioneers thought that it was caused by gas emitted from the newly turned sod. Moreover, pioneers had few ways to relieve even common colds or toothaches.

Early life on the Iowa prairie was sometimes made more difficult by the death of family members. Some pioneer women wrote of the heartache caused by the death of a child. One women, Kitturah Belknap, had lost one baby to lung fever. When a second child died, she confided in her diary:

"I have had to pass thru another season of sorrow. Death has again entered our home. This time it claimed our dear little John for its victim. It was hard for me to give him up but dropsy on the brain ended its work in four short days... We are left again with one baby and I feel that my health is giving way."

But for the pioneers who remained on the land, and most did, the rewards were substantial. These early settlers soon discovered that prairie land, although requiring some adjustments, was some of the richest land to be found anywhere in the world. Moreover, by the late 1860s, most of the state had been settled and the isolation and loneliness associated with pioneer living had quickly vanished.

Transportation: Railroad Fever

As thousands of settlers poured into Iowa in the mid-1800s, all shared a common concern for the development of adequate transportation. The earliest settlers shipped their agricultural goods down the Mississippi River to New

Orleans, but by the 1850s, Iowans had caught the nation's railroad fever. The nation's first railroad had been built near Baltimore in 1831, and by 1860, Chicago was served by almost a dozen lines. Iowans, like other Midwesterners, were anxious to start railroad building in their state.

In the early 1850s, city officials in the river communities of Dubuque, Clinton, Davenport, and Burlington began to organize local railroad companies. City officials knew that railroads building west from Chicago would soon reach the Mississippi River opposite the four Iowa cities. With the 1850s, railroad planning took place which eventually resulted in the development of the Illinois Central, the Chicago and North Western, reaching Council Bluffs in 1867. Council Bluffs had been designated as the eastern terminus for the Union Pacific, the railroad that would eventually extend across the western half of the nation and along with the Central Pacific, provide the nation's first transcontinental railroad. A short time later a fifth railroad, the Chicago, Milwaukee, St. Paul, and Pacific, also completed its line across the state.

The completion of five railroads across Iowa brought major economic changes. Of primary importance, Iowans could travel every month of the year. During the latter ninetieth and early twentieth centuries, even small Iowa towns had six passenger trains a day. Steamboats and stagecoaches had previously provided transportation, but both were highly dependent on the weather, and steam boats could not travel at all once the rivers had frozen over. Railroads also provided year-round transportation for Iowa's farmers. With Chicago's pre-eminence as a railroad center, the corn, wheat, beef, and pork raised by Iowa's farmers could be shipped through Chicago, across the nation to eastern seaports, and from there, anywhere in the world.

Railroads also brought major changes in Iowa's industrial sector. Before 1870, Iowa contained some manufacturing firms in the eastern portion of the state, particularly all made possible by year-around railroad transportation. Many of the new industries were related to agriculture. In Cedar Rapid, John and Robert Stuart, along with their cousin, George Douglas, started an oats processing plant. In time, this firm took the name Quaker Oats. Meat packing plants also appeared in the 1870s in different parts of the state: Sinclair Meat Packing opened in Cedar Rapids and John Morrell and Company set up operations in Ottumwa.

Education and Religion

As Iowa's population and economy continued to grow, education and religious institutions also began to take shape. Americans had long considered education important and Iowans did not deviate from that belief. Early in any neighborhood, residents began to organize schools. The first step was to set up township elementary schools, aided financially by the sale or lease of section 16 in each of the state's many townships. The first high school was established in the 1850s, but in general, high schools did not become widespread until after 1900. Private and public colleges also soon appeared. By 1900, the Congregationalists had established Grinnell College. The Catholics and Methodists were most visible in private higher education, however. As of 1900, they had each created five colleges: Iowa Wesleyan, Simpson, Cornell, Morningside, and Upper Iowa University by the Methodists; and Marycrest, St. Ambrose, Briar Cliff, Loras, and Clarke by the Catholics. Other church colleges present in Iowa by 1900 were

Coe and Dubuque (Presbyterian); Wartburg and Luther (Lutheran); Central (Baptist); and Drake (Disciples of Christ).

The establishment of private colleges coincided with the establishment of state educational institutions. In the mid-1800s, state officials organized three state institutions of higher learning, each with a different mission. The University of Iowa, established in 1855, was to provide classical and professional education for Iowa's young people; Iowa State College of Science and Technology (now Iowa State University), established in 1858; was to offer agricultural and technical training. Iowa State Teachers' College (now University of Northern Iowa), founded in 1876 was to train teachers for the state's public schools.

Iowans were also quick to organize churches. Beginning in the 1840s, the Methodist Church sent out circuit riders to travel throughout the settled portion of the state. Each circuit rider typically had a two-week circuit in which he visited individual families and conducted sermons for local Methodist congregations. Because the circuit riders' sermons tended to be emotional and simply stated, Iowa's frontiers-people could readily identify with them. The Methodists profited greatly from their "floating ministry," attracting hundreds of converts in Iowa's early years. As more settled communities appeared, the Methodist Church assigned ministers to these stationary charges.

Catholics also moved into Iowa soon after white settlement began. Dubuque served as the center for Iowa Catholicism as Catholics established their first diocese in that city. The leading Catholic figure was Bishop Mathias Loras, a Frenchman, who came to Dubuque in the late 1830s. Bishop Loras helped establish Catholic churches in the area and worked hard to attract priests and nuns from foreign countries. Before the Civil War, most of Iowa's Catholic clergy were from France, Ireland, and Germany. After the Civil War, more and more of that group tended to be native-born. Bishop Loras also helped establish two Catholic educational institutions in Dubuque, Clarke College and Loras College.

Congregationalists were the third group to play an important role in Iowa before the Civil War. The first group of Congregationalist ministers here were known as the Iowa Band. This was a group of 11 ministers, all trained at Andover Theological Seminary, who agreed to carry the gospel into a frontier region. The group arrived in 1843, and each minister selected a different town in which to establish a congregation. The Iowa Band's motto was "each a church; all a college." After a number of years when each minister worked independently, the ministers collectively helped to establish Iowa College in Davenport. Later church officials move the college to Grinnell and changed its name to Grinnell College.

Throughout the nineteenth century, many other denominations also established churches within the state. Quakers established meeting houses in the communities of West Branch, Springdale, and Salem. Presbyterians were also well represented in Iowa communities. Baptists often followed the practice of hiring local farmers to preach on Sunday mornings. And as early as the 1840s, Mennonite Churches began to appear in eastern Iowa. The work of the different denominations meant that during the first three decades of settlement, Iowans had quickly established their basic religious institutions.

The Civil War

By 1860, Iowa had achieved statehood (December 28, 1846), and the state continued to attract many settlers, both native and foreign-born. Only the extreme northwestern part of the state remained a frontier area. But after almost 30 years of peaceful development, Iowans found their lives greatly altered with the outbreak of the Civil War in 1861. While Iowans had no battles fought on their soil, the state paid dearly through the contributions of its fighting men. Iowa males responded enthusiastically to the call for Union volunteers and more than 75,000 Iowa men served with distinction in campaigns fought in the East and in the South. Of that number, 13,001 died in the war, many of disease rather than from battle wounds. Some men died in the Confederate prison camps, particularly Andersonville, Georgia. A total of 8,500 Iowa men were wounded.

Many Iowans served with distinction in the Union Army. Probably the best known was Grenville Dodge, who became a general during the war. Dodge fulfilled two important functions: he supervised the rebuilding of many southern railroad lines to enable Union troops to move more quickly through the South; and he directed the counter intelligence operation for the union Army, locating Northern sympathizers in the South who, in turn, would relay information on Southern troop movements and military plans to military men in the North.

Another Iowan, Cyrus Carpenter, was 31 years old when he entered the army in 1861. Living in Ft. Dodge, Carpenter requested a commission from the army rather than enlisting. He was given the rank of captain and was installed as quartermaster. Carpenter had never served in that capacity before, but with the aid of an army clerk, he proceeded to carry out his duties. Most of the time, Carpenter was responsible for feeding 40,000 men. Not only was it difficult to have sufficient food for the men, but Carpenter constantly had to keep his supplies and staff on the move. Carpenter found it an immensely frustrating task, but most of the time, he managed to have the food and other necessities at the right place at the right time.

Iowa women also served their nation during the war. Hundreds of women knitted sweaters, sewed uniforms, rolled bandages, and collected money for military supplies. Women formed soldiers' relief societies throughout the state. Annie Wittenmyer particularly distinguished herself through volunteer work. She spent much time during the war raising money and needed supplies for Iowa soldiers. At one point, Mrs. Wittenmyer visited her brother in a Union army hospital. She objected to the food served to the patients, contending that no one could get well on greasy bacon and cold coffee. She suggested to hospital authorities that they establish diet kitchens so that the patients would receive proper nutrition. Eventually, some diet kitchens were established in military hospitals. Mrs. Wittenmyer also was responsible for the establishment of several homes for soldiers' orphans.

The Political Arena

The Civil War era brought considerable change to Iowa and perhaps one of the most visible changes came in the political arena. During the 1840's, most Iowans voted Democratic although the state also contained some Whigs. Iowa's first two United States Senators were Democrats as were most state officials. During the 1850s, however, the state's Democratic Party developed serious internal problems as well as being unsuccessful in getting the national Democratic Party to respond to their needs. Iowans soon turned to the newly emerging Republican Party; the political career of James Grimes illustrates this change. In 1854, Iowans elected Grimes governor on the Whig ticket. Two years later, Iowans elected Grimes governor on the Republican ticket. Grimes would later serve as a Republican United States Senator from Iowa. Republicans took over state politics in the 1850s and quickly instigated several changes. They moved the state capital from Iowa City to Des Moines, they established the University of Iowa and they wrote a new state constitution. From the late 1850s until well into the twentieth century, Iowans remained strongly Republican. Iowans sent many highly capable Republicans to Washington, particularly William Boyd Allison of Dubuque, Jonathan P. Dolliver of Ft. Dodge, and Albert Baird Cummins of Des Moines. These men served their state and their nation with distinction.

Another political issue facing Iowans in the 1860s was the issue of women's suffrage. From the 1860s on, Iowa contained a large number of women, and some men, who strongly supported the measure and who worked endlessly for its adoption. In keeping with the general reform mood of the latter 1860s and 1870s, the issue first received serious consideration when both houses of the General Assembly passed a women's suffrage amendment in 1870. Two years later, however, when the legislature had to consider the amendment again before it could be submitted to the general electorate, interest had waned, opposition had developed, and the amendment was defeated.

For the next 47 years, Iowa women worked continually to secure passage of a women's suffrage amendment to Iowa's state constitution. During that time, the issue was considered in almost every session of the state legislature, but an amendment was offered (having passed both houses of the state legislature in two consecutive sessions) to the general electorate only once, in 1916. In that election, voters defeated the amendment by about 10,000 votes.

The arguments against women's suffrage ranged from the charge that women were not interested in the vote to the charge that women's suffrage would bring the downfall of the family and would cause delinquency in children. Regarding the defeat of the 1916 state referendum on the female vote, Iowa-born Carrie Chapman Catt, a leader for the women's suffrage cause, argued that the liquor interests in the state should accept responsibility as they had worked hard to defeat the measure. During the long campaign to secure the vote, however, the women themselves were not always in agreement as to the best approach to secure a victory. Catt herself led the final victorious assault in 1918 and 1919 in Washington with her "winning plan." This called for women to work for both state (state constitutions) and national (national constitution) amendments. Finally, in 1920, after both houses of the United States Congress passed the measure and it had been approved by the proper number of states, woman's suffrage became a reality for American women everywhere.

Iowa: Home for Immigrants

While Iowans were debating the issues of women's suffrage in the post Civil War period, the state itself was attracting many more people. Following the Civil War, Iowa's population continued to grow dramatically, from 674,913 people in 1860 to 1,194,020 in 1870. Moreover, the ethnic composition of Iowa's population also changed substantially. Before the Civil War, Iowa had attracted some foreign-born settlers, but the number remained small. After the Civil War, the number of immigrants increased. In 1869, the state encouraged immigration by printing a 96-page booklet entitled Iowa: The Home of Immigrants. The publication gave physical, social, educational, and political descriptions of Iowa. The legislature instructed that the booklet be published in English, German, Dutch, Swedish, and Danish.

Iowans were not alone in their efforts to attract more northern and western Europeans. Throughout the nation, Americans regarded these new comers as "good stock" and welcomed them enthusiastically. Most immigrants from these countries came in family units. Germans constituted the largest group, settling in every county within the state. The great majority became farmers, but many also became craftsmen and shopkeepers. Moreover, many German-Americans edited newspapers, taught school, and headed banking establishments. In Iowa, Germans exhibited the greatest diversity in occupations, religion, and geographical settlement.

The Marx Goettsch family of Davenport serves well as an example of German immigrants. At the time of his emigration in 1871, Goettsch was 24 years old, married and the father of a young son. During a two-year term in the German Army, Goettsch had learned the trade of shoemaking. Goettsch and his family chose to settle in Davenport, among Germans from the Schleswig-Holstein area. By working hard as a shoemaker, Goettsch managed not only to purchase a building for his home and shop, but also to purchased five additional town lots. Later, Goettsch had homes built on the lots which he rented out. He had then become both a small business man and a landlord.

During the next 25 years, Goettsch and his wife, Anna, raised six children and enjoyed considerable prosperity. For Marx and Anna, life in America, surrounded by fellow German-Americans, did not differ greatly from life in the old country. For their children, however, life was quite different. The lives of the Goettsch children - or the second generation - best illustrate the social and economic opportunities available to immigrants in the United States. If the family had remained in Germany, probably all five sons would have followed their father's occupation of shoemaker. In the United States, all five pursued higher education. Two sons received Ph.D. s, two sons received M.D.s, and one son became a professional engineer. With the third generation, education was also a crucial factor. Of seven grandchildren, all became professionals. Moreover, five of the seven were female. As the Goettsch experience indicates, opportunities abounded for immigrants settling in Iowa in the nineteenth and twentieth centuries. The newcomers and their children could take up land, go into business, or pursue higher education. For most immigrants, these areas offered a better, more prosperous life than their parents had known in the old country.

Iowa also attracted many other people from Europe, including Swedes, Norwegians, Danes, Hollanders, and many emigrants from the British Isles as shown by the following table. After 1900, people also emigrated from southern and eastern Europe. In many instances, immigrant groups were identified with particular occupations. The Scandinavians, including Norwegians, who settled in Winneshiek and Story Counties; Swedes, who settled in Boone County; and Danes, who settled in southwestern Iowa; were largely associated with farming. Many Swedes also became coal miners. The Hollanders made two major settlements in Iowa, the first in Marion County, and the second in northwest Iowa.

Proportionately far more southern and eastern immigrants, particularly Italians and Croatians, went into coal mining than did western and northern Europeans. Arriving in Iowa with little money and few skills, these groups gravitated toward work that required little or no training and provided them with immediate employment. In Iowa around the turn of the century, that work happened to be coal mining.

Coal Miners

Italian emigration differed from earlier emigration in that it tended to be male dominated. Typically, the Italian male emigrated with financial support of family or friends. Once in Iowa, he worked in the mines to pay back his sponsors; then he began to save to bring his wife and family from Italy. For two generations, Italian males worked in coal mines scattered throughout central and southern Iowa. Beginning around 1925, however, the Iowa coal industry began to decline. By the mid-1950s only a few underground mines remained in the state.

Life in a coal camp differed greatly from life in more settled Iowa communities. Most residents described the camps as bleak and dismal. The typical coal camp contained a company store, a tavern and pool hall, a miners' union hall, and an elementary school. Only rarely did coal camps contain churches or high schools. Coal camp residents had few social or economic opportunities. Most sons followed their fathers into the mines, and daughters tended to marry miners and continued to live in the camps.

The majority of blacks who migrated to Iowa during the late nineteenth and early twentieth centuries also worked as coal miners. Before the Civil War, Iowa had only a small black population, but in the 1880s that number increased considerably. Unfortunately, many of the early blacks were hired as strike breakers by Iowa coal operators. In later decades, however, coal companies hired blacks as regular miners.

The most notable coal community in Iowa was Buxton. Located in northern Monroe County, Buxton contained almost 5,000 people. By contrast, most coal camps averaged around 200 residents. Consolidation Coal Company owned and operated Buxton and instigated many progressive policies. Perhaps most unusual, Buxton had a high black population, at one time almost 54 percent. Most social and economic institutions were racially integrated, and the town contained many black professionals. Buxton existed from 1900 to 1922 when coal seams around the area were depleted. Black families then moved on to Des Moines, Waterloo, Cedar Rapids and to communities outside the state.

The Family Farm

After the Civil War, Iowa's agriculture also underwent considerable change. By the 1870s, farms and small towns blanketed the entire state. Also, in that decade, Iowa farmers established definite production patterns, which led to considerable prosperity. During the Civil War, Iowa farmers had raised considerable wheat. After the war, however, prominent Iowa farmers like "Tama Jim" Wilson, later to be national secretary of agriculture for 16 years, urged farmers to diversify their production, raise corn rather than wheat, and convert that corn into pork, beef, and wool whenever possible. For many generations, Iowa farmers have followed Wilson's advice.

Even though farmers changed their agricultural production, farm work continued to be dictated by the seasons. Wintertime meant butchering, fence mending, ice cutting, and wood chopping. In the spring, farmers prepared and planted their fields. Summertime brought sheep shearing, haying, and threshing. In the fall, farmers picked corn, the most difficult farm task of all.

Farm women's work also progressed according to the seasons. During the winter, women did their sewing and mending, and helped with butchering. Spring brought the greatest activity. Then women had to hatch and care for chickens, plant gardens, and do spring housekeeping. During the summer, women canned large amounts of vegetables and fruit. Canning often extended into the fall. Foods like apples and potatoes were stored for winter use. Throughout all the seasons, there were many constants in farm women's routines. Every-day meals had to be prepared, children cared for, and housekeeping done. With gardens to tend and chickens to feed and water, farm women had both indoor and outdoor work. Through their activities however, women produced most of their families' food supply.

During the late 1800s and early 1900s, social activities for farm families were limited. Most families made few trips to town. Some Iowans remember that even in the 1920s, they went to town only on Saturday night. Family members looked to each other for companionship and socializing. Moreover, the country church and the country school were important social centers. Families gathered at neighborhood schools several times each year for Christmas programs, spelling bees, and annual end-of-the-year picnics.

Many rural neighborhoods had distinct ethnic identifications, often merged into religion. Throughout the Iowa countryside, churches abounded with designations such as German Lutheran, German Catholic, German Methodist, Swedish Lutheran, Swedish Methodist, and Swedish Baptist.

Vast Changes

In 1917, the United States entered World War I and farmers as well as all Iowans experienced a wartime economy. For farmers, the change was significant. Since the beginning of the war in 1914, Iowa farmers had experienced economic prosperity. Along with farmers everywhere, they were urged to be patriotic by increasing their production. Farmers purchased more land and raised more corn, beef, and pork for the war effort. It seemed that no one could lose as farmers expanded their operations, made more money, and at the same time, helped the Allied war effort.

After the war, however, Iowa farmers soon saw wartime farm subsidies eliminated. Beginning in 1920, many farmers had difficulty making the payment for debts they had incurred during the war. The 1920s were a time of hardship for Iowa's farm families and for many families, these hardships carried over into the 1930s.

As economic difficulties worsened, Iowa farmers sought to find local solutions. Faced with extremely low farm prices, including corn at 10 cents a bushel and pork at three cents a pound, some Iowa farmers joined the Farm Holiday Association. This group, which had its greatest strength in the area around Sioux City, tried to withhold farm products from markets. They believed this practice would force up farm prices. The Farm Holiday Association had onlylimited success as many farmers did not cooperate and the withholding itself did little to raise prices. Farmers experienced little relief until 1933 when the federal government, as part of Franklin Roosevelt's New Deal, created a federal farm program.

In 1933, native Iowan Henry A. Wallace went to Washington as secretary of agriculture and served as principle architect for the new farm program. Wallace, former editor of the Midwest's leading farm journal, Wallace's Farmer, believed that prosperity would return to the agricultural sector only if agricultural production was curtailed. Further, he believed that farmers would be monetarily compensated for withholding agricultural land from production. These two principles were incorporated into the Agricultural Adjustment Act passed in 1933. Iowa farmers experienced some recovery as a result of the legislation but like all Iowans, they did not experience total recovery until the 1940s.

Since World War II, Iowans have continued to undergo considerable economic, political, and social change. In the political area, Iowan experienced a major change in the 1960s when liquor by the drink came into effect. During both the nineteenth and early twentieth centuries, Iowans had strongly supported prohibition, but in 1933 with the repeal of national prohibition, Iowans established a state liquor commission. This group was charged with control and regulation of Iowa's liquor sales. From 1933 until the early 1960s, Iowans could purchase packaged liquor only. In the 1970s, Iowans witnessed a reapportionment of the General Assembly, achieved only after a long struggle for an equitably-apportioned state legislature. Another major political change was in regard to voting. By the mid-1950s, Iowa had developed a fairly competitive two-party structure, ending almost 100 years of Republican domination within the state.

In the economic sector, Iowa also has undergone considerable change. Beginning with the first farm-related industries developed in the 1870s, Iowa has experienced a gradual increase in the number of business and manufacturing operations. The period since World War II has witnessed a particular increase in manufacturing operations. While agriculture continues to be the state's dominant industry, Iowans also produce a wide variety of products including refrigerators, washing machines, fountain pens, farm implements, and food products that are shipped around the world.

Strong Traditions

At the same time, some traditions remain unchanged. Iowans are still widely known for their strong educational systems, both in secondary as well as in higher education. Today, Iowa State University and the University of Iowa continue to be recognized nationally and internationally as outstanding educational institutions. Iowa remains a state composed mostly of farms and small towns, with a limited number of larger cities. Moreover, Iowa is still a place where most people live stable, comfortable lives, where family relationships are strong and where the quality of life is high. In many peoples' minds, Iowa is "middle America." Throughout the years, Iowans have profited from their environment and the result is a progressive people and a bountiful land.

6. Burlington, Iowa

Prior to European settlement, the area was neutral territory for the Sac and Fox Indians, who called it Shoquoquon (Shok-ko-kon), meaning Flint Hills.

In 1803, President Thomas Jefferson organized two parties of explorers to map the Louisiana Purchase. The Lewis and Clark Expedition followed the Missouri River, while Lt. Zebulon Pike followed the Mississippi River. In 1805, Pike landed at the bluffs below Burlington and raised the United States Flag for the first time on what would become Iowa soil and recommended construction of a fort. The recommendation went unheeded.

The American Fur Company of John Jacob Astor established a post in the area in 1829. Settlement began in 1833, shortly after the Black Hawk Purchase, when Samuel (aka Simpson) White, Amzi Doolitle, and Morton M. McCarver crossed the Mississippi River from Big Island and staked claims there. According to an account A.T. Andreas wrote in 1875. White erected a cabin in the area later platted to be Front Street between Court and High streets. Andreas called White and Doolittle the Romulus and Remus of their settlement, referring to the mythic heroes who founded Rome, a city surrounded by hills. A few weeks later, William R. Ross joined them and established a general store. In November and December, he surveyed the settlement for White and Doolittle.

In the spring of 1834 they allowed John Gray, who purchased the first lot with his wife Eliza Jane, to rename the town for $50. Gray chose to name it Burlington in honor of his hometown in Vermont. The Grays' daughter Abigail was born in Burlington that same year, the first American settler child born on Iowa soil.

In 1837, Burlington was designated the second territorial capital of the Wisconsin Territory. The Iowa Territory was organized in the following year, and Burlington was named as its first territorial capital. The government used "Old Zion," the first Methodist Church in Iowa (located near what is now Third and Washington streets), to conduct its business. A historical marker commemorates the site of the church and early territorial government.

On May 22, 1849, Maj. William Williams visited Burlington, writing a brief description in his journal:

This town [was] originally called Flint Hill- the Indian name was Shoquokon, Flint or Rock Hill. [It is] beautifully elevated, situated on the west side of the Mississippi River, a place of very considerable business. The town is very well built. Houses are good, generally taste[ful], brick dwellings. A great many handsome residences on the more elevated parts of the bluff. The number of inhabitants between 3,000 and 3,500. ... Was the first seat of government after the formation of the Territory of Iowa. The view of the city is extremely picturesque from the river. The main part of the city is situated like an amphitheater formed by the surrounding hills, beautiful buildings and private residences on the eminences around. From the location of Burlington, it must always be a place of considerable trade. The city is well built [in the] modern style, a very intelligent population... The river here is over 3/4 of mile wide and steam ferry boats constantly plying between this and the Illinois shore. — Maj. William Williams

7. 18th Century Social Order: Peasants and Aristos

The pattern of Europe's social organization, first established in the Middle Ages, continued well into the eighteenth century. Social status was still largely determined not by wealth and economic standing, but by the division into the traditional "orders" or "estates," determined by heredity and quality. This divinely sanctioned division of society into traditional orders was supported by Christian teaching, which emphasized the need to fulfill the responsibilities of one's estate. Inequality was part of that scheme and could not be eliminated. In the eighteenth century, this emphasis on a fixed order was expressed in secular terms as well.

One observer wrote in 1747 that "a reasonable man is always happy if he has what is necessary for him according to his condition [his place in the social order], that is to say, if he has the protection of the laws, and can live as his father lived before him: so that one of the essential things to the good of a nation is being governed in one constant and uniform manner."

Although Enlightenment intellectuals attacked these traditional distinctions, they did not die easily. In the Prussian law code of 1794, marriage between noble males and middle-class females was forbidden without a government dispensation. In cities, sumptuary legislation designated what dress different urban groups should wear so as to keep them separate. Even without government regulation, however, different social groups remained easily distinguished everywhere in Europe by the distinctive, traditional clothes they wore.

Such social conservatism was reinforced by society's ongoing preoccupation with local and regional differences. Local rivalries and local grievances greatly outweighed any loyalty to the larger state. Even local dialects continued to separate people. A French magistrate at Riom was unable to question a young itinerant from a town only fifteen miles away because "the speech of Courpire differs considerably from that of Riom." Nevertheless, some forces of change were at work in this traditional society. The ideas of the Enlightenment made headway as reformers argued that the idea of an unchanging social order based on privilege was hostile to the progress of society.

Moreover, especially in some cities, the old structures were more difficult to maintain as new economic structures, especially the growth of larger industries, brought new social contrasts that destroyed the old order. Despite these forces of change, however, it would take the revolutionary upheavals at the end of the eighteenth century before the old order would finally begin to disintegrate.

The Peasants

Since society was still mostly rural in the eighteenth century, the peasantry constituted the largest social group, making up as much as 85 percent of Europe's population. There were rather wide differences, however, between peasants from area to area. The most important distinction at least legally was between the free peasant and the serf. Peasants in Britain, northern Italy, the Low Countries, Spain, most of France, and some areas of western Germany shared freedom despite numerous regional and local differences. Legally free peasants, however, were not exempt from burdens.

Some free peasants in Andalusia in Spain, southern Italy, Sicily, and Portugal lived in poverty more desperate than that of many serfs in Russia and eastern Germany. In France, 40 percent of free peasants owned little or no land whatever by 1789. As the century progressed and new agricultural methods developed, small peasant proprietors were often unable to compete in efficiency with large estates.

Small peasant proprietors or tenant farmers in western Europe were also not free from compulsory services. Most owed tithes, often one-third of their crops. Although tithes were intended for parish priests, in France only 10 percent of the priests received them. Instead they wound up in the hands of towns and aristocratic landowners. Moreover, peasants could still owe a variety of dues and fees. Local aristocrats claimed hunting rights on peasant land and had monopolies over the flour mills, community ovens, and wine and oil presses needed by the peasants. Hunting rights, dues, fees, and tithes were all deeply resented.

Eastern Europe continued to be dominated by large landed estates owned by powerful lords and worked by serfs. Serfdom had come late to the east having largely been imposed in the sixteenth and seventeenth centuries. Peasants in eastern Germany were bound to the lord's estate, had to provide labor services on the lord's land, and could not marry or move without permission and payment of a tax.

By the eighteenth century, the landlord also possessed legal jurisdiction, giving him control over the administration of justice. Only in the Habsburg Empire had a ruler attempted to improve the lot of the peasants through a series of reforms. In Russia, peasants were not attached to the land but to the landlord and thus existed in a condition approaching slavery. In 1762, landowners were given the right to transfer their serfs from one estate to another. Unlike the rest of Europe and with the exception of the clergy and a small merchant class, eighteenth-century Russia was largely a society of landlords and serfs. Although eastern Europe, especially Poland, Russia, and some Habsburg provinces, experienced revolts by desperate peasants, they were easily crushed.

The local villages in which they dwelt remained the centers of peasants, social lives. Villages, especially in Western Europe, maintained public order, provided poor relief, a village church, and sometimes a schoolmaster, collected taxes for the central government, maintained roads and bridges, and established common procedures for sowing, ploughing, and harvesting crops. But villages were often dominated by richer peasants and proved highly resistant to innovations, such as new crops and agricultural practices.

The diet of the peasants in the eighteenth century did not vary much from that of the Middle Ages. Dark bread, made of roughly ground wheat and rye flour, remained the basic staple. It was quite nourishing and high in vitamins, minerals, and even proteins since the bran and germ were not ground out.

Peasants drank water, wine, and beer and ate soups and gruel made of grains and vegetables. Especially popular were peas and beans, eaten fresh in summer but dried and used in soups and stews in winter. The new foods of the eighteenth century, potatoes and American corn, added important elements to the peasant diet. Of course, when harvests were bad, hunger and famine became the peasants' lot in life, making them even more susceptible to the ravages of disease.

The Nobility

The nobles, who constituted about 2 or 3 percent of the European population, played a dominating role in society. Being born a noble automatically guaranteed a place at the top of the social order, with all of its attendant special privileges and rights. The legal privileges of the nobility included judgment by their peers, immunity from severe punishment, exemption from many forms of taxation, and rights of jurisdiction. Especially in central and eastern Europe, the rights of landlords over their serfs were overwhelming. In Poland until 1768, the nobility even possessed the right of life or death over their serfs. Other aristocratic privileges included the sole right to carry a sword, occupy a special pew in church, and possess a monopoly on hunting rights.   In many countries, nobles were self-conscious about their unique style of life that set them apart from the rest of society. This did not mean, however, that they were unwilling to bend the conventions of that lifestyle if there were profits to be made. For example, nobles by convention were expected to live off the yields of their estates. But although nobles almost everywhere talked about trade as being beneath their dignity, many were not averse to mercantile endeavors. Many were also, only too eager to profit from industries based on the exploitation of raw materials found on their estates; as a result, many nobles were involved in mining, metallurgy, and glassmaking.

Their diet also set them off from the rest of society. Aristocrats consumed enormous quantities of meat and fish dishes accompanied by cheeses, nuts, and a variety of sweets. Nobles also played important roles in military and government affairs. Since medieval times, landed aristocrats had functioned as military officers. While monarchs found it impossible to exclude commoners from the ranks of officers, the tradition remained that nobles made the most natural and hence the best officers. Moreover, the eighteenth-century nobility played a significant role in the administrative machinery of state. In some countries, such as Prussia, the entire bureaucracy reflected aristocratic values. Moreover, in most of Europe, the landholding nobility controlled much of the local government in their districts.

The nobility or landowning class was not a homogeneous social group. Landlords in England leased their land to tenant farmers while those in Eastern Europe used the labor services of serfs. Nobles in Russia and Prussia served the state while those in Spain and Italy had few official functions. Differences in wealth, education, and political power also led to differences within countries as well. In France, where there were about 350,000 nobles, only 4,000 noble families were allowed access to the court. The gap between rich and poor nobles could be enormous. According to figures for the poll tax in France, the richest nobles were assessed 2,000 livres a year while some nobles, because of their depressed economic state, paid only 6. Both groups were legally nobles. In

Poland, where the legal nobility constituted 10 to 15 percent of the population or about 750,000 people, most were poor and owned little or no land.

While these nobles had special pews in church and wore special dress, they were often as poor as the peasants. As the century progressed, these poor nobles increasingly sank into the ranks of the unprivileged masses of the population. lt has been estimated that the number of European nobles declined by one-third between 1750 and 1815. Although the nobles clung to their privileged status and struggled to keep others out, almost everywhere the possession of money made it possible to enter the ranks of the nobility. Rights of nobility were frequently attached to certain lands so purchasing the lands made one a noble; the acquisition of government offices also often conferred noble status.

The Aristocratic Way of Life

The Comte Charles-Maurice de Talleyrand-Perigord, the arch-survivor of the French revolutionary era, once commented that "no one who did not live before the Revolution" could know the real sweetness of living. Of course, he spoke not for the peasants whose labor maintained the system, but for the landed aristocrats. For them the eighteenth century was a final century of "sweetness" before the Industrial Revolution and bourgeois society diminished their privileged way of life.

In so many ways, the court of Louis XIV had provided a model for other European monarchs who, built palaces and encouraged the development of a court society as a center of culture. As at Versailles, these courts were peopled by members of the aristocracy whose income from rents or office-holding enabled them to participate in this lifestyle. This court society, whether in France, Spain, or Germany, manifested common characteristics: participation in intrigues for the king's or prince's favor, serene walks in formal gardens, and duels to maintain one's honor. Hierarchy and status were all important. A complex mixture of family heritage, title, and wealth determined the position one occupied in this society.

KJ The majority of aristocratic landowners, however, remained on their country estates and did not participate in court society; their large houses continued to give witness to their domination of the surrounding countryside. This was especially true in England where the court of the Hanoverian kings Georges I-III from 1714 to 1820, made little impact on the behavior of upper-class society. English landed aristocrats invested much time, energy, and money in their rural estates, giving the English country house an important role in English social life. One American observer remarked: "Scarcely any persons who hold a leading place in the circles of their society live in London. They have houses in London, in which they stay while Parliament sits, and occasionally visit at other seasons; but their homes are in the country."

After the seventeenth century, the English referred to their country homes, regardless of size, not as chateaus or villas but merely houses. Although there was much variety in country houses, many in the eighteenth century were built in the Georgian style named after the Hanoverian kings. This style was greatly influenced by the classical serenity and sedateness of the sixteenth-century Venetian architect, Andrea Palladio, who had specialized in the design of country villas. The Georgian country house combined elegance with domesticity, and its interior was often characterized as possessing a comfort of home that combined visual delight and usefulness.

The country house also fulfilled a newfound desire for greater privacy. Domestic etiquette militated against unannounced visits, and the rooms were designed to serve specialized purposes while their arrangement ensured more privacy. The central entrance hall contained a large staircase to the upstairs and also led to, the common rooms of the downstairs. The entrance hall, whose coats of arms and suits of armor still reflected its medieval ancestry, now also provided the setting for the ceremonial arrival and departure of guests on formal occasions. The lower floors of the country house held a series of common rooms for public activities. The largest was the drawing room of larger houses possessed two, which contained musical instruments and was used for dances or card games, a favorite pastime.

Other common rooms included a formal dining room, informal breakfast room, library, study, gallery, billiard room, and a conservatory. The downstairs common rooms were used for dining, entertaining, and leisure. Upstairs rooms consisted of bedrooms for husbands and wives, sons, and daughters. These were used not only for sleeping but also for private activities, such as playing for the children and sewing, writing, and reading for wives. This arrangement reflected the new desire for privacy and to some extent the growing awareness of individuality. "Going upstairs" literally meant leaving the company of others in the downstairs common rooms to be alone in the privacy of the bedroom. This eighteenth-century desire for privacy also meant keeping servants at a distance. They were now housed in their own wing of rooms and alerted to their employers, desire for assistance by a new invention long-distance cords connected to bells in the servants, quarters.

Although the arrangement of the eighteenth-century Georgian house originally reflected male interests, the influence of women was increasingly evident by the second half of the eighteenth century. Already in the seventeenth century, it had become customary for the sexes to separate after dinner; while the men preoccupied themselves with brandy and cigars in the dining room, women would exit into a "withdrawing room" for their own conversation. In the course of the eighteenth century, the drawing room became a larger, more feminine room with comfortable furniture grouped casually in front of fireplaces to create a cozy atmosphere.

8. Tecklenburg, Germany

A town in the district of Steinfurt, in North Rhine-Westphalia, Germany. It is located at the foothills of the Teutoburg Forest, southwest of Osnabrück.

In the 12th century the county of Tecklenburg emerged in the region that is now called the "Tecklenburger Land" in the western foothills of the Teutoburg Forest.

It was annexed by the neighbouring county of Bentheim in 1263, and Tecklenburg still had a count until the 19th century. Even today, some local descendents of the Bentheim / Tecklenburg families are sometimes considered as aristocrats. Much like many other European aristocrats, their family can be traced back to Charlemagne (800's) or is linked with the blood lines of old European royal families (e.g. in the case of the Bentheim-Tecklenburg there is a link with the House of Orange - the Dutch royal family).

Tecklenburg has retained some of its medieval townscape to date. Main sites include the ruined castle (now serving as open air theatre during the Summer) and the *Stadtkirche* (the main, old church) including tombs of the dukes of Tecklenburg and others prominent in the history of the county and city.

Today, the city of Tecklenburg (from a perspective of size really not a city but a town) is a tourist destination.

Burg Tecklenburg is a castle ruin in Tecklenburg, used today as an outdoor theatre.

The castle was built around 1250. Anna von Tecklenburg-Schwerin made a lot of construction changes. Around 1700 the castle was old and the bricks were used for other buildings in Tecklenburg. Only a ruin was the result.

9. Westphalia Parishes at the Family History Library

Kory L. Meyerink, MLS, AG, FUGA

The Family History Library has extensively collected church registers from the protestant and Catholic parishes in the former Prussian province of Westphalia (Westfalen in German). The following is a list (almost 1,000 places) of those parishes and other locales in Westphalia for which the library has cataloged materials. This list was extracted from the catalog in March 2006. Some localities may be added after that date, but this provides a useful starting place for identifying parishes in Westphalia.

Note that this is primarily a list of parishes, so most of the smaller villages, hamlets and similar locales do not appear in this list. However, since there is no similar list on the Internet of places in Westphalia, this provides a useful starting place for identifying locales in that important province.

A study of the Family History Library Catalog showed that there were 469 Evangelical (protestant) and 774 Catholic parishes in the province in 1910. This accounted for 87% of the protestant and 75% of the Catholic parishes. So, together, this list must account for at least 80% of all the parishes in one way or another. Indeed, that percentage is likely even higher. Certainly, some towns were parishes for both religions, yet the library may only hold copies of the registers for one of the religions in that town.

In the following list, several places include an additional name in parenthesis. When preceded by "Kr." this designates the German Kreis (county) to which the place belonged. Without the Kreis designation, the added word is usually a nearby town, river, region or another geographic feature name. In both cases, these are "descriptors" used in the catalog to distinguish that place from other places in the German empire with the same or a similar name. In a very few cases, that descriptor designates that the place is a different kind of political unit (such as a judicial office or a grafschaft), rather than a town or parish.

10. Steinfurt, Germany

A *Kreis* (district) in the northern part of North Rhine-Westphalia, Germany. Neighboring districts are Bentheim, Emsland, district-free Osnabrück and the Osnabrück district, Warendorf, district-free Münster, Coesfeld, and Borken.
In late medieval times Steinfurt became an independent earldom. Originally it was a part of the earldom of Bentheim, before it became independent in 1454. 1804 Steinfurt was reunited with Bentheim, before it became a part of the Prussian province of Westphalia in 1815. The new government in 1816 created the districts Steinfurt and Tecklenburg.

In 1975 the old district Steinfurt was merged with the district Tecklenburg, and together with Greven and Saerbeck from the former district Münster the current district was formed.

11. Rhineland

At the earliest historical period, the territories between the Ardennes and the Rhine were occupied by the Treveri, the Eburones and other Celtic tribes, who, however, were all more or less modified and influenced by their Germanic neighbours. On the right bank of the Rhine, between the Main and the Lahn, were the settlements of the Mattiaci, a branch of the Germanic Chatti, while farther to the north were the Usipetes and Tencteri.

Julius Caesar conquered the tribes on the left bank, and Augustus established numerous fortified posts on the Rhine, but the Romans never succeeded in gaining a firm footing on the right bank. As the power of the Roman Empire declined the Franks pushed forward along both banks of the Rhine, and by the end of the 5th century had conquered all the lands that had formerly been under Roman influence. The Germanic conquerors of the Rhenish districts were singularly little affected by the culture of the Roman provincials they subdued, and all traces of Roman civilization were submerged. By the 8th century the Frankish dominion was firmly established in western Germany and northern Gaul.

On the division of the Carolingian Empire at the Treaty of Verdun the part of the province to the east of the river fell to East Francia, while that to the west remained with the kingdom of Lotharingia.

By the time of Otto I. (d. 973) both banks of the Rhine had become part of the Holy Roman Empire, and the Rhenish territory was divided between the duchies of Upper Lorraine, on the Mosel, and Lower Lorraine on the Meuse. As the central power of the Holy Roman Emperor weakened, the Rhineland split up into numerous small independent principalities, each with its separate vicissitudes and special chronicles. The old Lotharingian divisions became obsolete, and the name of Lorraine became restricted to the district that still bears it.

In spite of its dismembered condition, and the sufferings it underwent at the hands of its French neighbours in various periods of warfare, the Rhenish territory prospered greatly and stood in the foremost rank of German culture and progress. Aachen was the place of coronation of the German emperors, and the ecclesiastical principalities of the Rhine bulked largely in German history.

Prussia first set foot on the Rhine in 1609 by the occupation of the Duchy of Cleves and about a century later Upper Guelders and Moers also became Prussian. At the peace of Basel in 1795 the whole of the left bank of the Rhine was resigned to France, and in 1806 the Rhenish princes all joined the Confederation of the Rhine.

After the Congress of Vienna, Prussia was awarded with the entire Rhineland, which included the Grand Duchy of Berg, the ecclesiastic electorates of Trier and Cologne, the free cities of Aachen and Cologne, and nearly a hundred small lordships and abbeys. The Prussian Rhine province was formed in 1822 and Prussia had the tact to leave them in undisturbed possession of the liberal institutions they had become accustomed to under the republican rule of the French. In 1920, the districts of Eupen and Malmedy were transferred to Belgium.

12. North Rhine-Westphalia, Germany

The state of North Rhine-Westphalia was established by the British military administration's "Operation Marriage" on 23 August 1946, by merging the province of Westphalia and the northern parts of the Rhine Province, both being political divisions of the former state of Prussia within the German Reich. On 21 January 1947, the former state of Lippe was merged with North Rhine-Westphalia. The constitution of North Rhine-Westphalia was then ratified through a referendum.

Geography

North Rhine-Westphalia encompasses the plains of the Lower Rhine region and parts of the Central Uplands (*die Mittelgebirge*) up to the gorge of Porta Westfalica. The state covers an area of 34,083 km^2 (13,160 sq mi) and shares borders with Belgium in the southwest and the Netherlands in the west and northwest. It has borders with the German states of Lower Saxony to the north and northeast, Rhineland-Palatinate to the south and Hesse to the southeast.

Approximately half of the state is located in the relative low-lying terrain of the Westphalian Lowland and the Rhineland, both extending broadly into the

North German Plain. A few isolated hill ranges are located within these lowlands, among them the Hohe Mark, the Beckum Hills, the Baumberge and the Stemmer Berge.

The terrain rises towards the south and in the east of the state into parts of Germany's Central Uplands. These hill ranges are the Weser Uplands - including the Egge Hills, the Wiehen Hills, the Wesergebirge and the Teutoburg Forest in the east, the Sauerland, the Bergisches Land, the Siegerland and the Siebengebirge in the south, as well as the left-Rhenish Eifel in the southwest of the state. The Rothaargebirge in the border region with Hesse rises to height of about 800 m above sea level. The highest of these mountains are the Langenberg, at 843.2 m above sea level, the Kahler Asten (840.7 m) and the Clemensberg (839.2 m).

The planimetrically-determined centre of North Rhine-Westphalia is located in the south of Dortmund-Aplerbeck in the Aplerbecker Mark (51° 28' N, 7° 33' Ö). Its westernmost point is situated near Selfkant close to the Dutch border, the easternmost near Höxter on the Weser. The southernmost point lies near Hellenthal in the Eifel region. The northernmost point is the NRW-Nordpunkt near Rahden in the northeast of the state. The Nordpunkt is located only 100 km to the south of the North Sea coast. The deepest natural dip is arranged in the district Zyfflich in the city of Kranenburg with 9.2 m above sea level in the northwest of the state. Though, the deepest point overground results from mining. The open-pit Hambach reaches at Niederzier a deep of 293 m below sea level. At the same time, this is the deepest man-made dip in Germany.

The most important rivers flowing at least partially through North Rhine-Westphalia include: the Rhine, the Ruhr, the Ems, the Lippe, and the Weser. The Rhine is the by far most important river in North Rhine-Westphalia: it enters the state as Middle Rhine near Bad Honnef, where still being part of the Mittelrhein wine region. It changes into the Lower Rhine near Bad Godesberg and leaves North Rhine-Westphalia near Emmerich at a width of 730 metres. Almost immediately after entering the Netherlands, the Rhine splits into many branches.

The Pader, which flows entirely within the city of Paderborn, is considered Germany's shortest river.

For many, North Rhine-Westphalia is synonymous with industrial areas and urban agglomerations. However, the largest part of the state is used for agriculture (almost 52%) and forests (25%).

Cologne is the largest city of North Rhine-Westphalia

North Rhine-Westphalia has a population of approximately 17.5 million inhabitants (more than the entire former East Germany, and slightly more than the Netherlands) and is centred around the polycentric Rhine-Ruhr metropolitan region, which includes the industrial Ruhr region and the Rhenish cities of Bonn, Cologne and Düsseldorf. 30 of the 80 largest cities in Germany are located within North Rhine-Westphalia. The state's capital is Düsseldorf; the state's largest city is Cologne.

According to studies of the Ruhr University Bochum 42.24% of the North Rhine-Westphalian population adheres to the Roman Catholic Church, 28.35% are members of the Evangelical Church in Germany, 23.76% are unaffiliated, non-religious or atheists, 2.78% are Muslims, 0.49% are adherents of the Eastern Orthodox Church, 1.05% are members of smaller Christian groups (half of them the New Apostolic Church), 1.0% are adherents of new religions or esoteric groups, 0.2% are adherents of Indian religions, and 0.17% are Jews.

North Rhine-Westphalia ranks first in population among German states for both Catholics and Protestants.

Politics

The politics of North Rhine-Westphalia takes place within a framework of a federal parliamentary representative democratic republic. The two main parties, as on the federal level, the centre-right Christian Democratic Union and the centre-left Social Democratic Party. From 1966 to 2005, North Rhine-Westphalia was continuously governed by the Social Democrats or SPD-led governments.
The state's legislative body is the Landtag ("state diet"). It may pass laws within the competency of the state, e.g. cultural matters, the education system, matters of internal security, i.e. the police, building supervision, health supervision and the media; as opposed to matters that are reserved to Federal law.

North Rhine-Westphalia uses the same electoral system as the Federal level in Germany: "*Personalized proportional representation*". Every five years the citizens of North Rhine-Westphalia vote in a general election to elect at least 181 members of the Landtag. Only parties who win at least 5% of the votes cast may be represented in parliament.

The Landtag, the parliamentary parties and groups consisting of at least 7 members of parliament have the right to table legal proposals to the Landtag for deliberation. The law that are passed by the Landtag is delivered to the Minister-President, who, together with the ministers involved, is required to sign it and announce it in the Law and Ordinance Gazette.

Culture

The flag of North Rhine-Westphalia is green-white-red with the combined coats of arms of the Rhineland (white line before green background, symbolizing the river Rhine), Westfalen (the white horse) and Lippe (the red rose).

According to legend the horse in the Westphalian coat of arms is the horse that the Saxon leader Widukind rode after his baptism. Other theories attribute the horse to Henry the Lion. Some connect it with the Germanic rulers Hengist and Horsa.

In the 1950s and 1960s, Westphalia was known as *Land von Kohle und Stahl* or the land of coal and steel. In the post-WWII recovery, the Ruhr was one of the most important industrial regions in Europe and contributed to the German Wirtschaftswunder. As of the late 1960s, repeated crises led to contractions of these industrial branches. On the other hand, producing sectors, particularly in mechanical engineering and metal and iron working industry, experienced substantial growth. Despite this structural change and an economic growth which was under national average, the 2007 GDP of 529.4 billion euro (21.8 percent of the total German GDP) made the land the economically most important in Germany, as well as one of the most important economical areas in the world. Of Germany's top 100 corporations, 37 are based in North Rhine-Westphalia. On a per capita base, however, Northrhine-Westphalia remains one of the weaker among the Western German states. As of November 2010, the unemployment rate is 8.1%, second highest among all western German states.

North Rhine-Westphalia attracts companies from both Germany and abroad. In 2009, the state had the most foreign direct investments (FDI) anywhere in

Germany. Around 13,100 foreign companies from the most important investment countries control their German or European operations from bases in North Rhine-Westphalia.

In February 2014 North Rhine-Westphalia was ranked as the European Region of the Future in the 2014/15 list by FDi Magazine.

There have been many changes in the state's economy in recent times. Among the many changes in the economy, employment in the creative industries is up while the mining sector is employing fewer people. Industrial heritage sites are now workplaces for designers, artists and the advertising industry. The Ruhr region, formerly known as the "land of coal and steel" (*Land von Kohle und Stahl*), has – since the 1960s – undergone a significant structural change away from coal mining and steel industry. Many rural parts of Eastern Westphalia, Bergisches Land and the Lower Rhine ground their economy on "Hidden Champions" in various sectors.

Education

RWTH Aachen is one of Germany's leading universities of technology and was chosen by DFG as one of the German Universities of Excellence in 2007 and again in 2012.

North Rhine-Westphalia is home to 14 universities and over 50 partly postgraduate colleges, with a total of over 500,000 students. Largest and oldest university is the University of Cologne *(Universität zu Köln)*, originally founded in 1388 AD, since 2012 also one of Germany's eleven Universities of Excellence.

13. Food and Drink in Europe

by Gunther Hirschfelder, Manuel Trummer Original in German, displayed in English Published: 2013-08-20

There is scarcely an aspect of daily cultural practice which illustrates the processes of transformation in European culture as clearly as daily nutrition. Indeed, securing the latter was essential for the daily fight for survival right up to the mid-19th century, with large sections of the population frequently being confronted with harvest failures and food shortages resulting from wars, extreme weather, pests, fire, and changes in the agrarian order, and population growth. Consequently, food and drink were central both in daily life and in the celebration of feasts and provided an opportunity for social differentiation. The hope for better nutrition was the primary impetus for many migration processes and a canvas onto which desires were projected. The "Land of Cockaigne" motif, which can be traced from the Frenchman Fabliau de Coquaignes in the 13th century to Erich Kästner's (1899–1974) children's book "Der 35. Mai oder Konrad reitet in die Südsee" (1931), is a classic example of this.

Introduction

Daily nutrition has in the past been dependent on many exogenous factors and remains so. Individual preferences have only begun to play a more significant role in nutrition since the second half of the 20th century. Particularly in pre-modern society, what people ate was decided to a far greater degree by political, economic, and religious factors. The selection of foods, but also the dining culture and the norms of behaviour at the table were defined by tradition and were considered to be binding on all members of society.

For much of the modern era, European culinary culture exhibited enormous spatial and social diversity, which persisted well into the 20th century. However, this broad spectrum of traditions, which in effect only had an emphasis on energy-rich foods and protein-rich products in common, began to narrow from the 16th century onward – at least among the European social elite – as French aristocratic cuisine became the example for others to follow. In the 20th century, another dominant culinary culture, the American, arrived on the scene, but this was now based on industrial production, products aimed at a mass market, and in particular on a new dining context, which over time played a central role in the dissolution of established dining chronologies.

Many aspects of daily nutrition have left little trace in the historical sources. This is particularly true of the rural context and of foodstuffs which were neither traded nor taxed, such as herbs and vegetables from garden plots, and mushrooms and berries gathered in the autumn. We nevertheless know, for example, that turnips, cabbages, beans, and peas, along with leeks, celery, and pumpkins formed the basis of the diet of the rural population. At the beginning of the 16th century, white cabbage, red cabbage, and savoy cabbage were added to the diet, and Brussels sprouts, swedes, cauliflowers, mangolds and lettuce were added from the late 16th century. The fertile soils of southwest Germany, the low countries and, in particular, France were far superior to the less fertile soils of eastern Europe and Russia when it came to growing these new vegetables. In the sparsely populated Scandinavian north, horticulture was not possible at all. However, gathering fruits and plants in forests played a more important role there.

We have more detailed information regarding the consumption of alcohol, as this has left deeper traces in the historical sources – for both fiscal reasons and reasons of public order – which is why this topic is dealt with in greater detail in this article. There are a number of distinct phases in the history of nutrition in the modern period, though these overlap to a considerable degree, affecting one another but also diverging. For this reason, it is difficult to draw a hard and fast distinction between them. However, two large phases emerge rather clearly. There was the Reformation period, which ended with the Thirty Years' War (1618–1648) and which gave rise to different dietary systems in close proximity due to the differences between the confessions of the issue of fasting. And there was the Little Ice Age, which caused numerous harvest failures and continuing undernourishment up to the 19th century. However, new foods from other continents and the colonies also appeared on the menu in Europe during this period, and table manners which were formerly only observed among the aristocracy gradually became the norm among broader sections of the population.

The End of Medieval Cuisine?

At the beginning of the modern period, the diet in Europe remained very similar to the medieval period, and old traditions were only replaced gradually. For the majority of the population – particularly in the towns and cities of central Europe – this meant that the calorie intake was higher compared to the preceding centuries and compared to the 18th century and the early 19th century. It is estimated that roughly 200 kilograms of cereals was consumed per person annually. Recent research suggests that the consumption of meat was lower during this period than academics had previously assumed though it is likely that roughly 50 kilograms of meat per person was consumed annually in the territory north of the Alps. Meat consumption was considerably higher in the northern part of the German-speaking territory than in the Mediterranean region, for example.

A complete daily ration usually consisted of a morning meal after the morning work had been completed ("prandium" or "imbs") and an evening meal. In addition to these, up to three other meals were consumed daily: morning soup, supper and nightcap. Among the poor, the dietary staples were primarily bread and a kind of porridge (a puree made with grain, usually cooked in lard). The whiter the bread, the more refined it was considered to be. In the case of meat, boiled soup meat was the simplest and the cheapest option. Roasts, poultry, and game were more prestigious, and they were the preserve of the nobility.

There were also differences between rich and poor with regard to the consumption of fish, which was primarily consumed on fast days, of which there were up to 150 annually. The wealthier section of the population availed of a range of fresh salt-water and fresh-water fish. Salmon was the most popular species. As a fresh-water fish, it could be caught relatively easily almost everywhere in central Europe. In addition to native river crabs, the poor primarily ate salted or dried sea fish, even in regions far from the coast. From the mid-14th century, fish farming flourished in a broad belt stretching from Bohemia, Poland and Silesia through Lusatia to Württemberg and Lorraine, providing a good supply of fresh-water fish up to the early 16th century. There were also dramatic differences between the social classes when it came to the supply of vegetables. The poor could scarcely afford anything other than dried legumes, while the rich could purchase fresh seasonal vegetables, and in the larger cities they could even buy citrus fruits from time to time.

The consumption of alcohol underwent a fundamental change at the beginning of the modern period. From the late medieval period onward, less wine was produced and consumed, primarily due to the increasingly unsuitable climate. Additionally, from the 14th century to the 16th century, the bottom-fermented hops beers, which could be stored for much longer, increasingly replaced the older gruit ales, which were brewed using a mixture of herbs. Wine – often spiced, sugared, and heated – then became a central element of the drinks culture of the higher social classes throughout Europe. However, the volume of alcoholic drinks consumed was not nearly as large as earlier studies of customs and culture had assumed. According to realistic estimations, the average consumption in Cologne, one of the wealthiest cities during that period, lay at most between 175 and 295 litres of beer per person annually. However, many people drank mainly – or exclusively – water, as pre-modern agrarian society was not capable of producing ingredients of sufficient quality for brewing in sufficient quantities.

The combination of food, the community, and public display played a central role in social and cultural life. This was fundamentally true of the agrarian context. Painted in Flanders around 1568 and still medieval in structure, *De Boerenbruiloft* (*The Peasant Wedding*) by Pieter Bruegel the Elder (ca. 1525–1569) depicts this phenomenon. Due to numerous saints' days, feast days, and public holidays, urban artisans worked no more than 265 days annually, which is equivalent to the modern five-day week. The food consumed on work-free days differed to that consumed on workdays for it was richer and higher in protein. However, just like during the week, it was consumed in a group, usually with work colleagues rather than with the family, and the dining context reflected hierarchies and traditions.

Elaborate and formal public feasts served to demonstrate hierarchical structures. For example, the aldermen of the wealthy city of Constance on Lake Constance put on a feast in December 1452 in honour of the mayor and the reeve. As the city accounts record "100 mannen" as guests, we can conclude that no women were invited. The city accounts detail exactly what was served. The organizers purchased 95 pounds of beef, 37 pounds of pork and 18 pounds of sausage, as well as 30 fat hens, 31 ducks, and 121 thrushes. They also procured spices, sugar, almonds, saffron, and 110 eggs, in addition to 300 carp and pike, and 140 smaller fish in order to prepare the stock for the popular *Galrey* fish galantine. In addition to these enormous quantities of fish and meat, bread, rice, cake, cheese, confectionery, and nuts were provided. 537 litres of wine were served. Compared to the vast expenditure on food, the crockery provided was decidedly modest. 120 bowls and 120 wooden plates were bought, as well as *Tellerbrot* (literally "plate bread"), i.e. bread which was used to eat on.

However, it is debatable whether these details can be taken at face value in a cultural analysis of the feast. Did each guest really eat two kilos of meat, numerous fish, and trimmings, and drink five litres of wine? That was certainly not the case. We must assume instead that the leftovers were brought home, donated to the poor, or given to employees of the city as a form of inflation-free payment-in-kind.

The transition from the medieval to the modern period had comparatively little effect at the dinner table, and many basic structures of medieval mealtimes persisted well into the 16th century. However, this does not apply to behaviour at the table. A range of French rules of behaviour from the mid-15th century clearly demonstrate how difficult it was even for people in the higher social classes to depart from older norms, for example to not dig into all the bowls with their hands at the beginning of the meal, to not toss gnawed bones back into the bowl or over their shoulders, or even just to wash their hands before eating. The "Prozeß der Zivilisation" ("civilizing process") proceeded at best very gradually. In the late 15th century, many archaic characteristics persisted. On the one hand, people were still placing gnawed chicken bones back in the bowl, while, on the other hand, there was much discussion about the rules regarding fasting and the godlessness of gluttony.

During the course of the 15th century, *Tischzucht* (table discipline) was also discussed in the more urbanized regions of the German-speaking territory. One of the earliest such documents was a book entitled *Von tisch zucht* published in 1471 by Clara Hätzlerin (1430–1476), whose family were burgesses of Augsburg. This work discusses among other things the hierarchy at the table and the importance of saying grace. Hätzlerin also encourages her readers not to use the tablecloth to blow their nose. Such rules soon became standard for the entire European bourgeoisie and they signalled the emerging homogenization of the dining culture of the European bourgeoisie and aristocracy.

During the transition to the modern period, hostelries also emerged as an integrative component of the European culture of dining and imbibing. Particularly along trade routes and in cities, multifunctional hostelries became common and served as centres of communication_ and the exchange of news, while in the countryside and in the sparsely populated regions of northern and eastern Europe, the older, archaic hospitality remained dominant.

We can summarize that the structure of the European diet changed comparatively little between 1450 and 1550, even in spite of the discovery_ of the New World. However, the Reformation brought about more abrupt changes because it fundamentally changed the culture of fasting and feasting by getting rid of the feast days for saints in many territories (those that became Protestant). Additionally, the Calvinist Reformation_ in particular resulted in a fundamentally more critical reappraisal of food consumption. Martin Luther (1483–1546)_ condemned the supposed drunkenness of the Germans, but he himself did not fundamentally reject earthly indulgences. John Calvin (1509–1564)_ and Huldrych Zwingli (1484–1531)_, on the other hand, condemned all gluttony. Additionally, the strict fasting regulations which had persisted up to the Reformation were relaxed in the Protestant territories, or even reversed. Thus, a bitter controversy soon emerged at the borders between Catholic and Protestant milieus over the supposedly correct diet, and this controversy had a considerable effect on people's daily habits. What was served at mealtimes in the northern Netherlands, in Switzerland, and in Scandinavia_ and how public taverns_ were evaluated and, in particular, regulated, now differed considerably from those territories which had remained Catholic.

Consumption and Innovation at the Beginning of the Modern Period – Rice, Buckwheat, and Meat

At the beginning of the modern period, the cuisine of the ruling elite and the dietary culture of the broader masses, which remained medieval in structure and heavily spiced, still received their primary impulses from Italy. In particular, the old trading port_ of Venice dominated the cuisines of central Europe. Rice cultivation blossomed in northern Italy in the late 15th century, and soon spread to central Europe as a result of trans-Alpine trade. While *riso* had previously been cultivated in monasteries and ground to make a binding agent for ointment, the political campaigns of individual rulers – particularly the Milanese duke Gian Galeazzo Sforza (1469–1494)_ – resulted in the large-scale cultivation of rice south of the Alps_. Compared to the established cereals, rice offered the prospect of a much higher yield and thus of an additional support in the event of food shortages. Promoted by advisory tracts such as the *Discorsi* ("Speeches", 1544)_ of Pietro Andrea Mattioli (1500–1577)_, the cultivation of rice spread throughout the whole of northern Italy during the course of the 16th century. In the well-watered Po Plain, the "treasure of the swamps" (Mattioli) was already a standard component in the meals of the broader population by 1550.

The Italian courts also influenced the refined cuisine of the European ruling class. The kitchen at the court of Naples was one of the main centres of innovation into the 16th century, where cooks like Ruperto de Nola_ introduced numerous Catalan, Castilian, and Moorish influences, as detailed in early cookbooks such as Nola's *Lybre de doctrina Pera ben Servir: de Tallar: y del Art de Coch* ("Textbook of Good Serving, of Cutting, and of the Art of Cooking", 1520)_. The Florentine court of Caterina de Medici (1519–1589)_ also became something of a guiding example of European court dining. The Florentine influence brought about a strong refinement of courtly table manners. Thus, eating with a fork instead of with one's hands reached France via the court of Caterina de Medici, who became queen of France when her husband Henry II (1519–1559)_ acceded to the throne in 1547. During the course of the 16th century, the table cutlery became more diversified until French aristocratic dining ultimately established the standard place setting which still applies today_.

The broader population in Europe was not initially affected by the civilising process which was led by the Italian courts and subsequently the French court. Instead, Eastern Europe became an innovative space for simple rural cooking during the transition from the medieval to the modern period. Among the more significant innovations was the widespread cultivation of buckwheat, which entered eastern central Europe from Russia and subsequently spread to the countries south of the Alps, and Carinthia and Tirol via Black Sea trade. The cultivation of buckwheat ultimately spread to the Netherlands and northwestern Germany via seaborne trade between Venice and Antwerp.

The large livestock herds from the territory of present-day Hungary, Poland, and Ukraine, which were driven to the cities of central Europe, also played a large role in the food supply of central Europe. Consequently, the consumption of meat in central Europe reached a level during the 16th century which has not been replicated until the 21th century. It is estimated that more than 100 kilograms of meat was consumed per person per annum in the first decades of the 1500s, which corresponds to a daily meat consumption of nearly 1 kilogram for a family of three. Descriptions of the supposedly sparse diet of the rural population are somewhat contradicted by these figures. Although Johannes Boemus (1485–1535)_ wrote of the peasant diet in 1520 that "[g]eringes Brot, Haferbrei oder gekochte Bohnen bildet die Speise der Bauern, Wasser oder Molken ihren Trank", the available figures show that a more nuanced understanding is required. The consumption of meat in the daily diet of the rural population was indeed mainly limited to boiled pieces of meat, which were eaten with porridge, soup, or coarse bread. This form of preparation involved only a small loss of fat compared to roasting, especially since all edible parts could be used. Meat as a dish on its own or roasted – as enjoyed by the aristocracy – was a prestige food which was reserved for important religious feasts and other important customary occasions, such as weddings and kermises.

The relative cultural prestige of the various types of meat also requires a more nuanced understanding. For example, the meat content of the daily diet of the rural population of central Europe was almost exclusively pig meat. Thus, Hieronymus Bock (1498–1554)_ wrote in his work *Teutsche Speißkammer (für gesunde und Kranke)_*, which was published in 1555, that "Vnsere Bawren essen viel lieber feißt Schweinenfleisch gesotten vnd gebraten, dann alle hüner. Sie sagen auch, wann ein Saw federn hett, vnnd könt über ein Zaun fliegen, übertreffe sie alles gevögel vnd federspil." However, dietary orders, invoices and other sources pertaining to cities and their citizenry show that pork and (in contrast to the present day) beef were less preferred in the cities. Roast veal and mutton were the highest status meats.

An extraordinarily detailed dietary order of the imperial count Joachim von Öttingen (1470–1520)_ gives detailed information regarding the quantities consumed, sorts of meat and preparation techniques in the kitchens of the aristocracy and the commoners. According to the order, serfs received:

Des morgens ain suppen oder gemues [im Sinne von Mus = Brei]. ain millich den arbeittern. den andern ain suppen. – Des Mittags suppen vnd flaisch. ain kraut, ain pfeffer oder eingemacht flaisch. ain gemues oder mylich. IIII essen. – Des Nachts. Suppen vnd flaisch. ruben vnd flaisch oder eingemacht flaisch. ain gemues oder millich. III essen. This was in stark contrast to the roast dishes of game, poultry, and innards on the table of the imperial count:

An aim flaischtag auff vnsern tisch. Ain voressen. täglich geendert. Alß von voglen, wildpret. wurst. Kalbskopf. kröß. gelung. leber. kudlfleck etc. – Suppen des morgens offt eingeschniten vnd flaisch Henne oder Höner. so, die wol vorhanden sind. darain. – kraut vnd ruben gesatten. So gut ochsen da sind ain stuck des flaisch. – Ain pfeffer. darjnn wildpret. zungen. Ejtter etc. – Ain gemues verendert all tag. – Ain eingebickts [Gepökeltes]. Sülts oder kaltfues [Kalbsfuß] etc. Ain prättes [Gebratenes] zwayer oder dreyerley. – So, man sew metziget. ain stuck schweines prötlin. Ain reys. gersten. kern. lynsin etc. – Er mag auch geben für ein vor oder mittelessen. Ochsenhyrn gesotten oder gebachen. ein gebaiß [gebeizt] lendpratten von ochssen. Des Nachts sollen zway essen minder gegeben werden. alß ain pfeffer vnd ain gemues. ist VI essen.

It is furthermore necessary to be cognisant of regional differences, as the types and quantities of meat consumed varied considerably between northern Europe, southern Germany, Austria, and eastern Europe. Thus, hospital accounts and other sources for southern Germany demonstrate that the rural diet there was considerably sparser that in the regions between the Netherlands and the Central German Uplands. While in the latter regions boiled meat eaten with bread was an integral part of the daily diet, the diet in southern Germany at the beginning of the 16th century was more herbivorous. Bread was even less common in southern Germany, where soups, porridge, and flour-based foods played a more significant role.

Vegetarian food became dominant throughout central Europe from the second half of the 16th century at the latest. While the consumption of meat in the Mediterranean region remained relatively constant during this period at approximately 30 kilograms per person per annum, a shortage of meat and animal fats became a permanent feature of the diet in central and northern Europe, which in some regions persisted right into the 20th century. The decisive factor in this development was the sharp rise in food prices in the 16th century while wages remained relatively constant and the population grew strongly. Additionally, the area of land devoted to the cultivation of cereals in central Europe grew at the expense of the area devoted to livestock farming. Areas in southern Germany and the Alpine region which were particularly affected compensated for the scarcity of meat in the daily diet with the introduction of flour-based dishes – Swabian noodles (*Spätzle*), Bavarian dumplings (*Klöße*) and Austrian pancakes (*Palatschinken*) are present-day reminders of this change. The boarder population now scarcely consumed meat at all outside of the important feast days, and the general consumption of meat in the German-speaking territory fell drastically from about 100 kilograms per person per annum around 1500 to only 16 kilograms per person per annum around 1800.

The proverbial "daily bread" gained its position of central importance in the European daily diet during this period, accounting for up to 75 per cent of the calorie intake of the total population in the German-speaking territory between the 16th and the 18th centuries. Numerous customs (for example, the large significance of the *Gebildbrote*, i.e. bread which is shaped to represent or symbolize something, such as an animal), proverbs, and expressions are continuing evidence of the central importance of bread in the historical daily culture of central Europe. Generally speaking, in central Europe bread was consumed from an earlier period and in larger quantities than in western Europe, where maize played a much bigger role, and the Mediterranean region. However, it is important to note both geographical and social variations when discussing bread consumption in pre-industrial Europe. While bread had become the predominant staple in rural areas of central Germany where tillage farming predominated as early as the early 16th century, porridge dishes – which were harder to digest but could be prepared using less energy and were viewed as more primitive – continued to be eaten for a considerable period in the poorer rural regions of Europe, for example in the Central German Uplands. The same is true for the broad tillage plains of eastern Europe, such as those in Hungary.

Health surveys (*Physikatsberichte*) from the mid-19th century illustrate, for example, that the population in east Bavaria, which was rural and had hardly experienced any industrial development, only ate bread on feast days, and otherwise predominantly ate soup, potatoes, and porridge. The types of bread consumed are also subject to geographical and social variation. While bread made of wheat flour was baked almost exclusively in the Mediterranean region, in the German-speaking territory fine wheaten bread was viewed as a prestige food of the higher social classes. North of the Alps, bread was primarily made using rye flour, with regional variations in terms of the spices added and the fineness to which the rye was ground.

Early Internationalisation and Innovations in the 17th and 18th Centuries – Potatoes, Maize and Hot Drinks

Some of the most significant innovations in European culinary culture resulted from the importation of new foodstuffs and stimulants from the New World. As regards its essential structural elements, modern European cuisine is essentially a product of the "Columbian exchange". Starting in Britain and the Netherlands, the potato entered the dietary culture of the broad masses of central Europe during the 17th century, as one of the first new crops to do so. The integration of the potato into the system of daily meals in Europe was one of the most significant innovations in modern European cuisine. It was also one of the most important steps towards overcoming subsistence crises of the *type ancien*. Thus, the potato, along with coffee and liquor, can be viewed as the decisive innovation – even as a central cultural norm – during the emergence of the modern system of dishes and meals in the 18th century. The potato brought about the ultimate decline of the porridge dishes which had been the main staple for broad sections of the population from the medieval period.

However, the potato only established its position as a staple gradually. Here again we can see the significance of social status struggles in the cultural history of the European diet. In contrast to colonial produce like coffee, tea, and chocolate, the potato was viewed as a low-status foodstuff of the lower social classes from France to Austria-Hungary well into the 18th century. In fact, the potato was originally viewed as an emergency foodstuff in the rural diet, and its spread was hampered by the continued cultivation of traditional crops up to the great famines of the 1770s. It was not until 1770–1772 and the introduction of comprehensive political measures to promote cultivation of the potato that the potato became a staple in all regions north of the Alps.

Simultaneously, the cultivation of maize across large swathes of southern Europe, particularly in Spain, Italy, and the Balkans, helped to bring an end to famines in these territories. Due to its adaptability to different climatic conditions and its comparatively high and stable yields, maize spread more quickly than the potato. As early as the 1520s – just 30 years after Christopher Columbus's (1451–1506) first voyage to America – Andalusian peasants began to cultivate maize. During the course of the 16th century, maize cultivation spread through Spain and along the cisalpine region as far as Carinthia, replacing millet in many cases. In the 17th century, maize cultivation spread to southeastern Europe through the Venetian Republic. Maize played a particularly important role in overcoming famines and assisting population growth in the latter region.

While the potato, as a rare example of an "upwardly mobile cultural good", spread comparatively quickly, the example of coffee demonstrates how slowly changes were often adopted. Probably originating in Yemen and Ethiopia, coffee initially reached the Mediterranean region, and then spread northward in the 17th century by means of sea-borne trade from Venice, before spreading from Britain and the Netherland to central Europe. The earliest reports of the consumption of these exotic beans from the Middle East come from the courts of rulers. Again the nobility functioned as a testing ground for innovation, albeit hesitantly, as the European palate took some time to get used to the bitter taste of coffee. In 1710, Liselotte of the Palatinate, who was Elisabeth Charlotte of Orléans (1652–1722) from 1671 onward, compared the beverage – which she had presumably become acquainted with at the court of Versailles – with "Ruß und Feigbohnen" ("soot and lupin beans").

It was not until the mid-17th century that the gustatory conservatism of the broader European population was overcome, with the urban bourgeois coffee houses acting as a catalyst. The fashionable aristocratic beverage and luxury good now became very popular in broader, bourgeois circles also. The further spread of the consumption of coffee in the 18th century can be summarized using the term "sinking cultural good". That is to say, coffee, formerly a luxury good, "sank" from the nobility via the urban bourgeoisie right down to the broad rural masses, and it gradually became a drink of the masses during the late 18th century and the 19th century. It ultimately became affordable for even the poorer sections of society – often in a diluted form or in the form of coffee surrogates. The fall in the price of coffee which made this development possible resulted from the expanding cultivation of coffee in the British and French colonies.

As the practice of drinking coffee became increasingly common among the bourgeoisie, it lost its significance in aristocratic circles, and it was replaced there during the course of the 17th century by black and green tea imported from China. At the court of Charles II (ca. 1630–1685) in London, tea replaced coffee in the beverage culture of the court in the 1660s. The first deliveries of tea had reached Europe around 1580 via the Portuguese trading post in Macau. In 1610, the Dutch merchant fleet had also entered the tea trade via its ports on Java and Sumatra, before the British East India Company became the dominant player in the global tea trade in the early 18th century. The volume of tea shipped by the East India Company from east Asia to London grew from 50 tonnes in 1700 to 15,000 tonnes in 1800. Between 1799 and 1833, the quantity of tea imported annually into Europe as a whole was around 73,000 tonnes.

With the exception of the Netherlands and neighbouring Frisia, continental Europe only gradually acquired the tea-drinking habit, if at all. In Britain, on the other hand, tea-drinking quickly spread through all section of the population during the 18th century. There are a number of reasons why tea reached broader sections of the population much more quickly than coffee and cocoa, the other two hot drinks of colonial trade. In particular, it was much easier to prepare tea at home from the ready-to-use leaves than was the case with cocoa, for example, and the quantity of leaves needed was comparatively small. The tea leaves could also be supplemented with native herbs if necessary. It was thus easier to integrate the cup of tea into the existing system of meals, which was particularly important in the era of factory work with its short breaks.

Just as the tankard of coffee replaced the morning and evening beer in central and northern Europe, in Britain tea became the main drink at meal times, but it also became the social drink in the bourgeois milieus. The customary 5 o'clock tea with sweet cake, marmalade, and scones is still integral to British tea culture in the present day. And just as in central Europe Enlightenment writers criticized the consumption of coffee by peasants, the new fashion for tea in Britain also drew criticism, such as that expressed by the Scottish writer William Mackintosh (1662–1743):

When I came to a friend's house of a morning, I used to be asked if I had my morning draught yet? I am now asked if I have had my tea? And in lieu of the big Quaigh with strong ale and toast, and after a dram of good wholesome Scots spirits, there is now a tea-kettle put to the fire, the tea-table and silver and china equipage brought in, and marmalade and cream!

However, reactions to tea, which was believed to be stimulating and to improve one's health, were predominantly positive, and already in the 18th century traditional European medicinal herbs were used to produce a substitute tea for the broader population.

Cocoa also began its career in Europe under medicinal auspices in the form of drinking chocolate. Due to its fat content and the calories it contains, cocoa can be considered a foodstuff. However, it was also considered a stimulant – due to its caffeine content – when the cocoa beans were roasted, peeled, and ground, in order to be served as a hot drink with sugar, vanilla, and cinnamon.

Europe's first contact with the cocoa bean occurred during the Spanish conquest of central America in the 16th century. Cocoa cultivated in this region found its way to the European courts in the form of drinking chocolate during the course of the 17th century. Spain met the rapidly growing demand for this fashionable new drink by means of new plantations and by spreading the cultivation to the Caribbean and Venezuela as well, using the labour of west African slaves. Raw cocoa exports from the Spanish colonies thus grew from about 28 tonnes per annum around 1650 to about 5,000 tonnes around the end of the 18th century. However, Britain, France, and the Dutch Republic managed to break the Spanish monopoly on cocoa in the 17th century by conquering the Caribbean, and Portugal also began to cultivate cocoa around this time in Brazil.

As with tea and coffee, cocoa initially spread in Europe during the 17th century as a high-status beverage of the aristocracy, before public coffee houses and chocolate houses – initially in Spain and Italy – began to serve the hot beverage as a sociable drink. The spread of cocoa was assisted by the decision of the Catholic Church to allow it during Lent, as well as by the medical profession, which sang its praises as a laxative and prescribed it as an aid to the recovery of strength after childbirth. Nevertheless, cocoa only reached the broader population during the course of industrialization around the mid-19th century, after

Coenraad Johannes van Houten (1801–1887) had invented inexpensive, long-life cocoa powder, which considerably reduced the quantity of cocoa needed to prepare a drink, and thus the price, as well as the time and effort involved. Starting in Switzerland, cocoa subsequently became the predominant chocolate product in Europe in the form of sweetened eating chocolate.

In addition to tea, cocoa, and coffee, sugar became very important in the cuisine and economy of Europe, as the consumption of these bitter drinks was only made attractive to the masses by the addition of sugar. The numerous sweet foods and cakes which were served as an accompaniment to tea and coffee were also only made possible by the modern European sugar trade. Christian crusaders encountered the cultivation of sugarcane in the Middle East as early as the 11th century. In the High Middle Ages, sugar reached Europe primarily through Venice, and it initially adorned the tables at royal courts as a luxury product, for example in the form of elaborate sugar figures. In aristocratic dining, cane sugar replaced honey as the main sweetening agent during the early modern period. Sugar was used by physicians and apothecaries to sweeten bitter medicines, and it was also considered a fortifier due to its energy content. The exceptional status of sugar as a luxury product is also emphasized by its very high price. At the beginning of the modern period, 1 kilogram of sugar was equivalent in price to 100 kilograms of wheat. Only spice from Asia enjoyed a comparable status.

Sugar prices only began to fall after the discovery of the Americas. Portugal and Spain had begun to cultivate sugarcane in the 15th century on the Canaries and in the Spanish Caribbean colonies. The plantation economy of the 16th century, which depended on the labour of millions of kidnapped African slaves, is among the worst chapters of European dietary history. Britain, the Netherlands, and France all participated in the triangular trade between Europe, Africa, and America, raising the volume of exported sugar to approximately 140,000 tonnes per annum by 1750 by mercilessly exploiting the slaves. The massive quantities of sugar imported into Europe also enabled it to be integrated into bourgeois dining culture in the 18th century. By 1800, the annual consumption of sugar in Germany had reached 1.1 kilograms per person – a twentyfold increase since the 16th century. But it was not till the discovery and mass cultivation of sugar beet in the late 19th century, in conjunction with the agricultural reforms of the time, industrialisation and European customs reform, that sugar became ubiquitous as a sweetening agent. Subsequently, sugar was the essential ingredient in the success of the modern chocolate and sweets industry.

The colonial trade in sugar, coffee, tea, and cocoa gave rise to massive changes in the dietary culture of pre-industrial Europe. First of all, the integration of the new stimulants and foodstuffs into European culture went hand in hand with the emergence of European coffee house culture. The first oriental-style coffee house opened its doors in Paris, the metropolis of fashion at the time, in 1643. Others followed in Venice, London, and Hamburg in 1645, 1652, and 1671 respectively, and, after its first coffee house had opened in 1685, Vienna became the heart of European coffee house culture. During the Enlightenment period in particular, coffee houses spread rapidly as a public place of discussion and of sociable consumption, and they increasingly replaced the late medieval taverns as formal gathering places in bourgeois and petit bourgeois circles, even in smaller towns. By virtue of its role as a meeting place for the various social classes, the coffee house also started the process of spreading coffee consumption to the rural and proletarian milieus.

The integration of colonial stimulants into European culture played a decisive role in the emergence of another cultural and economic innovation, one which relates to dining culture. With the arrival of the early high-status drinks of tea, cocoa, and coffee, Chinese crockery made of porcelain also made its appearance in Europe. Again, it was the royal courts that adopted the precious material first. As it did not affect the taste of food, it was superior to tin and silver receptacles. It was also more robust and less likely to crack than European earthenware and glass receptacles. Not surprisingly, this new precious material was initially the preserve of the aristocratic courts. The establishment of the European porcelain industry in the first half of the 19th century with its centres in Germany and Britain resulted in porcelain becoming common in the homes of the wealthy urban middle classes.

The 19th Century – Urbanisation and the Food Industry

Prior to the beginning of the industrial era, European societies, in spite of all their differences, had a number of structural characteristics in common. An absolute majority of the population lived in the countryside and was directly or indirectly employed in agriculture. Additionally, the people – and consequently the economy and culture – were heavily influenced by local factors such as soil composition and the climate. The years around 1800 witnessed fundamental change in a number of areas; this applies in particular to dietary habits.

These changes had been coming for a long time beforehand, and they are also conspicuous when one examines dietary habits. The potato and liquor, which had become increasingly widespread during the second half of the 18th century, were, to an extent, harbingers of the industrial age. Other harbingers were a strong growth in the economy and in the population. Processes of industrialisation certainly did not occur in parallel throughout all parts of Europe. In the Mediterranean region of southern Europe in particular, structures which were at least partially preindustrial persisted right up to the mid-20th century. However, the political and socio-economic changes of the 19th century nonetheless manifested themselves particularly clearly in dietary habits.

The technological innovations of early industrialisation manifested themselves directly in rapid demographic changes. Workers were drawn to the newly founded factories, resulting in an explosion in the population of the cities. This fundamentally changed daily dietary habits in two regards. Firstly, the density of urban development in the industrial conurbations excluded the possibility of growing one's own food in gardens or on larger plots of land. The agrarian subsistence farming of rural Europe was now replaced by a modern commercial system of food supply. Particularly in periods of economic stagnation, disease, and high unemployment, this change resulted in nutritional crises among the new urban proletariat. Secondly, the daily meals changed as a result of the new rhythm of working life. Particularly in the dynamic early phase of industrialisation, machines and the attendance clock hardly permitted any time for family meals. Eating on one's own to fend off hunger replaced collective mealtimes.

In spite of serious social problems, industrialisation in the first half of the 19th century nonetheless raised the standard of living of large sections of the population. In particular, the rising consumption of meat can be viewed as an indicator that famines and the previously unstable food supply were being overcome. In 1845, Friedrich Engels' (1820–1895) description of nutritional circumstances among the working classes of Manchester emphasized the fact that the availability of various foods was very wage-dependent:

The habitual food of the individual working-man naturally varies according to his wages. The better-paid workers, especially those in whose families every member is able to earn something, have good food as long as this state of things lasts; meat daily and bacon and cheese for supper. Where wages are less, meat is used only two or three times a week, and the proportion of bread and potatoes increases. Descending gradually, we find the animal food reduced to a small piece of bacon cut up with the potatoes; lower still, even this disappears, and there remain only bread, cheese, porridge, and potatoes, until on the lowest round of the ladder, among the Irish, potatoes form the sole food, As an accompaniment, weak tea, with perhaps a little sugar, milk, or spirits, is universally drunk.

While early industrialisation was concentrated in a small number of European regions, the processes of innovation nonetheless quickly also affected the smaller towns and the rural sphere. In addition to the demographic changes, the transformative processes of the first half of the 19th century also manifested themselves in an expansion of the range of foods available and the adoption of new foodstuffs. Three main developments can be identified. Firstly, the proliferation of the cultivation of potatoes resulted in profound change in the daily diet and replaced the early modern system of bread and porridge in many parts of Europe. The pace at which change occurred also depended on how readily the new foodstuff could be integrated into the existing dietary systems. It took a long time, for example, for the potato to integrate into the cuisine of southern Germany and Austria, which had been dominated by flour-based dishes. In northern Germany, by contrast, the potato replaced bread as an accompaniment to the main dish very quickly. In the Central German Uplands, the potato secured its place in the diet as an ingredient in soups and in the form of mash, which was comparable in texture and consistency to the porridge which had long been a part of the local diet. By the mid-19th century, the perception of the potato as the food of the impoverished classes had finally abated, and middle class European cuisine increasingly benefitted from the versatility of the potato.

Secondly, the distilling trade expanded, with the potato and other substances increasingly being used in the distilling process. For example, in Prussia, the amount of liquor distilled doubled between 1820 and 1840. Societal criticism of the consumption of hard liquor soon followed, but the available sources show that the phrase "scourge of drink" greatly exaggerates the reality of alcohol consumption. Thirdly, the extensive cultivation of sugar beet resulted in a dramatic reduction in the price of sugar, which had previously been an expensive imported commodity. It became commonly used among an ever-increasing portion of the population from the second half of the 19th century.

The general European perspective nonetheless indicates that, in spite of the great innovations in the area of nutrition as a result of industrialisation, the 19th century was characterized by the contemporaneity of phenomena that belonged to different eras. While the new factories fundamentally transformed life in some places, elsewhere medieval influences and the dependence on locally produced foods, which were dictated to a considerable degree by climatic and geographical factors, persisted. For example, the gathering of wild plants continued to play an important role in nutrition in 19th-century Scandinavia, as it did in the cuisines of eastern Europe and Russia, with mushrooms and berries providing a significant portion of daily nutrition. In the well-watered regions of northern Europe and in Scandinavia, the availability of fish all year round also helped to compensate to a degree for the prevalent dramatic shortage of protein in the diet.

The industrial era initially also had little effect in the Mediterranean region. Agrarian structures remained largely intact, and older dietary traditions persisted. However, these traditions came under pressure from another source, as the growth in population resulted in a narrowing of the dietary spectrum. The diet became even more cereal-dependent in many cases. Two main changes occurred: Maize finally established itself as a staple in the cuisine of the broader population, and noodles, which had been known in southern Europe since antiquity, finally became common in the diet in southern Italy. Fresh and dried noodles made to meet the needs of one's own family using flour, water, and eggs assumed a similar importance here to that enjoyed by the potato north of the Alps. This innovation gave rise to the stereotype of the southern Italian as "macaroni eater".

At the opposite end of Europe, a combination of a population explosion, adverse political and agrarian conditions, and harvest failures resulted in the last great European nutritional disaster. Between 1845 and 1849, the "Great Famine" cost the lives of 800,000 people in Ireland. It was the earliest indication of the negative consequences of monocultures. The higher yields which the potato made possible had already resulted in its widespread cultivation in Ireland in the late 18th century, which had swept away the existing dietary system. Consequently, it was not possible to compensate with other crops when potato blight resulted in widespread failure of the potato crop.

The growing importance of sugar beet during the early 19th century, or more precisely the production of industrially refined sugar, indicates another development which would continue to fundamentally transform nutrition in Europe: Science and technology became decisive factors in the production and distribution of food. The most significant innovations after 1850 were the application of technological advances to food (particularly in the area of preservation), the industrially standardized mass production and uniformization of food by means of newly developed machines, and the production of completely new food products, such as margarine, baking powder, artificial honey, and powdered milk.

In 1840, Justus von Liebig (1803–1873) published his *Die organische Chemie in ihrer Anwendung auf Agricultur und Physiologie* ("Organic Chemistry as Applied to Agriculture and Physiology"), which became a standard work. Liebig and his colleagues Gerardus Johannes Mulder (1802–1880) and Jacob Molescott (1822–1893) revolutionized the nutritional sciences by identifying protein, fat, carbohydrates, water, and mineral salts as individual nutrients, thereby laying the foundations for modern nutritional physiology. Building on these theoretical discoveries, Liebig established the foundations of modern preservation methods.

The French chemist Nicolas Appert (1748–1841) had already published his *Art de conserver, pendant plusieurs années, toutes les substances animales et végétales* ("The Art of Preserving all Animal and Vegetable Substances for a Period of Years") in 1810, which had indicated the far-reaching possibilities for the preservation ("Appertisieren") of food. However, it was not until the second half of the 19th century that the full potential of the new preservation techniques and the industrial pasteurisation developed by Louis Pasteur (1822–1895)_ became apparent. The development of the industrial production of canned foods, pasta, and jam, the use of Liebig's meat extracts for the production of soups and sauces, and the invention of refrigeration by Carl von Linde (1842–1934)_ in 1874 made it possible for broad sections of the population to live on commercially produced food. This also helped to accelerate the industrialisation of Europe.

In Germany, this development resulted in Braunschweig becoming a "Stadt der Konserven" ("city of canned food") in the decades after 1850. It was a particularly important centre for the industrial production of canned vegetables. The *Erbswurst* (pease-flour sausage), which was developed by the Berlin chef Johann Heinrich Grüneberg (ca. 1819–1872) and which was first used as a cheap, easily transportable, and nutritious food for the frontline soldiers during the Franco-Prussian War in 1870, was subsequently consumed throughout Germany. Increasing regulation of the materials used in cans, as well as of the contents of the cans, and other technological innovations – such as the invention of the sealing machine in 1889 – advanced the development of canned food, brought down prices, and made canned food a permanent component in the diet_ of the lower-paid sections of the population. In return, the making of homemade preserves declined.

In tandem with important changes in farming techniques and land usage (such as the use of artificial fertilisers and the development of agricultural machinery) and economic policies facilitating the easier circulation of goods (such as the foundation of the German *Zollverein* in 1834 as a precursor to further economic integration), these developments made it possible for the first time since the Middle Ages to ensure that the broad masses of the European population had a dependable food supply. Whereas around 1800 the work of four peasants had been required to provide sufficient food for one non-agrarian consumer, 100 years later one farmer was able to provide for four consumers. The last large famine that was not caused by war occurred in Europe in 1846/1847. The demographic development in Europe in the 19th century impressively reflects the improvement in nutritional circumstances. The population grew by one third between 1850 and 1900, from 266 million to 401 million people.

The continuing expansion of the railway network in Europe_ and of the infrastructure of the retail trade, which further assisted an accelerated and comprehensive supply of basic food requirements, also contributed to the fundamental improvements in the supply of food during the 19th century. In the larger cities, large modern stores emerged to complement the smaller retailers. Intercontinental steam shipping also enabled a diversification of diets even in the rural parts of Europe. Colonial goods, tropical fruits, and imported spices now became part of the diet of broader sections of the population.

Conclusion: 1900–1950

The enormous economic and social transformations which characterised the first half of the 20th century hardly manifested themselves in the dietary culture at all because the world wars precluded large structural changes in this area – apart from the destruction they wrought. However, that destruction occurred on a massive scale. Initially, the wars resulted in a drastic reduction of the supply of food, and emergency foods such as "stretched bread" (*gestrecktes Brot*) and turnip soup became increasingly common. In the southeast of Europe, a restructuring of the dietary culture occurred in the second decade of the 20th century as the disintegration of the ailing Ottoman Empire_ brought an end to Turkish dominance over the Balkans. As the Turkish officials and merchants departed, their dietary habits left southeastern Europe also. In Hungary, in the southern Slavic territory, and in Bulgaria, native dietary traditions became increasingly dominant, and they served as constitutive factors in the coalescing of new national identities. The end of Ottoman rule also brought a widespread departure from Muslim dietary regulations.

The foundation of the Soviet Union also set a chain of processes in motion which resulted in the collectivisation of agriculture_ from the Elbe to the Urals, which had the effect of suppressing regional and ethnic dietary differences. Simultaneously, the fundamental restructuring of the societies under Soviet influence resulted in bourgeois practices losing their significance and in the spread of a culture which purported to be proletarian, and which emphasized the communal provision of food. The famine referred to as the *Holodomor* was a special case, which came about in the context of complex economic and political circumstances. With the Soviet regime not taking the measures required to prevent it, this disaster cost the lives of more than 3.5 million people in 1932 and 1933 primarily in the territory of present-day Ukraine. In the aftermath of the Second World War, large-scale displacements of populations_ occurred in the eastern part of the German-speaking territory, but also in the Polish territory. A number of regional cuisines all but disappeared as a result, such as the East Prussian, the Silesian, and the eastern Galician cuisines. Much more dramatic was the almost total demise of the Jewish culinary tradition in Europe as a result of the Holocaust.

The communal provision of food not only played a central role in the territories under Soviet influence_, but also in National Socialist Germany. The most prominent example of this was the party decree pertaining to the *Eintopfsonntag*_ ("Stew Sunday"), which attached ideological importance to the traditional stew and introduced communal dining in the public space as a visible display of commitment to the national community (*Volksgemeinschaft*).

There was a degree of stasis in the area of commercial hospitality during the first half of the 20th century. From the last third of the 19th century, middle class restaurants had begun to replace the old taverns, particularly in the urban space, and these became an integrative component in middle class urban life. They experienced something of a golden age in the 20th century, which only came to an end in the 1970s. While the range of dishes offered was very broad during the early phase in the late 19th century, by the 1920s most restaurants only offered set meals with four or five courses. The restaurants were points where middle class life crystallised, both on work days and on the weekends, with the emphasis being on the midday meal, which usually consisted of soup as a starter, a main course (consisting of meat, a bulk ingredient – usually potatoes – and vegetables) and a sweet dish as a dessert.

In the late 1940s, enormous geopolitical shifts occurred as a result of the independence of the former colonies of British India and Dutch India (Indonesia), which had a lasting effect on European culinary culture. Curry dishes and chutneys had been party of British cuisine from the 18th century, and from 1945 these foods were increasingly on offer in fast food restaurants in British cities, where large sections of the population became familiar with, and partial to, these dishes. Similarly, Dutch fast food features peanut sauce and chicken satay dishes besides *Frikandel* and French fries.

At the end of the 1940s, the way was prepared for the "pluralisation of the palate" in West Germany also. For example, the fast food restaurant *Puszta-Hütte* in Cologne sold Hungarian goulash from 1948 onward using a recipe which the founder had apparently learned during a period of captivity in Hungary during the war. The presence of foreign soldiers in various parts of Europe after the end of the war also had a pronounced influence on the culinary culture. In the case of Germany, the natives – particularly the children – became acquainted with, and partial to, bubble gum, Coca Cola, and Hershey chocolate through contact with the American GIs. The broad acceptance which these products had attained by 1950 was a slight foretaste of what would happen in the second half of the century: a European dining culture which is heavily influenced by American fast food.

In the mid-20th century, the European dietary culture was still divided on the basis of social class. It was dominated by middle class habits, it exhibited regional variation, and, in terms of the food consumed, it was highly seasonal. However, the emergence of uniformity and standardisation_ had already begun. Maggi sausages and Knorr pease-flour sausage were already in existence, and margarine of industrialised and uniform quality was already on offer. Food was increasingly sold in aestheticised packaging and could thus no longer be examined or handled before being bought. Of course, hardly anyone would have predicted the trend which was about to develop. In the 1950s, consumers became acquainted with frozen food, which had been common in the USA from the 1930s. In 1958, the first ready-made meal came on the market in the form of *Maggi ravioli_*, which became remarkably widely popular. From 1952, pizzerias began to spread, followed by Spanish, Greek, and Yugoslavian restaurants. The fast food chains followed from 1972 onward, greatly undermining the traditional meal consisting of three successive courses. Thus, the European dietary culture of the first half of the 20th century can be viewed in retrospect as a period of relative calm in a world of rapid change. Gunther Hirschfelder / Manuel Trummer, Regensburg.

Translated by: Niall Williams Editor: Ruth-Elisabeth Mohrmann Copy Editor: Christina Müller

14. Dresden, Germany

The capital city of the Free State of Saxony in Germany. It is situated in a valley on the River Elbe, near the Czech border. The Dresden conurbation is part of the Saxon Triangle metropolitan area with 2.4 million inhabitants.

Dresden has a long history as the capital and royal residence for the Electors and Kings of Saxony, who for centuries furnished the city with cultural and artistic splendor. The city was known as the Jewel Box, because of its baroque and rococo city center. The controversial British and American bombing of Dresden in World War II towards the end of the war killed approximately 25,000, many of whom were civilians, and destroyed the entire city center. The bombing gutted the city, as it did for other major German cities. After the war restoration work has helped to reconstruct parts of the historic inner city, including the Katholische Hofkirche, the Semper Oper and the Dresdner Frauenkirche as well as the suburbs.

Before and since German reunification in 1990, Dresden was and is a cultural, educational, political and economic center of Germany and Europe. The Dresden University of Technology is one of the 10 largest universities in Germany and part of the German Universities Excellence Initiative.

15. Keokuk, Iowa

Named for Chief Keokuck, a chief of the Sac and Fox Indians. His bones were brought here in 1883 from Franklin County, Kansas, and reinterred in Rand Park beneath a massive stone pedestal which is surrounded by a life-sized statute of an Indian chieftain. On the east side of this monument is embedded the marble slab taken from the grave in Kansas which is lettered as follows: "Sacred to the memory of Keokuck, a distinguished Sac chief born at Rock Island in 1788. Died in April 1848" Keokuck, "The Watchful Fox", was not a hereditary chief, but raised him to the dignity by the force of talent and enterprise. He was a man of extraordinary eloquence in council and never at a loss in an emergency. He was a noble looking man about six feet tall, portly and weighing over 200 pounds. He had an eagle eye, dignified bearing, and a manly, intelligent expression of countenance.

On November 23, 1985 a new Keokuk Hamilton (IL) bridge was opened. This bridge which is 3,340 feet long and 64 feet wide eliminates the tie up of traffic from the former swing span bridge, allowing both automobile and barge traffic to move more efficiently.

http://www.cityofkeokuk.org/community/history-of-keokuk/

16. Illinois

Before Illinois became a State, it was known as the *Illinois Territory*. In early 1818, the General Assembly of the Illinois Territory sent a petition to the United States Congress asking to be admitted into the Union. Part of the process for being admitted as a State was for Illinois to adopt its own constitution.

The word Illinois comes from the French word meaning Illini or Land of Illini. It is an Algonquin word meaning Men or Warriors. Illinois was discovered in 1673, settled in 1720 and entered the Union on December 3, 1818. Illinois is surrounded by bodies of water on nearly every border: the Mississippi River on the west; the Ohio and Wabash Rivers in the south, and Lake Michigan in the North. The States that border Illinois are: Kentucky, Iowa, Wisconsin, Missouri, and Indiana. The first Railroad train crossed the Mississippi River on the river's first bridge in Rock Island, Illinois on April 21, 1856. The highest point in Illinois is Charles Mound in JoDaviess County, elevation, 1,235 feet, and the lowest point is in Cairo, Alexander county at the Mississippi River, elevation 279 feet.

Early Villages in Illinois
Courtesy Illinois State Museum

Thousands of years before the French reached Illinois, Paleo-Indians, a nomadic people, and their descendants, archaic Indians, had explored Illinois. The culture of these hunters, dated before 5000 BC, can be studied at the Modoc Rock Shelter in Randolph County. Woodland Indians were their descendants. By 900 AD, Middle Mississippi Indians, who succeeded the Woodland Indians, built large earthen mounds and developed complex urban areas. These cities disappeared possibly because of overpopulation, disease, and exhaustion of resources. The descendants of the Mississippians were the Illiniwek tribes of the 17th, 18th, and 19th centuries. After years of losing land and wars to other Indian groups and European colonists, the Illiniweks were moved to a Kansas reservation.

The French controlled areas along the Mississippi River valley in the American Bottoms between Cahokia and Kaskaskia. Their occupation, from about 1675 to 1763, left few lasting marks, as did the ineffective British rule. European control was ended by the U.S. militia of George Rogers Clark in 1778, whereupon Virginia claimed Illinois as within its territory.

The Northwest Ordinance of 1787 charted this region and organized counties, and in 1809 the Territory of Illinois was created. During the early years of settlement by fur trappers, southern Illinois was the focus of migration to the area, especially along the Mississippi River valley and the Wabash and Ohio rivers. Granting of statehood in 1818 was controversial. The population numbered less than the required 60,000. Moreover, in order to include the Chicago port area, territorial representatives induced the U.S. Congress to draw the Illinois border 51 miles to the north of the original boundary as delimited by the Northwest Ordinance. The first capital was Kaskaskia, followed by Vandalia, along the Kaskaskia River, which held the position for 20 years. After strong pressure from Abraham Lincoln, the capital was moved to Springfield by an 1837 legislative vote.

Early statehood problems engulfed Illinois.

The state population in 1830 was 157,445. By then the state was near bankruptcy because of government financing of canals and railroad construction. The Black Hawk War in 1832 was fought by the Indians and newly arrived settlers over possession of Illinois land.

In 1833 Chicago was founded, and the final Indian treaty pertaining to Illinois land, the Treaty of Chicago, was concluded with the Potawatomi, Chippewa, and Ottawa tribes. Also, the first higher education institution for women in Illinois, the Jacksonville Female Seminary, was opened.

In 1839, the state capital was moved to Springfield, while the population in Illinois had grown to nearly 500,000. The first railroad, The Northern Cross, started running from the Illinois River to Springfield. Later in 1844, the Mormon prophet Joseph Smith and his brother Hyrum were killed by a mob at Carthage, prompting the Mormons to move out of Illinois by 1848. The Illinois and Michigan Canal opened the same year. By that time, the population was nearly one million.

By 1860, debates were held in seven Illinois communities. The state's population was 1,711,951. In 1861, Abraham Lincoln of Springfield is inaugurated as president. The Civil War caused mixed loyalties among Illinoisans, many of whom were first- or second-generation Southerners; however, many took pride in the fact that the Union was led by a native son, Lincoln, and the state provided 250,000 soldiers to the Union army. Illinois also was the weapons manufacturer, supplier of iron products, and major grain and meat supplier for the North. The Civil War ended in 1865, and Lincoln was assassinated.

In 1867, the Illinois Industrial University (later the University of Illinois) was established. In 1868, a new statehouse was authorized, and construction began, but would not be completed for 20 years. By 1870, the state's population is 2,539,891.

By 1880, Illinois had become the fourth most populous state. It was a leader in grain production and manufacturing. Large-scale European immigration provided labor to mine coal, run steel mills, and enhance the economy and culture of the state. Its leadership was achieved despite the economic slumps of the 1880s, 1890s, and early 1900s; the labor disputes in coal mining and railroading; the Chicago fire of 1871. By 1890, the state's population was 3,836,352, and Chicago became a metropolis of 1,099,850.

By 1910, the state's population was 5,638,591. In 1911, Starved Rock State park became the first state park in Illinois. In 1912, Poetry magazine was founded in Chicago by Harriet Monroe, and it helped to launch the careers of Vachel Lindsay, Carl Sandburg, and other notable poets. In 1913, the Women's Suffrage Act was passed, extending voting rights for Illinois women. In 1917, the United States entered World War I, in which 314,504 Illinois men participated. In 1918, Illinois celebrated its centennial. Also, an influenza epidemic killed thousands of Illinois residents and more than 600,000 people nationwide.

By 1920, Illinois was counted among the foremost states in nearly every significant growth variable—coal mining, industry, farming, urbanization, transportation, and wholesaling. WWII saw Illinois send thousand of its residents to fight in Europe and the Pacific.

The post-World War II era was a time of industrial modification for the production of consumer goods. Even though meat-packing companies began to move away from Chicago and East Saint Louis, in part because of obsolete physical plants, Illinois farms were being mechanized and upgraded for increased output. The use of hybrid seed, chemical fertilizer, herbicides, and insecticides resulted in larger crop yields. Post-World War II Illinois experienced rapid population growth. The rising number of school-age children brought public school reform, rural school consolidations, and huge suburban educational plants. Migration streams of blacks from the South, Hispanics from Mexico and Puerto Rico, and whites from Appalachia reshaped neighborhoods in Chicago, its suburbs, and other large Illinois cities.

As of the census of 2000, Illinois currently has the 6th largest population of the 50 U.S. states. Chicago, in terms of population, is the third largest city in the country.

http://www.illinoiscourts.gov/kids/IL_Hist/default.asp

17. Ohio

In prehistoric times Ohio was inhabited by the Mound Builders, many of whose mounds are preserved in state parks and in the Hopewell Culture National Historical Park (see National Parks and Monuments, table). Before the arrival of Europeans, E Ohio was the scene of warfare between the Iroquois and the Erie, which resulted in the extermination of the Erie. In addition to the Iroquois, other Native American tribes soon prominent in the region were the Miami, the Shawnee, and the Ottawa.

La Salle began his explorations of the Ohio valley in 1669 and claimed the entire area for France. The Ohio River became a magnet for fur traders and landseekers, and the British, attempting to move in (see Ohio Company), hotly contested the French claims. Rivalry for control of the forks of the Ohio River led to the outbreak (1754) of the last of the French and Indian Wars. The defeat of the French gave the land to the British, but British possession was disturbed by Pontiac's Rebellion. The British government issued a proclamation in 1763 forbidding settlement W of the Appalachian Mts. Then in 1774, with the Quebec Act, the British placed the region between the Ohio River and the Great Lakes within the boundaries of Canada. The colonists' resentment over these acts contributed to the discontent that led to the American Revolution, during which military operations were conducted in the Ohio country.

From the Settlement of the Old Northwest to Statehood

Ohio was part of the vast area ceded to the United States by the Treaty of Paris 1783. Conflicting claims to land in that area made by Connecticut, Massachusetts, and Virginia were settled by relinquishment of almost all of the claims and the organization of the Old Northwest by the Ordinance of 1787. Ohio was the first region developed under the provisions of that ordinance, with the activities of the Ohio Company of Associates promoted by Rufus Putnam and

Manasseh Cutler. Marietta, founded in 1788, was the first permanent American settlement in the Old Northwest.

In the years that followed, various land companies were formed, and settlers poured in from the East, either down the Ohio on flatboats and barges, or across the mountains by wagon—their numbers varying with conditions but steadily expanding the area's population. The Native Americans, supported by the British, resisted American settlement. They successfully opposed campaigns led by Josiah Harmar and Arthur St. Clair but were decisively defeated by Anthony Wayne in the battle of Fallen Timbers (1794). The British thereafter (1796) withdrew their outposts from the Northwest under the terms of Jay's Treaty, and the area was pacified. Ohio became a territory in 1799. General St. Clair, as the first governor, ruled in an arbitrary fashion that made Ohioans for many years afterward distrustful of all government. In 1802 a state convention drafted a constitution, and in 1803 Ohio entered the Union, with Chillicothe as its capital. Columbus became the permanent capital in 1816.

The War of 1812 and Further Settlement

In the War of 1812 the Americans lost many of the early battles of the war that took place in the Old Northwest, and their military frontier was pushed back to the Ohio River. Two British attacks on Ohio soil were successfully resisted: one against Fort Meigs at the mouth of the Maumee River and the other against Fort Stephenson on the Sandusky. The area was further secured by Oliver Hazard Perry's naval victory on Lake Erie near Put-in-Bay, Ohio, and William Henry Harrison's victory in the battle of the Thames on Canadian soil.

After the war Ohio's growth was spurred by the building of the Erie Canal, other canals, and toll roads. The National Road was a vital settlement and commercial artery. Settlement of the Western Reserve by New Englanders (especially those from Connecticut) gives NE Ohio a decidedly New England cultural landscape. Ohio's society of small farmers exported their produce down the Ohio and the Mississippi rivers to St. Louis and New Orleans. In 1837 Ohio won a territorial struggle with Michigan usually called the Toledo War. The Loan Law, adopted in the Panic of 1837, encouraged railroad and industrial development. Railroads gradually succeeded canals, preparing the way for the industrial expansion that followed the Civil War.

The Civil War, Industrialization, and Politics

Most Ohioans were sympathetic with the Union in the Civil War, and many Ohioans served in the Union army. Native sons such as Joshua R. Giddings, Salmon P. Chase, and Edwin M. Stanton had long been prominent opponents of slavery. Nevertheless, the Peace Democrats, the Knights of the Golden Circle, and the Copperheads were very active; Clement L. Vallandigham drew many votes in the gubernatorial election of 1863. Ohio was the scene of the northernmost penetration of Confederate forces in the war—the famous raid (1863) of John Hunt Morgan, which terrorized the people of the countryside until Morgan and most of his men were finally captured in the southeast corner of the state.

After the Civil War industrial development grew rapidly when shipments of ore from the upper Great Lakes region increased and the development of the petroleum industry in NE Ohio shifted the center of economic activity from the banks of the Ohio River to the shores of Lake Erie, particularly around Cleveland. Immigrants began to swell the population, and huge fortunes were made.

Ohio became very important politically. The state contributed seven American presidents: Ulysses S. Grant, Rutherford B. Hayes, James A. Garfield, Benjamin Harrison, William McKinley, William Howard Taft, and Warren G. Harding. Big business and politics became entwined as in the relations of Marcus A. Hanna and McKinley. City bosses such as Cincinnati's George B. Cox also followed this pattern. The state as a whole was for many years steadily Republican, despite the rise of organized labor in the late 19th cent. and considerable labor strife. In the 1890s the reform-minded mayor of Toledo, Samuel "Golden Rule" Jones, won national fame for his espousal of city ownership of municipal utilities.

Twentieth-Century Developments

Floods in the many rivers flowing to the Ohio and in the Ohio River itself have long been a problem; a devastating flood in 1913 led to the establishment of the Miami valley conservation project. Continuing long-term state and federal projects have improved locks and dams along the entire length of the Ohio and its major tributaries, for navigation as well as flood control purposes.

Both farms and industries in Ohio were hard hit by the Great Depression that began in 1929. In the 1930s the state was wracked by major strikes such as the sit-down strikes in Akron (1935–36) and the so-called Little Steel strike (1937). World War II brought great prosperity to Ohio, but labor strife later resumed, as in the steel strikes of 1949 and 1959. Political unrest also affected the state in the protests of the 1960s and most violently in 1970 when four students were killed by national guardsmen who fired on a group of Vietnam War protesters at Kent State Univ.

Ohio's economy went into massive decline in the 1970s and 80s as the automobile, steel, and coal industries virtually collapsed, causing unemployment to soar. Akron, once world famous as a rubber center, stopped manufacturing rubber products altogether by the mid-1980s. During this period, the state's northern industrial centers were especially hard hit and lost much of their population. Since then, Ohio has concentrated on diversifying its economy, largely through expansion of the service sector. The state became an important center for the health-care industry with the opening of the Cleveland Clinic. Industrial research is also important, with Nela Park near Cleveland and Battelle Memorial Institute in Columbus among the more notable research centers; there are also still important rubber research laboratories in Akron.

http://www.infoplease.com/encyclopedia/us/ohio-state-united-states-history.html

18. Massachusetts

The coast of what is now Massachusetts was probably skirted by Norsemen in the 11th cent., and Europeans of various nationalities (but mostly English) sailed offshore in the late 16th and early 17th cent. Settlement began when the Pilgrims arrived on the Mayflower and landed (1620) at a point they named

Plymouth (for their port of embarkation in England). Their first governor, John Carver, died the next year, but under his successor, William Bradford, the Plymouth Colony took firm hold. Weathering early difficulties, the colony eventually prospered.

Other Englishmen soon established fishing and trading posts nearby— Andrew Weston (1622) at Wessagusset (now Weymouth) and Thomas Wollaston (1625) at Mt. Wollaston, which was renamed Merry Mount (now Quincy) when Thomas Morton took charge. The fishing post established (1623) on Cape Ann by Roger Conant failed, but in 1626 he founded Naumkeag (Salem), which in 1628 became the nucleus of a Puritan colony led by John Endecott of the New England Company and chartered by the private Council for New England.

The Puritan Colonies

In 1629 the New England Company was reorganized as the Massachusetts Bay Company after receiving a more secure patent from the crown. In 1630 John Winthrop led the first large Puritan migration from England (900 settlers on 11 ships). Boston supplanted Salem as capital of the colony, and Winthrop replaced Endecott as governor. After some initial adjustments to allow greater popular participation and the representation of outlying settlements in the General Court (consisting of a governor, deputy governor, assistants, and deputies), the "Bay Colony" continued to be governed as a private company for the next 50 years. It was also a thoroughgoing Puritan theocracy, in which clergymen such as John Cotton enjoyed great political influence. The status of freeman was restricted (until 1664) to church members, and the state was regarded as an agency of God's will on earth. Due to a steady stream of newcomers from England, the South Shore (i.e., S of Boston), the North Shore, and the interior were soon dotted with firmly rooted communities.

The early Puritans were primarily agricultural people, although a merchant class soon formed. Most of the inhabitants lived in villages, beyond which lay their privately-owned fields. The typical village was composed of houses (also individually owned) grouped around the common—a plot of land held in common by the community. The dominant structure on the common was the meetinghouse, where the pastor, the most important figure in the community, held long Sabbath services. The meetinghouse of the chief village of a town (in New England a town corresponds to what is usually called a township elsewhere in the United States) was also the site of the town meeting, traditionally regarded as a foundation of American democracy. In practice the town meeting served less to advance democracy than to enforce unanimity and conformity, and participation was as a rule restricted to male property holders who were also church members.

Because they were eager for everyone to have the ability to study scripture and always insisted on a learned ministry, the Puritans zealously promoted the development of educational facilities. The Boston Latin School was founded in 1635, one year before Harvard was established, and in 1647 a law was passed requiring elementary schools in towns of 50 or more families. These were not free schools, but they were open to all and are considered the beginning of popular education in the United States.

Native American resentment of the Puritan presence resulted in the Pequot War of 1637, after which the four Puritan colonies (Massachusetts Bay,

Plymouth, Connecticut, and New Haven) formed the New England Confederation, the first voluntary union of American colonies. In 1675–76, the confederation broke the power of the Native Americans of southern New England in King Philip's War. In the course of the French and Indian Wars, however, frontier settlements such as Deerfield were devastated.

The population of the Massachusetts Bay Colony naturally rejoiced at the triumph of the Puritan Revolution in England, but with the restoration of Charles II in 1660 the colony's happy prospects faded. Its recently extended jurisdiction over Maine was for a time discounted by royal authority, and, worse still, its charter was revoked in 1684. The withdrawal of the charter of the Massachusetts Bay Colony had long been expected because the colony had consistently violated the terms of the charter and repeatedly evaded or ignored royal orders by operating an illegal mint, establishing religious rather than property qualifications for suffrage, and discriminating against Anglicans.

A New Royal Colony

In 1691 a new charter united Massachusetts Bay, Plymouth, and Maine into the single royal colony of Massachusetts. This charter abolished church membership as a test for voting, although Congregationalism remained the established religion. Widespread anxiety over loss of the original charter contributed to the witchcraft panic that reached its climax in Salem in the summer of 1692. Nineteen persons were hanged and one crushed to death for refusing to confess to the practice of witchcraft. The Salem trials ended abruptly when colonial authorities, led by Cotton Mather, became alarmed at their excesses.

By the mid-18th cent. the Massachusetts colony had come a long way from its humble agricultural beginnings. Fish, lumber, and farm products were exported in a lively trade carried by ships built in Massachusetts and manned by local seamen. That the menace of French Canada was removed by 1763 was due in no small measure to the unstinting efforts of England, but the increasing British tendency to regulate colonial affairs, especially, without colonial advice, was most unwelcome. Because of the colony's extensive shipping interests, e.g., the traffic in molasses, rum, and slaves (the "triangular trade"), it sorely felt these restrictions.

Discontent and Revolution

In 1761 James Otis opposed a Massachusetts superior court's issuance of writs of assistance (general search warrants to aid customs officers in enforcing collection of duties on imported sugar), arguing that this action violated the natural rights of Englishmen and was therefore void. He thus helped set the stage for the political controversy which, coupled with economic grievances, culminated in the American Revolution. In Massachusetts a bitter struggle developed between the governor, Thomas Hutchinson, and the anti-British party in the legislature led by Samuel Adams, John Adams, James Otis, and John Hancock. The Stamp Act (1765) and the Townshend Acts (1767) preceded the Boston Massacre (1770), and the Tea Act (1773) brought on the Boston Tea Party. The rebellious colonials were punished for this with the Intolerable Acts (1774), which troops under Gen. Thomas Gage were sent to enforce.

Through committees of correspondence Massachusetts and the other colonies had been sharing their grievances, and in 1774 they called the First Continental Congress at Philadelphia for united action. The mounting tension in Massachusetts exploded in Apr. 1775, when General Gage decided to make a show of force. Warned by Paul Revere and William Dawes, the Massachusetts militia engaged the British force at Lexington and Concord. Patriot militia from other colonies hurried to Massachusetts, where, after the battle of Bunker Hill (June 17, 1775), George Washington took command of the patriot forces.

The British remained in Boston until Mar. 17, 1776, when Gen. William Howe evacuated the town, taking with him a considerable number of Tories. British troops never returned, but Massachusetts soldiers were kept busy elsewhere fighting for the independence of the colonies. In 1780 a new constitution, drafted by a constitutional convention under the leadership of John Adams, was ratified by direct vote of the citizenry.

The New Nation

Victorious in the Revolution, the colonies faced depressing economic conditions. Nowhere were those conditions worse than in W Massachusetts, where discontented Berkshire farmers erupted in Shays's Rebellion in 1786. The uprising was promptly quelled, but it frightened conservatives into support of a new national constitution that would displace the weak government created under the Articles of Confederation; this constitution was ratified by Massachusetts in 1788.

Independence had closed the old trade routes within the British Empire, but new ones were soon created, and trade with China became especially lucrative. Boston and lesser ports boomed, and the prosperous times were reflected politically in the commonwealth's unwavering adherence to the Federalist party, the party of the dominant commercial class. European wars at the beginning of the 19th cent. at first further stimulated maritime trade but then led to interference with American shipping. To avoid war Congress resorted to Jefferson's Embargo Act of 1807, but its provisions dealt a severe blow to the economy of Massachusetts and the rest of the nation.

War with Great Britain came anyway in 1812, and it was extremely unpopular in New England. There was talk of secession at the abortive Hartford Convention of New England Federalists, over which George Cabot presided. As it happened, however, the embargo and the War of 1812 had an unexpectedly favorable effect on the economy of Massachusetts. With English manufactured goods shut out, the United States had to begin manufacturing on its own, and the infant industries that sprang up after 1807 tended to concentrate in New England, and especially in Massachusetts. These industries, financed by money made in shipping and shielded from foreign competition by protective tariffs after 1816, grew rapidly, transforming the character of the commonwealth and its people.

Labor was plentiful and often ruthlessly exploited. The power loom, perfected by Francis Cabot Lowell, as well as English techniques for textile manufacturing (based on plans smuggled out of England) made Massachusetts an early center of the American textile industry. The water power of the Merrimack River became the basis for Lowell's cotton textile industry in the 1820s. The manufacture of shoes and leather goods also became important in the state. Agriculture, on the other hand, went into a sharp decline because Massachusetts could not compete with the new agricultural states of the West, a region more readily accessible after the opening of the Erie Canal (1825). Farms were abandoned by the score; some farmers turned to work in the new factories, others moved to the West.

In 1820 Maine was separated from Massachusetts and admitted to the Union as a separate state under the terms of the Missouri Compromise. In the same year the Massachusetts constitution was considerably liberalized by the adoption of amendments that abolished all property qualifications for voting, provided for the incorporation of cities, and removed religious tests for officeholders. (Massachusetts is the only one of the original 13 states that is still governed under its original constitution, the one of 1780, although this was extensively amended by the constitutional convention of 1917–19.)

Reform Movements and Civil War

In the 1830s and 40s the state became the center of religious and social reform movements, such as Unitarianism and transcendentalism. Of the transcendentalists, Ralph Waldo Emerson and Henry Thoreau were quick to perceive and decry the evils of industrialization, while Bronson Alcott, Margaret Fuller, Nathaniel Hawthorne, and Emerson had some association with Brook Farm, an outgrowth of Utopian ideals. Horace Mann set about establishing an enduring system of public education in the 1830s. During this period Massachusetts gave to the nation the architect Charles Bulfinch; such writers and poets as Richard Henry Dana, Emily Dickinson, Oliver Wendell Holmes, Henry Wadsworth Longfellow, James Russell Lowell, and John Greenleaf Whittier; the historians George Bancroft, John Lothrop Motley, Francis Parkman, and William Hickling Prescott; and the scientist Louis Agassiz.

In the 1830s reformers began to devote energy to the antislavery crusad. This was regarded with great displeasure by the mill tycoons, who feared that an offended South would cut off their cotton supply. The Whig party split on the slavery issue, and Massachusetts turned to the new Republican party, voting for John C. Frémont in 1856 and Abraham Lincoln in 1860. Massachusetts was the first state to answer Lincoln's call for troops after the firing on Fort Sumter. Massachusetts soldiers were the first to die for the Union cause when the 6th Massachusetts Regiment was fired on by a secessionist mob in Baltimore. In the course of the war over 130,000 men from the state served in the Union forces.

Industrialization and Immigration

After the Civil War Massachusetts, with other northern states, experienced rapid industrial expansion. Massachusetts capital financed many of the nation's new railroads, especially in the West. Although people continued to leave the state for the West, labor remained cheap and plentiful as European immigrants streamed into the state. The Irish, oppressed by both nature and the British, began arriving in droves even before the Civil War (beginning in the 1840s), and they continued to land in Boston for years to come. After them came French Canadians, arriving later in the 19th cent., and, in the early 20th cent., Portuguese, Italians, Poles, Slavs, Russian Jews, and Scandinavians. Also, from the British Isles came the English, the Scots, and the Welsh. Of all the immigrant groups, English-speaking and non-English-speaking, the Irish came to be the most influential, especially in politics. Their religion (Roman Catholic) and their political faith (Democratic) definitely set them apart from the old native Yankee stock.

Practically all the immigrants went to work in the factories. The halcyon days of shipping were over. The maritime trade had bounded back triumphantly after the War of 1812, but the supplanting of sail by steam, the growth of railroads, and the destruction caused by Confederate cruisers in the Civil War helped reduce shipping to its present negligible state—a far cry from the colorful era of the clipper ships, which were perfected by Donald McKay of Boston. Whaling, once the glory of New Bedford and Nantucket, faded quickly with the introduction of petroleum.

The Growth of the Cities and the Labor Movement

The rise of industrialism was accompanied by a growth of cities, although the small mill town, where the factory hands lived in company houses and traded in the company store, remained important. Labor unions struggled for recognition in a long, weary battle marked by strikes, sometimes violent, as was the case in the Lawrence textile strike of 1912.

World War I, which caused a vast increase in industrial production, improved the lot of workers, but not of Boston policemen, who staged and lost their famous strike in 1919. For his part in breaking the strike, Gov. Calvin Coolidge won national fame and went on to become vice president and then president, the third Massachusetts citizen to hold the highest office in the land. The Sacco-Vanzetti Case, following the police strike, attracted international attention, as liberals raged over the seeming lack of regard for the spirit of the law in a state that had given the nation such an eminent jurist as Oliver Wendell Holmes (1841–1935). Labor unions finally came into their own in the 1930s under the New Deal.

Industry spurted forward again during World War II, and in the postwar era the state continued to develop. Politically, the state again assumed national importance with the 1960 election of Senator John F. Kennedy as the nation's 35th President. In 1974, Michael S. Dukakis, a Democrat, was elected governor. He lost to Edward King in 1978 but won again in 1982 and was reelected in 1986. In 1988 he ran for president, losing to George H. W. Bush. Dukakis decided not to run again for governor.

During the postwar period the decline of textile manufacturing was offset as the electronics industry, attracted by the skilled technicians available in the Boston area, boomed along Route 128. Growth in the computer and electronics sectors, much of it spurred by defense spending, helped Massachusetts prosper during much of the 1980s. At the end of the decade effects of a nationwide recession and the burden of a huge state budget hit Massachusetts hard, but in the 1990s there was a substantial economic recovery, spearheaded by growth in small high-tech companies.

http://www.infoplease.com/encyclopedia/us/massachusetts-history.html

19. Oregon

Initial European interest in the region was aroused by the search for the Northwest Passage. Spanish seamen skirted the Pacific coast from the 16th to the 18th cent., hoping to claim the area. The English may first have arrived in the person of Sir Francis Drake, who sailed along the coast in 1579, possibly as far as Oregon.

Two centuries later, in 1778, Capt. James Cook, seeking the award of £20,000 for the discovery of the Northwest Passage, charted some of the coastline. By this time the Russians were pushing southward from posts in Alaska and the British fur companies were exploring the West. Oregon's furs promised to become an important factor in the rapidly expanding China trade, and the Oregon coast was soon active with the vessels of several nations engaged in fur trade with the Native Americans. British captains, among them John Meares and George Vancouver, made the coastal area known, but it was an American, Robert Gray, who first sailed up the Columbia River (1792), thus establishing U.S. claim to the areas that it drained.

Canadian traders of the North West Company were approaching the Columbia River country when the overland Lewis and Clark expedition arrived in 1805. David Thompson was already making his way to the lower river when John Jacob Astor's agents (in the Pacific Fur Company) founded Astoria, the first permanent settlement in the Oregon country. In the War of 1812 the post was sold (1813) to the North West Company, but in 1818 a treaty provided for 10 years of joint rights for the United States and Great Britain in Oregon (i.e., the whole Columbia River area). This agreement was later extended. The North West Company merged with the Hudson's Bay Company in 1821, and soon the region was dominated by John McLoughlin at Fort Vancouver.

Settlement and Statehood

In 1842 and 1843 enormous wagon trains began the "great migration" westward over the Oregon Trail. Trouble between the settlers and the British followed. The Americans set out to form their own government, and demanded the British be removed from the whole of the Columbia River country up to lat. 54°40−N; one of the slogans of the 1844 election was "Fifty-four forty or fight." War with Britain was a threat momentarily, but diplomacy prevailed. In 1846 the boundary was set at the line of lat. 49°N, but disagreements over the interpretation of the 1846 treaty were not successfully arbitrated until 1872.

Two years later the Oregon Territory was created, embracing the area W of the Rockies from the 42d to the 49th parallel. The area was reduced with the creation of the Washington Territory in 1853, and Oregon became a state in 1859 with a constitution that prohibited slaveholding but also forbade free blacks from entering the state. Although the California gold rush caused a temporary exodus of settlers, it also brought a new market for Oregon's goods, and the Oregon gold strike that followed attracted some permanent settlement to the eastern hills and valleys.

Wheat farming prospered and in 1867–68 a surplus crop was shipped to England—the beginning of Oregon's great wheat export trade. Cattle and sheep were driven up from California to graze on the tallgrass of the semiarid plateaus, and soon cattle barons, such as Henry Miller, acquired huge herds. They dominated the industry until the late 19th cent., when sheepmen and homesteaders succeeded in reducing the cattle range. The 1850s, 60s, and 70s were plagued by Native American uprisings, but by 1880 troubles with the Native American were over, and the next few decades brought increasing settlement and internal improvements.

Railroads and Industrialization

During the 1880s, and largely under the management of Henry Villard of the Northern Pacific RR, transcontinental rail lines were completed to the coast and down the Willamette Valley into California, bringing new trade and stimulating the beginnings of manufacture. Lumbering, which had long been important, became a leading industry. Seemingly overnight logging camps and sawmills were built in the western foothills. The huge stands of Douglas fir and cedar brought fortunes to the lumbering kings, but the threat to natural resources led ultimately to the creation of national forests.

By the time of the Lewis and Clark Centennial Exposition at Portland in 1905, less than 50 years after statehood had been gained, the frontier era had passed. Most of the feuding on the eastern plateaus was over, and cattle and sheep grazed peacefully on fenced-in ranges. In spring the Willamette Valley was abloom with fruit blossoms, and the river cities were busy with trade and industry.

Reform Movements and Environmental Issues

Oregon has been a leader in social, environmental, and political reforms. It was the first state, for example, to institute initiative, referendum, and recall; to ease the laws governing the use of marijuana; and to initiate a ban against nonrecyclable containers. Several issues have sharply divided conservatives and liberals; one of the most important has been the question of minority groups. In the 1880s the influx of Chinese threatened the labor market and brought violent anti-Chinese sentiment, and in the 20th cent. there was opposition to the Japanese. Feeling against minorities has never been statewide, however, and large groups have vigorously opposed it.

In the 1930s one of the most disputed issues was the question of whether the development of power should be public or private. Today, however, it is widely recognized that the federal power and irrigation projects have had a profoundly positive effect on the economy of the entire Pacific Northwest. Many acres have been opened to irrigated farming, and the tremendous industrial expansion of World War II was to a large extent dependent on Bonneville power.

Environmental issues have dominated Oregon politics since the 1970s. Controversy arose in the late 1980s over the spotted owl, which has become endangered as old-growth forest has been cut down. Restrictions on logging on public lands were initiated in 1991 and attempts to establish forest policies acceptable to both environmentalists and the timber industry bogged down as other species were also shown to be in danger. There also is concern that the state's numerous hydroelectric dams are disrupting the migratory cycle of Pacific salmon.

http://www.infoplease.com/encyclopedia/us/oregon-state-united-states-history.html

20. Washington

Washington's early history is shared with that of the whole Oregon Territory. The perennial search for the Northwest Passage aroused initial interest in the area. Of the early explorers along the Pacific coast, Spanish expeditions under Juan Pérez (1774) and Bruno Heceta (1775) are the first known to have definitely skirted the coast of what is now Washington. Capt. James Cook's English expedition (1778) first opened up the area to the maritime fur trade with China, and British fur companies were soon exploring the West and encountering Russians pushing southward from posts in Alaska. In 1787, Charles William Barkley found the inland channel, which the following year John Meares named the Juan de Fuca Strait (after the sailor who is alleged to have discovered it). In 1792, the British explorer George Vancouver and the American fur trader Robert Gray crossed paths along the Washington coast. Vancouver sailed into Puget Sound and mapped the area; Gray, convinced of the existence of a great river that the other explorers rejected, found the entrance, crossed the dangerous bar, and sailed up the Columbia, establishing U.S. claims to the areas that it drained.

Early Settlement and Boundary Disputes

The Lewis and Clark expedition, which reached the area in 1805, and the establishment of John Jacob Astor's settlement, Astoria, both helped to further the American claim; but in 1807 the Canadian trader David Thompson traveled the length of the Columbia, mapping the region and establishing British counterclaims. After Astoria was sold to the North West Company in the War of 1812, British interests appeared paramount, although in 1818 a treaty provided for 10 years (later extended) of joint rights for the United States and Great Britain in the Columbia River country. The Hudson's Bay Company absorbed the North West Company in 1821 and, under the patriarchal guidance of Dr. John McLoughlin, dominated the region until challenged by the Americans in the 1840s.

Fort Vancouver, on the site of present-day Vancouver, sheltered American overland traders—particularly Jedediah Smith, Benjamin Bonneville, and Nathaniel Wyeth—and later the American missionaries, who were the first real settlers in the area north of the Columbia. Marcus Whitman established (1836) a mission at Waiilatpu (near present-day Walla Walla), which for a decade not only served Native Americans as a medical and religious center but also provided an indispensable rest stop for immigrants on the Oregon Trail. Meanwhile the British, although despairing of control over the area S of the Columbia, were still determined to retain the region to the north; the Americans, on the other hand, demanded the ouster of the British from the whole of the Columbia River country up to a lat. of 54°40–N. "Fifty-four forty or fight" became a slogan in the 1844 election campaign, and for a time war with Britain threatened. However, diplomacy prevailed, and in 1846 the boundary was set at lat. 49°N.

Native American Resistance and Territorial Status

Peace with the British did not, however, preclude Native American conflict. Partly as a protective measure, the Oregon Territory, embracing the Washington area, was created the following year; but in 1853 the region was divided, and Washington Territory (containing a part of what is now Idaho) was set up, with Isaac Stevens as the first governor. (The Idaho section was cut away when Idaho

Territory was formed in 1863.) Meanwhile, some of the pioneers on the oregon trail began to turn northward, and a small settlement sprang up at New Market, or Tumwater (near present-day Olympia).

After word of the needs of California gold-seekers for lumber and food spread northward, settlers recognized the commercial potential of the Puget Sound country and poured into the area in ever-increasing numbers. Lumber and fishing industries arose to satisfy the demand to the south, and new towns, including Seattle, were founded. Meanwhile Stevens, who also served as superintendent of Indian affairs, set about persuading the Native Americans to sell much of their lands and settle on reservations. Treaties with the coast tribes were quickly concluded, but the inland tribes revolted, and hostilities with the Cayuse, the Yakima, and the Nez Percé tribes continued for many years. Over the years, Native Americans remained a small but significant presence in the state; in the early 1990s their population was over 81,000.

Gold, Immigration, and Statehood

Gold was first discovered in Washington in 1852 by a Hudson's Bay Company agent at Fort Colville, but the Yakima War was then in progress and it hindered extensive mining activity. In 1860 the Orofino Creek and Clearwater River deposits were uncovered, bringing a rush of prospectors to the Walla Walla area. The major influx of settlers was delayed, however, until the 1880s, when transport by rail became possible (the first of three transcontinental railroads linked to Washington was completed in 1883).

The population almost quadrupled between 1880 and 1890; although the majority of the new settlers were from the East and Midwest, the territory also absorbed large numbers of foreign immigrants. Chinese laborers had been brought in during the 1860s to aid in placer mining; after 1870 they were followed by substantial groups of Germans, Scandinavians, Russians, Dutch, and Japanese immigrants. By the time Washington became a state in 1889, the wide sagebrush plains of E Washington had been given over to cattle and sheep, agriculture was flourishing in the fertile valleys, and the lumber industry had been founded.

Although some agrarian and labor dissatisfaction with the railroads and other big corporations existed, giving rise to the Granger movement and the Populist party, the discovery of gold in Alaska in 1897 brought renewed prosperity. Seattle, the primary departure point for the Klondike, became a boomtown. Labor and election reform laws were enacted, and the primary, the initiative, the referendum, and the recall were adopted.

The Early Twentieth Century

The turn of the century brought labor clashes that gave Washington a reputation as a radical state. The extreme policies of the Industrial Workers of the World (IWW; also known as the "Wobblies") proved appealing to the shipyard and dock workers and to the loggers, and in 1917 the U.S. War Dept. was forced to intervene in a lumber industry dispute. A general strike following World War I had a crippling effect on the state's economy; antilabor feeling increased, and the famous incident at Centralia resulted in bloody strife between the IWW and the American Legion. The alarmed and brutal reaction of management to radical labor policies produced a confrontational atmosphere that hindered the mediation until the onset of the lean days of the 1930s and the emergence of the New Deal. Washington was an important center of the defense industry during World War II, particularly with the immense aircraft industry in Seattle and the Manhattan Project's Hanford Works at Richland. (Decades later it was discovered that the Hanford facility had leaked large amounts of hazardous radioactive waste in the 1940s and 50s.) During the war, the large Japanese-American population in the state (more than 15,000 persons) was moved eastward to camps, where they suffered great physical and emotional hardship.

Postwar Change and New Industry

In the postwar period military spending continued to pour into such facilities as the Hanford nuclear reservation and the Bremerton naval shipyard, as well as into Boeing's bomber production. At the same time, trade with Asia boomed. Since the 1970s, Washington has attracted a large number of firms moving from California to a more favorable business climate. These include computer software manufacturers and other high-technology companies. The increased economic diversification and stepped-up activity in high-tech industries have cushioned the impact of job losses in the 1990s from post–cold war cutbacks, especially in aerospace orders for Boeing. At the same time, industrial and residential growth has brought the state face to face with environmental issues, among them the effects of continued massive logging and the impact of dams on fish populations.

http://www.infoplease.com/encyclopedia/us/washington-state-united-states-history.html

21.British Columbia, Canada

The earliest known inhabitants of the province are indigenous peoples of the Pacific Northwest (widely known for their totem poles and potlatches); carbon dating has confirmed their occupation of some sites 6,000 to 8,000 years ago. Juan Peréz was probably the first European to sail (1774) along the coast, but he did not make a landing. In 1778, Capt. James Cook, on his last voyage, explored the coast in his search for the Pacific entrance to the elusive Northwest Passage and claimed the area for Great Britain.

Rival British and Spanish claims for the area were partly resolved by the Nootka Conventions of 1790–92, which gave both equal trading rights but did not resolve ownership. The British sent George Vancouver to take possession of the land, and in 1792–94 he explored and mapped the coast from Oregon to Alaska. In 1793, Sir Alexander Mackenzie reached the Pacific overland; he was followed early in the 19th cent. by fur traders and explorers of the North West Company who crossed the mountains to establish posts in New Caledonia, as the region was then called.

The Hudson's Bay Company Era

After the Hudson's Bay Company (HBC) absorbed the North West Company in 1821, the region became a preserve of the new company. In 1843, Fort Victoria was established by James Douglas as an HBC trading post. Rival British and American claims to the area were settled three years later when the boundary was set at the 49th parallel, but further controversy led to the San Juan Boundary Dispute. Partly as protection against American expansion, Vancouver Island was ceded (1849) to Britain by the HBC and became a crown colony.

In 1858 gold was discovered in the sandbars and tributaries of the Fraser River. The gold rushes that resulted brought profound changes. Fort Victoria boomed as a supply base for miners, and a town sprang up around it. Officials of the crown were dispatched to keep order and to supervise government projects and the building of roads. Some 30,000 miners moved into what was then unorganized territory; this led to the creation (1858) of a new colony on the mainland, called British Columbia, and the end of the HBC's supremacy. In 1863 the newly settled territory about the Stikine River was added to British Columbia.

Confederation

In 1866, Vancouver Island and British Columbia were merged, and in 1871 the united British Columbia, lured by promises of financial aid and the building of a transcontinental railroad that would link it to the rest of Canada, voted to join the new Canadian confederation. The Canadian Pacific Railway finally reached the coast in 1885, and a new era began. By providing access to new markets, the railroad furthered agriculture, mining, and lumbering; steamship service with Asia was inaugurated, and Vancouver grew as a busy port, serving many provinces. The opening (1914) of the Panama Canal further boosted trade and commerce. A long dispute with the United States over the Alaska boundary was finally settled by the Alaska Boundary Commission in 1903.

The Twentieth Century

The Conservatives and Liberals alternated in power from 1903 (when the national parties were first introduced into local politics) until 1941, when a wartime coalition was formed. The Social Credit party came into power in 1952, under the leadership of W. A. C. Bennett, and retained control until 1972, when the New Democratic party, led by David Barrett, won a majority. The Social Credit party regained control in 1975 under Premier William Richards Bennett, who was succeeded in 1986 by William Vander Zalm and in 1991 by Rita Johnston, the province's first woman premier. The New Democratic party again took power in late 1991, with Michael Harcourt as premier, succeeded in 1996 by Glen Clark, in 1999 by Dan Miller, and in 2000 by Ujjal Dosanjh (Canada's first nonwhite provincial premier). In 2001, however, the Liberals, led by Gordon Campbell, won a landslide victory; they were returned to power in 2005 and 2009, albeit with narrower majorities. Liberal Christy Clark succeeded the retiring Campbell as premier in 2011; the Liberals remained in power after the 2013 elections.

This fastest growing of Canada's provinces increased its national political clout in 1995 when it was given its own veto power over constitutional amendments rather than being subsumed under the western regional vote. By the end of the 1990s, metropolitan Vancouver had become one of the Pacific Rim's most dynamic cities, with a population c.10% Chinese and c.7% Asian Indian. At the same time, land claims by indigenous peoples, claims that could return much of the province to aboriginal ownership, had become a significant political and economic issue in the province. British Columbia, unlike Canada's other provinces, largely did not have signed treaties with most indigenous peoples, despite a 1763 Crown directive requiring such treaties. As a result, the provincial and federal governments began negotiating with the native tribes in the 1990s to sign treaties with them.

British Columbia sends 6 senators and 32 representatives to the national parliament.

http://www.infoplease.com/encyclopedia/world/british-columbia-history-politics.html

BC's first people may have journeyed to the region from Asia via a land bridge across the Bering Sea. As the ice receded, forests advanced and fluctuating sea levels exposed the temporary land passage linking Asia to the New World.

It is thought that BC's coastal region became one of the most densely populated areas in North America. Prior to European contact, BC's First Nations populations may have numbered some 300,000. The Aboriginal way of life would continue undisturbed for thousands of years, until the arrival of the British in 1778.

When British naval explorer Captain James Cook reached the west coast of Vancouver Island in 1778, he was eager to trade with the Nuu-chah-nulth (Nootka) people. In his wake, waves of European settlers arrived, carrying smallpox and other diseases that decimated Aboriginal populations in the late 1700s.

Nearly a century later, British agent James Douglas was searching the Pacific Coast for a new Hudson's Bay Company headquarters. He was welcomed by the Lekwammen, whose villages dotted the shores of what is now Greater Victoria. Douglas settled in and selected a site called Camosack. A year later, in 1843, Fort Victoria was built in the area now known as Old Town, the heart of Victoria's downtown.

Gold Rush in BC

The discovery of gold in the Fraser River and the Cariboo brought a rapid influx of prospectors, merchants, pioneers and other colourful figures to BC in the 1860s. They came from around the world, arriving from as far away as China. It was a time of rapid economic expansion; sleepy hamlets became bustling cities, and new roads, railways and steamships were constructed to carry the extra load.

Boomtowns were born, and legends made, but not all experienced good fortune. The Aboriginal peoples lost most of their ancestral lands and, in 1876, First Nations populations were made subject to the federal Indian Act, which regulated every aspect of their lives.

Rapid Expansion in BC

Transportation and development marked another period of rapid economic expansion during the 1950s and 60s. Massive building projects changed the shape of the BC landscape. Expansive damming projects turned rivers into lakes; giant turbines powered dozens of new pulp mills and smelters; and the Trans Canada Highway was completed, while new bridges, railways, and BC Ferries linked land, people and technological progress.

BC's Cultural Diversity

Today, BC's population is wonderfully diverse. More than 40 major Aboriginal cultural groups are represented in the region. The province's large Asian communities have made Chinese and Punjabi the most spoken languages after English. There are also sizeable German, Italian, Japanese and Russian communities – all creating a vibrant cultural mosaic in which distinct cuisine, architecture, language and arts thrive.

In 1986 the City of Vancouver celebrated its centennial, hosting the Expo '86 World Exposition. That same year, the Sechelt Indian Band was the first Aboriginal group in BC to gain a municipal style of self-government.

In 2000, the Nisga'a Treaty came into being. The Nisga'a Nation, who has lived in the Nass area since time immemorial, negotiated with the provincial and federal governments to achieve BC's first modern-day, constitutionally protected self-governance agreement. This marked a momentous achievement in the history of the relationship among British Columbia, Canada and First Nations.

In February and March 2010, Vancouver was the host city for the 2010 Olympic and Paralympic Winter Games.

http://www.hellobc.com/british-columbia/about-bc/culture-history.aspx

22. Cannon Beach, Oregon

The first recorded journey by a European to what is now **Cannon Beach** was made by William Clark, one of the leaders of the Lewis and Clark Expedition in early 1805. The expedition was wintering at Fort Clatsop, roughly 20 miles (32 km) to the north near the mouth of the Columbia River. In December 1805, two members of the expedition returned to camp with blubber from a whale that had beached several miles south, near the mouth of Ecola Creek. Clark later explored the region himself. From a spot near the western cliffs of the headland he saw "...the grandest and most pleasing prospects which my eyes ever surveyed, in front of a boundless Ocean..." That viewpoint, later dubbed "Clark's Point of View," can be accessed by a hiking trail from Indian Beach in Ecola State Park.

Clark and several of his companions, including Sacagawea, completed a three-day journey on January 10, 1806, to the site of the beached whale. They encountered a group of Native Americans from the Tillamook tribe who were boiling blubber for storage. Clark and his party met with them and successfully bartered for 300 pounds (140 kg) of blubber and some whale oil before returning to Fort Clatsop. There is a wooden whale sculpture commemorating the encounter between Clark's group and the Tillamooks in a small park at the northern end of Hemlock Street.

Clark applied the name "*Ekoli*" to what is now Ecola Creek. *Ehkoli* is a Chinook word for "whale". Early settlers later renamed the creek "Elk Creek", and a community with the same name formed nearby.

In 1846, cannon from the US Navy schooner Shark washed ashore just north of Arch Cape, a few miles south of the community. The schooner hit land while attempting to cross the Columbia Bar, also known as the "Graveyard of the Pacific." The cannon, rediscovered in 1898, eventually inspired a name change for the growing community. In 1922, Elk Creek was redubbed Cannon Beach (after the name of the beach that extends south of Ecola Creek for 8 miles

(13 km), ending at Arch Cape) at the insistence of the Post Office Department because the name was frequently confused with Eola. Elk Creek itself was renamed Ecola Creek to honor William Clark's original name.

The cannon is now housed in the city's museum and a replica of it can be seen alongside U.S. Route 101. Two more cannons, also believed to have been from the *Shark*, were discovered on Arch Cape over the weekend of February 16, 2008.

U.S. Highway 101 formerly ran through Cannon Beach. In 1964, a tsunami generated by the Good Friday earthquake came ashore along the coast of the Pacific Northwest. The subsequent flooding inundated parts of Cannon Beach and washed away the highway bridge located on the north side of city. The city, now isolated from the highway, decided to attract visitors by holding a sand castle contest, an event that still continues annually every June.

Cannon Beach is an affluent tourist resort destination. Because of its proximity to Portland, Oregon, it is particularly known as a weekend getaway spot for Portlanders.

23. Lienen, Germany

A municipality in the district of Steinfurt, in North Rhine-Westphalia, Germany. It is situated approximately 15 km south-east of Osnabrück and 30 km north-east of Münster.

24. Münster, Germany

Is an independent city in North Rhine-Westphalia, Germany. It is in the northern part of the state and is considered to be the cultural centre of the Westphalia region. It is also capital of the local government region Münsterland. Münster was the location of the Anabaptist rebellion during the Protestant Reformation and the site of the signing of the Treaty of Westphalia ending the Thirty Years' War in 1648. Today it is known as the bicycle capital of Germany.

Münster gained the status of a *Großstadt* (major city) with more than 100,000 inhabitants in 1915. Currently there are 300,000 people living in the city, with about 55,500 students, only some of whom are recorded in the official population statistics as having their primary residence in Münster.

In 793, Charlemagne sent out Ludger as a missionary to evangelise the Münsterland. In 797, Ludger founded a school that later became the Cathedral School. Gymnasium Paulinum traces its history back to the school. Ludger was ordained as the first bishop of Münster. The first cathedral was completed by 850. The combination of ford and crossroad, market place, episcopal administrative centre, library and school, established Münster as an important centre. In 1040, Heinrich III became the first king of Germany to visit Münster.

Middle Ages and early modern period

In the Middle Ages, the Prince-Bishopric of Münster was a leading member of the Hanseatic League.

View from the south-west of Münster in 1570 as seen by Remigius Hogenberg. On the left is the Überwasserkirche, in the centre is St. Paul's Cathedral and to its right St. Lambert's Church, and on the far right is the Ludgerikirche

In 1534, the Anabaptists led by John of Leiden, took power in the Münster Rebellion and founded a democratic proto-socialistic state. They claimed all property, burned all books except the Bible, and called it the "New Jerusalem". John of Leiden believed he would lead the elect from Münster to capture the entire world and purify it of evil with the sword in preparation for the Second Coming of Christ and the beginning of the Millennium. They went so far as to require all citizens to be naked as preparation for the Second Coming. However, the town was recaptured in 1535; the Anabaptists were tortured to death, their corpses were exhibited in metal baskets (often confused with cages), which can still be seen hanging from the Tower of St. Lambert's steeple.

Part of the signing of the Peace of Westphalia of 1648 was held in Münster. This ended the Thirty Years' War and the Eighty Years' War. It also guaranteed the future of the prince-bishop and the diocese; the area was to be exclusively Roman Catholic.

18th, 19th and early 20th centuries

The last outstanding palace of the German baroque period was created according to plans by Johann Conrad Schlaun. The University of Münster (today called "Westphalian Wilhelms-University", WWU) was established in 1780. Now a major European centre for excellence in education and research with large faculties in the arts, humanities, theology, sciences, business and law. Currently there are about 40,000 undergraduate and postgraduate students enrolled. In 1802 Münster was conquered by Prussia during the Napoleonic Wars. It was also part of the Grand Duchy of Berg between 1806 and 1811 and the Lippe department of the First French Empire between 1811 and 1813, before returning to Prussian rule. It became the capital of the Prussian province of Westphalia. A century later in 1899 the city's harbour started operations when the city was linked to the Dortmund-Ems Canal.

25. Minden

A town of about 83,000 inhabitants in the north-east of North Rhine-Westphalia, Germany. The town extends along both sides of the River Weser. It is the capital of the district (*Kreis*) of Minden-Lübbecke, which is part of the region of Detmold. Minden is the historic political centre of the cultural region of Minden Land. It is widely known as the intersection of the Mittelland Canal and the River Weser. The town is over 1,200 years old and has many buildings in the

Weser Renaissance style, in addition to its architecturally symbolic 1,000-year-old cathedral.

Evidence of settlements in various parts of the town suggest that Minden has been settled since the 3rd century A.D. The Minden area shows continuing settlement activity from the 1st to the 4th century. The area then belonged to the Rhine-Weser-Germanic development sphere. This is apparent from the imperial age burial fields at Minden-Römerring and Porta Westfalica-Costedt.

The first recorded mention of Minden is a record in the Franconian Imperial Annals (*Reichsannalen*) of Charlemagne holding an imperial assembly in 798. Charlemagne founded a bishopric in Minden around the year 800. The rights to hold a market, to mint coins and to collect customs duties were granted in 977. Until the beginning of the 13th century, the bishop appointed the leader and administrator of the town, with the title of *Wichgraf*. The citizens of Minden and their Council obtained independence from the rule of the bishop around the year 1230 and received a town charter. They utilised these new rights to begin trading independently from the church. The profits from this led to the further growth of the town. Minden was a member of the Hanseatic League during the Middle Ages. The increased self-confidence of the citizens of Minden was demonstrated by the construction of the town hall, probably adjoining the separately governed cathedral precinct. As a result, Bishop Gottfried von Waldeck moved his official residence from Minden to Petershagen in 1306-7.

Middle Ages to Modern Era

The introduction of the Reformation to Minden in 1529 created much conflict in the town, leading to the formation of a 36-man unit that took over the role of town regiment. Nicholas Krage announced Minden's new evangelical church order from the pulpit of St. Martin's Church (*Martinikirche*) on 13 February 1530.

There were 128 prosecutions for witchcraft between 1603 and 1684. As in nearby regions, almost all those sentenced were women.

Imperial troops occupied Minden from 1625 to 1634, during the Thirty Years' War (1618–1648). Protestant Swedish troops laid siege to Minden and captured it in 1634. Queen Christina of Sweden (reigned 1632–1654) granted full sovereignty in internal and external affairs to Minden.

The Peace of Westphalia in 1648 gave the possession of Minden to Brandenburg-Prussia, and it remained with Prussia until its break-up in 1947. The rule of Frederick I of Prussia (in office 1688-1713) ended the 400-year self-determination or independence of the citizens of Minden. The 40-man unit was dissolved by the king and the town council was replaced by a town authority consisting of 16 businessmen, 16 tradesmen and eight representatives of the community who were elected for life.

The Battle of Minden took place in front of the gates of Minden on 1 August 1759 during the Seven Years' War. The allies of Great Britain, led by Duke Ferdinand of Brunswick, defeated the French and their allies in a decisive battle. The region remained Prussian and the adjacent Kingdom of Hanover remained in the possession of the English king.

The town was capital of the Territory of Minden-Ravensberg from 1719 to 1807 and capital of the District of Minden from 1816 to 1947.

19th century

The area around the cathedral was sovereign territory until 1806. It was governed by clerical rulers in contrast to other town quarters. French troops occupied the town on 13 November 1806. The town then became part of the Kingdom of Westphalia and, later, an actual part of France until 1810. After the defeat of Napoleon at the Battle of Leipzig, French troops abandoned Minden and it returned to Prussia. Minden Fortress was rebuilt in the time of district administrator (*Landrat*) von Arnim, from 1816 to 1820. This reconstruction of the fortifications had serious negative consequences because it hindered economic development, which almost totally by-passed Minden. During this time relatively, smaller towns like Bielefeld and Dortmund laid the foundation for their greater subsequent growth.

The Prussian era was very influential for Minden. This is apparent both in the townscape and town layout. Many buildings from this era remain. The first Fortress Commander was Ernst Michael von Schwichow. The town remained a Prussian fortress until 1873, when the *Reichstag* (Germany's Imperial Parliament) passed the law to remove the fortress status of Minden along with Stettin, Erfurt, Wittenber, Kosel, Graudenz, Kolberg and Stralsund. The fortress walls were razed at this time permitting the town to catch up economically. However, it was never able to regain its former political and economic importance.

26. Freeport, Illinois

Is the county seat and largest city of Stephenson County, Illinois. The population was 25,638 at the 2010 census. Freeport is known for hosting the second Lincoln-Douglas debate of 1858, and as "Pretzel City, USA", named after the heritage of its Germanic settlers in the 1850s and the Billerbeck Bakery pretzel company that started as a result of their arrival.

The community was originally called **Winneshiek**. When it was incorporated, the new municipality took its name from the generosity of Tutty Baker, who was credited with running a "free port" on the Pecatonica River. The name "Winneshiek" was later adopted, and is preserved to this day, by the Freeport Community Theatre Group.

In 1837, Stephenson County was formed, and Freeport became its seat of government in 1838. Linked by a stagecoach with Chicago, the community grew rapidly. In 1840, a frame courthouse was erected, and the first school was founded. Within two years, Freeport had two newspapers and in 1853, the two were joined by a third which published in German. By then, the community had a population of 2,000.

On August 27, 1858, the second debate between Abraham Lincoln and Stephen A. Douglas took place in Freeport and gave the nation direction in the following years. Although Stephen Douglas won the election and retained his U.S. Senate seat, his reply to a question on slavery alienated the South, which called it the "Freeport Heresy", and split the Democratic Party. This enabled Abraham Lincoln to win the Presidency in 1860.

Freeport is known as the "Pretzel City", and its public high school's team is named the Pretzels. The nickname is a reminder of Freeport's ethnic heritage; in the late 1850s, many Germans, both from Pennsylvania and from their European homeland, resettled in Stephenson County bringing with them their love of pretzel snacks. In 1869, a German immigrant named John Billerbeck established the Billerbeck Bakery, which distributed so many pretzels to residents that the local newspaper later dubbed Freeport the "Pretzel City". The city later capitalized on this nickname in 2003 by starting Freeport's first Pretzel Festival.

Freeport is home to the oldest Carnegie Library in Illinois and one of the first Carnegie Libraries designed by the famous Chicago architectural firm of Patton and Miller.

27. Elgin, Illinois

Is a city in Cook and Kane counties in the northern part of the U.S. state of Illinois. Located roughly 35 mi (56 km) northwest of Chicago, it lies along the Fox River. As of 2013, the city had a total population of 110,145, making it the eighth-largest city in Illinois.

The Indian Removal Act of 1830 and the Black Hawk Indian War of 1832 led to the expulsion of the Native Americans who had settlements and burial mounds in the area and set the stage for the founding of Elgin. Thousands of militiamen and soldiers of Gen. Winfield Scott's army marched through the Fox River valley during the war, and accounts of the area's fertile soils and flowing springs soon filtered east.

In New York, James T. Gifford and his brother Hezekiah Gifford heard tales of this area ripe for settlement and travelled west. Looking for a site on the stagecoach route from Chicago to Galena, Illinois, they eventually settled on a spot where the Fox River could be bridged. In April 1835, they established the city, naming it after the Scottish tune "Elgin".

Early Elgin achieved fame for the butter and dairy goods it sold to the city of Chicago. Gail Borden established a condensed milk factory here in 1866, and the local library is named in his honor. The dairy industry became less important with the arrival of the Elgin Watch Company. The watch factory employed three generations of Elginites from the late 19th to the mid 20th century, when it was the largest producer of fine watches in the United States (the factory ceased production in 1965 and was torn down in the summer of 1966) and the operator of the largest watchmaking complex in the world. Today, the clocks at Chicago's Union Station still bear the Elgin name.

Elgin has a long tradition of education and invention. Elgin is home to the Elgin Academy, the oldest coeducational, non-sectarian college preparatory school west of the Allegheny Mountains. Elgin High School boasts five navy admirals, a Nobel Prize winner, a Pulitzer Prize winner, a Tony Award winner, two Academy Award–winning producers, Olympic athletes and a General Motors CEO among its alumni. Elgin resident John Murphy invented the motorized streetsweeper in 1914 and later formed the Elgin Sweeper Corporation. Pioneering African-American chemist Lloyd Hall was an Elgin native, as was the legendary marketer and car stereo pioneer Earl "Madman" Muntz and Max Adler, founder of the Adler Planetarium in Chicago, America's first planetarium.

28. Akron, Ohio

The fifth-largest city in the U.S. state of Ohio and is the county seat of Summit County, the fourth most populous county in the state. The city is located in northeastern Ohio on the western edge of the Glaciated Allegheny Plateau, approximately 39 miles (63 km) south of Lake Erie and was co-founded along the Little Cuyahoga River in 1825 by Simon Perkins and Paul Williams. The name derived from the Greek word "ἄκρον" signifying a summit or high point. Due to Eliakim Crosby founding "North Akron" (Cascade) in 1833, "South" was added to the city's name until the two merged into an incorporated village in 1836. Neighboring settlements Kenmore and Ellet were annexed in 1929. As of the 2015 Census Estimate, the city proper had a total population of 197,542, making Akron the 119th largest city in the United States, and the fifth largest city in Ohio. The Akron, OH Metropolitan Statistical Area (MSA) covers Summit and Portage counties, and in 2010 had a population of 703,200. Akron is also part of the larger Cleveland-Akron-Canton, OH Combined Statistical Area, which in 2013 had a population of 3,501,538, ranking 15th. Creating the first Joint Economic Development Districts, it did so with Springfield, Coventry, and Copley, also Bath in conjunction with Fairlawn. Residents of Akron are called "Akronites". Akron has had many nicknames, three of which are "Rubber City" "Cross Roads of the Deaf", and "City of Invention".

The city became a manufacturing center owing to its location on the Ohio and Erie Canal, as well as being connected to numerous others and railroad lines. With Goodyear, Gojo Industries, FirstEnergy, FirstMerit Corporation, and Time Warner Cable among employers, Akron's economy has diversified sectors that include manufacturing, education, healthcare, and biomedical. Akron is home to the All-American Soapbox Derby. It is also the former home of Goodrich, Firestone, General Tire. Listed by Newsweek as one of ten Information Age high tech havens, it was awarded by the National Civic League and National Arbor Day Foundation, plus named one of the world's most livable cities. Residents Frank and Charles Menches have a disputable claim of inventing the hamburger thus the annual national festival is hosted in the city. A creature often referred to as the Kenmore Grassman is reported through history.

Three major civil unrest events took place during the riot of 1900, rubber strike of 1936, and the Wooster Avenue riots of 1968. Dr. W.E.B. Du Bois (1920) and President Bill Clinton (1997) both gave speeches on race relations in the city. Headquartered on the north side, mobster Rosario Borgio ran black hand operations, Pretty Boy Floyd's Walker-Mitchell mob was also headquartered in the city. Though Akron was part of the Underground Railroad while active, the city also had many officials who were members of the Ku Klux Klan which Wendell Willkie suppressed, and abolitionist John Brown as a resident.

Despite the number of rubber workers decreasing by approximately half from 2000–07, Akron's research in polymers gained an international reputation. It now centers the Polymer Valley which consist of 400 polymer-related companies, of which 94 were located in the city itself. Because of its contributions to the Information Age, *Newsweek's* listed Akron fifth of ten high tech havens in 2001. In 2008 "City of Invention" was added to the seal when the All-America City Award was received for the third time.

29. Columbus, Ohio

The capital and largest city of the U.S. state of Ohio. It is the 15th largest city in the United States, with a population of 850,106 (2015 estimate). It is the core city of the Columbus, OH Metropolitan Statistical Area (MSA), which encompasses a ten-county area. It is Ohio's third largest metropolitan area, behind Cleveland and Cincinnati.

It is also the fourth most populous state capital in the United States, and the third largest city in the Midwestern United States.

Columbus is the county seat of Franklin County. Named for explorer Christopher Columbus, the city was founded in 1812 at the confluence of the Scioto and Olentangy rivers and assumed the functions of state capital in 1816. The city has a diverse economy based on education, government, insurance, banking, fashion, defense, aviation, food, clothes, logistics, steel, energy, medical research, health care, hospitality, retail, and technology. Columbus is home to the Battelle Memorial Institute, the world's largest private research and development foundation; Chemical Abstracts Service, the world's largest clearinghouse of chemical information; and The Ohio State University, one of the largest universities in the United States.

In 2012, Columbus was ranked in *BusinessWeek*'s 50 best cities in America. In 2007, *fDi Magazine* ranked the city no. 3 in the U.S. for cities of the future, and the Columbus Zoo and Aquarium was rated no. 1 in 2009 by *USA Travel Guide*.

The National Road reached Columbus from Baltimore in 1831, which complemented the city's new link to the Ohio and Erie Canal and facilitated a population boom. A wave of European immigrants led to the creation of two ethnic enclaves on the city's outskirts. A large Irish population settled in the north along Naghten Street (presently Nationwide Boulevard), while the Germans took advantage of the cheap land to the south, creating a community that came to be known as the *Das Alte Südende* (The Old South End).

Before the abolition of slavery in the South in 1863, the Underground Railroad was active in Columbus; led, in part, by James Preston Poindexter. Poindexter arrived in Columbus in the 1830s and became a Baptist Preacher and leader in the city's African-American community until the turn of the century.

30. North Vancouver, British Columbia, Canada

Is a waterfront municipality on the north shore of Burrard Inlet, directly across from Vancouver, British Columbia. It is the smallest of the three North Shore municipalities, and the most urbanized as well. Although it has significant industry of its own, including shipping, chemical production, and film production, the city is usually considered to be a suburb of Vancouver. The city is served by the Royal Canadian Mounted Police.

Moodyville (at the south end of Moody Avenue, now Moodyville Park), is the oldest settlement on Burrard Inlet, predating Vancouver; only New Westminster is the older non-native settlement in the region. Logging came to the virgin forests of Douglas Fir in North Vancouver, as sailing ships called in to load. A water-powered sawmill was set up in the 1860s at Moodyville, by Sewell Moody. Subsequently, post offices, schools and a village sprang up. In time, the municipality of North Vancouver (which encompassed the entire North Shore from Deep Cove to Dundarave) was incorporated. In the 1880s, Arthur Heywood-Lonsdale and a relation James Pemberton Fell, made substantial investments in North Vancouver and in 1882 he financed the Moodyville investments. Several locations in the North Vancouver area are named after Lonsdale and his family. The financial collapses of the 1890s and 1907 aggrieved the young city into bankruptcy. As a result of this, the separate areas of West Vancouver, and District of North Vancouver came into being, with the city holding on to only a small portion of its former area.

Part of the reason was the cost of developing raw mountainous terrain. And, originally the ocean foreshore was primarily swamp. The great distances, and large rivers to span, hindered development. Bridges were built, only to have them washed out in a few years from winter floods. The city and district-built Keith Road in 1912, which undulated from West Vancouver to Deep Cove amid the slashed sidehills, swamps, and burnt stumps.

Yet the city did gain a strong foothold, with Lonsdale Avenue. Serviced by the North Vancouver Ferries, it proved a popular area. Commuters used the ferries to work in Vancouver. Street cars and early land speculation, spurred interest in the area. Streets, city blocks and houses were slowly built around lower Lonsdale.

31. Camas, Washington

A city in Clark County, Washington, with a population of 19,355 at the 2010 census. Officially incorporated on June 18, 1906, the city is named after the camas lily, a plant with an onion-like bulb prized by Native Americans. At the west end of downtown Camas is a large Georgia-Pacific paper-mill from which the high school teams get their name "the Papermakers". Accordingly, the city is about 20 miles east (upwind) from Portland, Oregon. Historically, the commercial base of the city was almost solely the paper mill; however, the diversity of industries has been enhanced considerably in recent years by the influx of several white-collar, high-tech companies including Hewlett-Packard, Sharp Microelectronics, Linear Technology, WaferTech and Underwriters Labs. Camas was founded as the LaCamas colony in 1883 by Henry Pittock who owned the Oregonian. The upriver location from Vancouver made it a good site for his new paper mill. The town was named after the Camas lilly which was used as food by the local chinook tribes. This agriculture town was incorporated in 1906 as an active Prohibition town. Its incorporation was done as a way to control alcohol. Due to hightech companies moving in the landscape of the town began to change.

32. Beaverton, Oregon

A city in Washington County, in the U.S. state of Oregon. The city center is 7 miles (11 km) west of downtown Portland in the Tualatin River Valley. As of the 2010 census, the population is 89,803.] This makes it the second-largest city in the county and Oregon's sixth-largest city. Fire protection and EMS services are provided through Tualatin Valley Fire and Rescue.

In 2010, Beaverton was named by *Money* magazine as one of the 100 "best places to live", among smaller cities in the country. Along with Hillsboro, Beaverton is one of the economic centers for Washington County, home to numerous corporations in a variety of industries.

According to *Oregon Geographic Names*, Beaverton got its name because of the settlement's proximity to a large body of water resulting from beaver dams. The area of Tualatin Valley which became Beaverton was originally the home of a Native American tribe known as the *Atfalati*, which settlers mispronounced as *Tualatin*. The Atfalati population dwindled in the latter part of the 18th century, and the prosperous tribe was no longer dominant in the area by the 19th century when settlers arrived.

19th century Early settlers

The natives had a village called *Chakeipi*, meaning *Place of the Beaver*, and early settlers referred to it as "Beaverdam". Early settlers include the Hall Family from Kentucky, the Denneys who lived on their claim near present-day Scholls Ferry Road and Hall Blvd, and Orin S. Allen, from western New York
Beginning of the town

After the American Civil War, numerous other settlers, including Joshua Welch, George Betts, Charles Angel, W. P. Watson, and John Henry, laid out what is now known as Beaverton hoping they could bring a railroad to an area once described as, "mostly swamps & marshes connected by beaver dams to create what looked like a huge lake." In 1872, Beaverton's first post office opened in a general store operated by Betts, who also served as the first postmaster of the community. Betts Street, where the current post office now stands, is named in honor of him. In 1893, Beaverton, which by that time had a population of 400, was officially incorporated. Alonzo Cady, a local businessman, served as the first mayor. Many major roads in Beaverton are named for these early settlers.

The city has tried to encourage transit-oriented development around the city's MAX Light Rail stations. The Round, a mixed-use development around Beaverton Central MAX Station on the site of a former sewer plant, was originally announced in 1996 It is only partially complete, due to the bankruptcy of one developer and the Great Recession. In 2014, the City of Beaverton moved its city hall into a vacant office building in The Round. Further development and an arts center have been proposed for the former site of the Westgate Theatre, adjacent to The Round.

33. Portland, Oregon

The largest city in the U.S. state of Oregon and the seat of Multnomah County. It is located in the Willamette Valley region of the Pacific Northwest, at the confluence of the Willamette and Columbia Rivers. The city covers 145 square miles (380 square kilometers) and had an estimated population of 632,309 in 2015, making it the 26th most populous city in the United States. Approximately 2,389,228 people live in the Portland metropolitan statistical. Roughly 60% of Oregon's population resides within the Portland metropolitan area.

Named after the city on the coast of Maine, the Oregon settlement began to be populated in the 1830s near the end of the Oregon Trail. Its water access provided convenient transportation of goods, and the timber industry was a major force in the city's early economy. At the turn of the 20th century, the city had developed a reputation as one of the most dangerous port cities in the world, a hub for organized crime and racketeering. After the city's economy experienced an industrial boom during World War II, its hard-edged reputation began to dissipate. Beginning in the 1960s, Portland became noted for its growing liberal political values, and the city has earned a reputation as a bastion of counterculture, which proceeded into the 21st century. According to a 2009 Pew

Research Center study, Portland ranks as the eighth most popular American city, based on where people want to live.

The city operates with a commission-based government guided by a mayor and four commissioners as well as Metro, the only directly elected metropolitan planning organization in the United States. The city government is notable for its land-use planning and investment in public transportation. Portland is frequently recognized as one of the most environmentally conscious cities in the world because of its high walkability, large community of bicyclists, farm-to-table dining, expansive network of public transportation options, and over 10,000 acres (4,000 hectares) of public parks. Its climate is marked by warm, dry summers and cold, rainy winters. This climate is ideal for growing roses, and Portland has been called the "City of Roses" for over a century. "Keep Portland Weird" is an unofficial slogan for the city.

During the prehistoric period, the land that would become Portland was flooded after the collapse of glacial dams from Lake Missoula, located in what would later become Montana. These massive floods occurred during the last ice age and filled the Willamette Valley with 300 to 400 feet (91 to 122 m) of water. Before American pioneers began arriving in the 1800s, the land that eventually became Portland and surrounding Multnomah County was inhabited for many centuries by two bands of indigenous Chinook people— the Multnomah and the Clackamas peoples. The Chinook people occupying the land which would become Portland were first documented by Meriwether Lewis and William Clark in 1805. Before its European settlement, the Portland Basin of the lower Columbia River and Willamette River valleys had been one of the most densely populated regions on the Pacific Coast.

Settlement

Significant numbers of pioneer settlers began arriving in the Willamette Valley in the 1830s via the Oregon Trail, though life was originally centered in nearby Oregon City. In the early 1840s a new settlement began emerging ten miles from the mouth of the Willamette River, roughly halfway between Oregon City and Fort Vancouver. This community was initially referred to as "Stumptown" and "The Clearing" because of the many trees being cut down to allow for its growth. In 1843 William Overton saw potential in the new settlement but lacked the funds.

At the time of its incorporation on February 8, 1851, Portland had over 800 inhabitants, a steam sawmill, a log cabin hotel, and a newspaper, the *Weekly Oregonian*. A major fire swept through downtown in August 1873, destroying twenty blocks on the west side of the Willamette along Yamhill and Morrison Streets, and causing $1.3 million in damage. By 1879, the population had grown to 17,500 and by 1890 it had grown to 46,385. In 1888, the city constructed the first steel bridge built on the West Coast.

Portland's access to the Pacific Ocean via the Willamette and the Columbia rivers, as well as its easy access to the agricultural Tualatin Valley via the "Great Plank Road" (the route of current-day U.S. Route 26), provided the pioneer city with an advantage over other nearby ports, and it grew very quickly. Portland remained the major port in the Pacific Northwest for much of the 19th century, until the 1890s, when Seattle's deepwater harbor was connected to the rest of the mainland by rail, affording an inland route without the treacherous navigation of the Columbia River.

Portland developed a reputation early on in its history as a hard-edged and gritty port town. In 1889, *The Oregonian* called Portland "the most filthy city in the Northern States," due to the unsanitary sewers and gutters, and, at the turn of the 20th century, it was considered one of the most dangerous port cities in the world. By the early 20th century, the city had lost its reputation as a "sober frontier city" and garnered a reputation for being violent and dangerous.

Between 1900 and 1930, the population of the city tripled from nearly 100,000 to 301,815. Following this population boom, Portland became a notorious hub for underground criminal activity and organized crime between the 1940s and 1950s. In 1957, *LIFE* Magazine published an article detailing the city's history of government corruption and crime, specifically its gambling rackets and illegal nightclubs. In spite of the city's seedier undercurrent of criminal activity, Portland was experiencing an economic and industrial surge during World War II. Ship builder Henry J. Kaiser had been awarded contracts to construct Liberty ships and aircraft carrier escorts, and chose sites in Portland and Vancouver, Washington for work yards.– During this time, Portland's population rose by over 150,000, largely attributed to recruited laborers.

During the 1960s, an influx of hippie subculture began to take root in the city in the wake of San Francisco's burgeoning countercultural scene. A large social activist presence evolved during this time as well, specifically concerning Native American rights, environmentalist causes, and gay rights. By the 1970s, Portland had well established itself as a progressive city, and experienced an economic boom for the majority of the decade; however, the slowing of the housing market in 1979 caused demand for the city and state timber industries to drop significantly.

In the 1990s, the technology industry began to emerge in Portland, specifically with the establishment of companies like Intel, which brought more than $10 billion in investments in 1995 alone. After the year 2000, Portland experienced significant growth, with a population rise of over 90,000 between the years 2000 and 2014. The city's increased presence within the cultural lexicon has established it a popular city for young people, and it was second only to Louisville, Kentucky as one of the cities to attract and retain the highest number of college-educated people in the United States. Between 2001 and 2012, Portland's gross domestic product per person grew fifty percent, more than any other city in the country.

The city has acquired a diverse range of nicknames throughout its history, though it is most frequently called "Rose City" or "The City of Roses", the latter of which being its unofficial nickname since 1888 and its official nickname since 2003. Another widely utilized nickname by local residents in everyday speech is "PDX", which is also the airport code for Portland International Airport. Other nicknames include Bridgetown, Stumptown, Rip City, Soccer City, P-Town, Portlandia, and the more antiquated Little Beirut.

34. Des Moines County, Iowa

A county located in the U.S. state of Iowa. As of the 2010 census, the population was 40,325. The county seat is Burlington. It is one of Iowa's two original counties along with Dubuque County; both were organized by the Michigan Territorial legislature in 1834.

Des Moines County should not be confused with the city of Des Moines, which is the capital of Iowa. Des Moines County sits on Iowa's eastern border alongside the Mississippi River. The city of Des Moines is in Polk County in south-central Iowa. Both places derive their name from the Des Moines River, which flows through the city of Des Moines and originally flowed through the county. When the county was divided early in Iowa's history, the river ended up further west, forming the border between Lee County, Iowa and the state of Missouri.

At an extra session of the Sixth Legislative Assembly of Michigan Territory held in September 1834, the Iowa District was divided into two counties by running a line due west from the lower end of Rock Island in the Mississippi River. The territory north of this line (which started just south of the present-day Davenport) was named Dubuque County, and all south of it was Demoine County. It was named after the Des Moines River. From July 3, 1836 until July 3, 1838, Des Moines County was part of Wisconsin Territory. The county underwent various border changes during this time. July 4, 1838, the named county became part of Iowa Territory (later the state of Iowa).

35. Lee County, Iowa

Was established in 1836. As of the 2010 census, the population was 35,862. It has two county seats — Fort Madison and Keokuk.

Fort Madison dates to the War of 1812. Lee County was the location of the Half-Breed Tract, established by treaty in 1824. Allocations of land were made to American Indian descendants of European fathers and Indian mothers at this tract. Originally the land was to be held in common. Some who had an allocation lived in cities, where they hoped to make better livings.

Lee County as a named entity was formed on December 7, 1836, under the jurisdiction of Wisconsin Territory. It would become a part of Iowa Territory when it was formed on July 4, 1838. Large-scale European-American settlement in the area began in 1839, after Congress allowed owners to sell land individually. Members of the Church of Christ (Latter Day Saints) fled persecutions in Missouri to settle in Illinois and Iowa. Nauvoo, across the border in Hancock County, Illinois, became the main center of Latter-day Saints settlement, but there was also a Latter-Day Saints stake organized in Lee County under the direction of John Smith, the uncle of Joseph Smith, land that was sold to them by Isaac Galland in 1839.

Lee has two county seats — Fort Madison and Keokuk. The latter was established in 1847 when disagreements led to a second court jurisdiction.

Lee County's population grew to about 19,000 in 1850, the first US census, to 37,000 per the 3rd census in 1870, peaking at 44,000 people in 1960. It has continuously decreased since and as of 2010, 35,862 people lived there, comparable to the years between 1860-1870.

36. The Commonwealth of Virginia

A state located in the Mid-Atlantic region of the United States. Virginia is nicknamed the "Old Dominion" due to its status as the first colonial possession established in mainland British America. The geography and climate of the

Commonwealth are shaped by the Blue Ridge Mountains and the Chesapeake Bay, which provide habitat for much of its flora and fauna. The capital of the Commonwealth is Richmond; Virginia Beach is the most populous city, and Fairfax County is the most populous political subdivision. The Commonwealth's estimated population as of 2014 is over 8.3 million.

The area's history begins with several indigenous groups, including the Powhatan. In 1607 the London Company established the Colony of Virginia as the first permanent New World English colony. Slave labor and the land acquired from displaced Native American tribes each played a significant role in the colony's early politics and plantation economy. Virginia was one of the 13 Colonies in the American Revolution and joined the Confederacy in the American Civil War, during which Richmond was made the Confederate capital and Virginia's northwestern counties seceded to form the state of West Virginia. Although the Commonwealth was under one-party rule for nearly a century following Reconstruction, both major national parties are competitive in modern Virginia.

The Virginia General Assembly is the oldest continuous law-making body in the New World.- The state government was ranked most effective by the Pew Center on the States in both 2005 and 2008.- It is unique in how it treats cities and counties equally, manages local roads, and prohibits its governors from serving consecutive terms. Virginia's economy has many sectors: agriculture in the Shenandoah Valley; federal agencies in Northern Virginia, including the headquarters of the Department of Defense and CIA; and military facilities in Hampton Roads, the site of the region's main seaport. Virginia's economy changed from primarily agricultural to industrial during the 1960s and 1970s, and in 2002 computer chips became the state's leading export.

"Jamestown 2007" marked Virginia's quadricentennial year, celebrating 400 years since the establishment of the Jamestown Colony. The celebrations highlighted contributions from Native Americans, Africans, and Europeans, each of which had a significant part in shaping Virginia's history. Warfare, including among these groups, has also had an important role. Virginia was a focal point in conflicts from the French and Indian War, the American Revolution and the Civil War, to the Cold War and the War on Terrorism. Stories about historic figures, such as those surrounding Pocahontas and John Smith, George Washington's childhood, or the plantation elite in the slave society of the antebellum period, have also created potent myths of state history, and have served as rationales for Virginia's ideology.

37. Canada

A country in the northern half of North America. Its ten provinces and three territories extend from the Atlantic to the Pacific and northward into the Arctic Ocean, covering 9.98 million square kilometres (3.85 million square miles), making it the world's second-largest country by total area and the fourth-largest country by land area. Canada's border with the United States is the world's longest land border. The majority of the country has a cold or severely cold winter climate, but southerly areas are warm in summer. Canada is sparsely populated; the majority of its land territory being dominated by forest and tundra and the Rocky Mountains. About four-fifths of the country's population of 36 million people is urbanized and live near the southern border. Its capital is Ottawa.

Canada has been inhabited for millennia by various Aboriginal peoples. Beginning in the 16th century, British and French claims were made on the area, with the colony of Canada first being established by the French in 1537. As a consequence of various conflicts, the United Kingdom gained and lost territories within British North America until it was left, in the late 18th century, with what mostly geographically comprises Canada today. Pursuant to the British North America Act, on July 1, 1867, the colonies of Canada, New Brunswick, and Nova Scotia joined to form the semi-autonomous federal Dominion of Canada. This began an accretion of provinces and territories to the mostly self-governing Dominion to the present ten provinces and three territories forming modern Canada.

In 1931, Canada achieved near total independence from the United Kingdom with the Statute of Westminster 1931, and full sovereignty was attained when the Canada Act 1982 removed the last remaining ties of legal dependence on the Parliament of the United Kingdom. Canada is a federal parliamentary democracy and a constitutional monarchy, with Queen Elizabeth II being the head of state. The country is officially bilingual at the federal level. It is one of the world's most ethnically diverse and multicultural nations, the product of large-scale immigration from many other countries. Its advanced economy is the eleventh largest in the world, relying chiefly upon its abundant natural resources and well-developed international trade networks. Canada's long and complex relationship with the United States has had a significant impact on its economy and culture.

Canada is a developed country and has the tenth highest nominal per capita income globally as well as the ninth highest ranking in the Human Development Index. It ranks among the highest in international measurements of government transparency, civil liberties, quality of life, economic freedom, and education. Canada is a Commonwealth realm member of the Commonwealth of Nations, a member of the Francophonie, and part of several major international and intergovernmental institutions or groupings including the United Nations, the North Atlantic Treaty Organization, the G8, the Group of Ten, the G20, the North American Free Trade Agreement and the Asia-Pacific Economic Cooperation forum.

38. The United States of America

Commonly referred to as America, is a federal republic composed of 50 states, a federal district, five major self-governing territories, and various possessions.- Forty-eight of the fifty states and the federal district are contiguous and located in North America between Canada and Mexico. The state of Alaska is in the far northwestern corner of North America, with a land border to the east with Canada and separated by the Bering Strait from Russia. The state of Hawaii is an archipelago in the mid-Pacific. The territories are scattered about the Pacific Ocean and the Caribbean Sea.

At 3.8 million square miles (9.8 million km²) and with over 324 million people, the United States is the world's fourth-largest country by total area (and fourth-largest by land area)- and the third-most populous. It is one of the world's most ethnically diverse and multicultural nations, the product of large-scale immigration from many other countries.Urbanization climbed to over 80% in

2010 and leads to growing megaregions. The country's capital is Washington, D.C. and its largest city is New York City; the other top metropolitan areas, all with around five million or more inhabitants, are Los Angeles, Chicago, Dallas, San Francisco, Boston, Philadelphia, Houston, Atlanta, and Miami.

Paleo-Indians migrated from Asia to the North American mainland at least 15,000 years ago.-European colonization began in the 16th century. The United States emerged from 13 British colonies along the East Coast. Numerous disputes between Great Britain and the colonies in the aftermath of the Seven Years' War led to the American Revolution, which began in 1775. On July 4, 1776, as the colonies were fighting Great Britain in the American Revolutionary War, delegates from the 13 colonies unanimously adopted the Declaration of Independence. The war ended in 1783 with recognition of the independence of the United States by Great Britain, and was the first successful war of independence against a European colonial empire.- The current constitution was adopted in 1788, after the Articles of Confederation, adopted in 1781, were felt to have provided inadequate federal powers. The first ten amendments, collectively named the Bill of Rights, were ratified in 1791 and designed to guarantee many fundamental civil liberties.

The United States embarked on a vigorous expansion across North America throughout the 19th century,- displacing American Indian tribes, acquiring new territories, and gradually admitting new states until it spanned the continent by 1848. During the second half of the 19th century, the American Civil War led to the end of legal slavery in the country. By the end of that century, the United States extended into the Pacific Ocean, and its economy, driven in large part by the Industrial Revolution, began to soar.- The Spanish–American War and World War I confirmed the country's status as a global military power. The United States emerged from World War II as a global superpower, the first country to develop nuclear weapons, the only country to use them in warfare, and a permanent member of the United Nations Security Council. It is a founding member of the Organization of American States (UAS) and various other Pan-American and international organisations. The end of the Cold War and the dissolution of the Soviet Union in 1991 left the United States as the world's sole superpower.

The United States is a highly developed country, with the world's largest economy by nominal GDP. It ranks highly in several measures of socioeconomic performance, including average wage, human development, per capita GDP, and productivity per person.- While the U.S. economy is considered post-industrial, characterized by the dominance of services and knowledge economy, the manufacturing sector remains the second-largest in the world.– Though its population is only 4.4% of the world total, the United States accounts for nearly a quarter of world GDP⌐ and almost a third of global military spending,- making it the world's foremost military and economic power. The United States is a prominent political and cultural force internationally, and a leader in scientific research and technological innovations.

Appendix D - Timelines

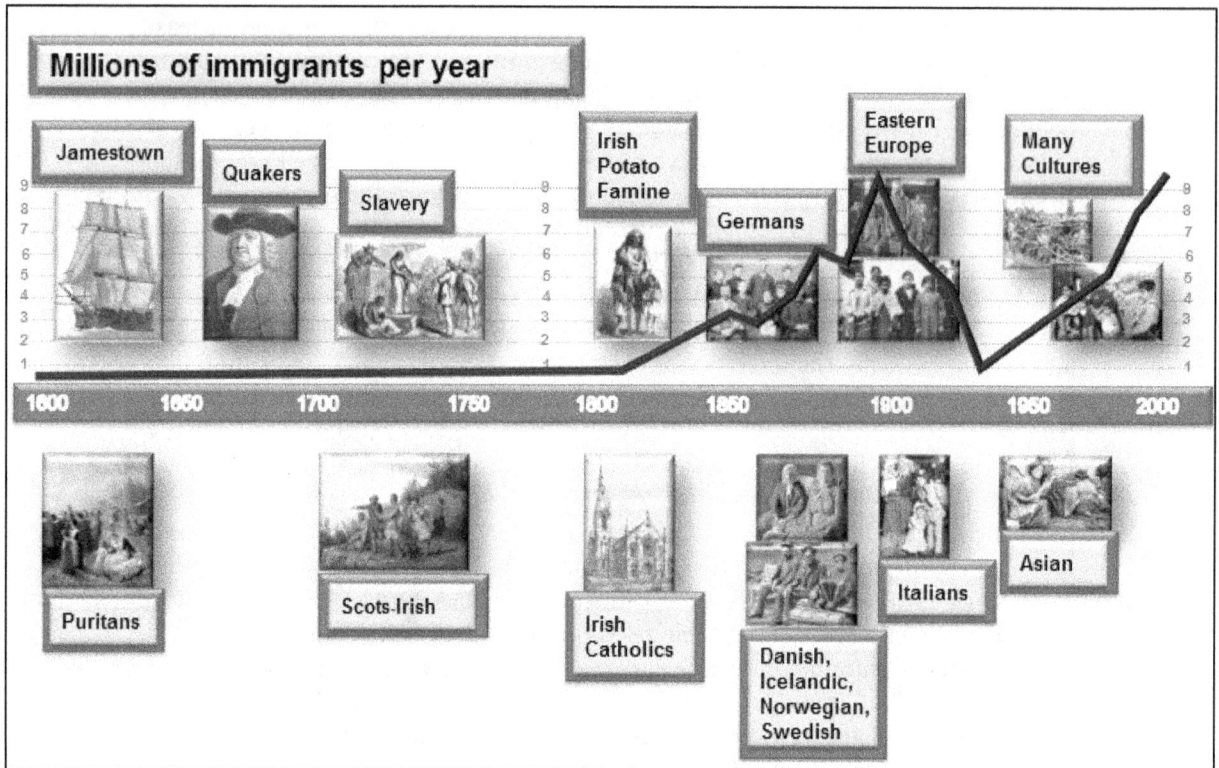

Millions of immigrants per year

Jamestown

Quakers

Slavery

Irish Potato Famine

Germans

Eastern Europe

Many Cultures

9 8 7 6 5 4 3 2 1

1600 1650 1700 1750 1800 1850 1900 1950 2000

Puritans

Scots-Irish

Irish Catholics

Danish, Icelandic, Norwegian, Swedish

Italians

Asian

Art History Timeline

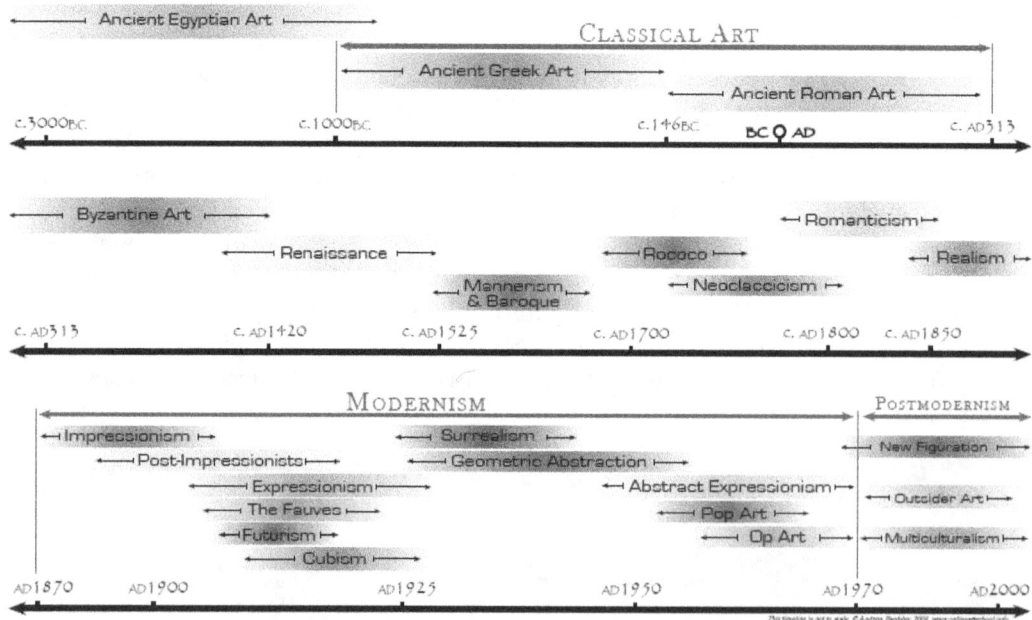

Ancient Egyptian Art

CLASSICAL ART

Ancient Greek Art

Ancient Roman Art

c.3000BC   c.1000BC   c.146BC   BC ○ AD   c. AD313

Byzantine Art

Romanticism

Renaissance

Rococo

Realism

Mannerism & Baroque

Neoclassicism

c. AD313   c. AD1420   c. AD1525   c. AD1700   c. AD1800   c. AD1850

MODERNISM

POSTMODERNISM

Impressionism

Surrealism

New Figuration

Post-Impressionists

Geometric Abstraction

Outsider Art

Expressionism

Abstract Expressionism

The Fauves

Pop Art

Multiculturalism

Futurism

Op Art

Cubism

AD1870   AD1900   AD1925   AD1950   AD1970   AD2000

This timeline is not to scale. © Andrew Bamber 2006 www.redboatschool.info

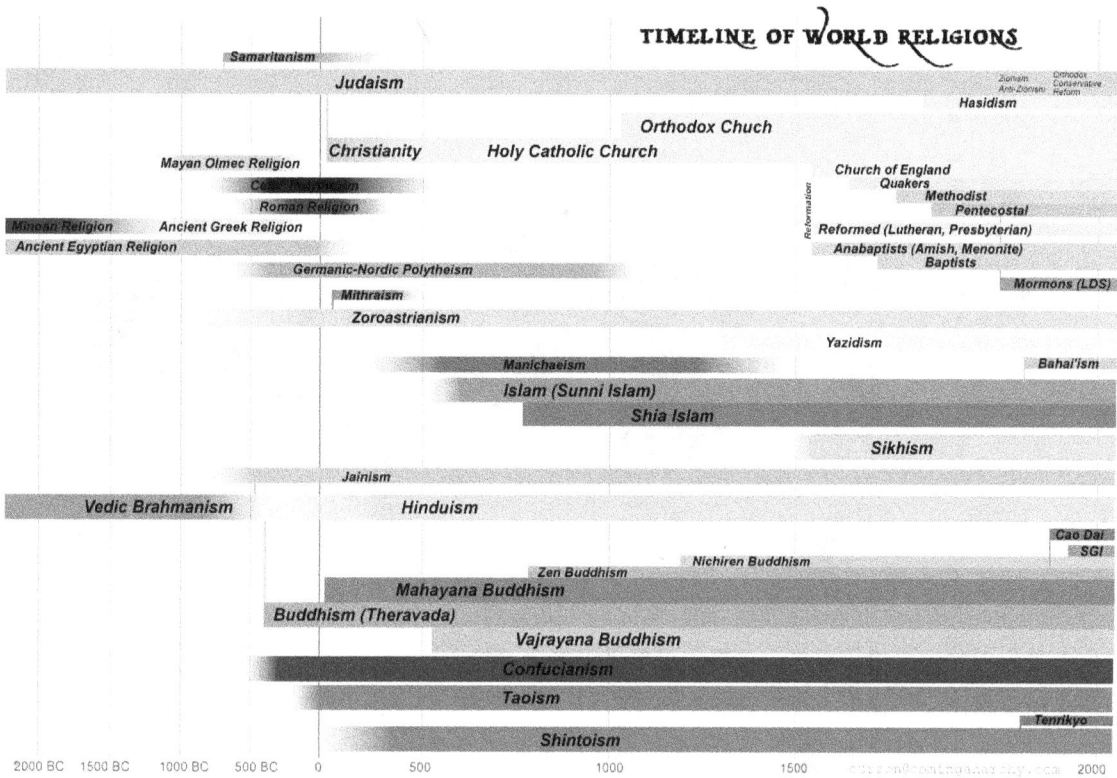

TIMELINE OF WORLD RELIGIONS

Appendix E - Clothes

GERMAN. 93. 1700.

1. 3. Peasants. 2. Travelling Costume. 4. Protestant Clergyman. 5. Costum of the Magistracy. 6. Bishop. 7. 8. Citizens. 9—19. Costumes of Female Citizens.

1. Empress Josephine.   2. Napoleon I. in Coronation Robes. 1804.   3. Minister. 1806.   4. Lady of the Court. 1808.   5. Gentleman 1807.   6. Gentleman. 181
7. 8. Ladies. 1808.   9. 10. Ladies 1810.   11. Gentleman. 1811.   12. Gentleman. 1812.   13. Lady. 1812.   14. 15 Lady and Gentleman. 1814.   16. Lady. 181
17. Gentleman. 1820   18. Gentleman in Court Costume. 1825.   19. Lady. 1827.   20. Lady. 1826.   21. Lady. 1829.   22. Lady. 1824.

GERMAN. 104. 1834—1881

1—20. Fashions from the Year. 1834 to 1881

Produced by: Michael Tieman, September 2016

Michael Tieman Family Portrait 2017

Michael Tieman Family -All of Us - Easter 2017, Corvalis, OR
Back: Michael Tieman, Connor Tieman-Woodward
Middle:Katie Tieman, Sam Woodward, R.J. Erwin, Nancy (Marshall) Tieman, Heather (Tieman) Erwin, Phillip Erwin
Front: Owen Tieman-Woodward, Alexis Tieman-Woodward, Jack Erwin

27. US Farmers 1800

28. US Workers 1800

26. US Farmers 1900

25. US Workers 1900

www.ingramcontent.com/pod-product-compliance
Lightning Source LLC
Chambersburg PA
CBHW081146270326

41930CB00014B/3047